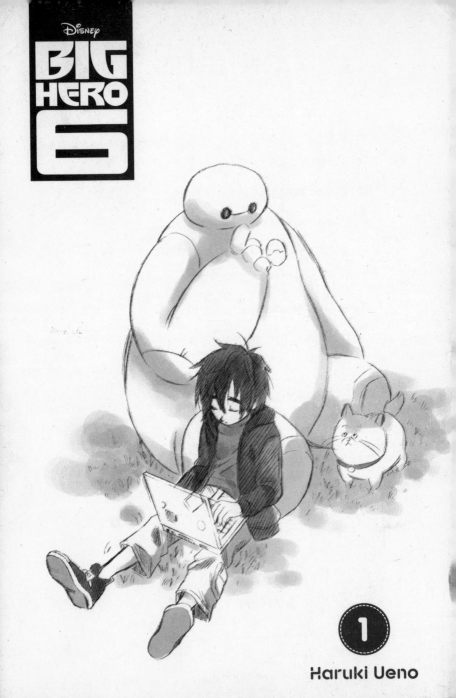

Disney

BIG HERO 6

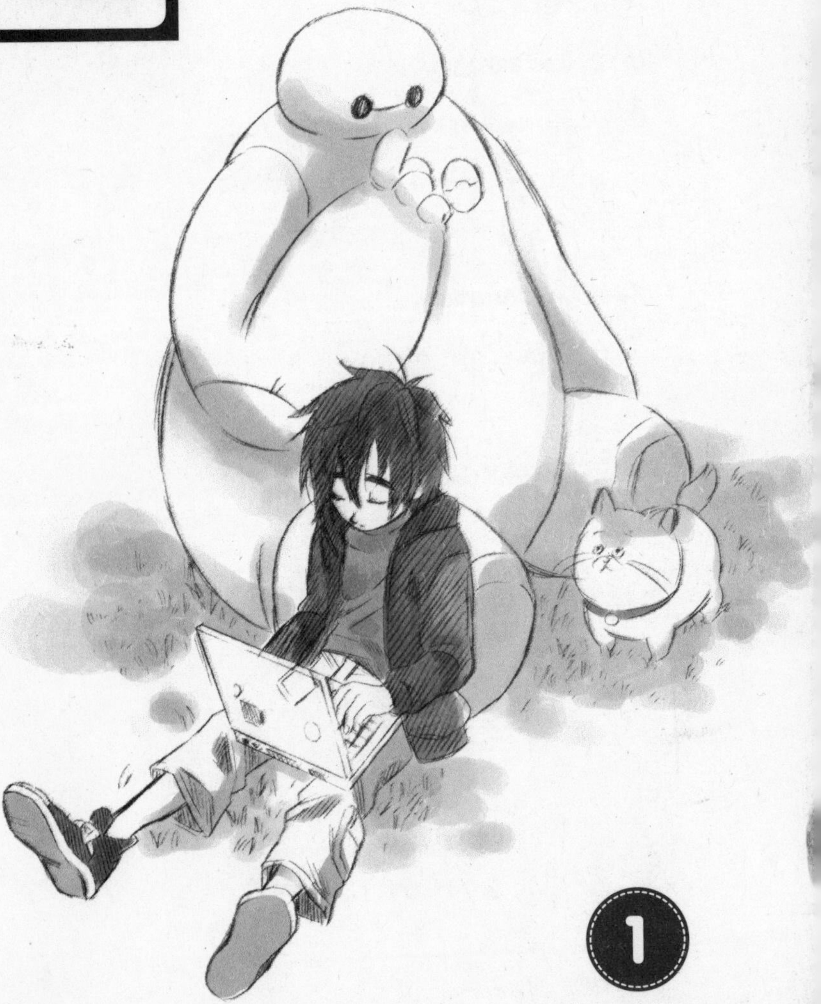

1

Haruki Ueno

CONTENTS

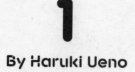

By Haruki Ueno

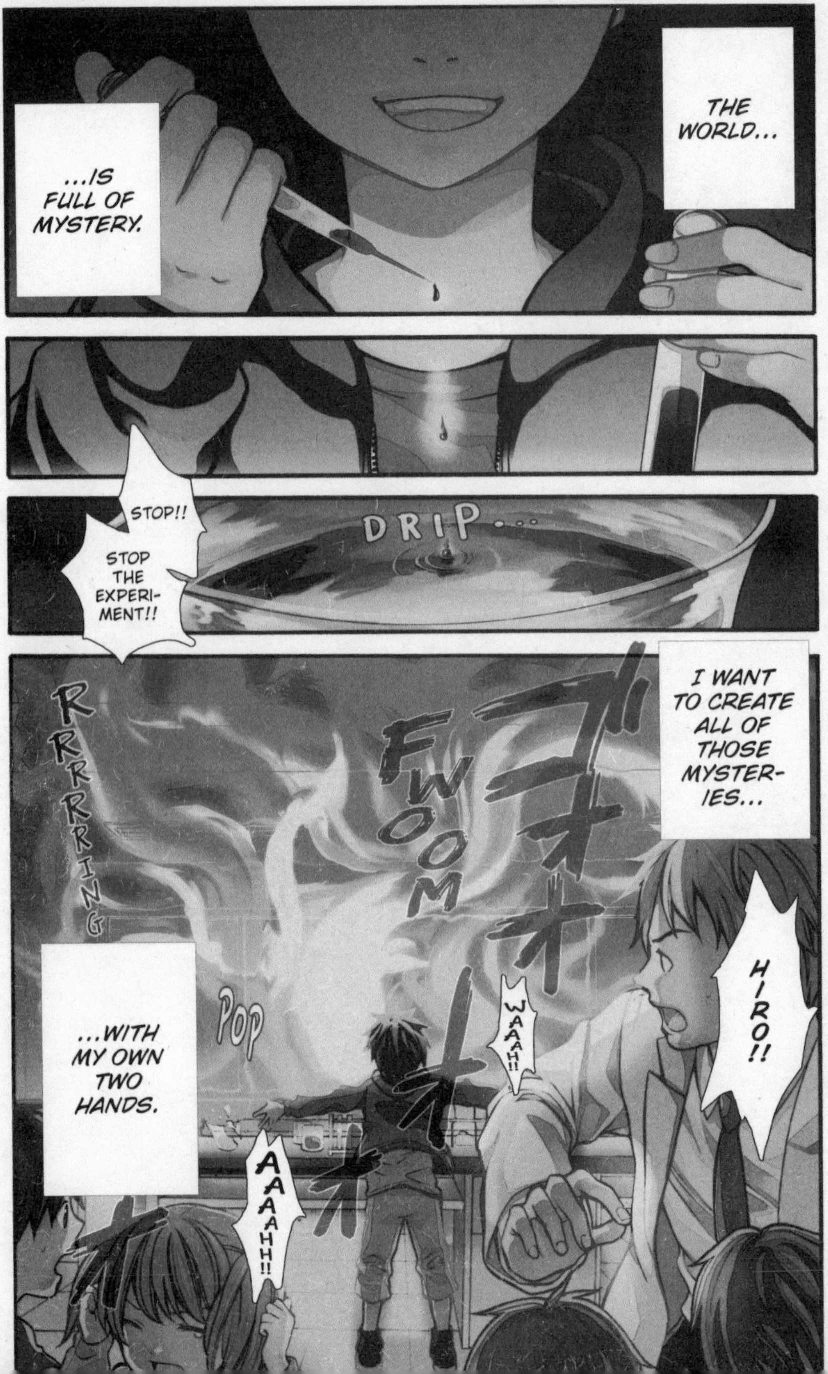
THE WORLD...
...IS FULL OF MYSTERY.
STOP!!
STOP THE EXPERIMENT!!
DRIP...
I WANT TO CREATE ALL OF THOSE MYSTERIES...
HIRO!!
FWOOOM
WAAAH!!
RRRRRING
POP
...WITH MY OWN TWO HANDS.
AAAAAHH!!

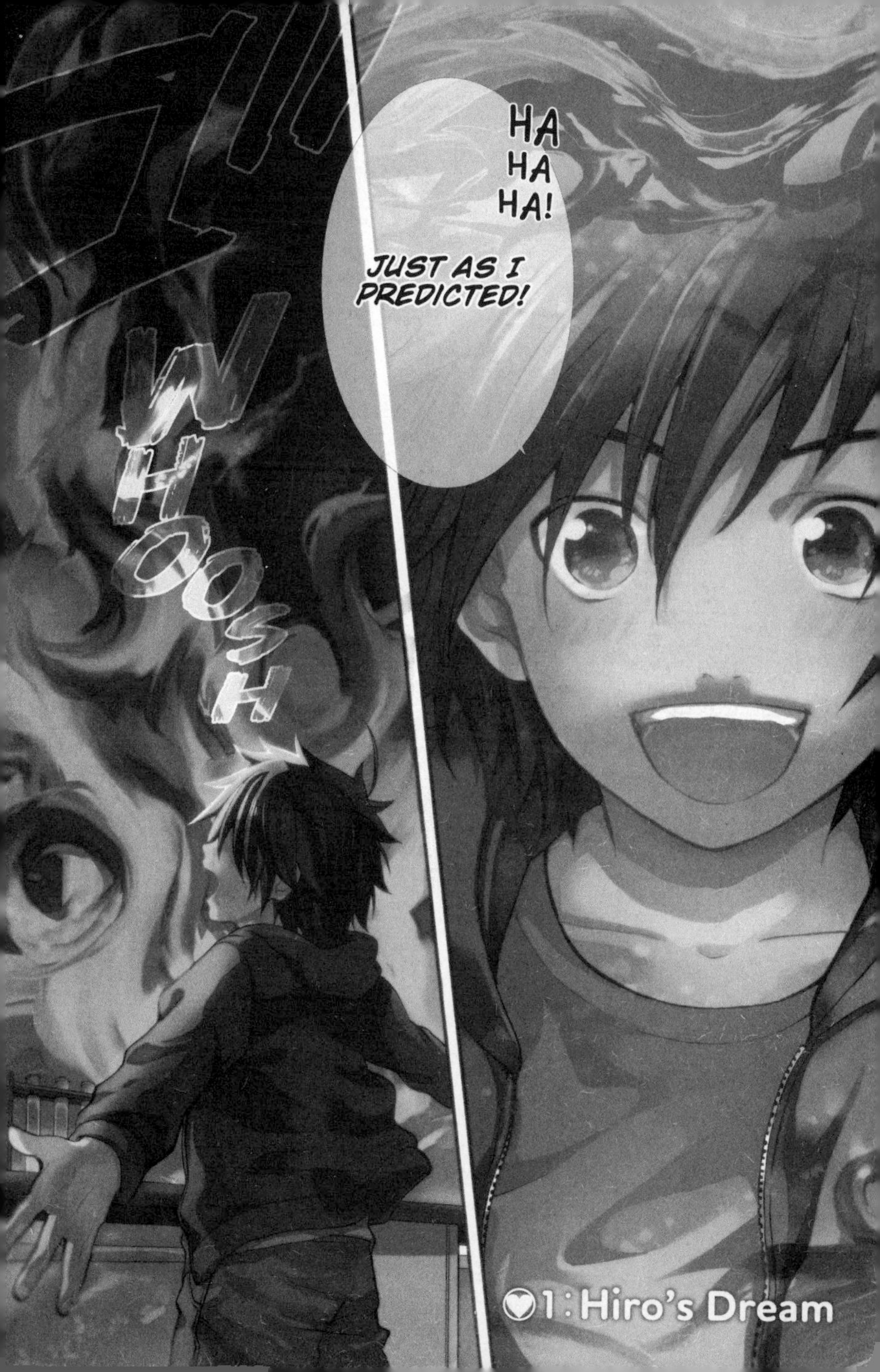
HA HA HA!
JUST AS I PREDICTED!
WHOOSH
1: Hiro's Dream

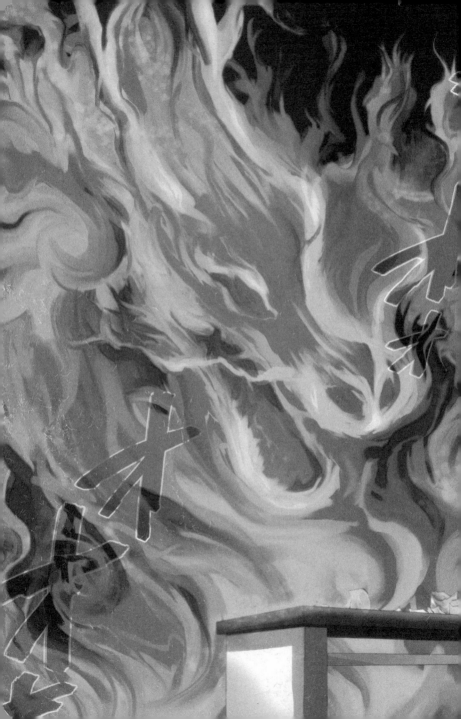

Disney

BIG HERO 6

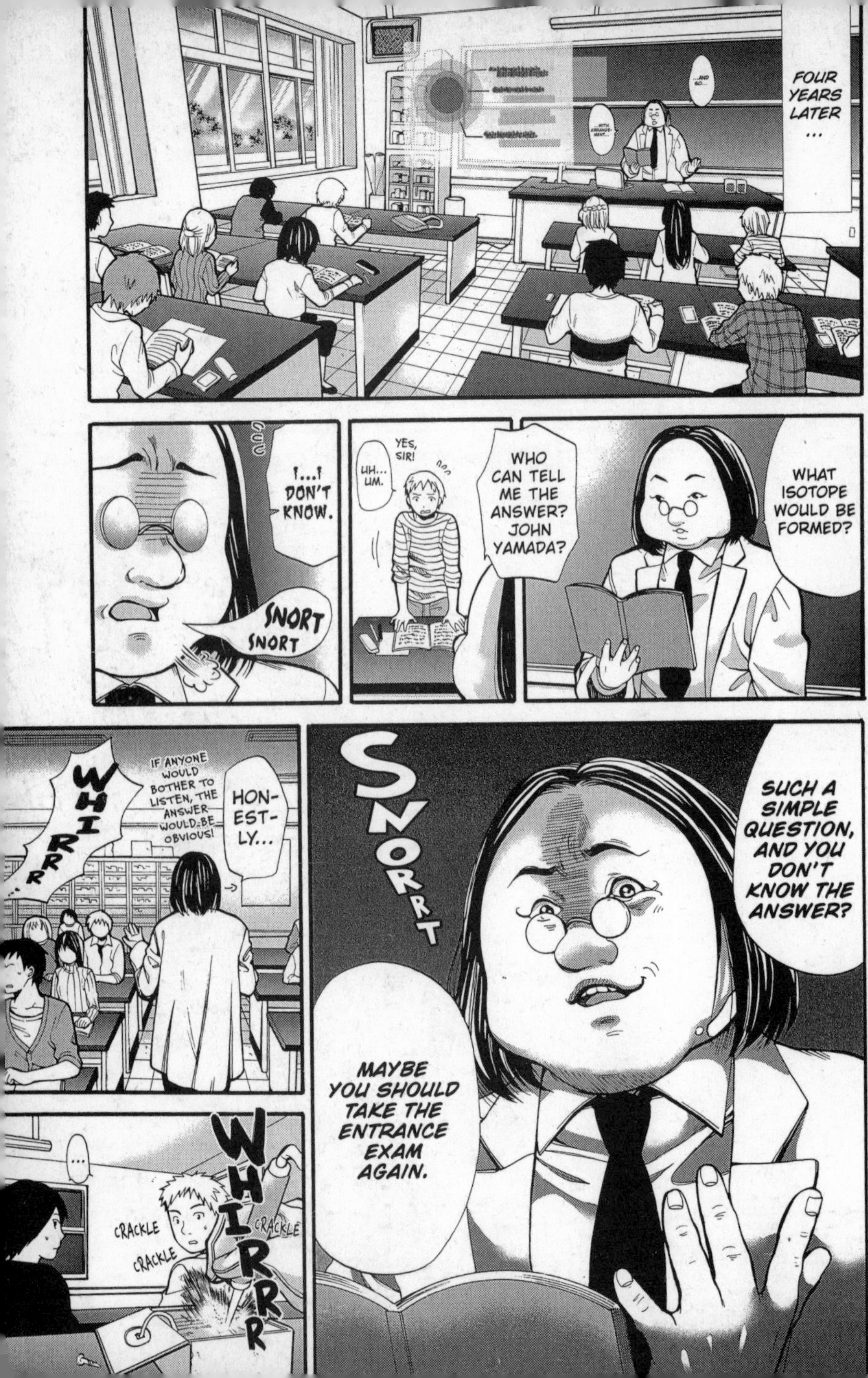
FOUR YEARS LATER …
…AND SO…
…WITH ARRANGEMENT…
WHAT ISOTOPE WOULD BE FORMED?
WHO CAN TELL ME THE ANSWER? JOHN YAMADA?
YES, SIR!
UH… UM.
I…I DON'T KNOW.
SNORT SNORT
SNORRT
SUCH A SIMPLE QUESTION, AND YOU DON'T KNOW THE ANSWER?
MAYBE YOU SHOULD TAKE THE ENTRANCE EXAM AGAIN.
HON-EST-LY…
IF ANYONE WOULD BOTHER TO LISTEN, THE ANSWER WOULD BE OBVIOUS!
WHIRRR
…
WHIRRR
CRACKLE
CRACKLE
CRACKLE

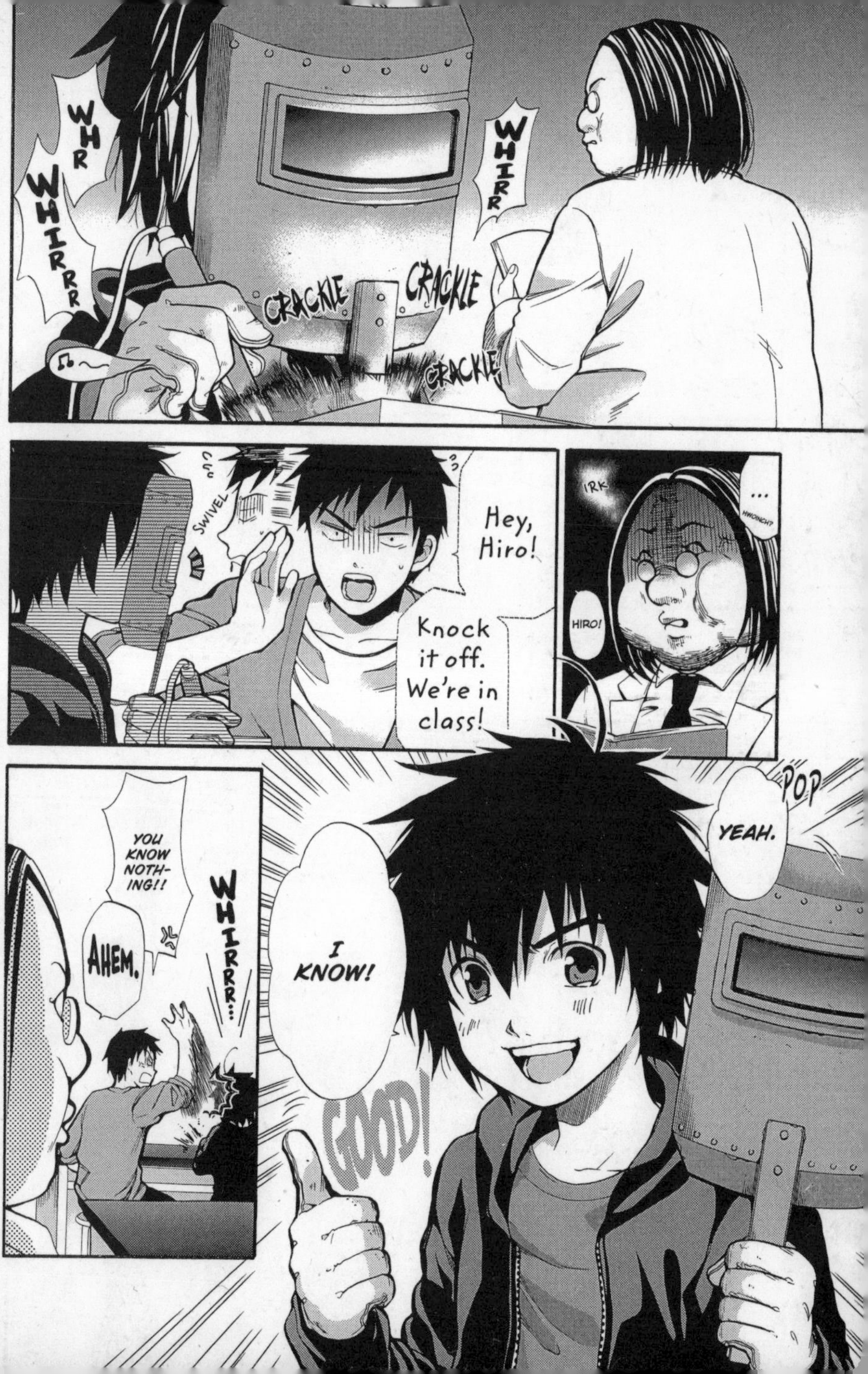

WHIRR
WHR
WHIRRR
CRACKLE
CRACKLE
CRACKLE
♪~
IRK
...
HWOINCH?
HIRO!
Hey, Hiro!
Knock it off. We're in class!
SWIVEL
POP
YEAH.
I KNOW!
GOOD!
YOU KNOW NOTHING!!
WHIRRR...
AHEM.

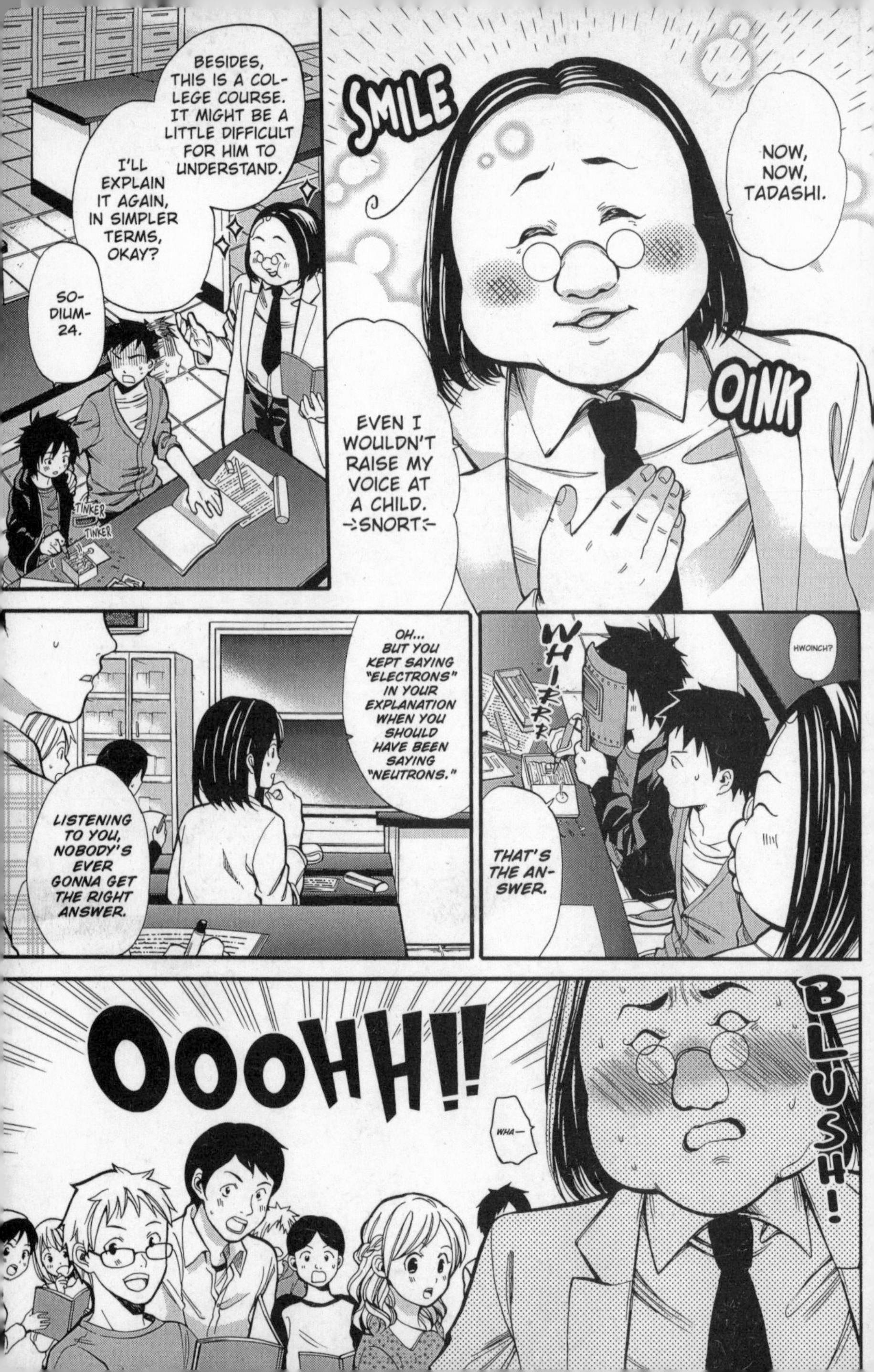
SMILE
NOW, NOW, TADASHI.
OINK
EVEN I WOULDN'T RAISE MY VOICE AT A CHILD. -SNORT-
BESIDES, THIS IS A COLLEGE COURSE. IT MIGHT BE A LITTLE DIFFICULT FOR HIM TO UNDERSTAND.
I'LL EXPLAIN IT AGAIN, IN SIMPLER TERMS, OKAY?
SODIUM-24.
TINKER
TINKER
HWOINCH?
WHIRRR
THAT'S THE ANSWER.
OH... BUT YOU KEPT SAYING "ELECTRONS" IN YOUR EXPLANATION WHEN YOU SHOULD HAVE BEEN SAYING "NEUTRONS."
LISTENING TO YOU, NOBODY'S EVER GONNA GET THE RIGHT ANSWER.
BLUSH!
WHA—
OOOHH!!

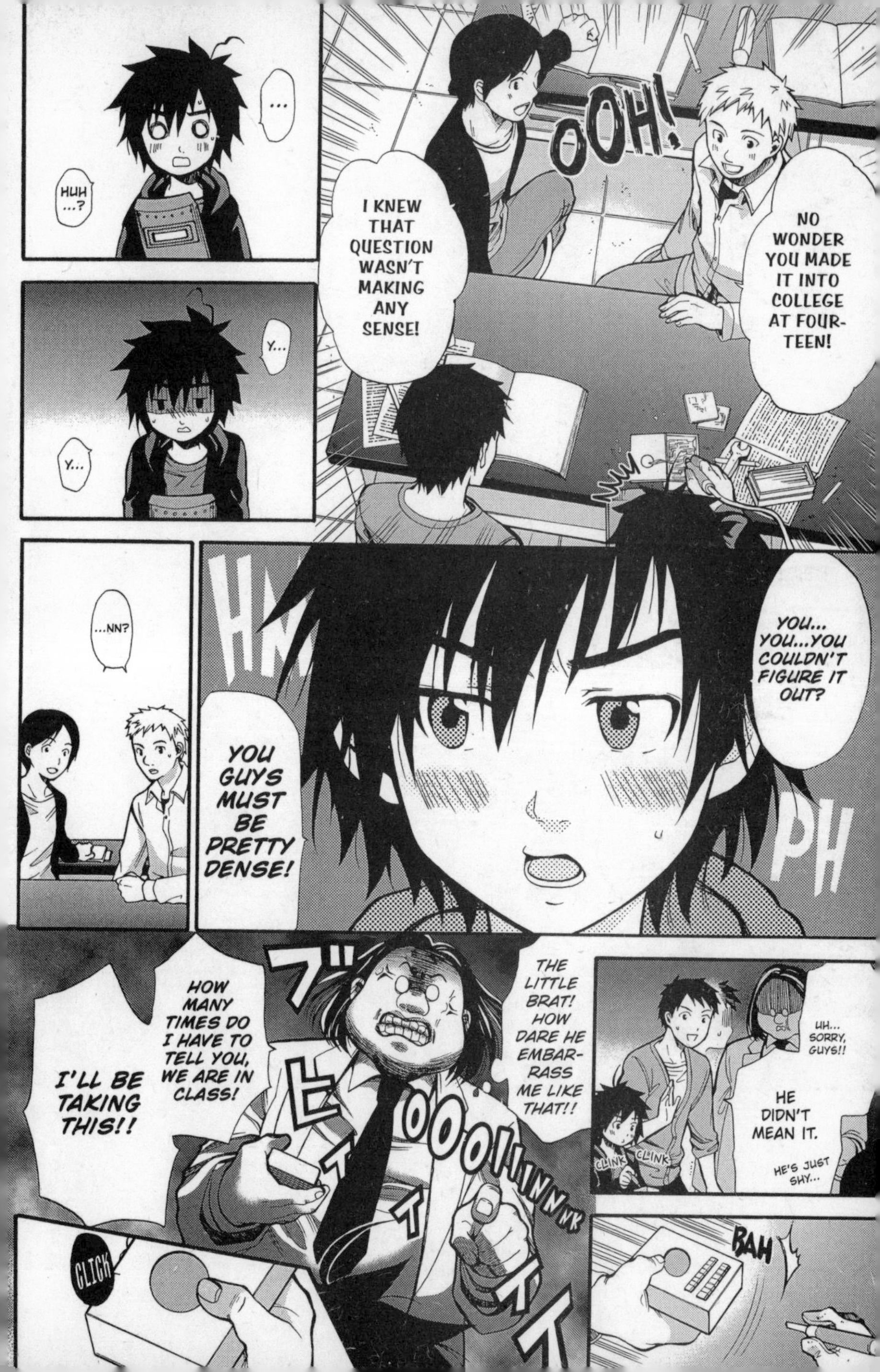
OOH!
NO WONDER YOU MADE IT INTO COLLEGE AT FOUR-TEEN!
I KNEW THAT QUESTION WASN'T MAKING ANY SENSE!
...
HUH ...?
Y...
Y...
YOU... YOU...YOU COULDN'T FIGURE IT OUT?
YOU GUYS MUST BE PRETTY DENSE!
...NN?
UH... SORRY, GUYS!!
HE DIDN'T MEAN IT.
HE'S JUST SHY...
CLINK
CLINK
THE LITTLE BRAT! HOW DARE HE EMBARRASS ME LIKE THAT!!
HOW MANY TIMES DO I HAVE TO TELL YOU, WE ARE IN CLASS!
I'LL BE TAKING THIS!!
OOOIIIINNNK
BAH
CLICK

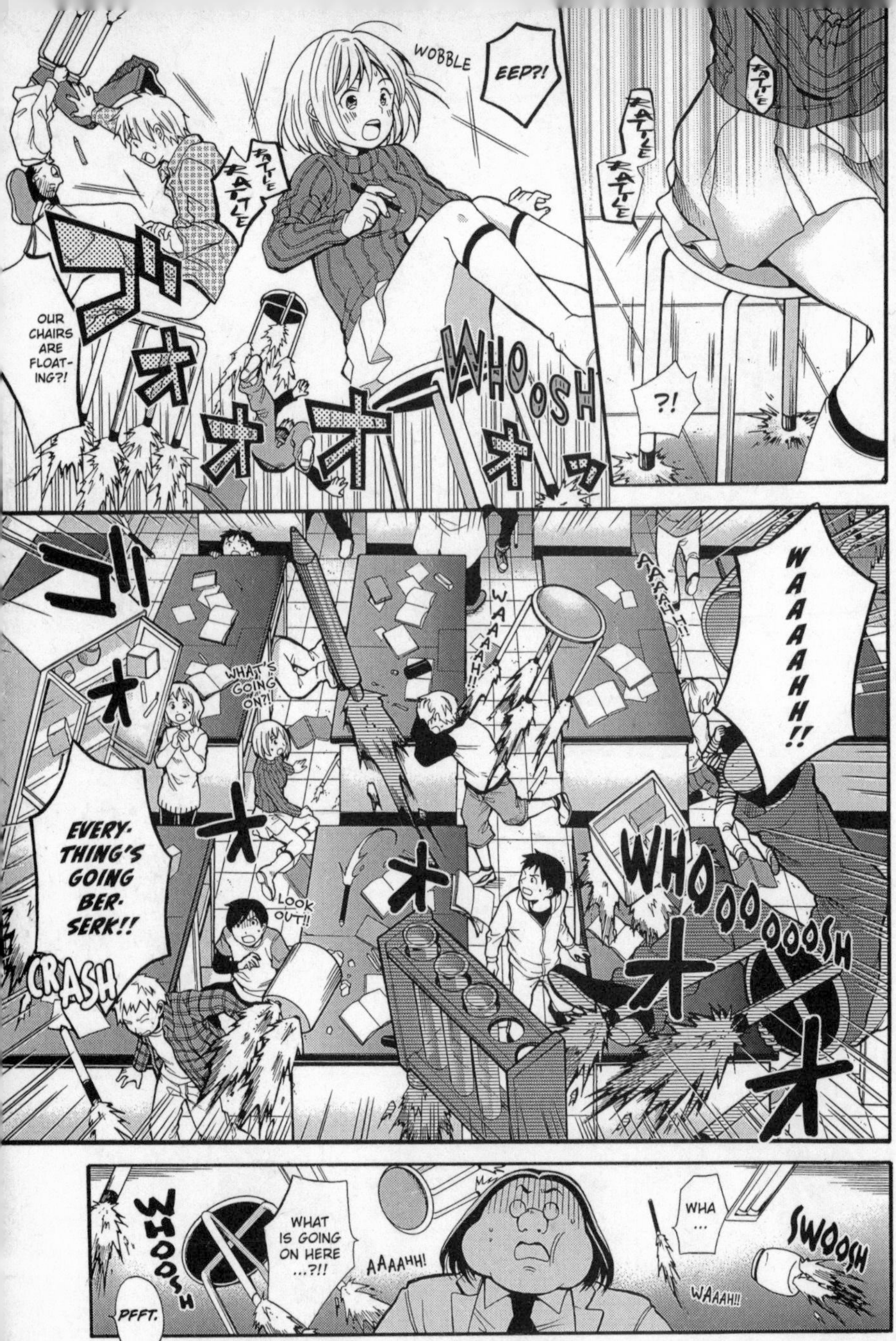

RATTLE
RATTLE
RATTLE
?!
WOBBLE
EEP?!
RATTLE
RATTLE
OUR CHAIRS ARE FLOATING?!
WHOOSH
WAAAAAHH!!
AAAAAH!!
WAAAAH!!
WHAT'S GOING ON?!
EVERYTHING'S GOING BERSERK!!
LOOK OUT!!
CRASH
WHOOOOOOOSH
SWOOSH
WHA...
WAAAH!!
WHAT IS GOING ON HERE...?!!
AAAAHH!
WHOOSH
PFFT.

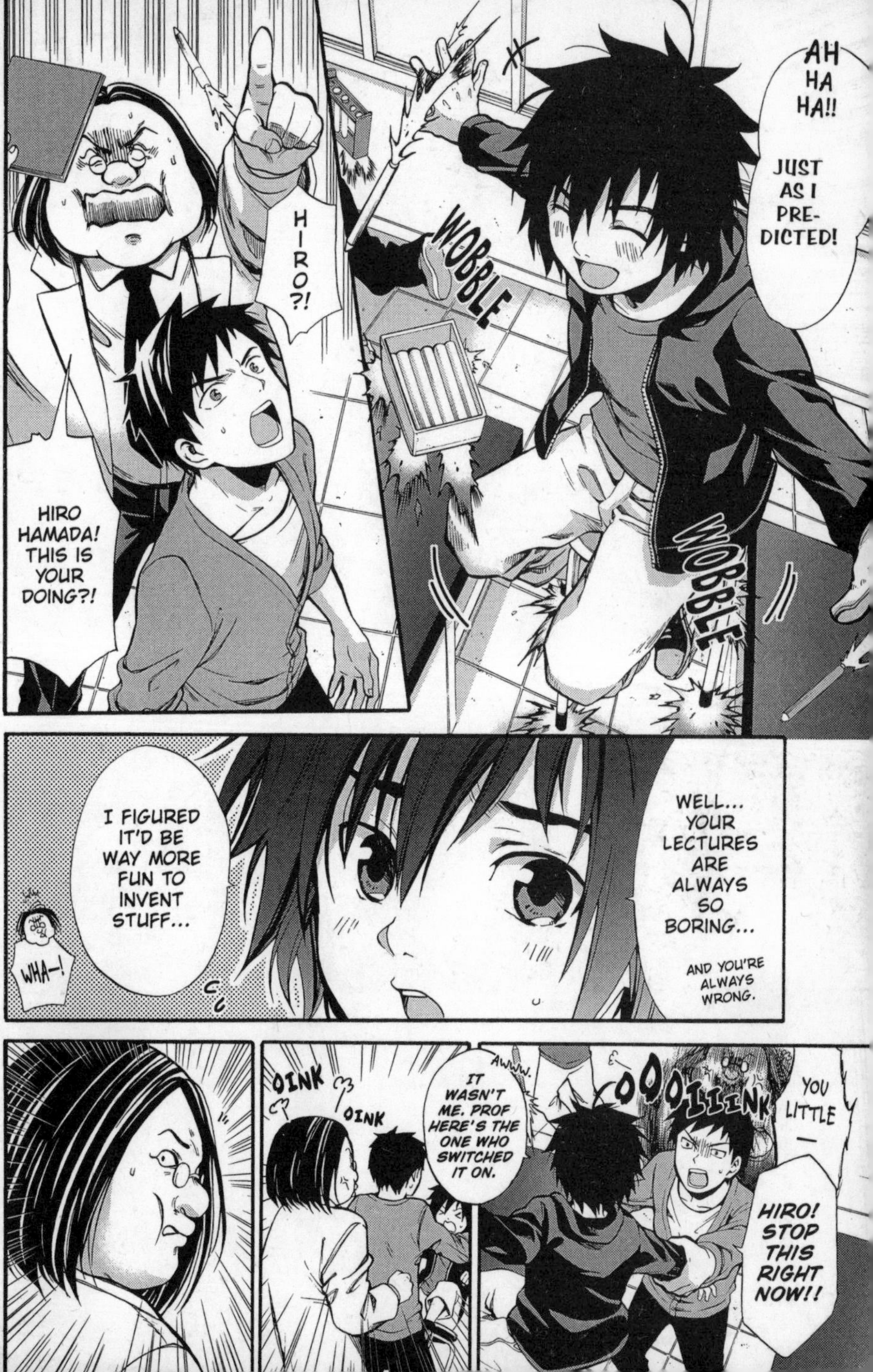
AH HA HA!!
JUST AS I PRE-DICTED!
WOBBLE
WOBBLE
HIRO?!
HIRO HAMADA! THIS IS YOUR DOING?!
WELL... YOUR LECTURES ARE ALWAYS SO BORING...
AND YOU'RE ALWAYS WRONG.
I FIGURED IT'D BE WAY MORE FUN TO INVENT STUFF...
WHA—!
YOU LITTLE —
OOOIIIINK
AWWW.
HIRO! STOP THIS RIGHT NOW!!
IT WASN'T ME. PROF HERE'S THE ONE WHO SWITCHED IT ON.
OINK
OINK

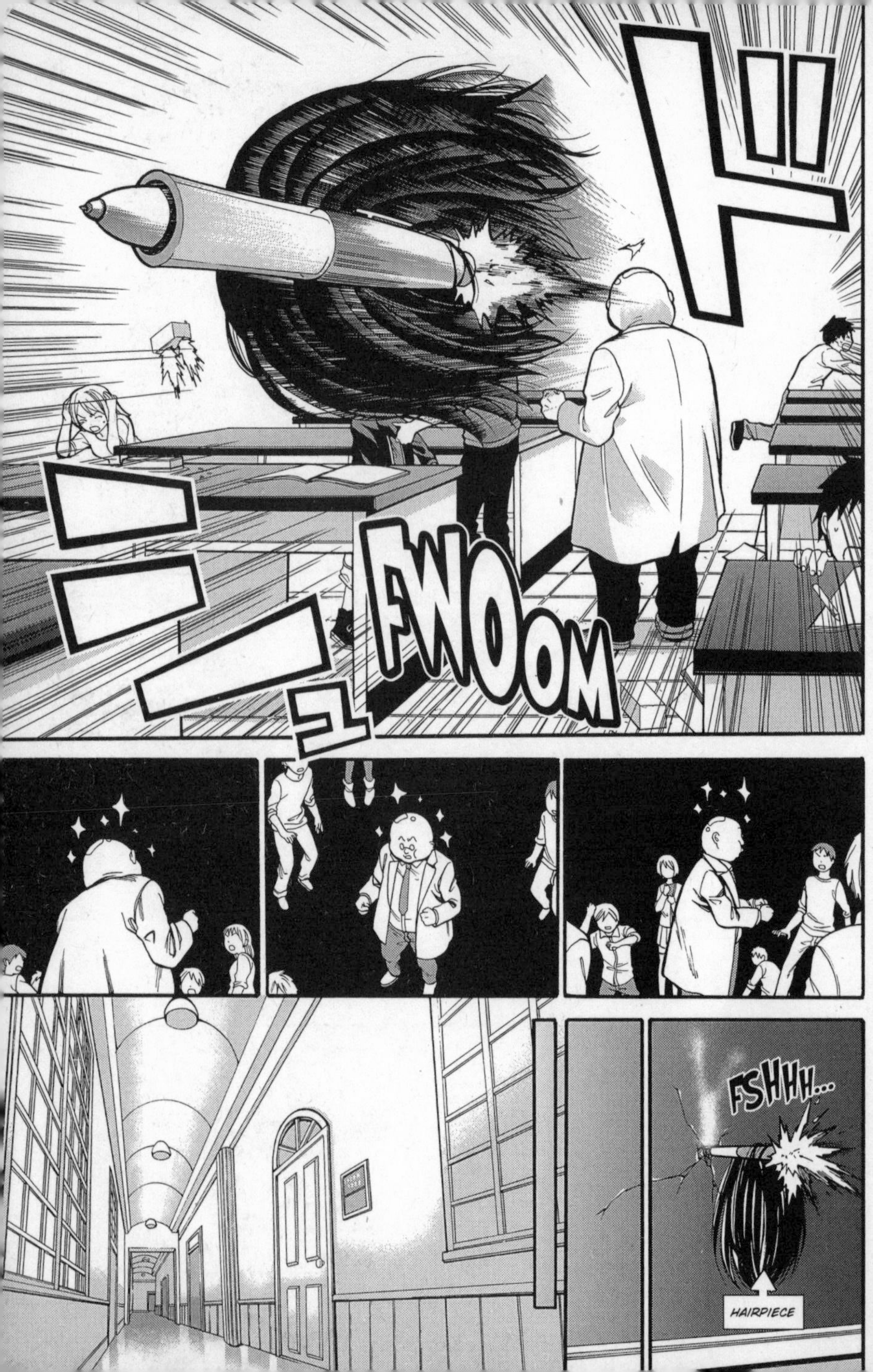
FWOOM
FSHHH...
HAIRPIECE

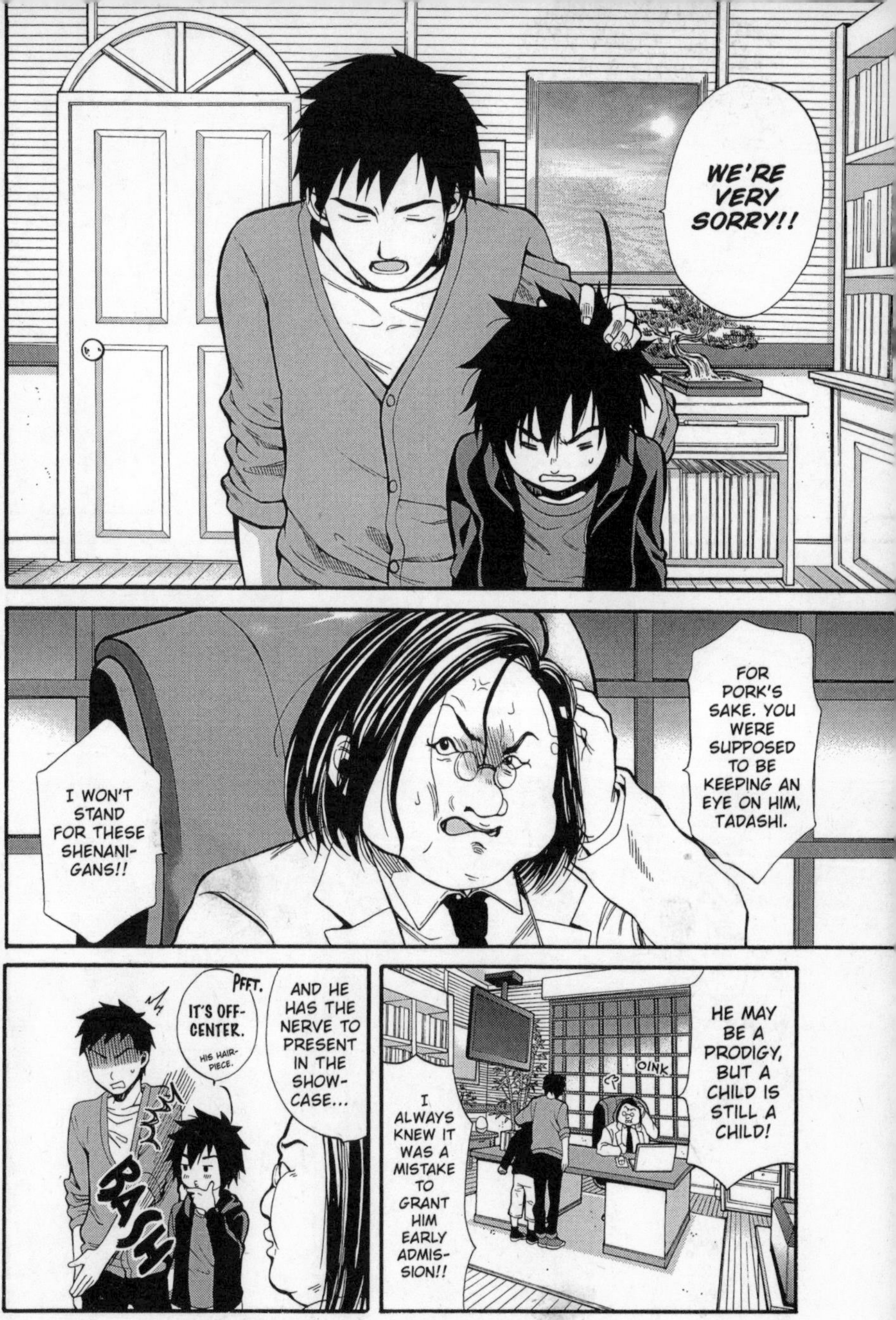
WE'RE VERY SORRY!!
FOR PORK'S SAKE. YOU WERE SUPPOSED TO BE KEEPING AN EYE ON HIM, TADASHI.
I WON'T STAND FOR THESE SHENANI-GANS!!
HE MAY BE A PRODIGY, BUT A CHILD IS STILL A CHILD!
OINK
I ALWAYS KNEW IT WAS A MISTAKE TO GRANT HIM EARLY ADMIS-SION!!
AND HE HAS THE NERVE TO PRESENT IN THE SHOW-CASE...
PFFT.
IT'S OFF-CENTER.
HIS HAIR-PIECE.
BASH

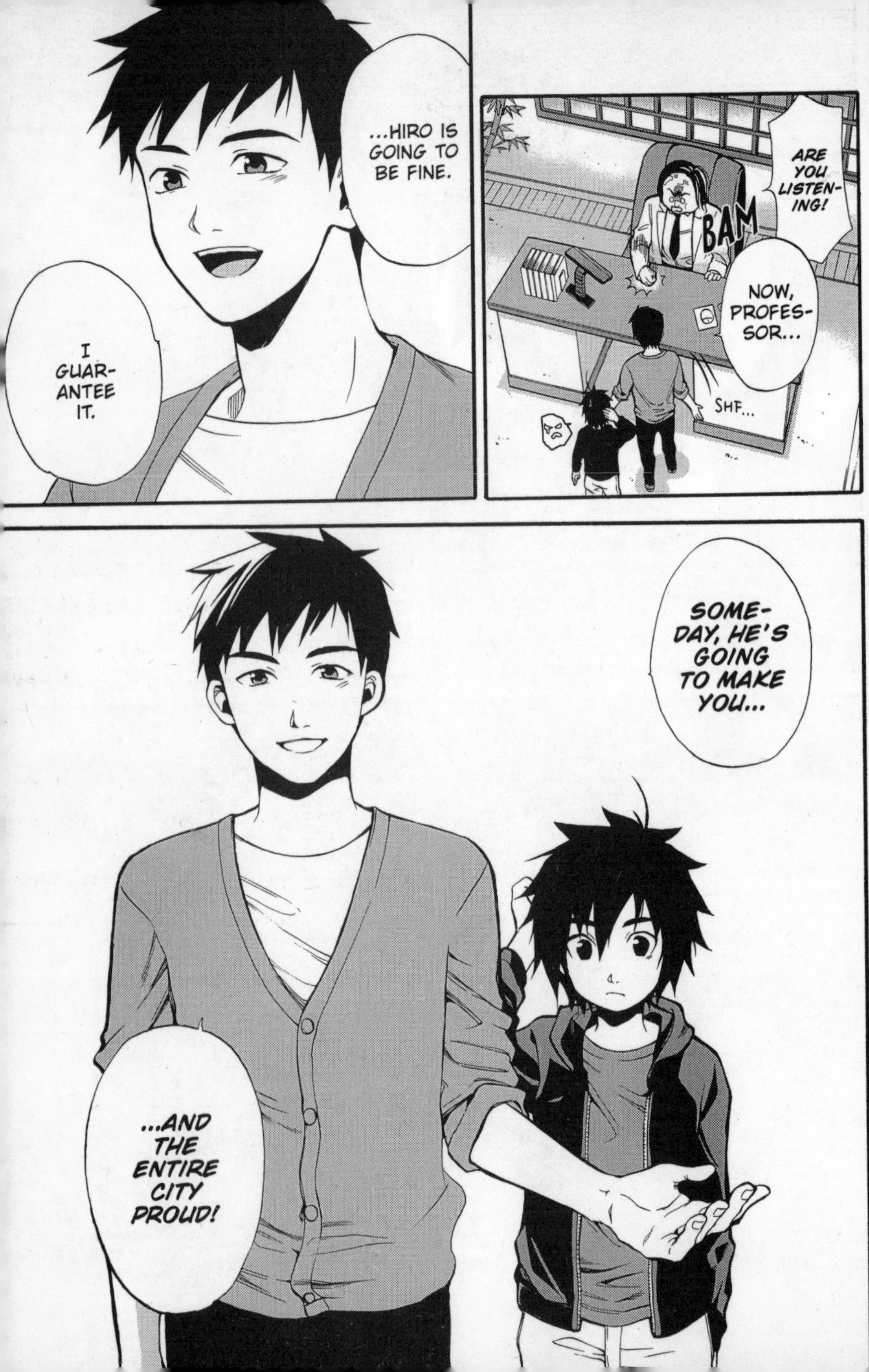
ARE YOU LISTENING!
BAM
NOW, PROFESSOR...
SHF...
...HIRO IS GOING TO BE FINE.
I GUARANTEE IT.
SOMEDAY, HE'S GOING TO MAKE YOU...
...AND THE ENTIRE CITY PROUD!

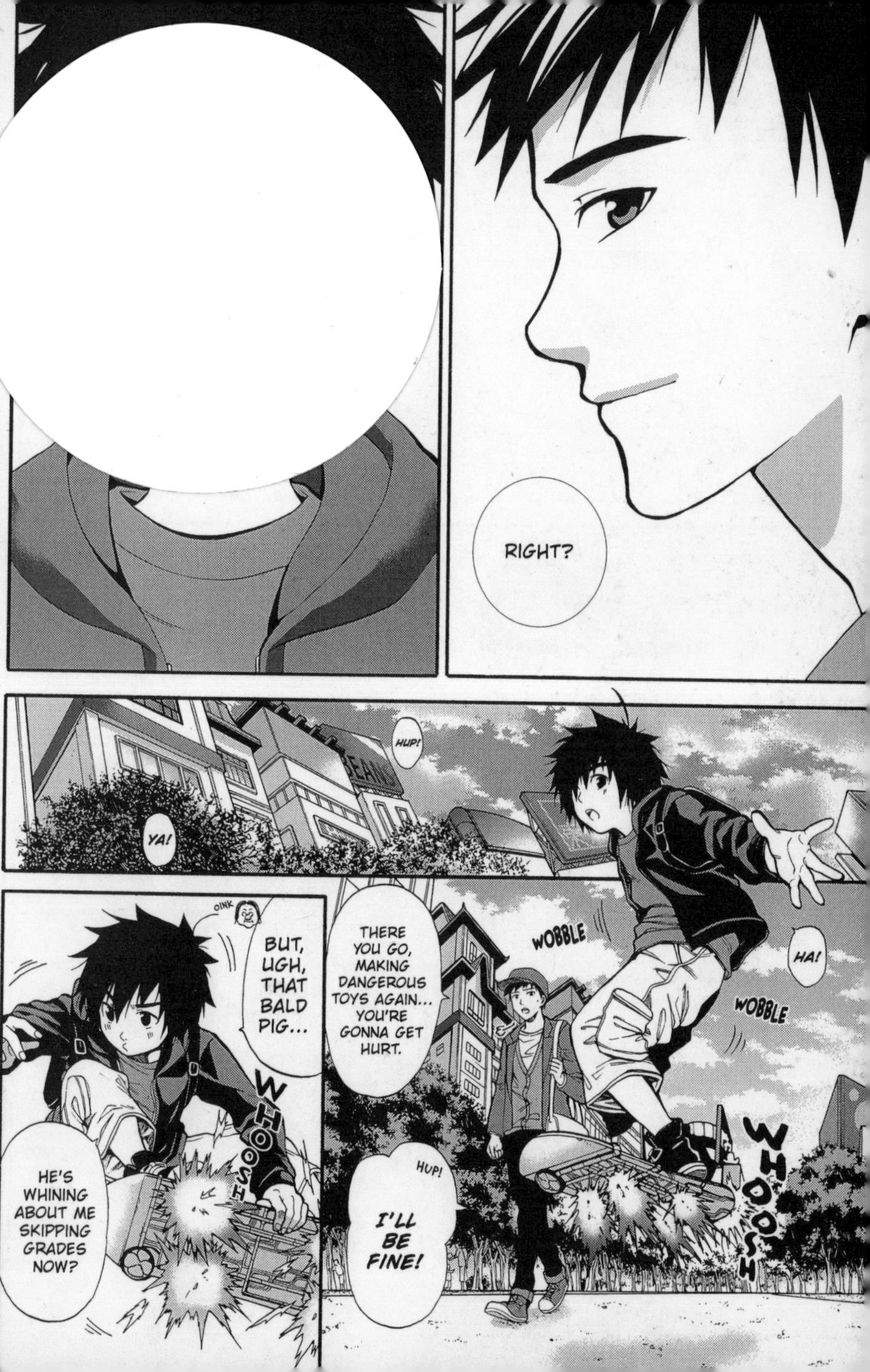
RIGHT?
HUP!
YA!
WOBBLE
HA!
WOBBLE
THERE YOU GO, MAKING DANGEROUS TOYS AGAIN... YOU'RE GONNA GET HURT.
WHOOSH
HUP!
I'LL BE FINE!
OINK
BUT, UGH, THAT BALD PIG...
WHOOSH
HE'S WHINING ABOUT ME SKIPPING GRADES NOW?

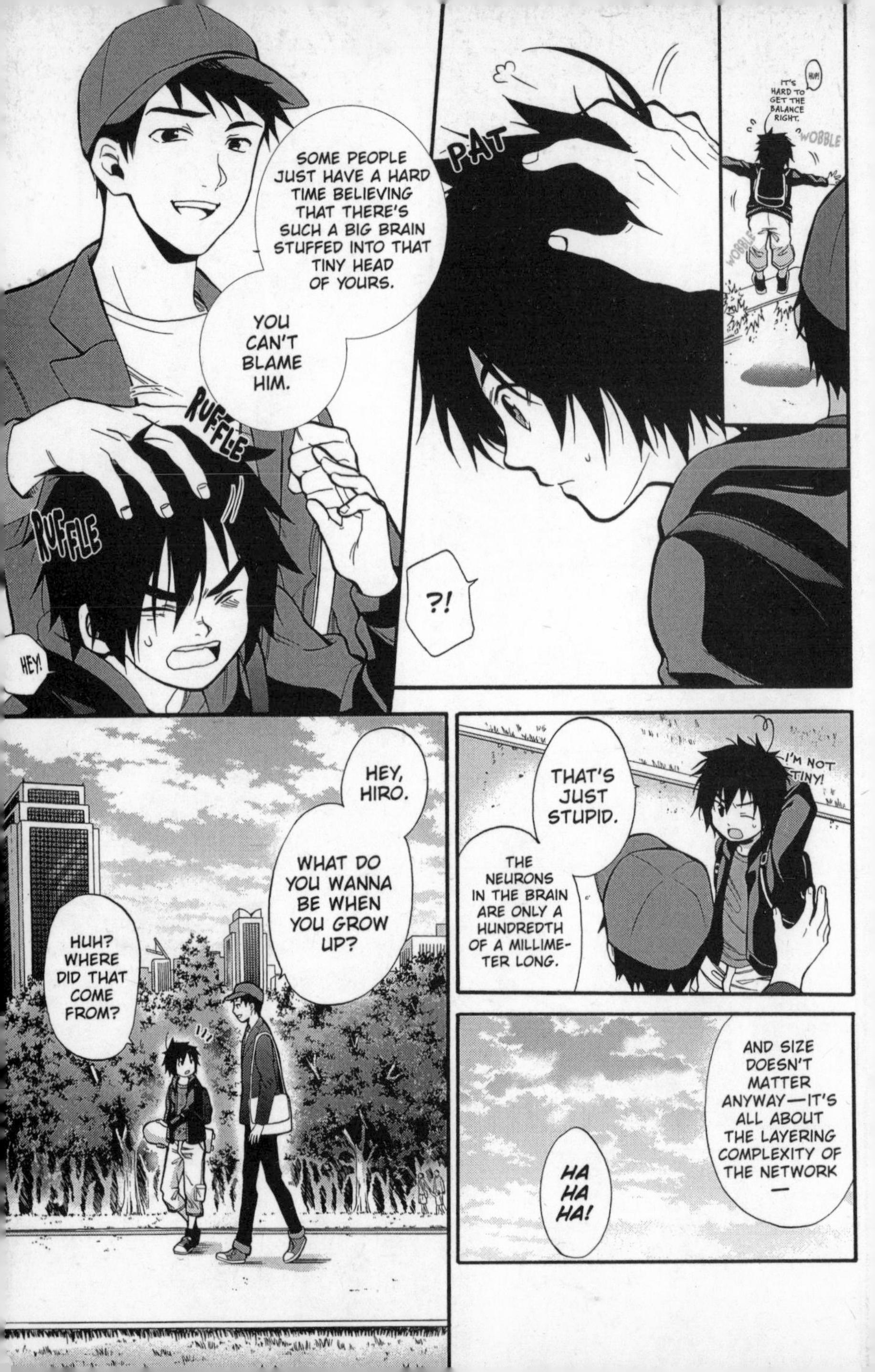
HUP!
IT'S HARD TO GET THE BALANCE RIGHT.
WOBBLE
WOBBLE
PAT
?!
SOME PEOPLE JUST HAVE A HARD TIME BELIEVING THAT THERE'S SUCH A BIG BRAIN STUFFED INTO THAT TINY HEAD OF YOURS.
YOU CAN'T BLAME HIM.
RUFFLE
RUFFLE
HEY!
I'M NOT TINY!
THAT'S JUST STUPID.
THE NEURONS IN THE BRAIN ARE ONLY A HUNDREDTH OF A MILLIME-TER LONG.
AND SIZE DOESN'T MATTER ANYWAY—IT'S ALL ABOUT THE LAYERING COMPLEXITY OF THE NETWORK —
HA HA HA!
HEY, HIRO.
WHAT DO YOU WANNA BE WHEN YOU GROW UP?
HUH? WHERE DID THAT COME FROM?

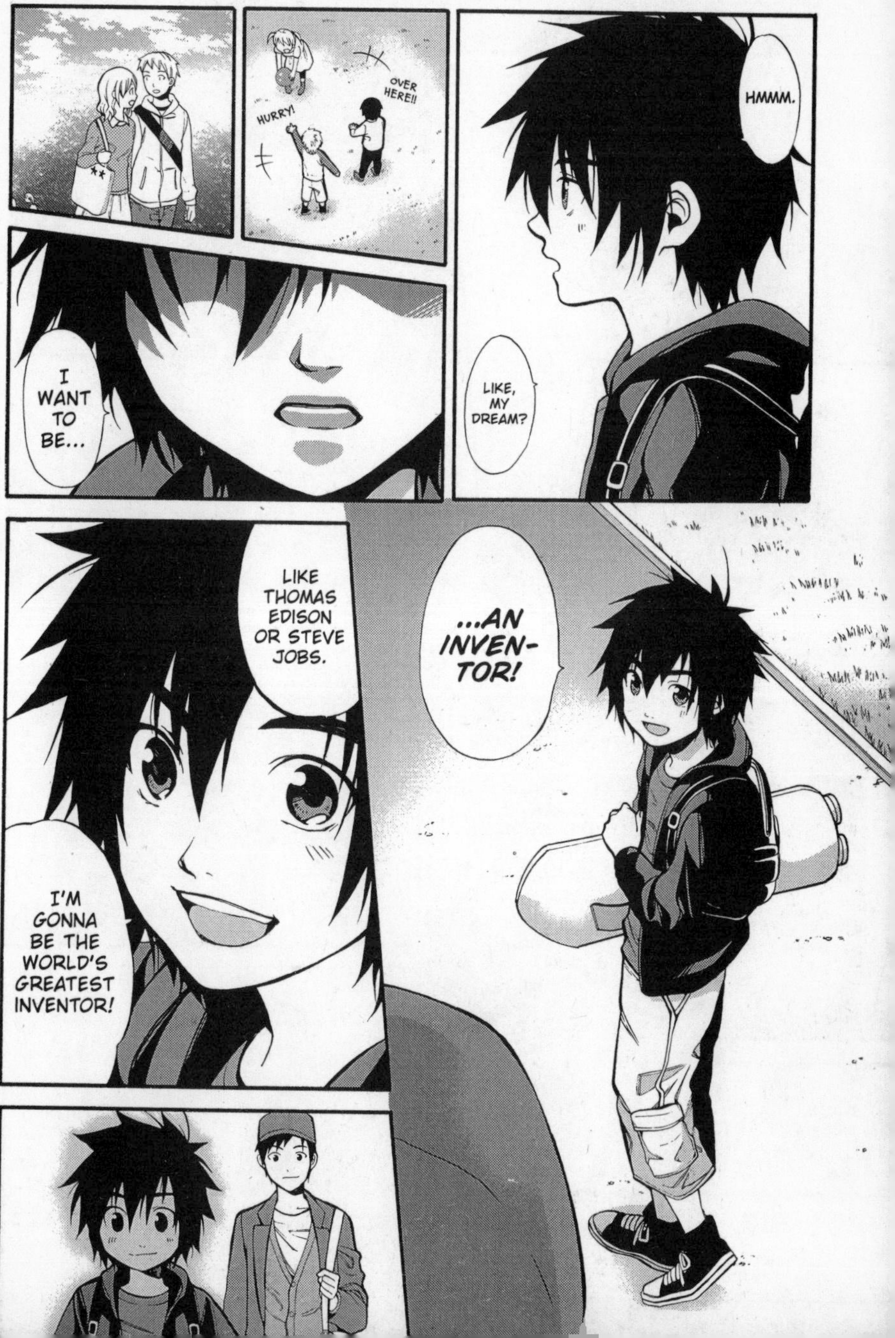
HMMM.
LIKE, MY DREAM?
OVER HERE!!
HURRY!
I WANT TO BE...
...AN INVEN-TOR!
LIKE THOMAS EDISON OR STEVE JOBS.
I'M GONNA BE THE WORLD'S GREATEST INVENTOR!

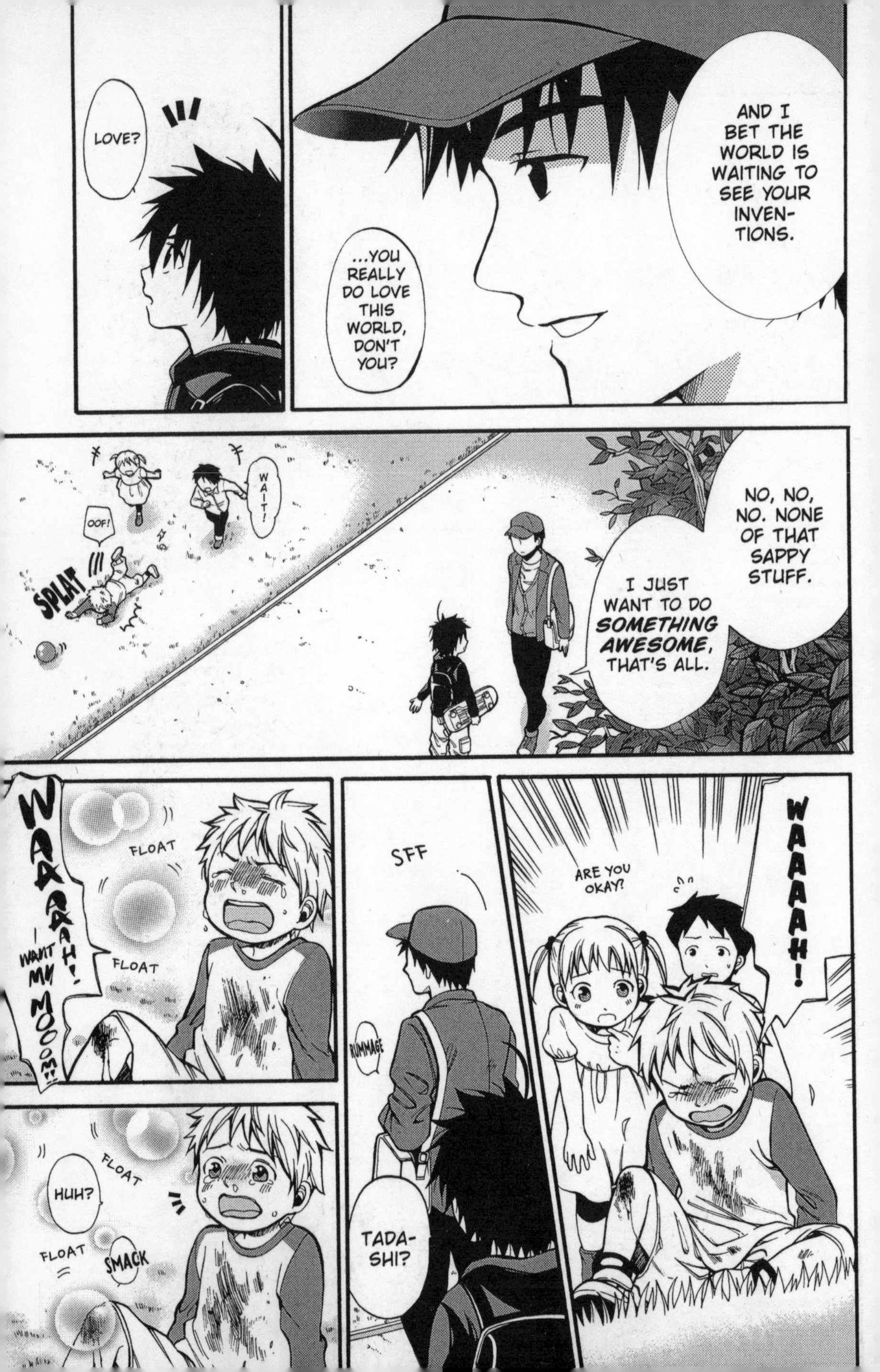
AND I BET THE WORLD IS WAITING TO SEE YOUR INVEN-TIONS.
...YOU REALLY DO LOVE THIS WORLD, DON'T YOU?
LOVE?
NO, NO, NO. NONE OF THAT SAPPY STUFF.
I JUST WANT TO DO *SOMETHING AWESOME*, THAT'S ALL.
WAIT!
OOF!
SPLAT
WAAAAAH!
ARE YOU OKAY?
SFF
RUMMAGE
TADA-SHI?
WAAAAAH! I WANT MY MOOOOM!!
FLOAT
FLOAT
FLOAT
HUH?
FLOAT
SMACK

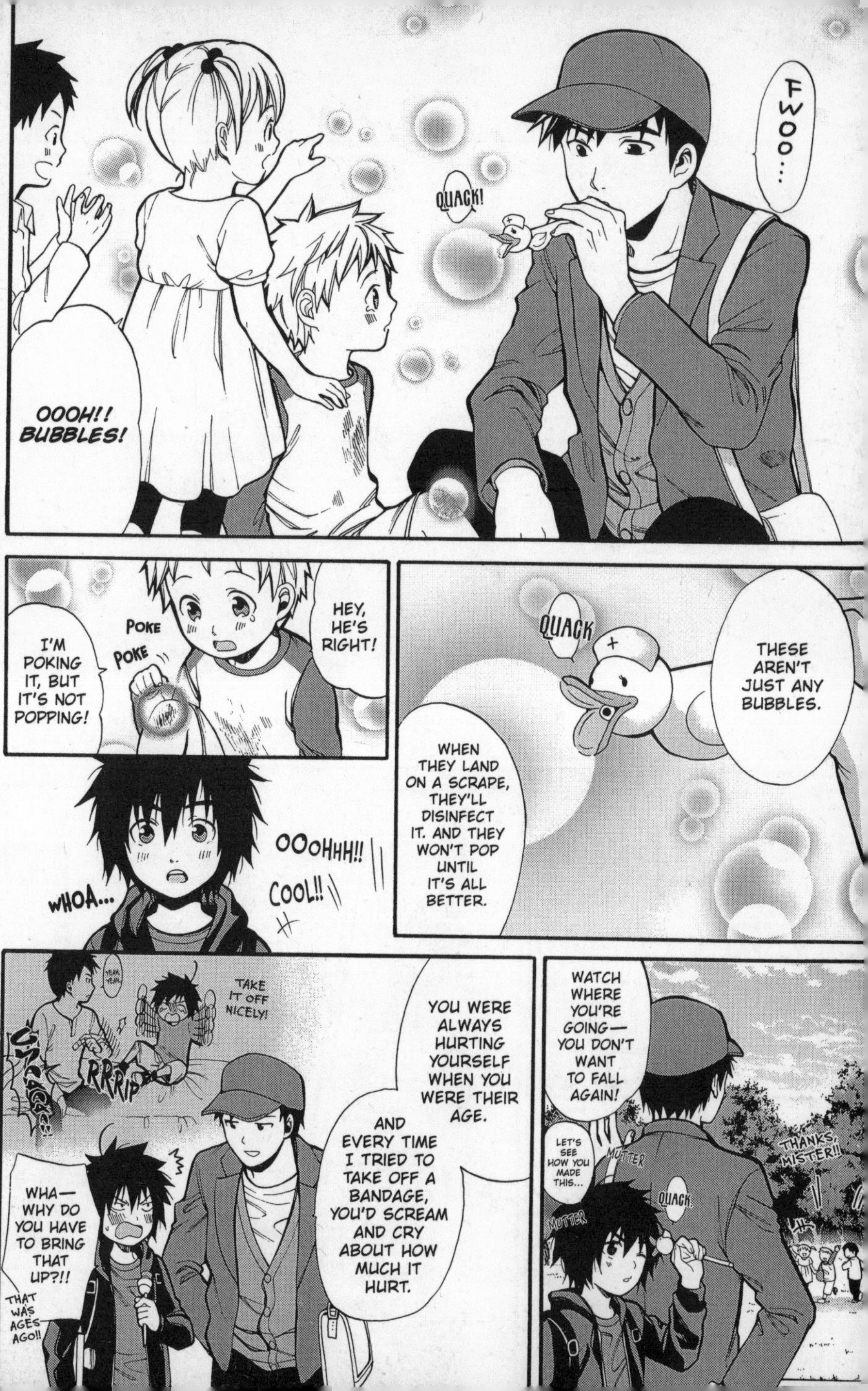
FWOO...
QUACK!
OOOH!! BUBBLES!
QUACK
THESE AREN'T JUST ANY BUBBLES.
WHEN THEY LAND ON A SCRAPE, THEY'LL DISINFECT IT. AND THEY WON'T POP UNTIL IT'S ALL BETTER.
HEY, HE'S RIGHT!
POKE
POKE
I'M POKING IT, BUT IT'S NOT POPPING!
OOOHHH!!
COOL!!
WHOA...
THANKS, MISTER!!
WATCH WHERE YOU'RE GOING— YOU DON'T WANT TO FALL AGAIN!
MUTTER
QUACK
LET'S SEE HOW YOU MADE THIS...
MUTTER
YOU WERE ALWAYS HURTING YOURSELF WHEN YOU WERE THEIR AGE.
AND EVERY TIME I TRIED TO TAKE OFF A BANDAGE, YOU'D SCREAM AND CRY ABOUT HOW MUCH IT HURT.
TAKE IT OFF NICELY!
YEAH YEAH
RRRIP
WHA— WHY DO YOU HAVE TO BRING THAT UP?!!
THAT WAS AGES AGO!!

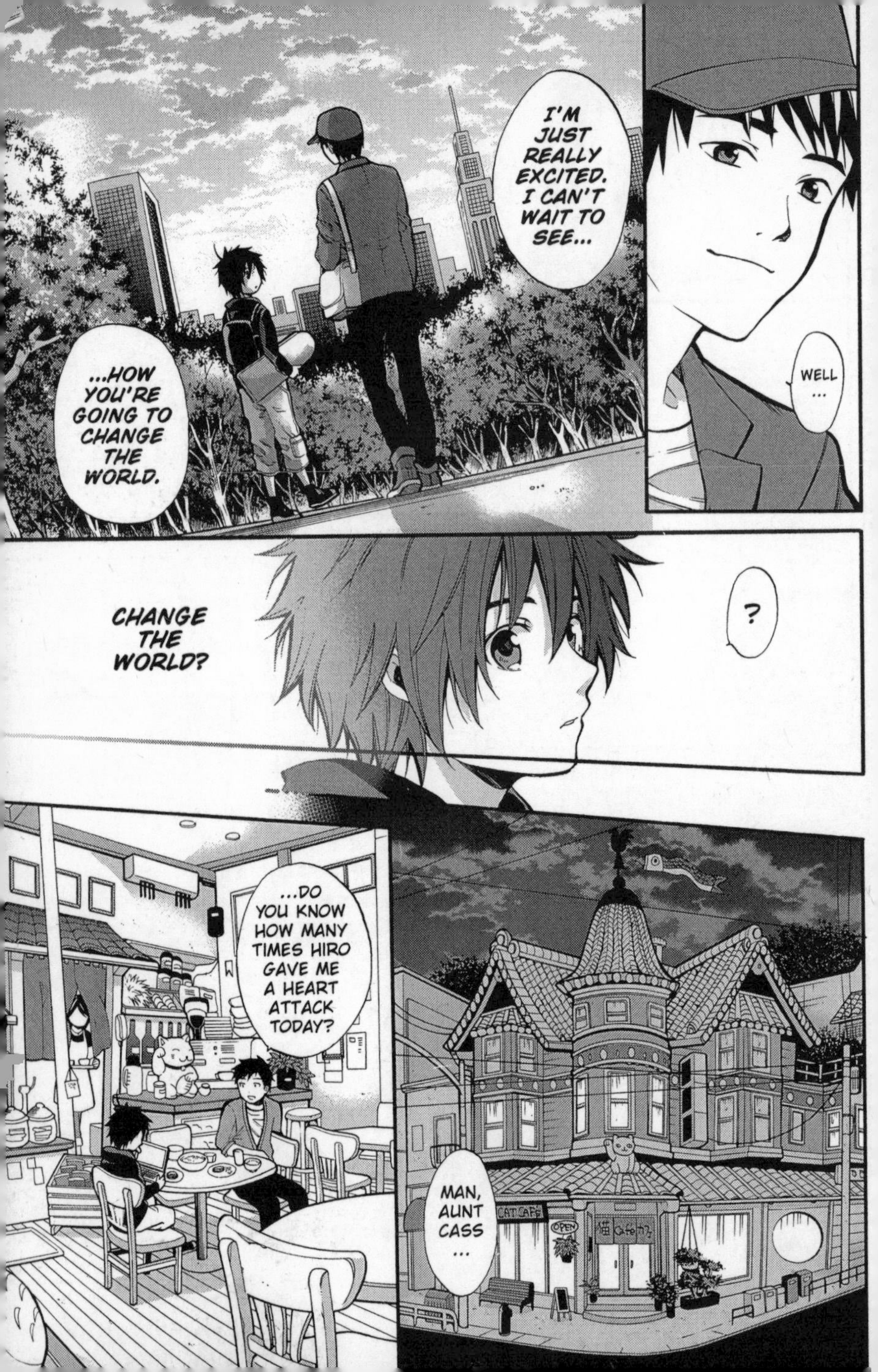
WELL ...
I'M JUST REALLY EXCITED. I CAN'T WAIT TO SEE...
...HOW YOU'RE GOING TO CHANGE THE WORLD.
...
?
CHANGE THE WORLD?
MAN, AUNT CASS ...
CAT CAFE
OPEN
...DO YOU KNOW HOW MANY TIMES HIRO GAVE ME A HEART ATTACK TODAY?

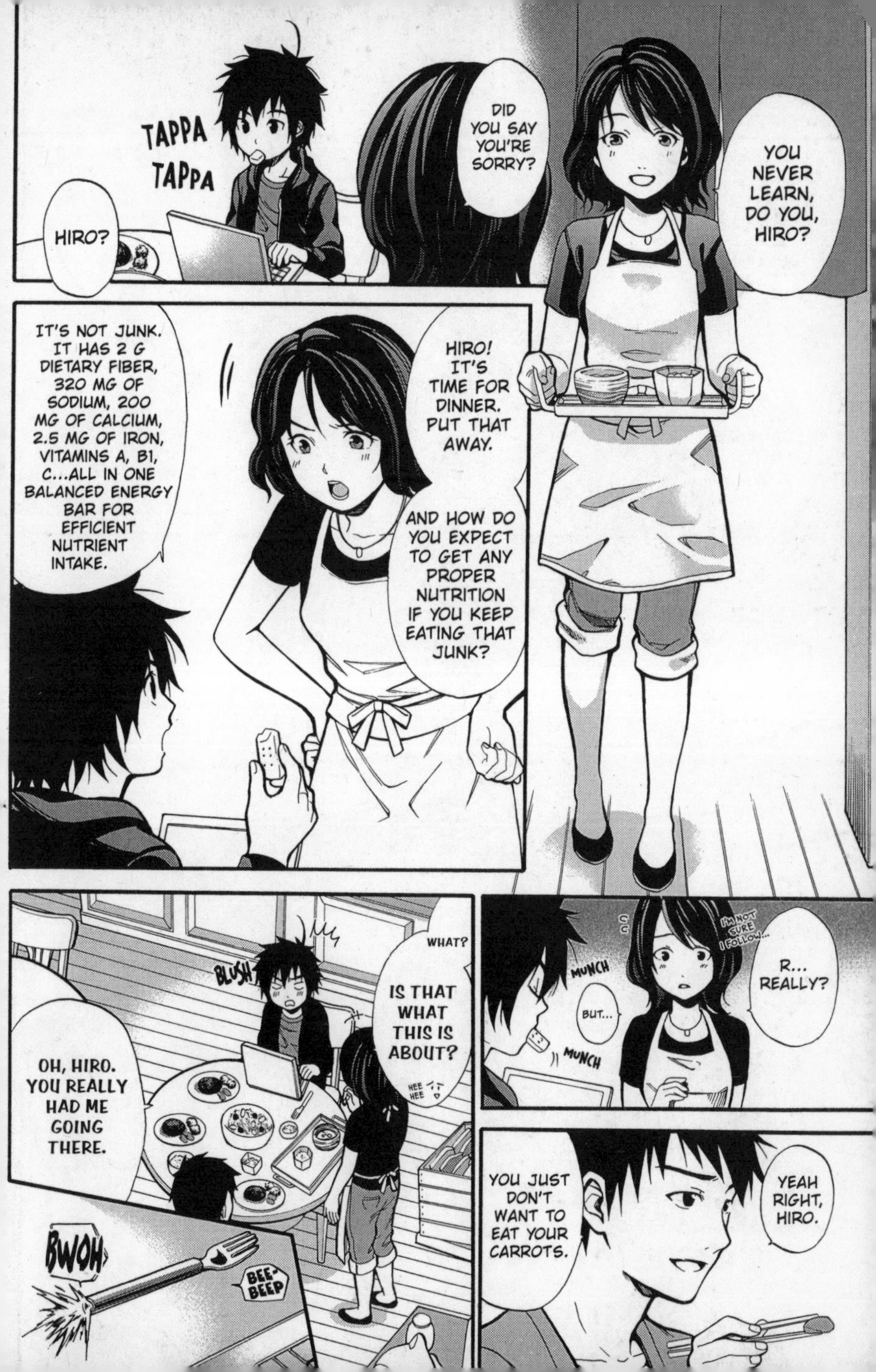
YOU NEVER LEARN, DO YOU, HIRO?
DID YOU SAY YOU'RE SORRY?
TAPPA TAPPA
HIRO?
HIRO! IT'S TIME FOR DINNER. PUT THAT AWAY.
AND HOW DO YOU EXPECT TO GET ANY PROPER NUTRITION IF YOU KEEP EATING THAT JUNK?
IT'S NOT JUNK. IT HAS 2 G DIETARY FIBER, 320 MG OF SODIUM, 200 MG OF CALCIUM, 2.5 MG OF IRON, VITAMINS A, B1, C...ALL IN ONE BALANCED ENERGY BAR FOR EFFICIENT NUTRIENT INTAKE.
I'M NOT SURE I FOLLOW...
R... REALLY?
MUNCH
BUT...
MUNCH
YEAH RIGHT, HIRO.
YOU JUST DON'T WANT TO EAT YOUR CARROTS.
WHAT?
IS THAT WHAT THIS IS ABOUT?
BLUSH
HEE HEE
OH, HIRO. YOU REALLY HAD ME GOING THERE.
BWOH
BEE-BEEP

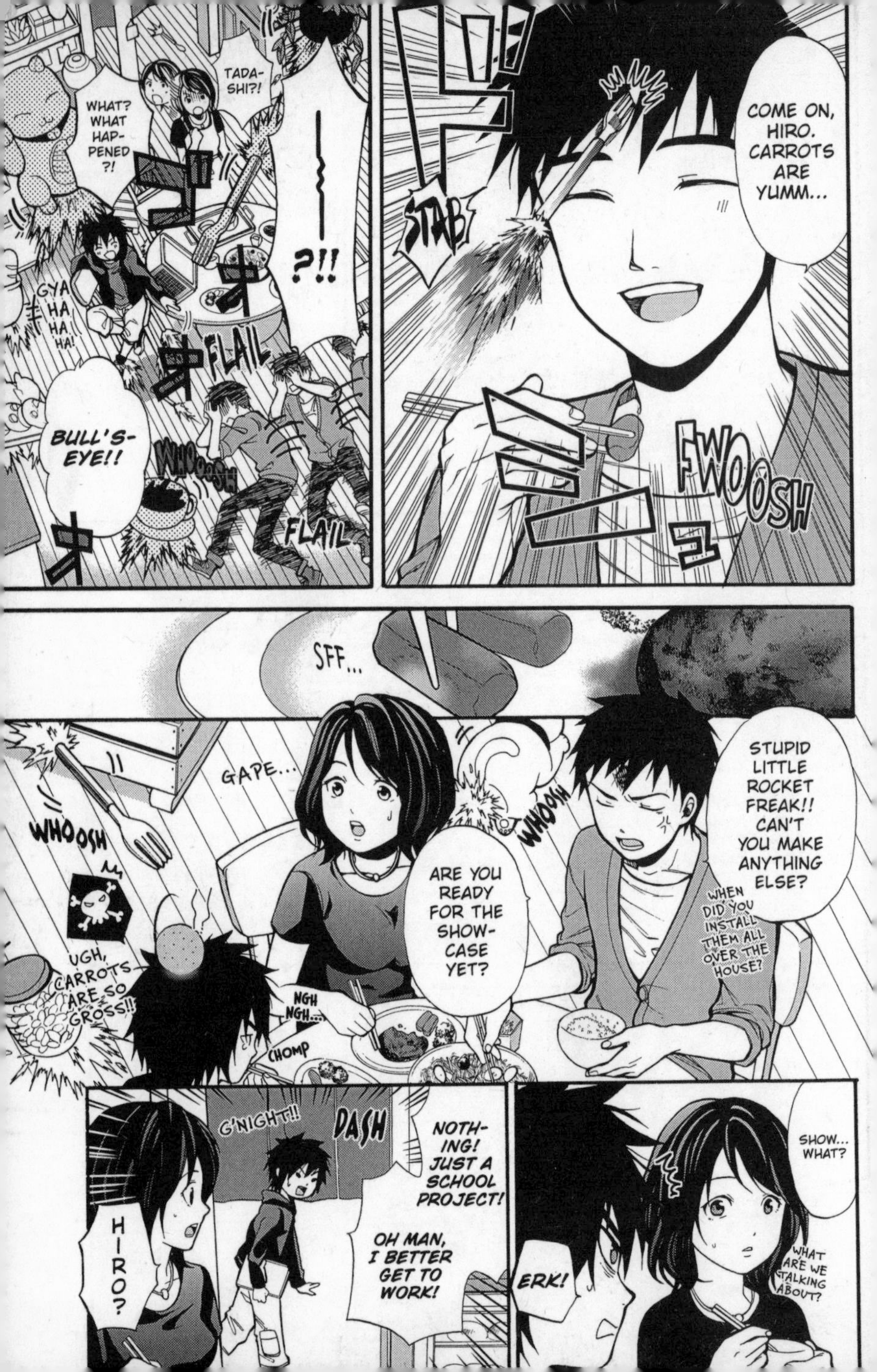
COME ON, HIRO. CARROTS ARE YUMM...
STAB
FWOOSH
TADA-SHI?!
WHAT? WHAT HAP-PENED?!
?!!
GYA HA HA HA!
FLAIL
BULL'S-EYE!!
WHOOOSH
FLAIL
SFF...
STUPID LITTLE ROCKET FREAK!! CAN'T YOU MAKE ANYTHING ELSE?
WHEN DID YOU INSTALL THEM ALL OVER THE HOUSE?
WHOOSH
GAPE...
ARE YOU READY FOR THE SHOW-CASE YET?
WHOOSH
NGH NGH...
UGH, CARROTS ARE SO GROSS!!
CHOMP
SHOW... WHAT?
WHAT ARE WE TALKING ABOUT?
ERK!
NOTH-ING! JUST A SCHOOL PROJECT!
DASH
G'NIGHT!!
OH MAN, I BETTER GET TO WORK!
HIRO?

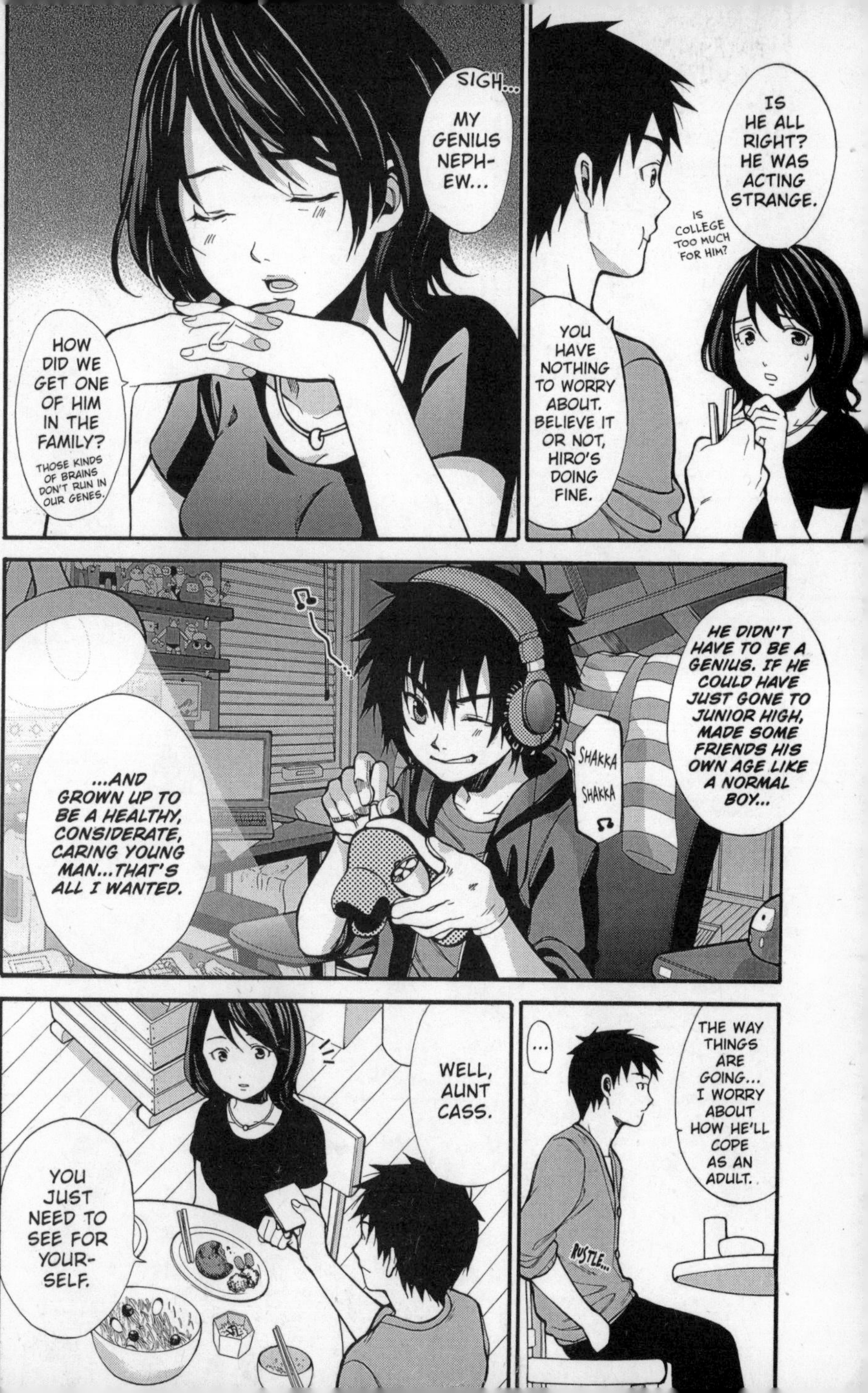
IS HE ALL RIGHT? HE WAS ACTING STRANGE.
IS COLLEGE TOO MUCH FOR HIM?
YOU HAVE NOTHING TO WORRY ABOUT. BELIEVE IT OR NOT, HIRO'S DOING FINE.
SIGH...
MY GENIUS NEPH-EW...
HOW DID WE GET ONE OF HIM IN THE FAMILY?
THOSE KINDS OF BRAINS DON'T RUN IN OUR GENES.
HE DIDN'T HAVE TO BE A GENIUS. IF HE COULD HAVE JUST GONE TO JUNIOR HIGH, MADE SOME FRIENDS HIS OWN AGE LIKE A NORMAL BOY...
SHAKKA SHAKKA
...AND GROWN UP TO BE A HEALTHY, CONSIDERATE, CARING YOUNG MAN...THAT'S ALL I WANTED.
THE WAY THINGS ARE GOING... I WORRY ABOUT HOW HE'LL COPE AS AN ADULT.
...
RUSTLE...
WELL, AUNT CASS.
YOU JUST NEED TO SEE FOR YOUR-SELF.

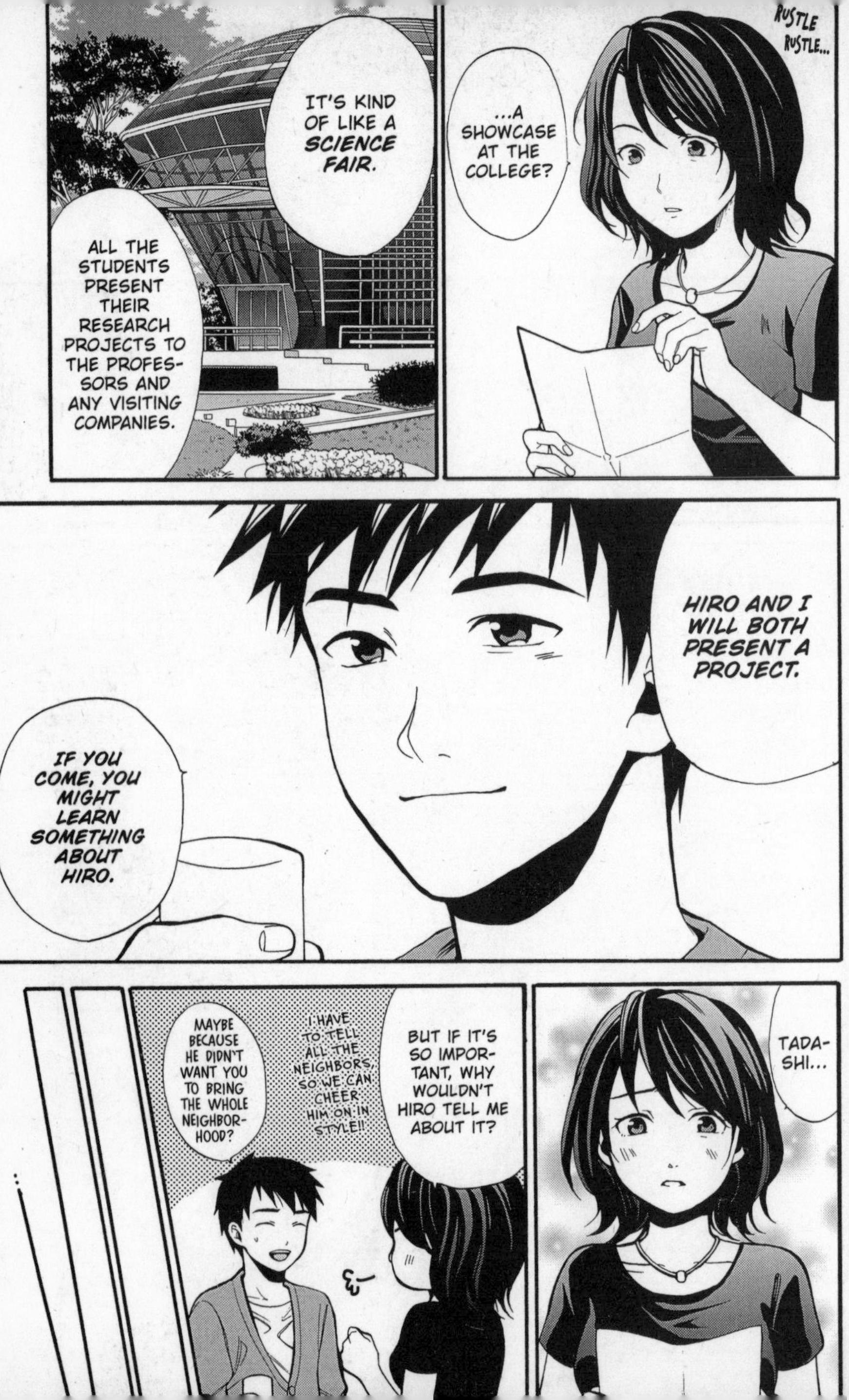
RUSTLE RUSTLE...
...A SHOWCASE AT THE COLLEGE?
IT'S KIND OF LIKE A SCIENCE FAIR.
ALL THE STUDENTS PRESENT THEIR RESEARCH PROJECTS TO THE PROFES-SORS AND ANY VISITING COMPANIES.
HIRO AND I WILL BOTH PRESENT A PROJECT.
IF YOU COME, YOU MIGHT LEARN SOMETHING ABOUT HIRO.
TADA-SHI...
BUT IF IT'S SO IMPOR-TANT, WHY WOULDN'T HIRO TELL ME ABOUT IT?
I HAVE TO TELL ALL THE NEIGHBORS, SO WE CAN CHEER HIM ON IN STYLE!!
MAYBE BECAUSE HE DIDN'T WANT YOU TO BRING THE WHOLE NEIGHBOR-HOOD?

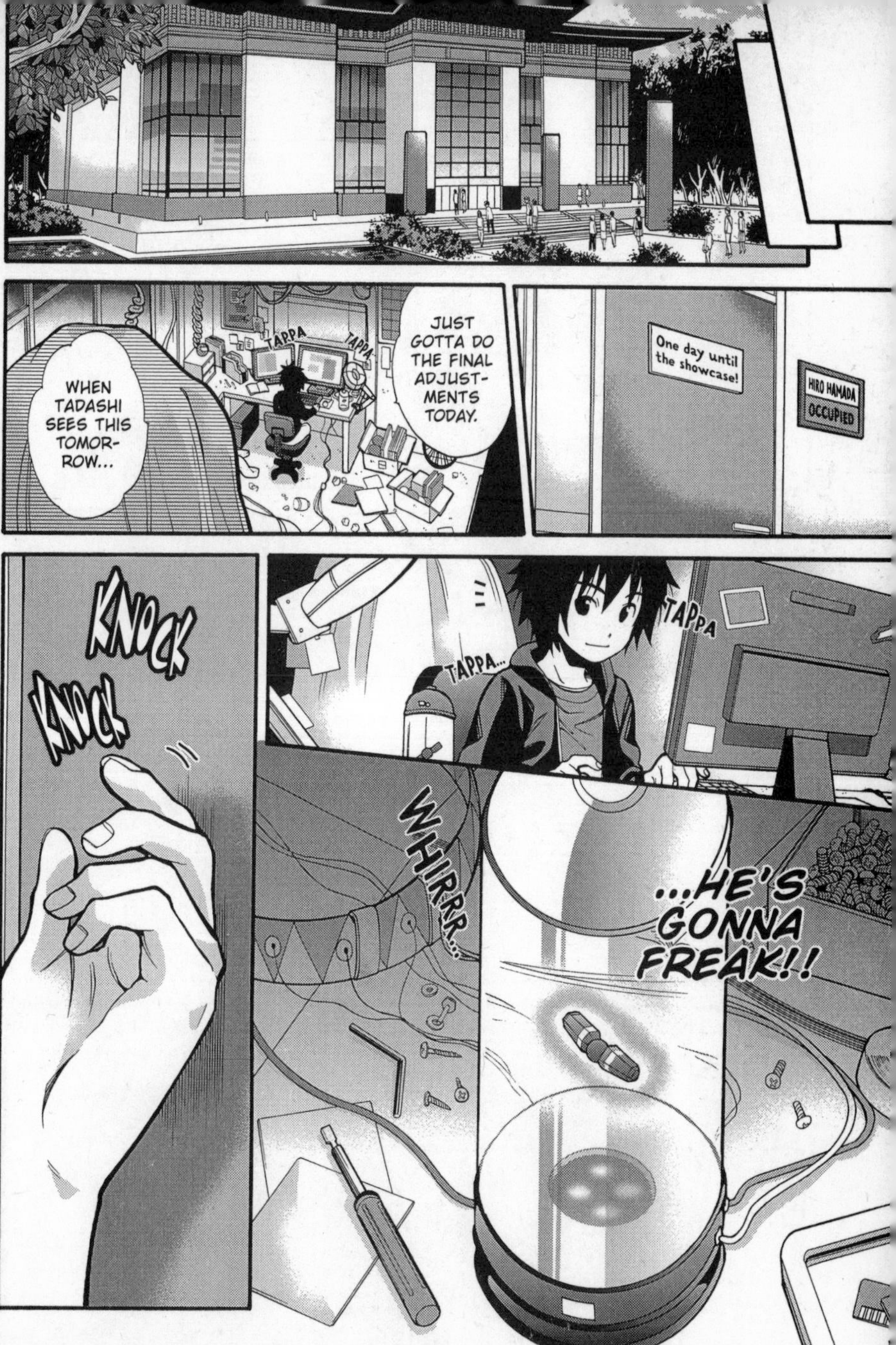
One day until the showcase!
HIRO HAMADA
OCCUPIED
JUST GOTTA DO THE FINAL ADJUSTMENTS TODAY.
TAPPA
TAPPA
WHEN TADASHI SEES THIS TOMORROW...
TAPPA
TAPPA...
...HE'S GONNA FREAK!!
WHIRRR...
KNOCK
KNOCK

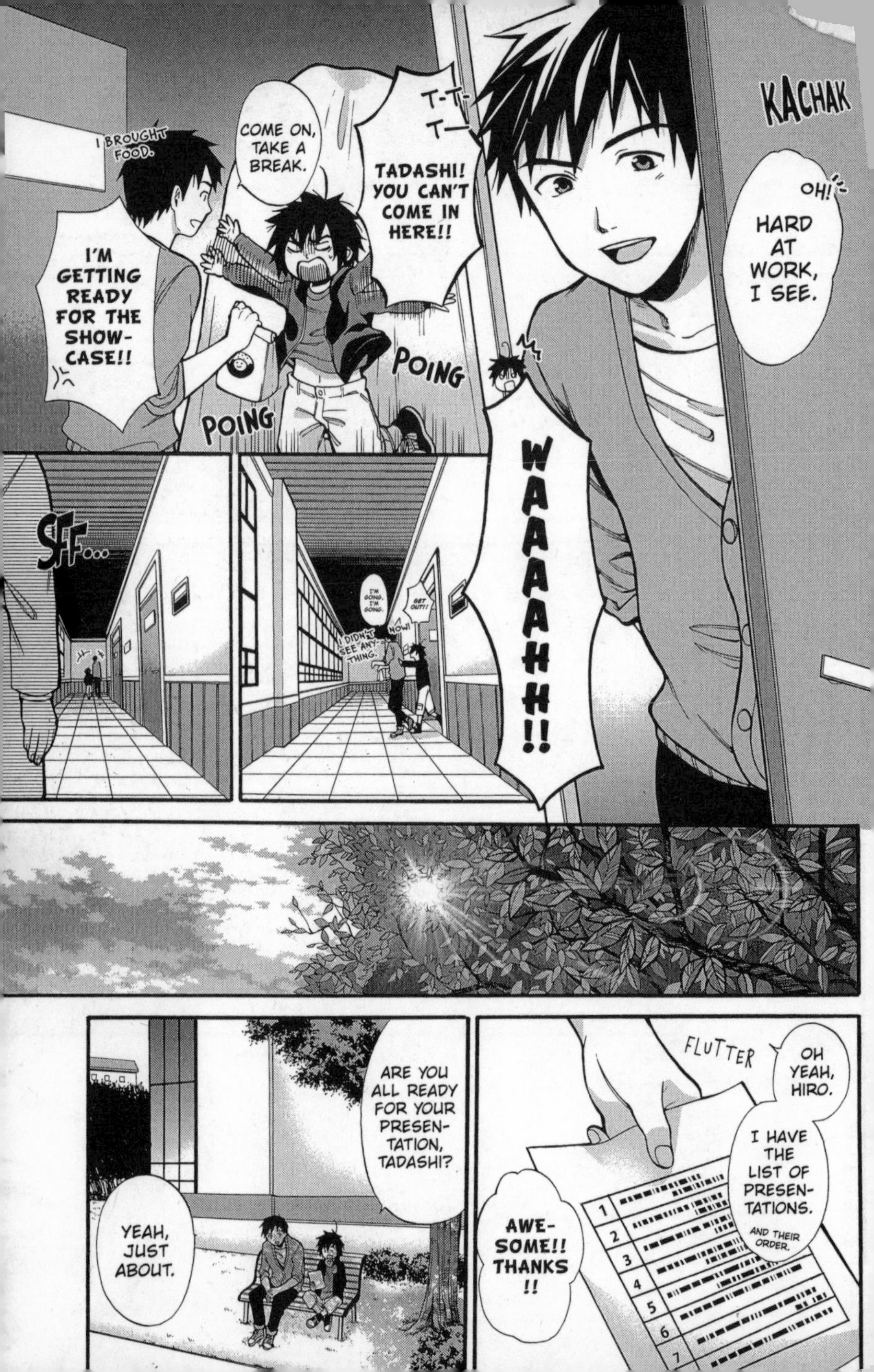
KACHAK
OH!
HARD AT WORK, I SEE.
WAAAAAHH!!
T-T-T-T—
TADASHI! YOU CAN'T COME IN HERE!!
COME ON, TAKE A BREAK.
I BROUGHT FOOD.
I'M GETTING READY FOR THE SHOW-CASE!!
POING
POING
I'M GOING, I'M GOING.
GET OUT!!
NOW!
I DIDN'T SEE ANY-THING.
SFF...
FLUTTER
OH YEAH, HIRO.
I HAVE THE LIST OF PRESEN-TATIONS.
AND THEIR ORDER.
AWE-SOME!! THANKS!!
ARE YOU ALL READY FOR YOUR PRESEN-TATION, TADASHI?
YEAH, JUST ABOUT.

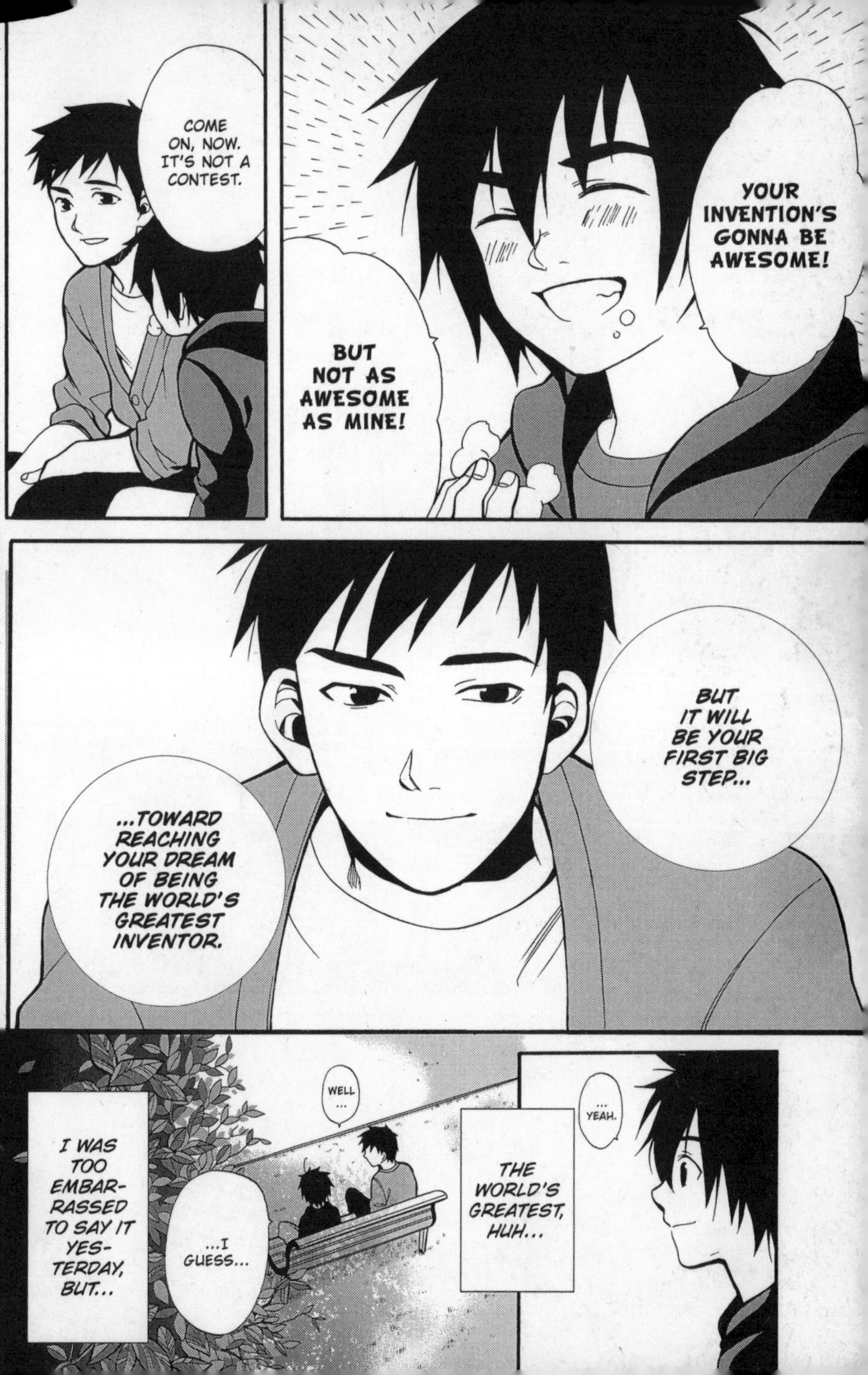
YOUR INVENTION'S GONNA BE AWESOME!
BUT NOT AS AWESOME AS MINE!
COME ON, NOW. IT'S NOT A CONTEST.
BUT IT WILL BE YOUR FIRST BIG STEP...
...TOWARD REACHING YOUR DREAM OF BEING THE WORLD'S GREATEST INVENTOR.
...YEAH.
THE WORLD'S GREATEST, HUH...
WELL...
...I GUESS...
I WAS TOO EMBARRASSED TO SAY IT YESTERDAY, BUT...

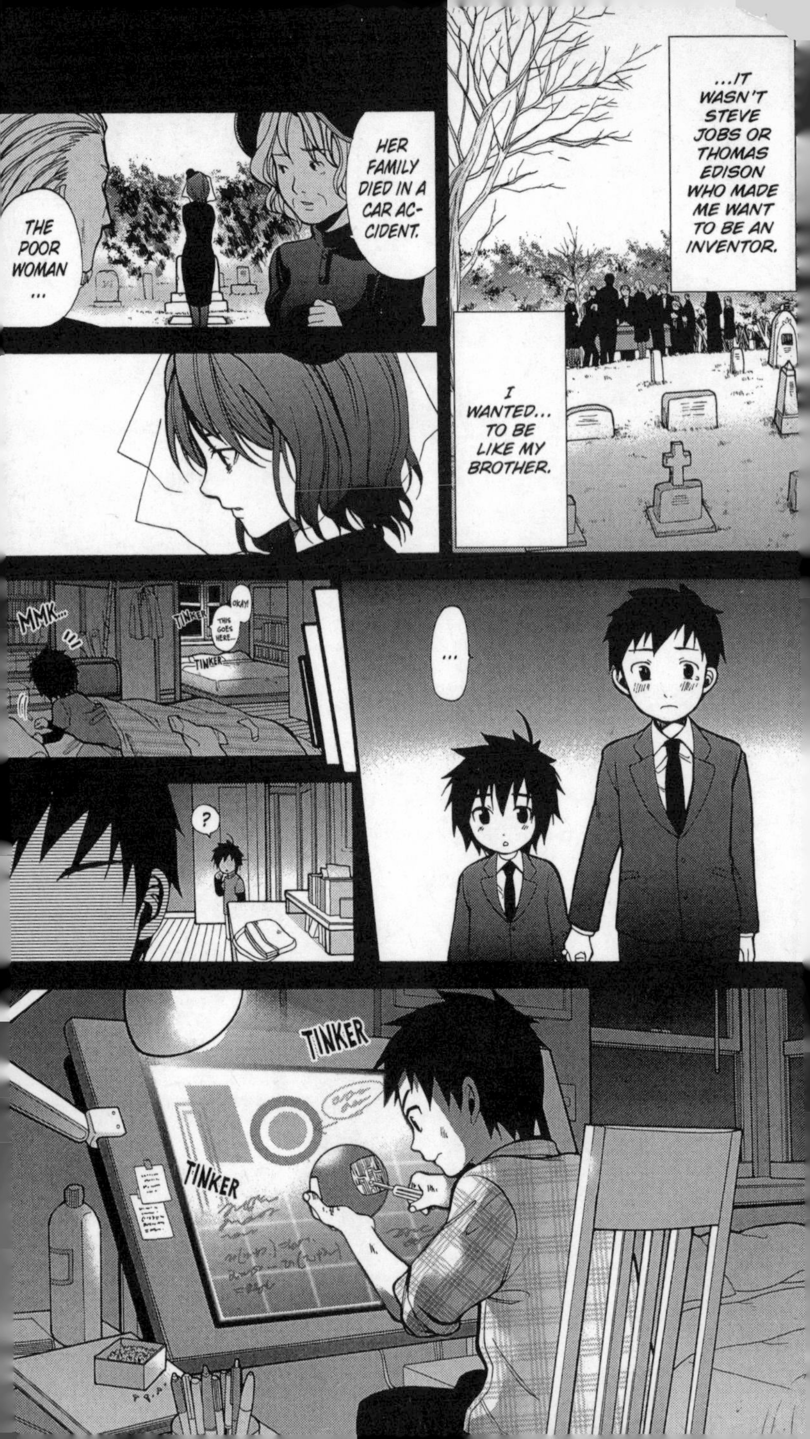
...IT WASN'T STEVE JOBS OR THOMAS EDISON WHO MADE ME WANT TO BE AN INVENTOR.
I WANTED... TO BE LIKE MY BROTHER.
HER FAMILY DIED IN A CAR ACCIDENT.
THE POOR WOMAN ...
...
OKAY!
THIS GOES HERE...
TINKER
TINKER
MMK...
?
TINKER
TINKER

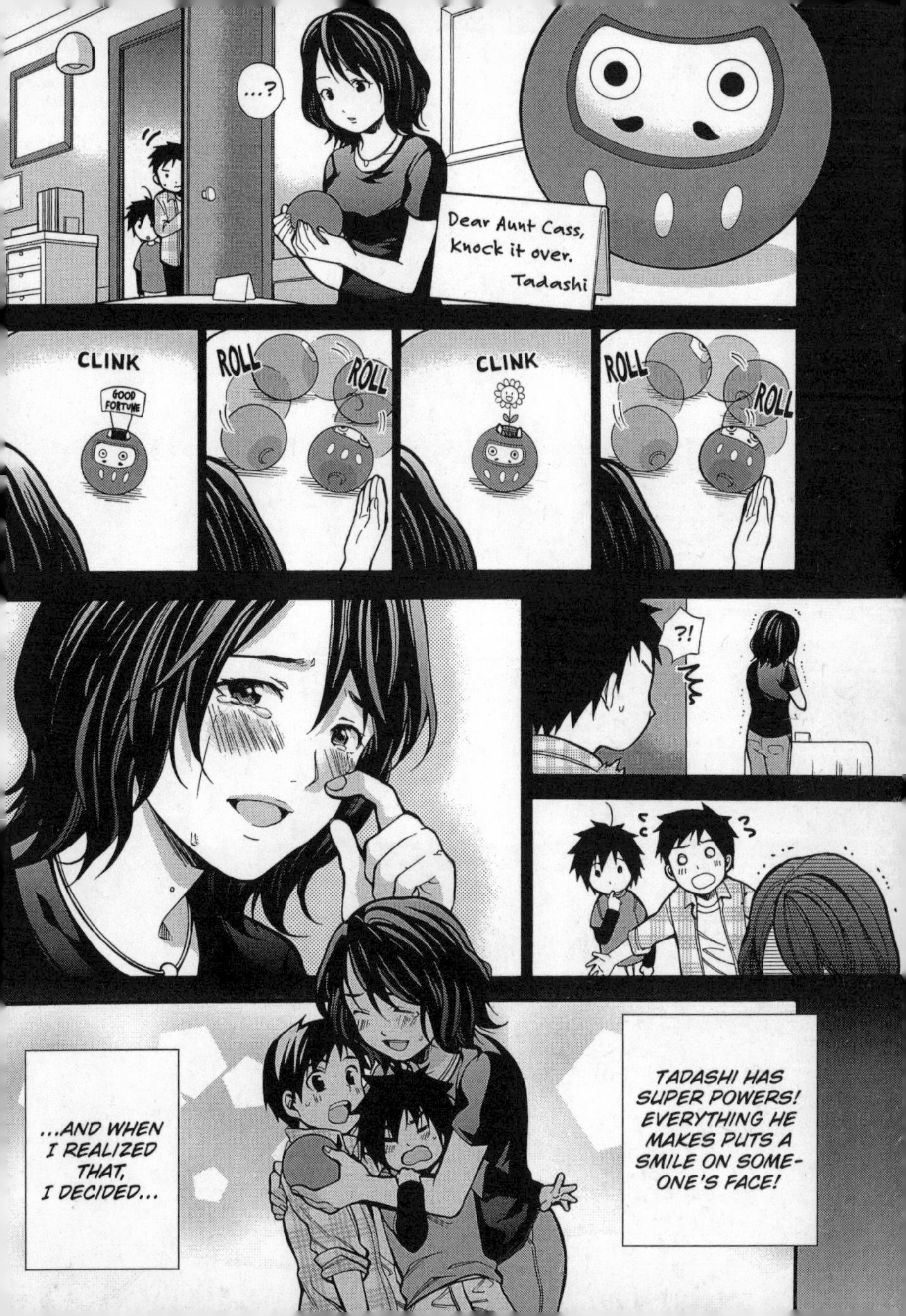
Dear Aunt Cass,
Knock it over.
Tadashi
...?
ROLL
ROLL
CLINK
ROLL
ROLL
CLINK
GOOD FORTUNE
?!
TADASHI HAS SUPER POWERS! EVERYTHING HE MAKES PUTS A SMILE ON SOME-ONE'S FACE!
...AND WHEN I REALIZED THAT, I DECIDED...

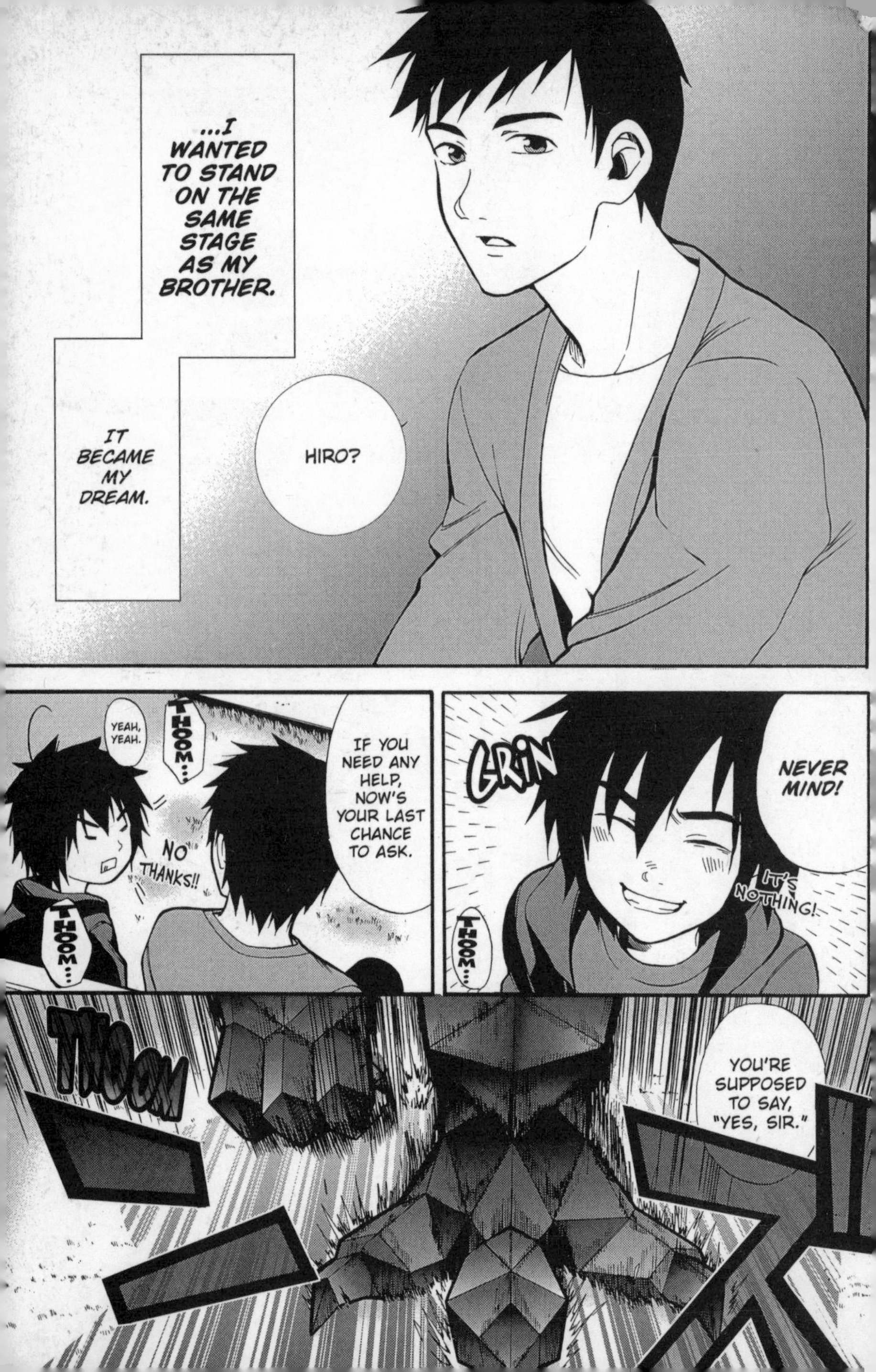
...I WANTED TO STAND ON THE SAME STAGE AS MY BROTHER.
IT BECAME MY DREAM.
HIRO?
NEVER MIND!
GRIN
IT'S NOTHING!
THOOM...
IF YOU NEED ANY HELP, NOW'S YOUR LAST CHANCE TO ASK.
THOOM...
YEAH, YEAH.
NO THANKS!!
THOOM...
YOU'RE SUPPOSED TO SAY, "YES, SIR."
THOOM

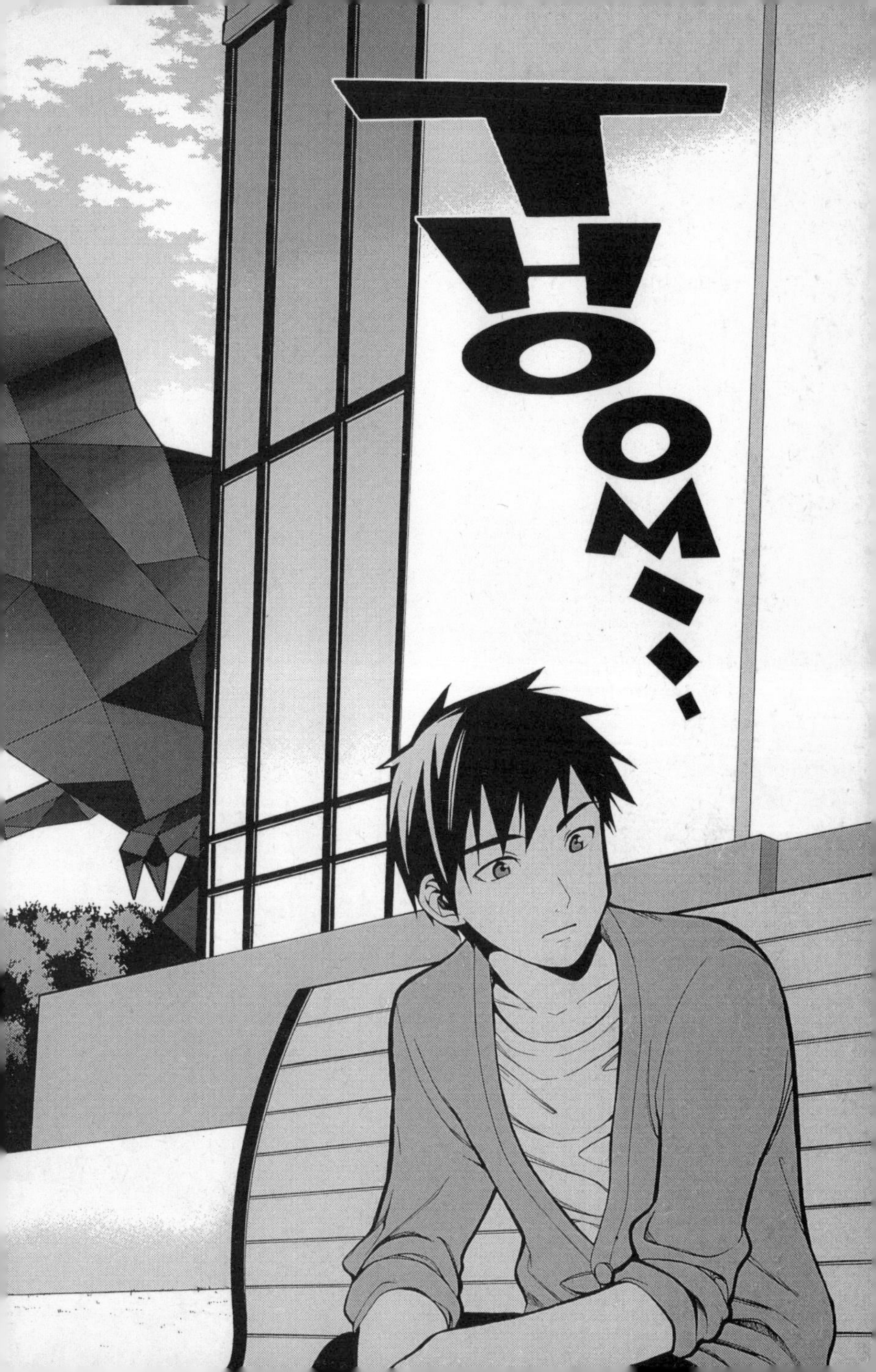
THOOM!!

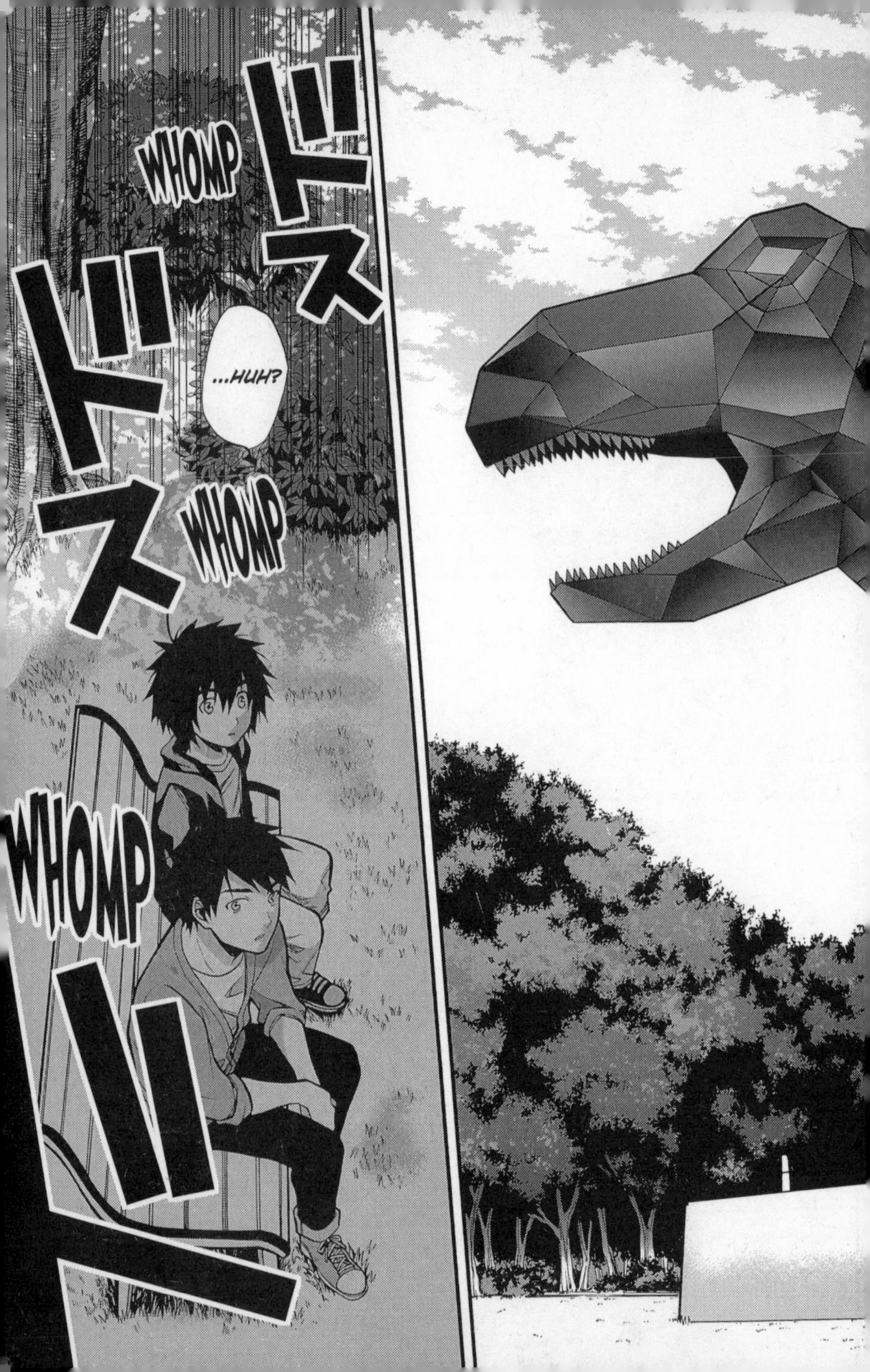
ドス
WHOMP
...HUH?
ドス
WHOMP
WHOMP

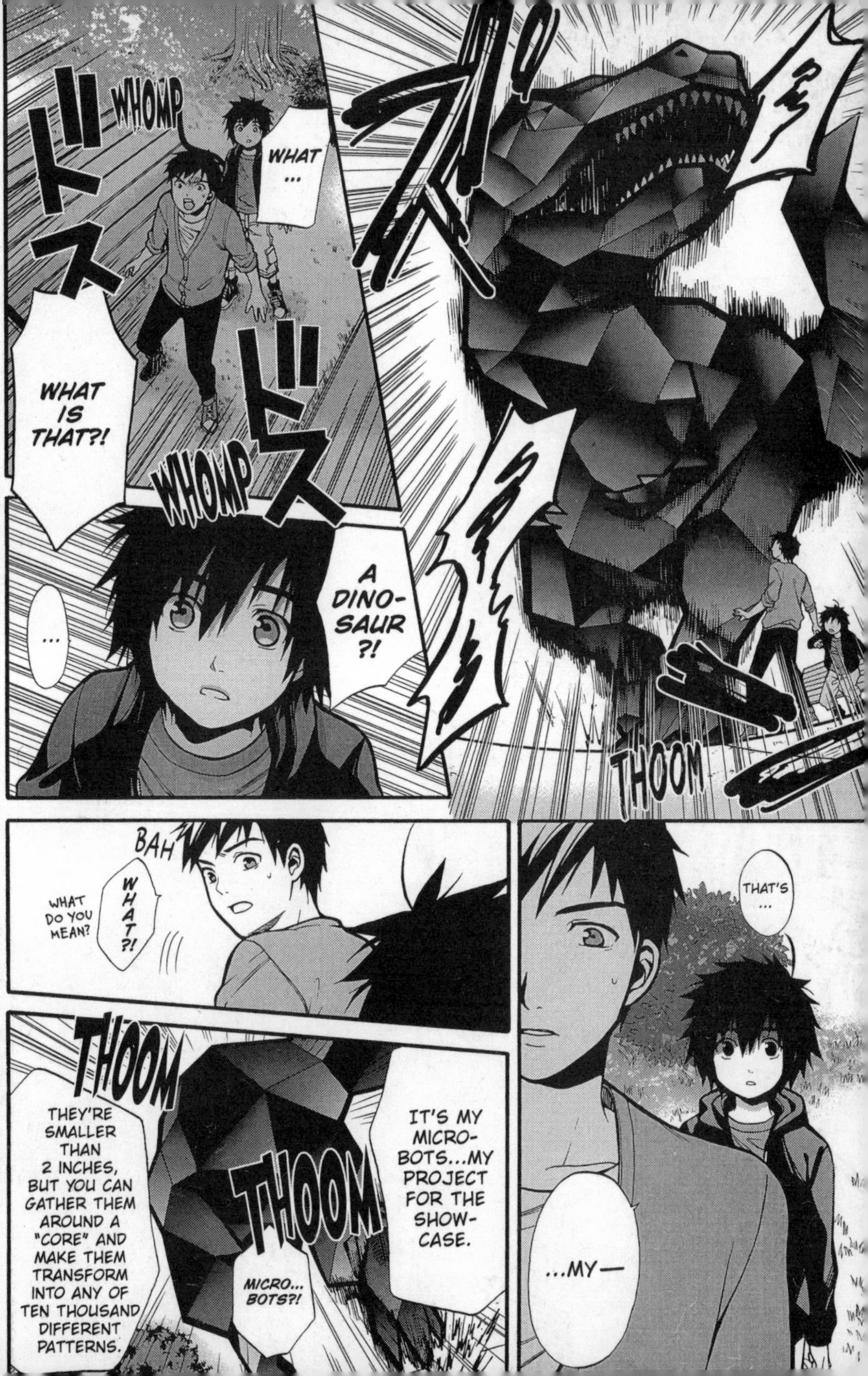

THOOM
WHAT ...
WHOMP
WHAT IS THAT?!
WHOMP
A DINO-SAUR?!
...
THAT'S ...
...MY—
BAH
WHAT?!
WHAT DO YOU MEAN?
IT'S MY MICRO-BOTS...MY PROJECT FOR THE SHOW-CASE.
THOOM
THOOM
THEY'RE SMALLER THAN 2 INCHES, BUT YOU CAN GATHER THEM AROUND A "CORE" AND MAKE THEM TRANSFORM INTO ANY OF TEN THOUSAND DIFFERENT PATTERNS.
MICRO... BOTS?!

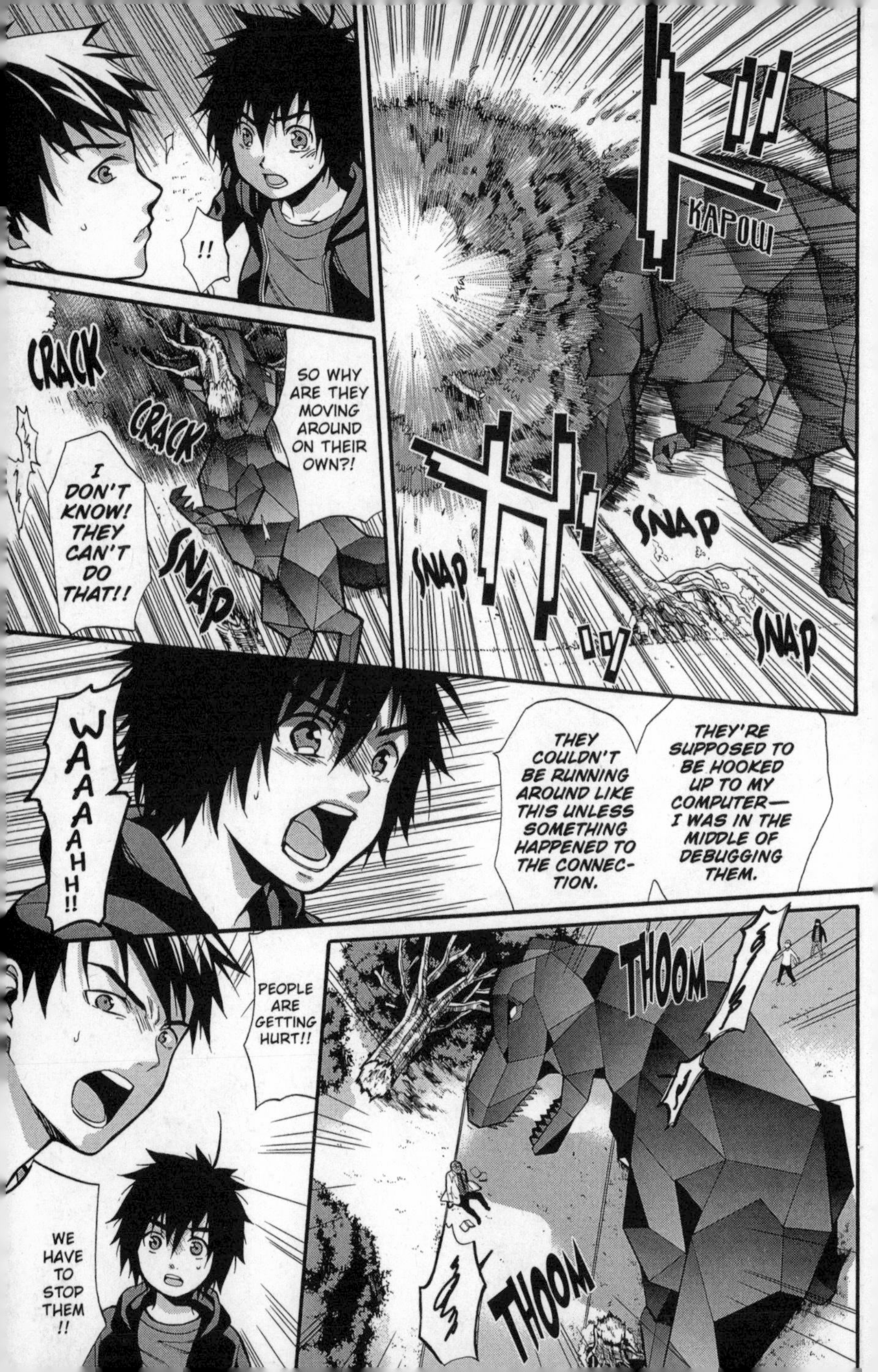
KAPOW
SNAP
SNAP
SNAP
!!
CRACK
CRACK
SO WHY ARE THEY MOVING AROUND ON THEIR OWN?!
I DON'T KNOW! THEY CAN'T DO THAT!!
SNAP
THEY'RE SUPPOSED TO BE HOOKED UP TO MY COMPUTER— I WAS IN THE MIDDLE OF DEBUGGING THEM.
THEY COULDN'T BE RUNNING AROUND LIKE THIS UNLESS SOMETHING HAPPENED TO THE CONNEC-TION.
WAAAAAHH!!
THOOM
THOOM
PEOPLE ARE GETTING HURT!!
WE HAVE TO STOP THEM!!

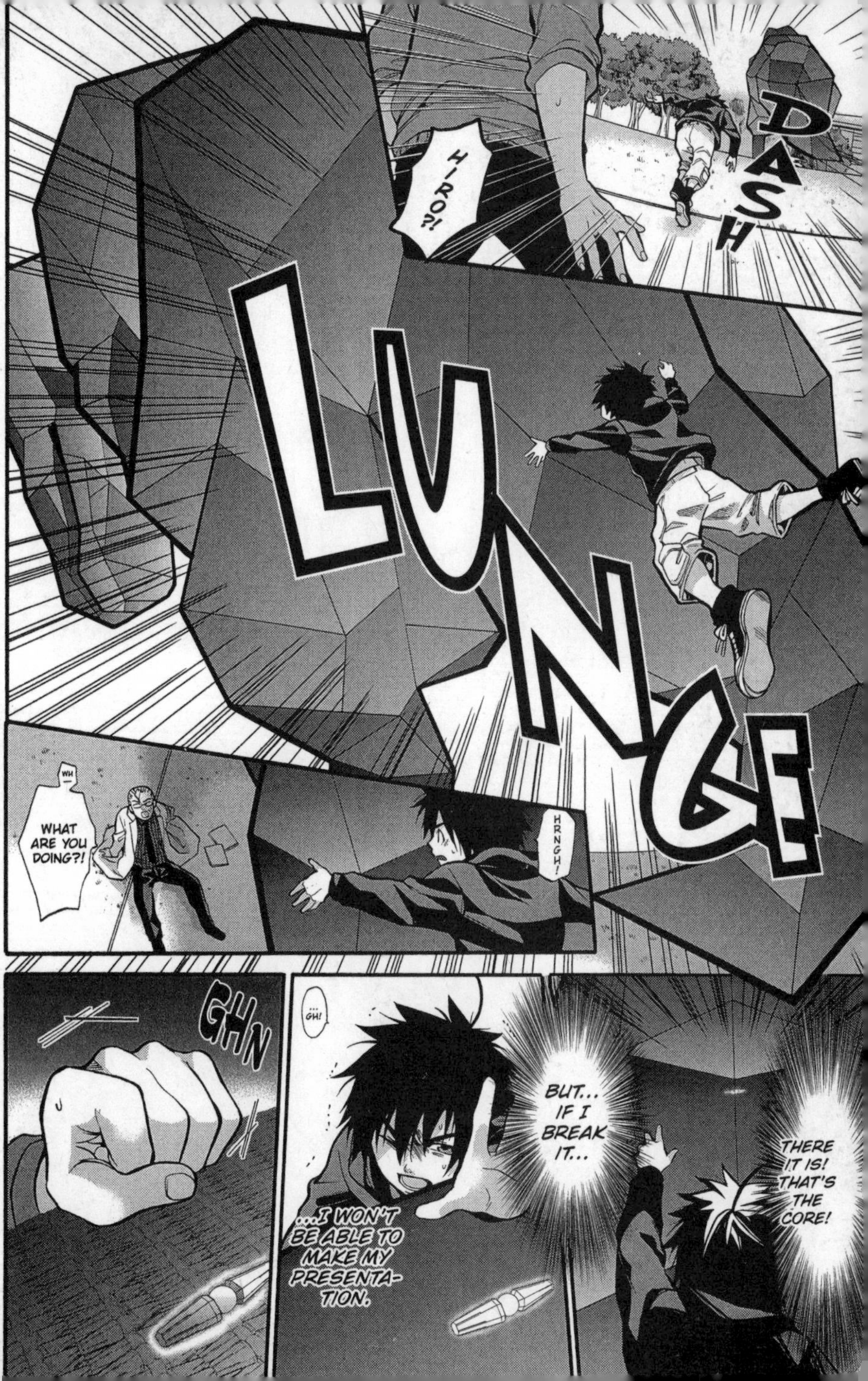
DASH
HIRO?!
LUNGE!
HRNGH!
WH—
WHAT ARE YOU DOING?!
THERE IT IS! THAT'S THE CORE!
...GH!
BUT... IF I BREAK IT...
...I WON'T BE ABLE TO MAKE MY PRESENTATION.
GHN

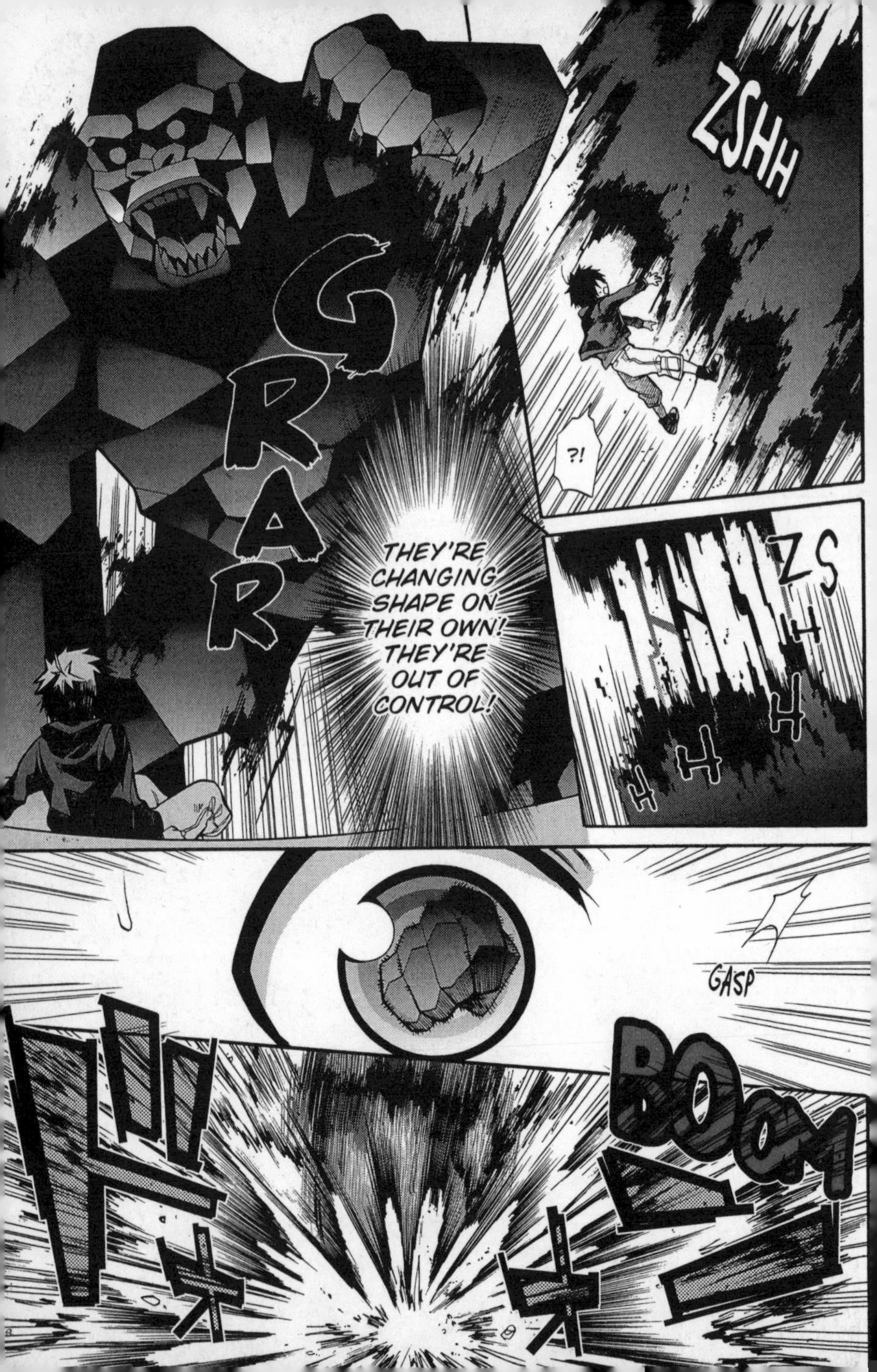
ZSHH
?!
ZSHHHHH
GRAR
THEY'RE CHANGING SHAPE ON THEIR OWN! THEY'RE OUT OF CONTROL!
GASP
BOOM

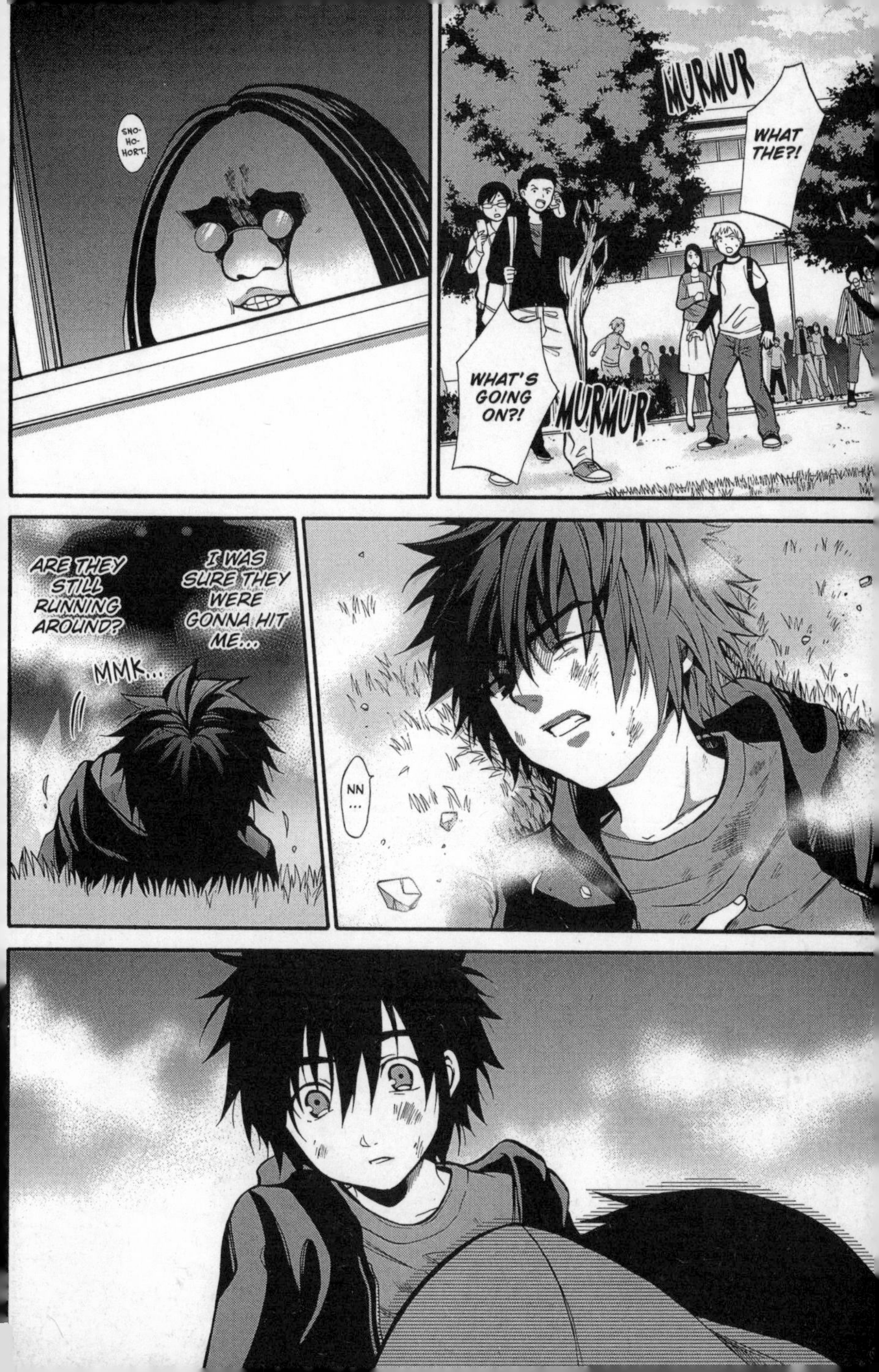
MURMUR
WHAT THE?!
WHAT'S GOING ON?!
MURMUR
SNO-HO-HORT.
NN...
I WAS SURE THEY WERE GONNA HIT ME...
ARE THEY STILL RUNNING AROUND?
MMK...

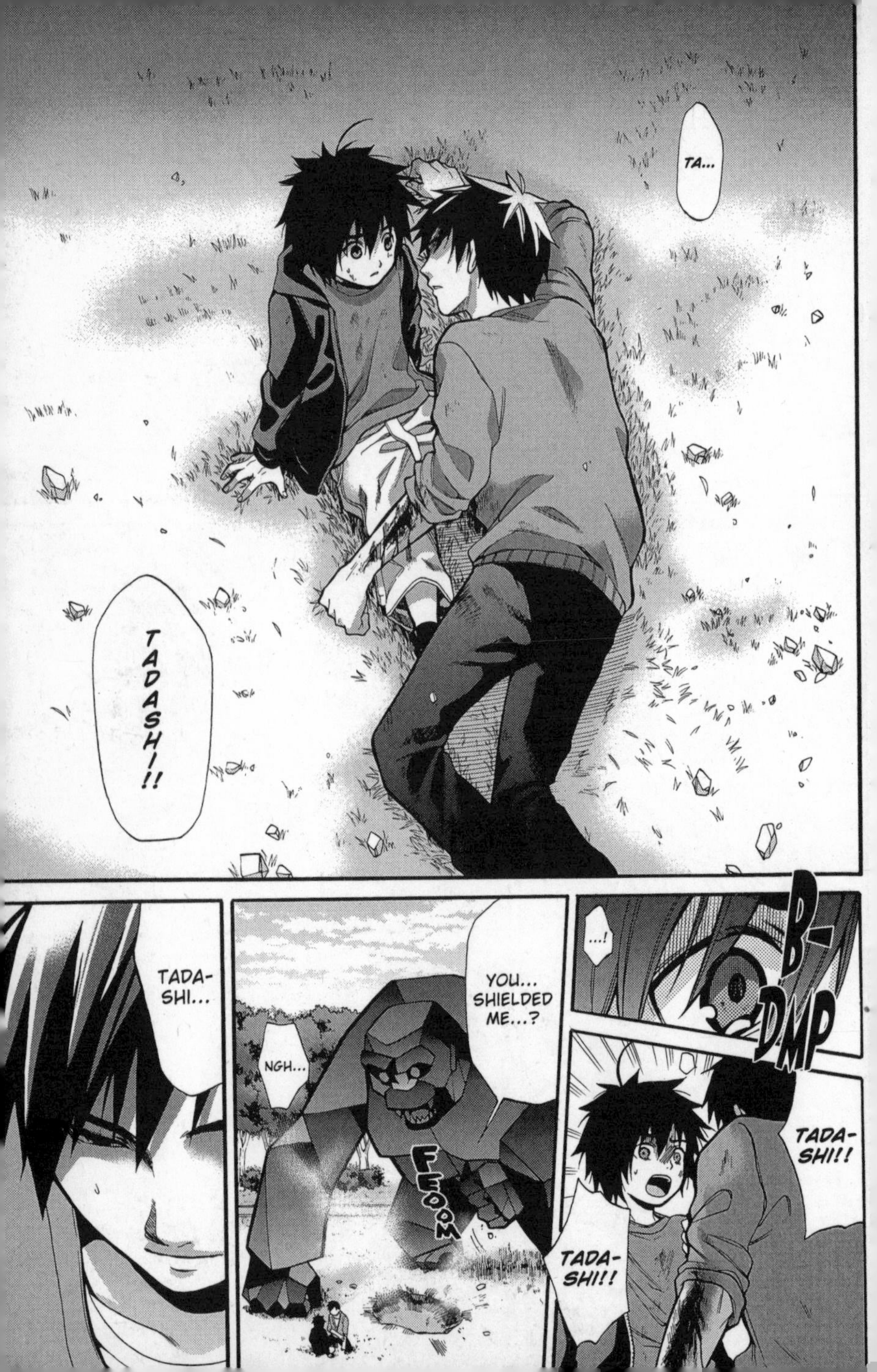
TA...
TADASHI!!
...!
B-DMP
TADA-SHI!!
TADA-SHI!!
YOU... SHIELDED ME...?
NGH...
FEOOM
TADA-SHI...

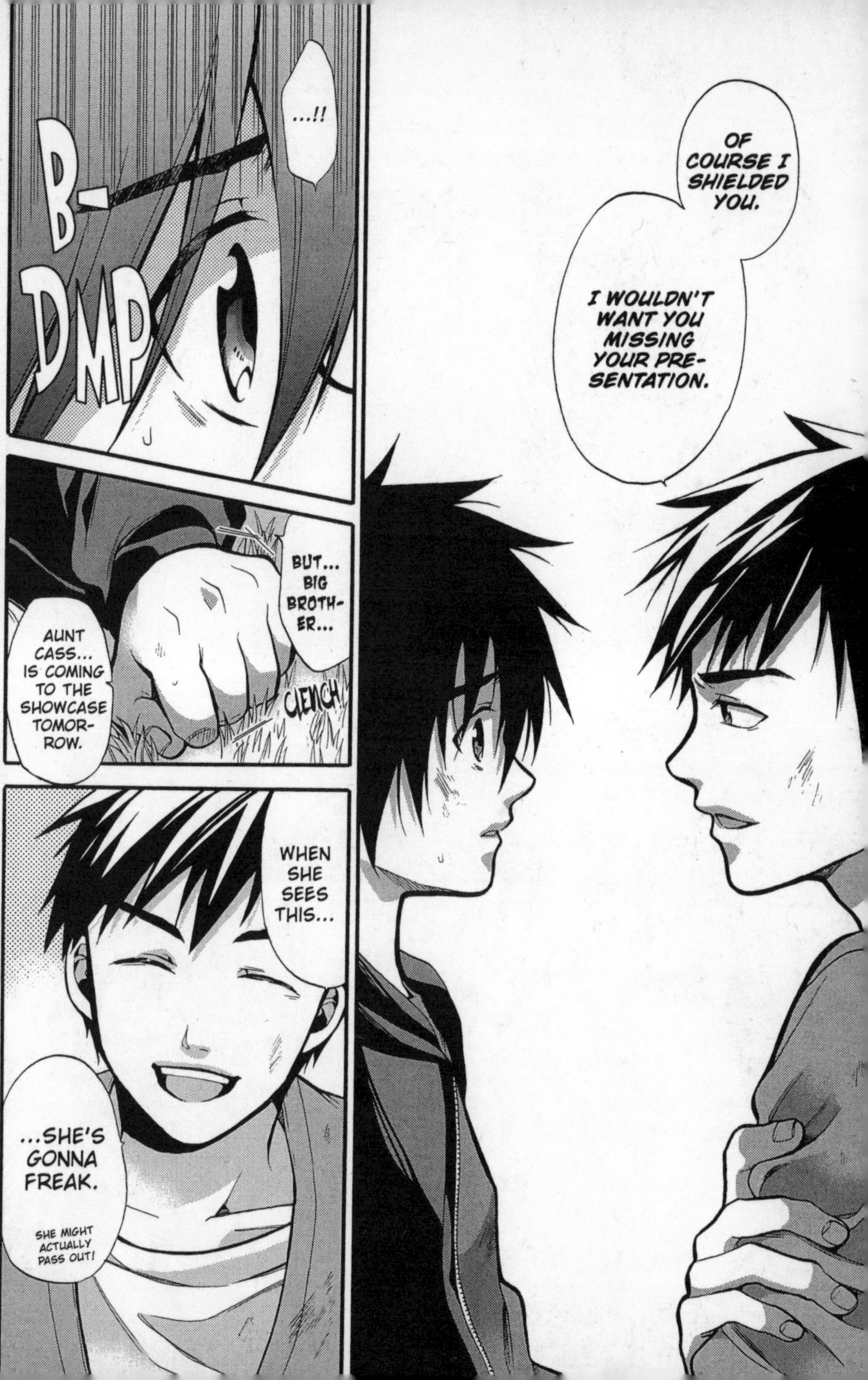
OF COURSE I SHIELDED YOU.
I WOULDN'T WANT YOU MISSING YOUR PRE-SENTATION.
...!!
B-DMP
BUT... BIG BROTHER...
CLENCH
AUNT CASS... IS COMING TO THE SHOWCASE TOMORROW.
WHEN SHE SEES THIS...
...SHE'S GONNA FREAK.
SHE MIGHT ACTUALLY PASS OUT!

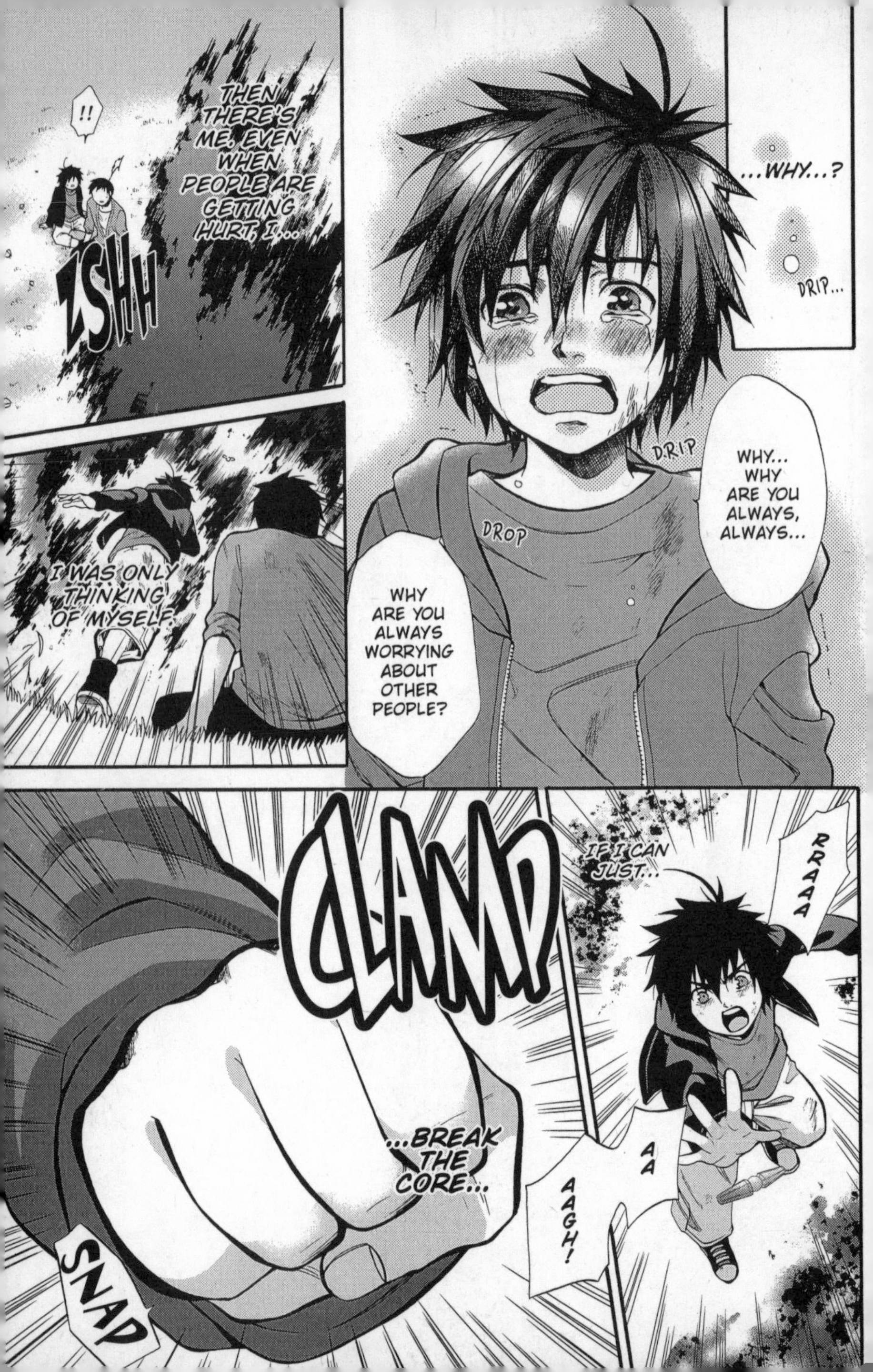
...WHY...?
DRIP...
DRIP
DROP
WHY... WHY ARE YOU ALWAYS, ALWAYS...
WHY ARE YOU ALWAYS WORRYING ABOUT OTHER PEOPLE?
!!
THEN THERE'S ME, EVEN WHEN PEOPLE ARE GETTING HURT, I...
ZSHH
I WAS ONLY THINKING OF MYSELF.
RRAAAA
IF I CAN JUST...
AAAAGH!
CLAMP
...BREAK THE CORE...
SNAP

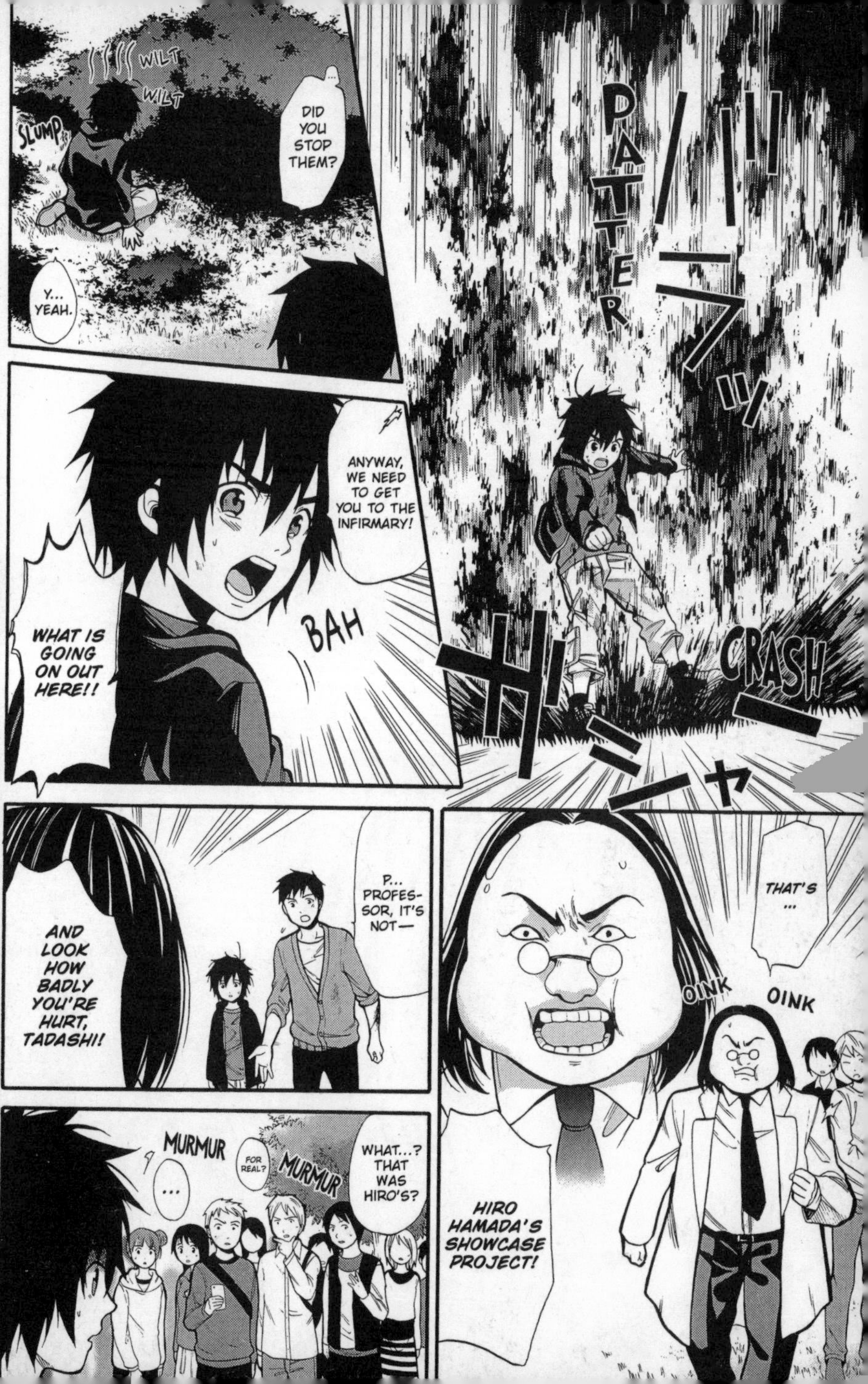
PATTER
CRASH
WILT
WILT
SLUMP
...
DID YOU STOP THEM?
Y... YEAH.
ANYWAY, WE NEED TO GET YOU TO THE INFIRMARY!
BAH
WHAT IS GOING ON OUT HERE!!
THAT'S ...
OINK
OINK
HIRO HAMADA'S SHOWCASE PROJECT!
P... PROFES-SOR, IT'S NOT—
AND LOOK HOW BADLY YOU'RE HURT, TADASHI!
WHAT...? THAT WAS HIRO'S?
MURMUR
FOR REAL?
MURMUR
...

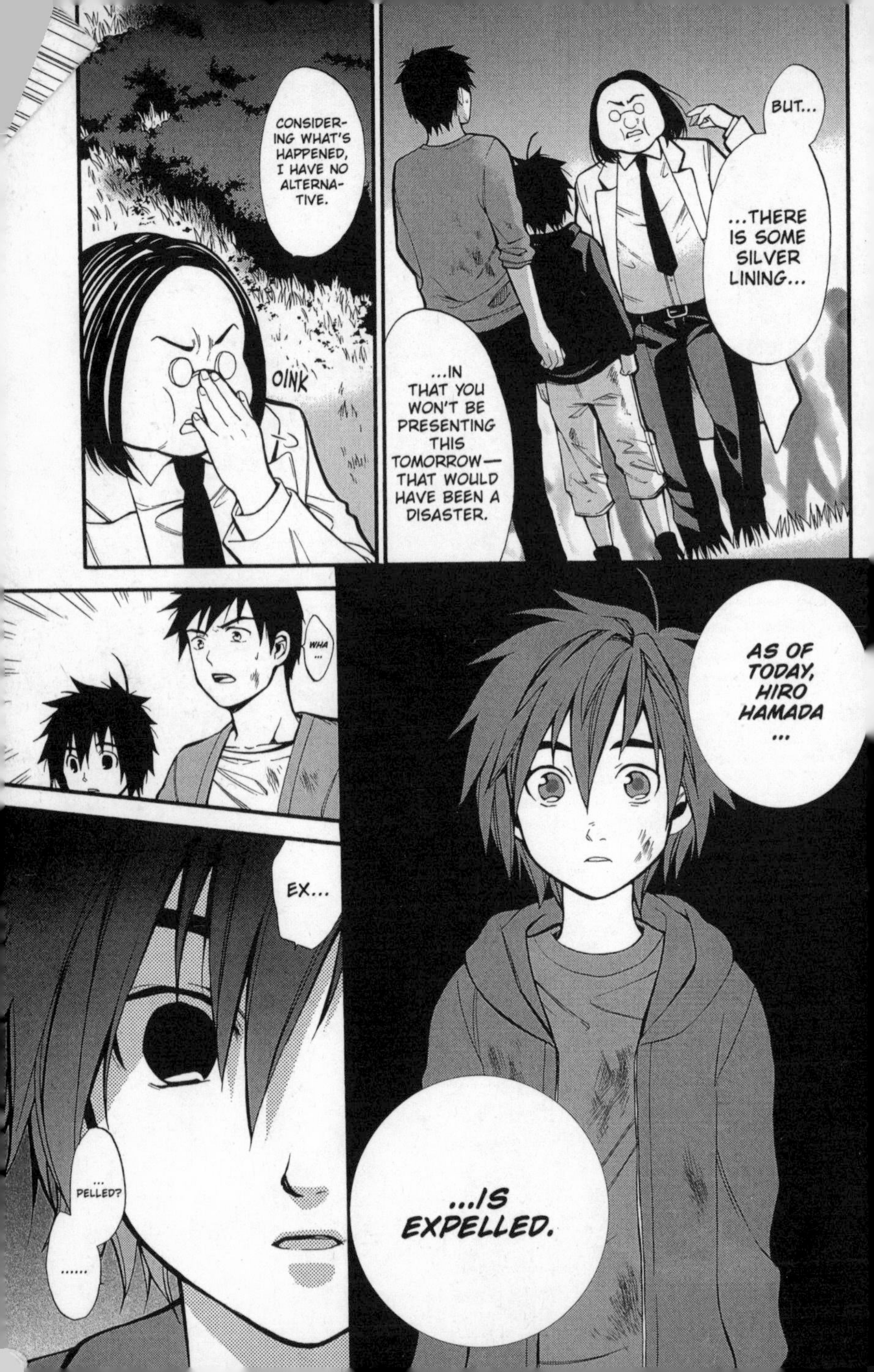
BUT...
...THERE IS SOME SILVER LINING...
...IN THAT YOU WON'T BE PRESENTING THIS TOMORROW—THAT WOULD HAVE BEEN A DISASTER.
CONSIDER-ING WHAT'S HAPPENED, I HAVE NO ALTERNA-TIVE.
OINK
AS OF TODAY, HIRO HAMADA ...
...IS EXPELLED.
WHA ...
EX...
... PELLED?
......

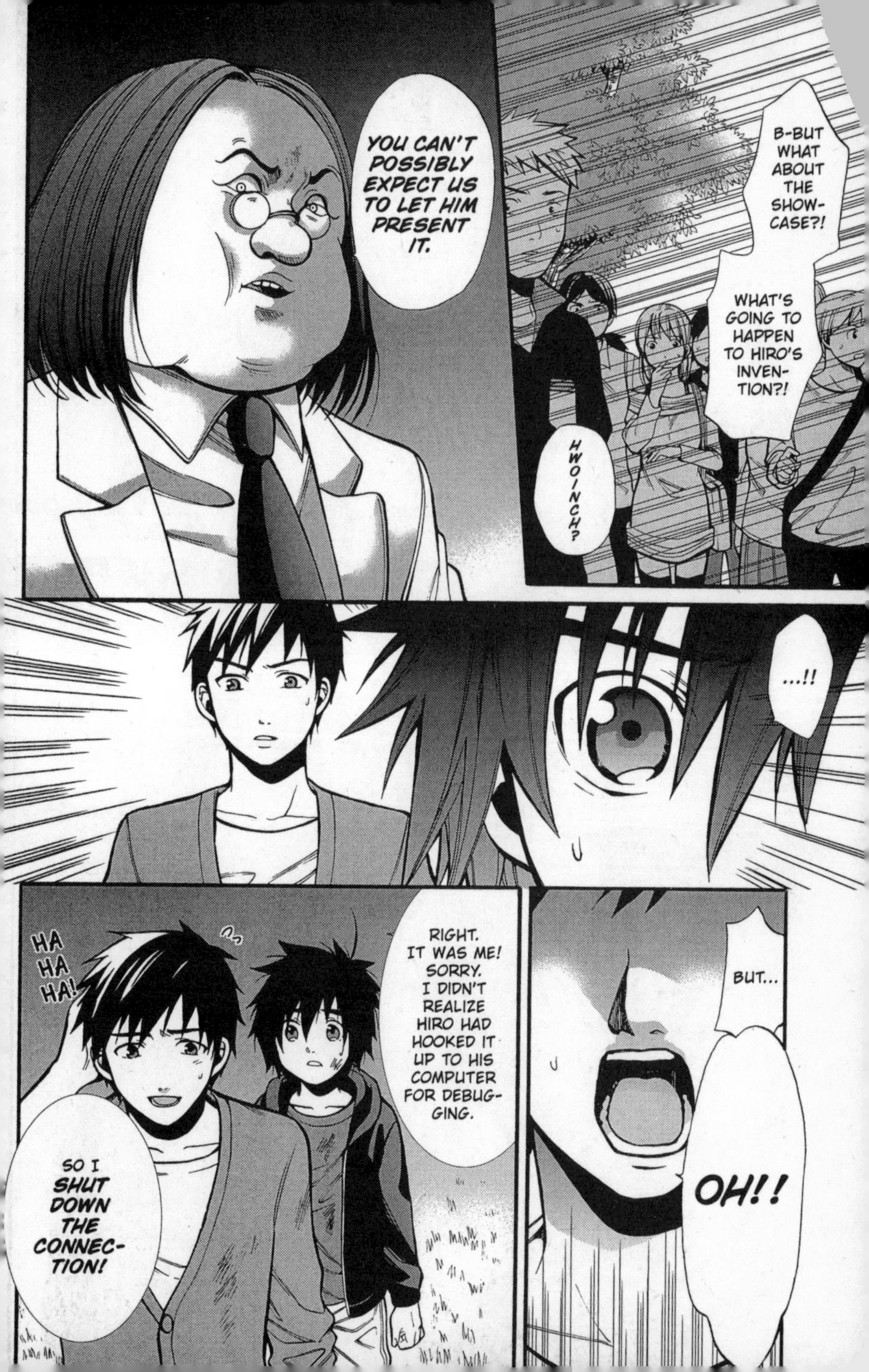
B-BUT WHAT ABOUT THE SHOW-CASE?!
WHAT'S GOING TO HAPPEN TO HIRO'S INVEN-TION?!
HWOINCH?
YOU CAN'T POSSIBLY EXPECT US TO LET HIM PRESENT IT.
...!!
BUT...
OH!!
RIGHT. IT WAS ME! SORRY. I DIDN'T REALIZE HIRO HAD HOOKED IT UP TO HIS COMPUTER FOR DEBUG-GING.
HA HA HA!
SO I SHUT DOWN THE CONNEC-TION!

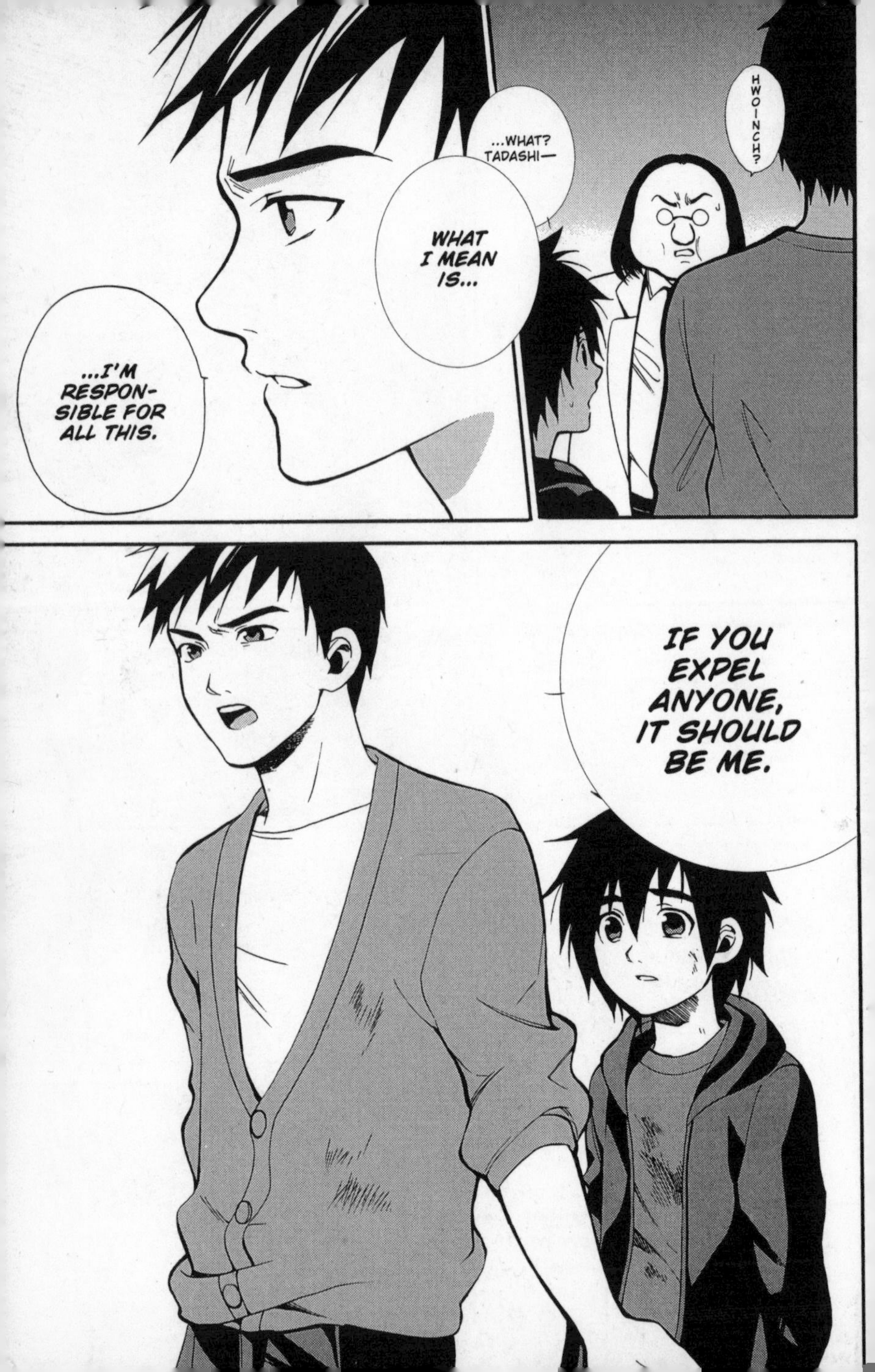
HWOINCH?
...WHAT? TADASHI—
WHAT I MEAN IS...
...I'M RESPONSIBLE FOR ALL THIS.
IF YOU EXPEL ANYONE, IT SHOULD BE ME.

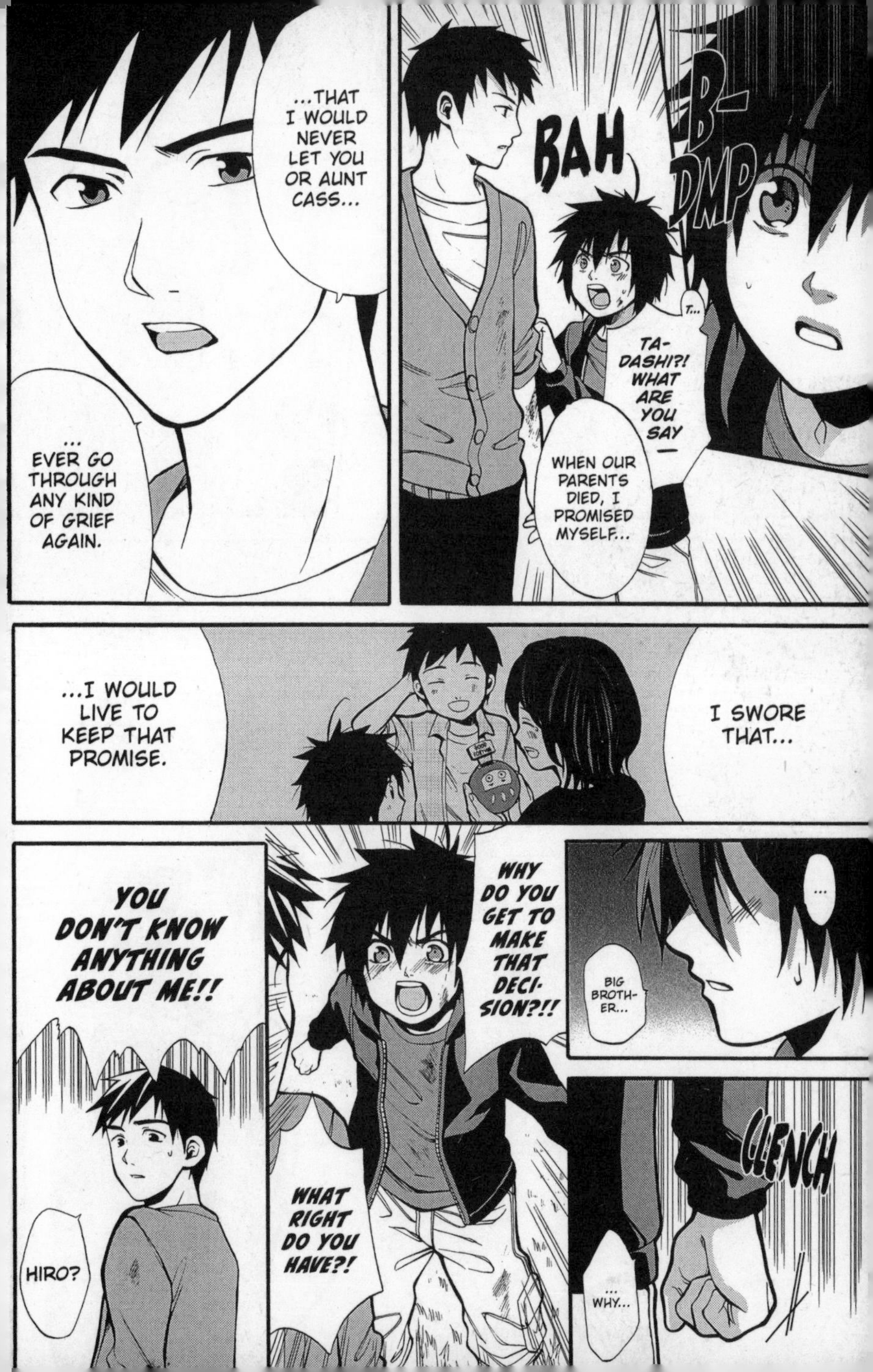
B-DMP
BAH
T...
TA-DASHI?! WHAT ARE YOU SAY—
WHEN OUR PARENTS DIED, I PROMISED MYSELF...
...THAT I WOULD NEVER LET YOU OR AUNT CASS...
...EVER GO THROUGH ANY KIND OF GRIEF AGAIN.
I SWORE THAT...
...I WOULD LIVE TO KEEP THAT PROMISE.
...
BIG BROTH-ER...
CLENCH
...WHY...
WHY DO YOU GET TO MAKE THAT DECI-SION?!!
WHAT RIGHT DO YOU HAVE?!
YOU DON'T KNOW ANYTHING ABOUT ME!!
HIRO?

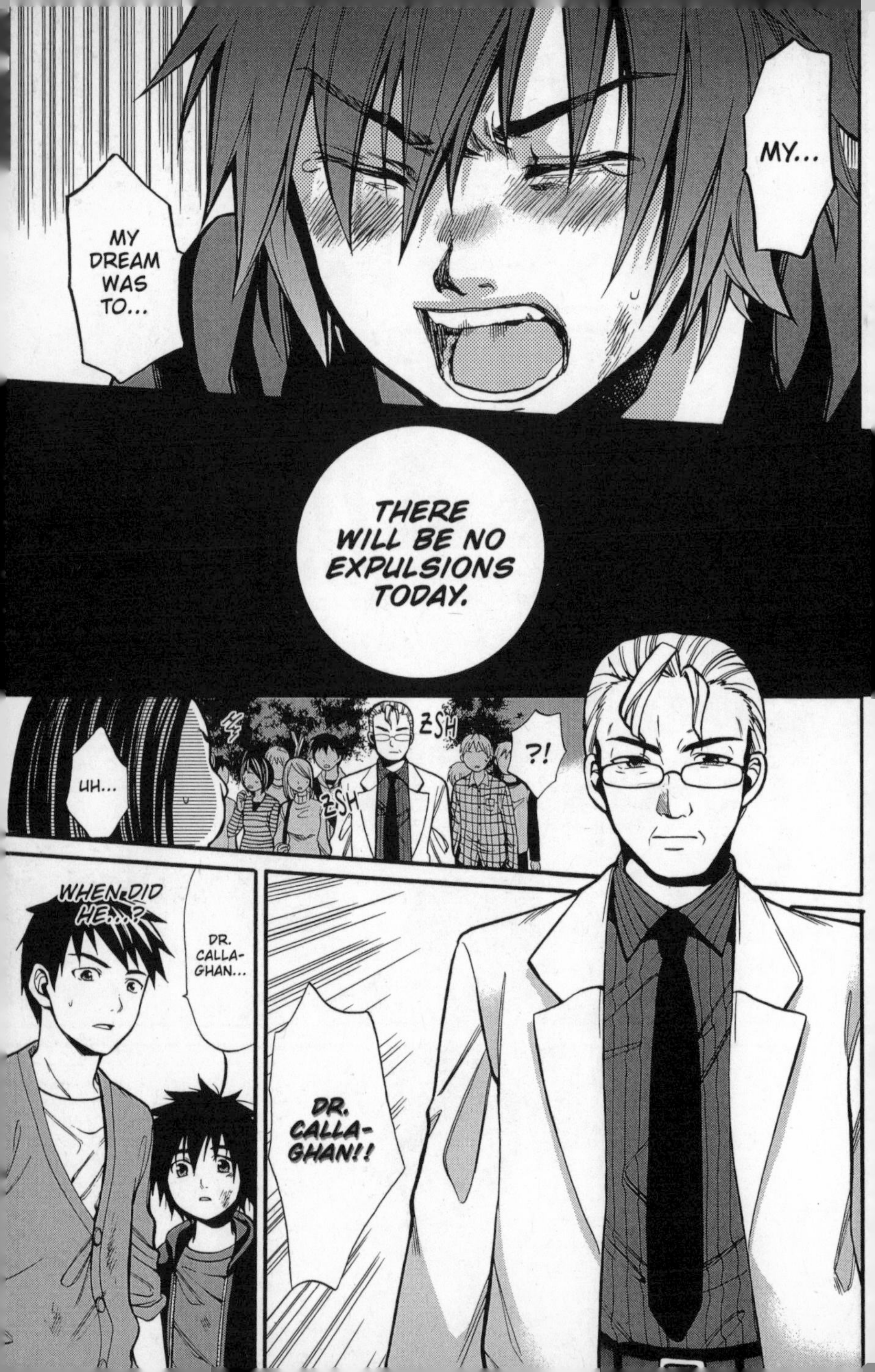
MY...
MY DREAM WAS TO...
THERE WILL BE NO EXPULSIONS TODAY.
?!
ZSH
ZSH
UH...
DR. CALLA-GHAN!!
DR. CALLA-GHAN...
WHEN DID HE...?

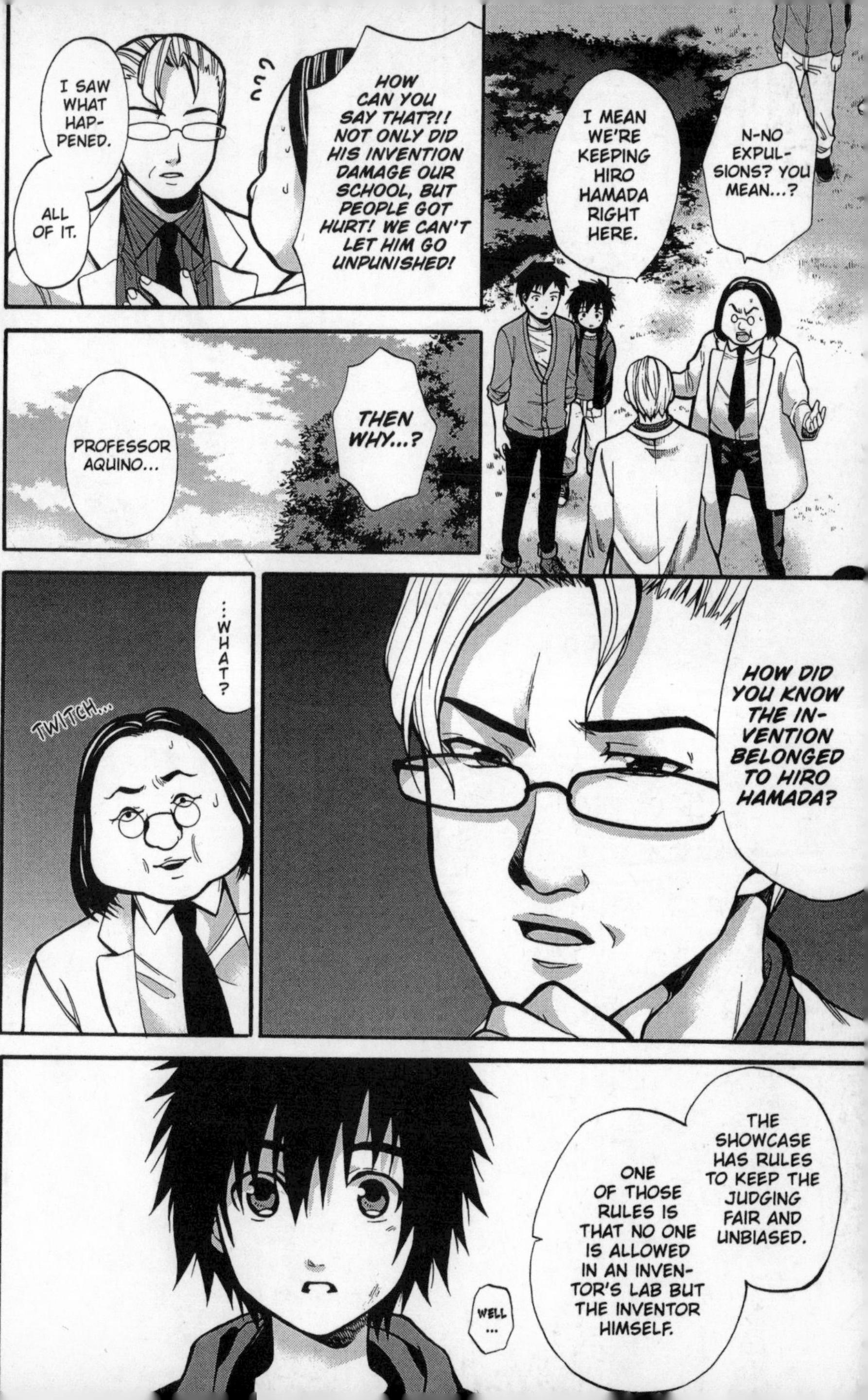
N-NO EXPULSIONS? YOU MEAN...?
I MEAN WE'RE KEEPING HIRO HAMADA RIGHT HERE.
HOW CAN YOU SAY THAT?!! NOT ONLY DID HIS INVENTION DAMAGE OUR SCHOOL, BUT PEOPLE GOT HURT! WE CAN'T LET HIM GO UNPUNISHED!
I SAW WHAT HAP-PENED.
ALL OF IT.
THEN WHY...?
PROFESSOR AQUINO...
HOW DID YOU KNOW THE IN-VENTION BELONGED TO HIRO HAMADA?
...WHAT?
TWITCH...
THE SHOWCASE HAS RULES TO KEEP THE JUDGING FAIR AND UNBIASED.
ONE OF THOSE RULES IS THAT NO ONE IS ALLOWED IN AN INVEN-TOR'S LAB BUT THE INVENTOR HIMSELF.
WELL...

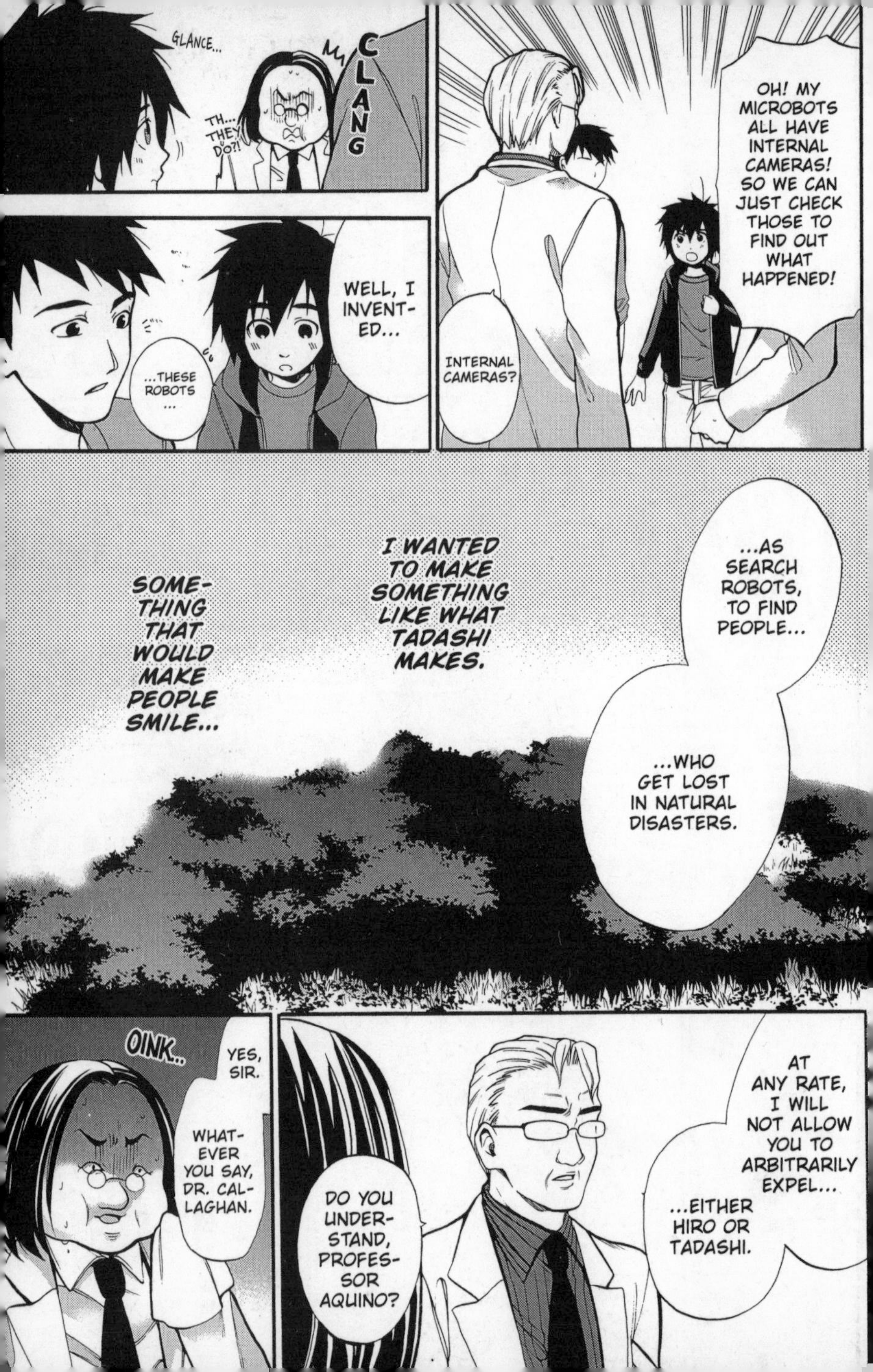
OH! MY MICROBOTS ALL HAVE INTERNAL CAMERAS! SO WE CAN JUST CHECK THOSE TO FIND OUT WHAT HAPPENED!
INTERNAL CAMERAS?
CLANG
GLANCE...
TH... THEY DO?!
WELL, I INVENT-ED...
...THESE ROBOTS ...
...AS SEARCH ROBOTS, TO FIND PEOPLE...
...WHO GET LOST IN NATURAL DISASTERS.
I WANTED TO MAKE SOMETHING LIKE WHAT TADASHI MAKES.
SOME-THING THAT WOULD MAKE PEOPLE SMILE...
AT ANY RATE, I WILL NOT ALLOW YOU TO ARBITRARILY EXPEL...
...EITHER HIRO OR TADASHI.
DO YOU UNDER-STAND, PROFES-SOR AQUINO?
YES, SIR.
OINK...
WHAT-EVER YOU SAY, DR. CAL-LAGHAN.

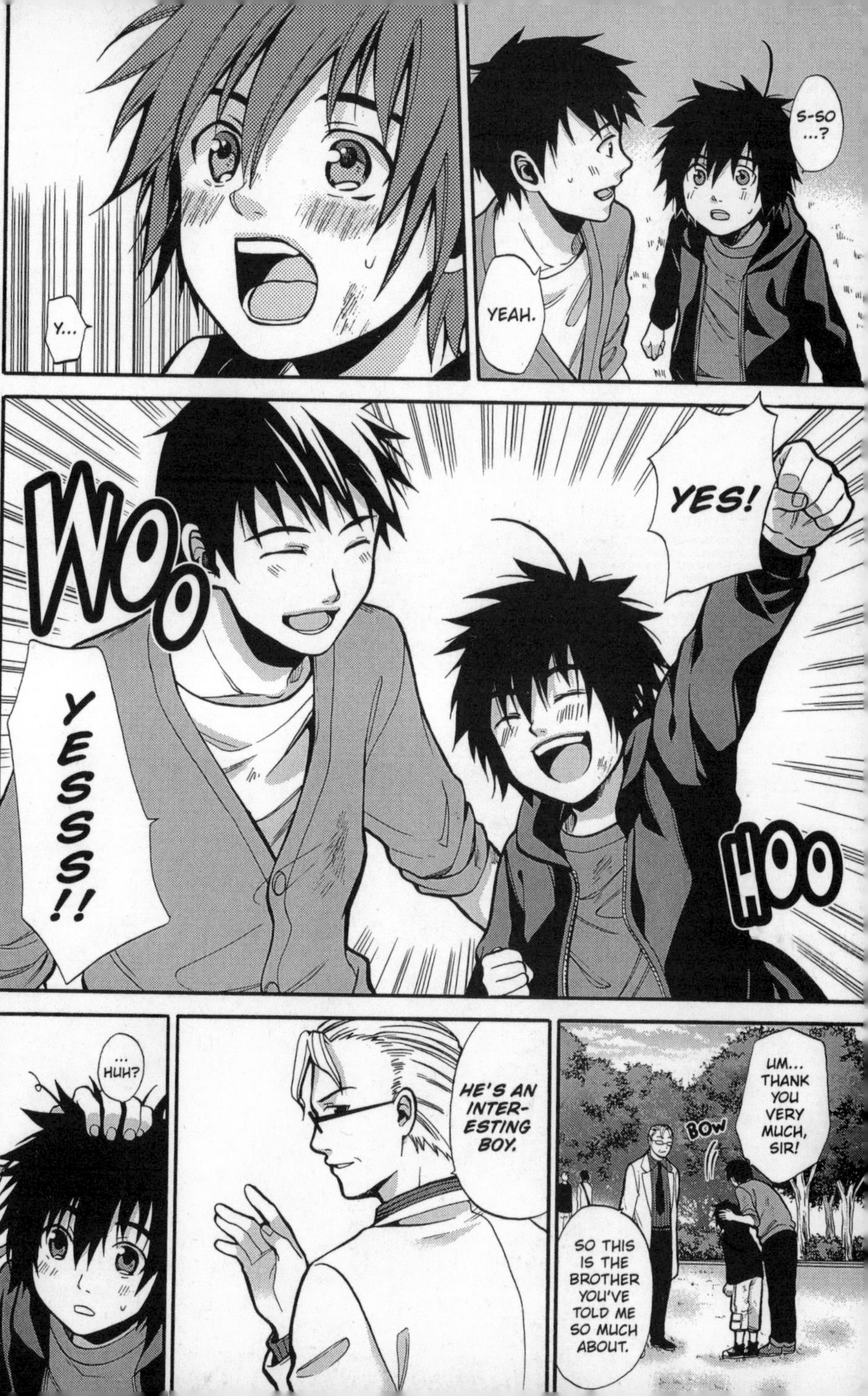
S-SO ...?
YEAH.
Y...
YES!
WOO
HOO
YESSSS!!
UM... THANK YOU VERY MUCH, SIR!
BOW
SO THIS IS THE BROTHER YOU'VE TOLD ME SO MUCH ABOUT.
HE'S AN INTER-ESTING BOY.
... HUH?

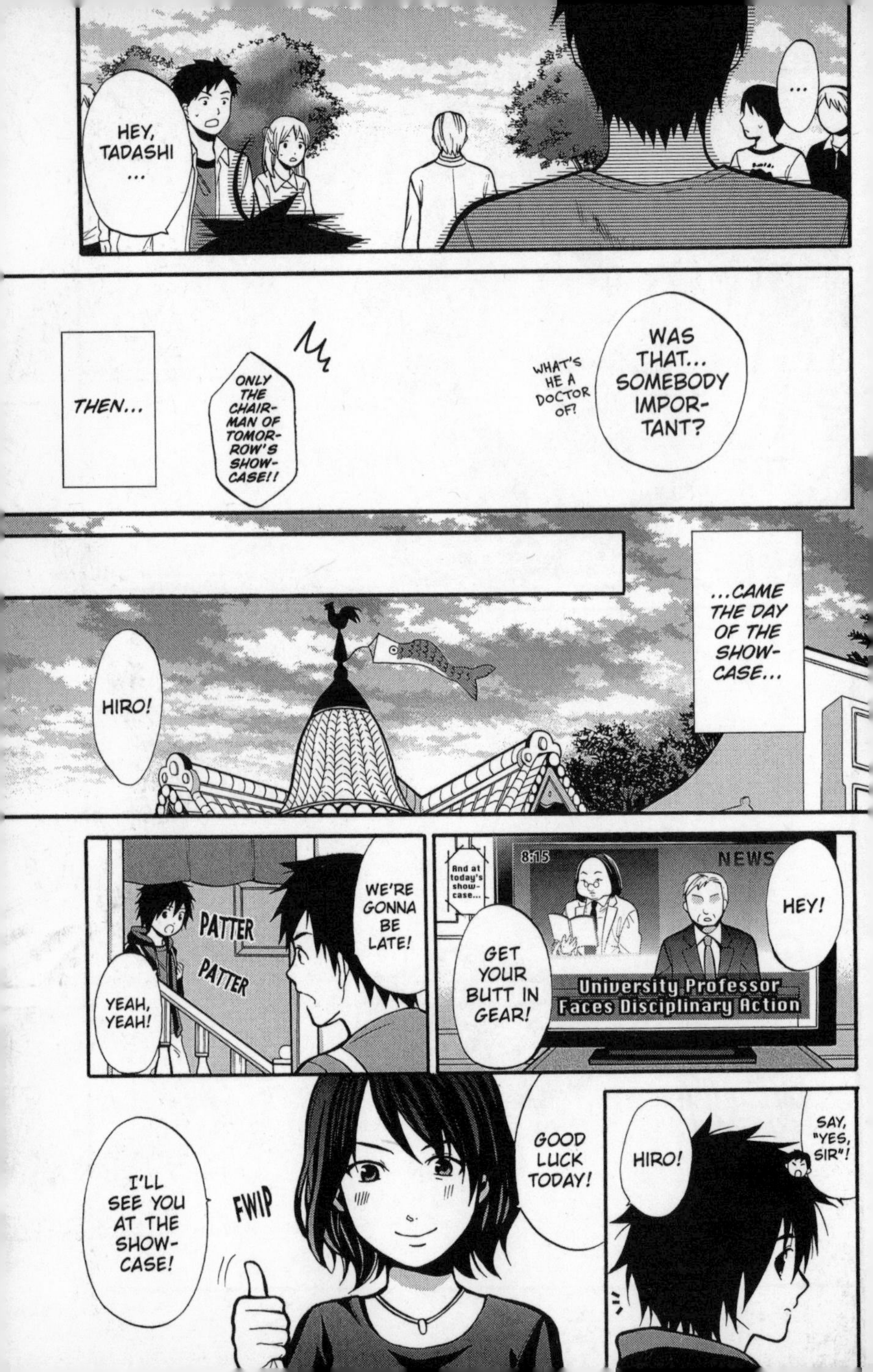

...
HEY, TADASHI ...
WAS THAT... SOMEBODY IMPORTANT?
WHAT'S HE A DOCTOR OF?
ONLY THE CHAIRMAN OF TOMORROW'S SHOWCASE!!
THEN...
...CAME THE DAY OF THE SHOWCASE...
HIRO!
8:15
NEWS
HEY!
And at today's showcase...
University Professor Faces Disciplinary Action
GET YOUR BUTT IN GEAR!
WE'RE GONNA BE LATE!
PATTER
PATTER
YEAH, YEAH!
HIRO!
SAY, "YES, SIR"!
GOOD LUCK TODAY!
FWIP
I'LL SEE YOU AT THE SHOWCASE!

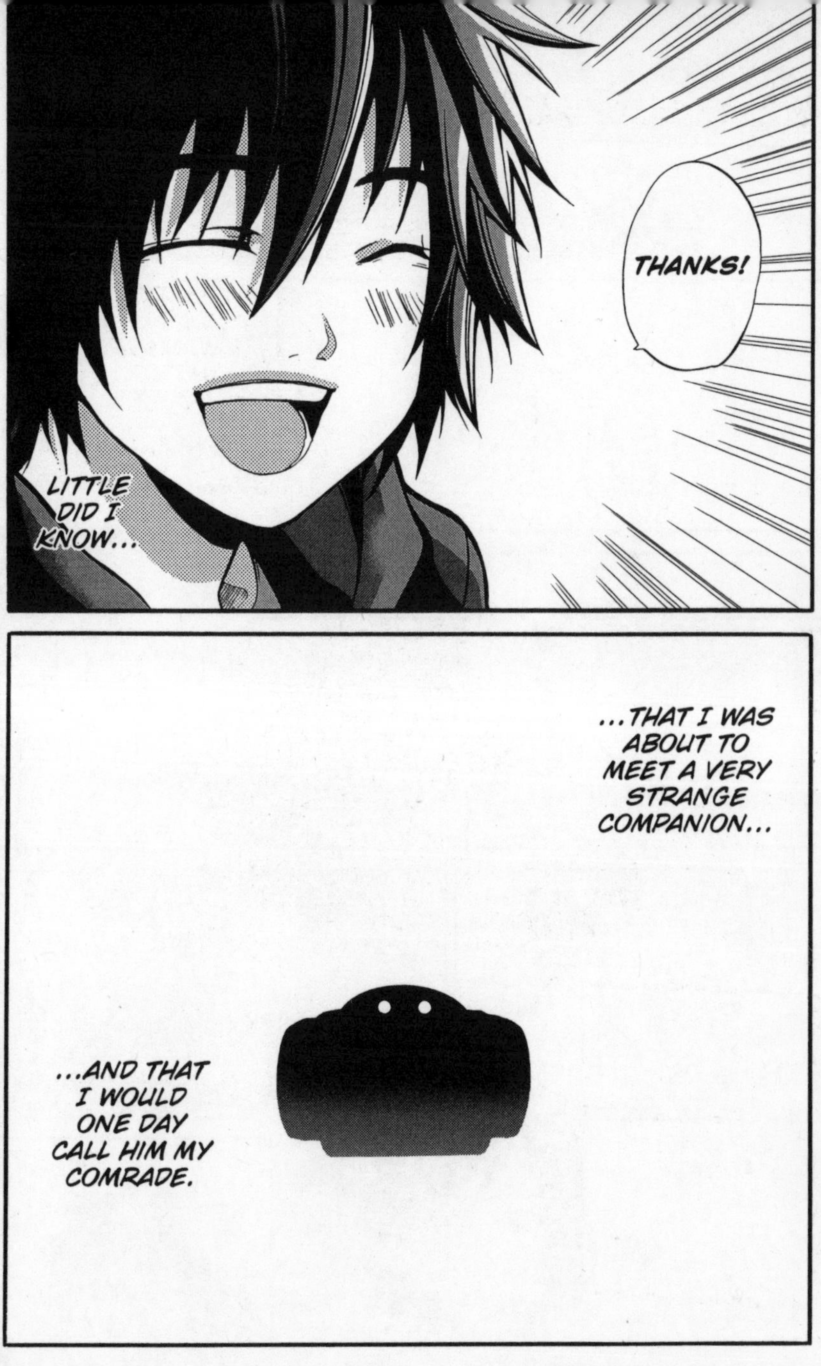
THANKS!
LITTLE DID I KNOW...
...THAT I WAS ABOUT TO MEET A VERY STRANGE COMPANION...
...AND THAT I WOULD ONE DAY CALL HIM MY COMRADE.

♥2: Tadashi's Wish

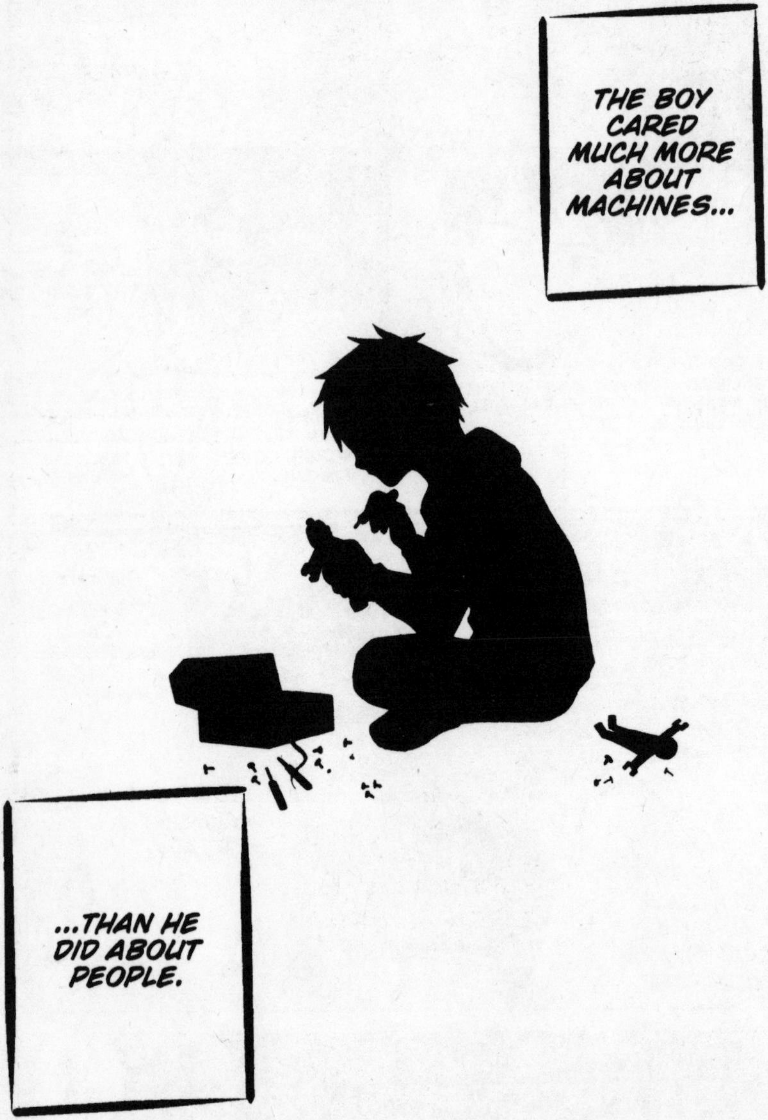
THE BOY CARED MUCH MORE ABOUT MACHINES...
...THAN HE DID ABOUT PEOPLE.

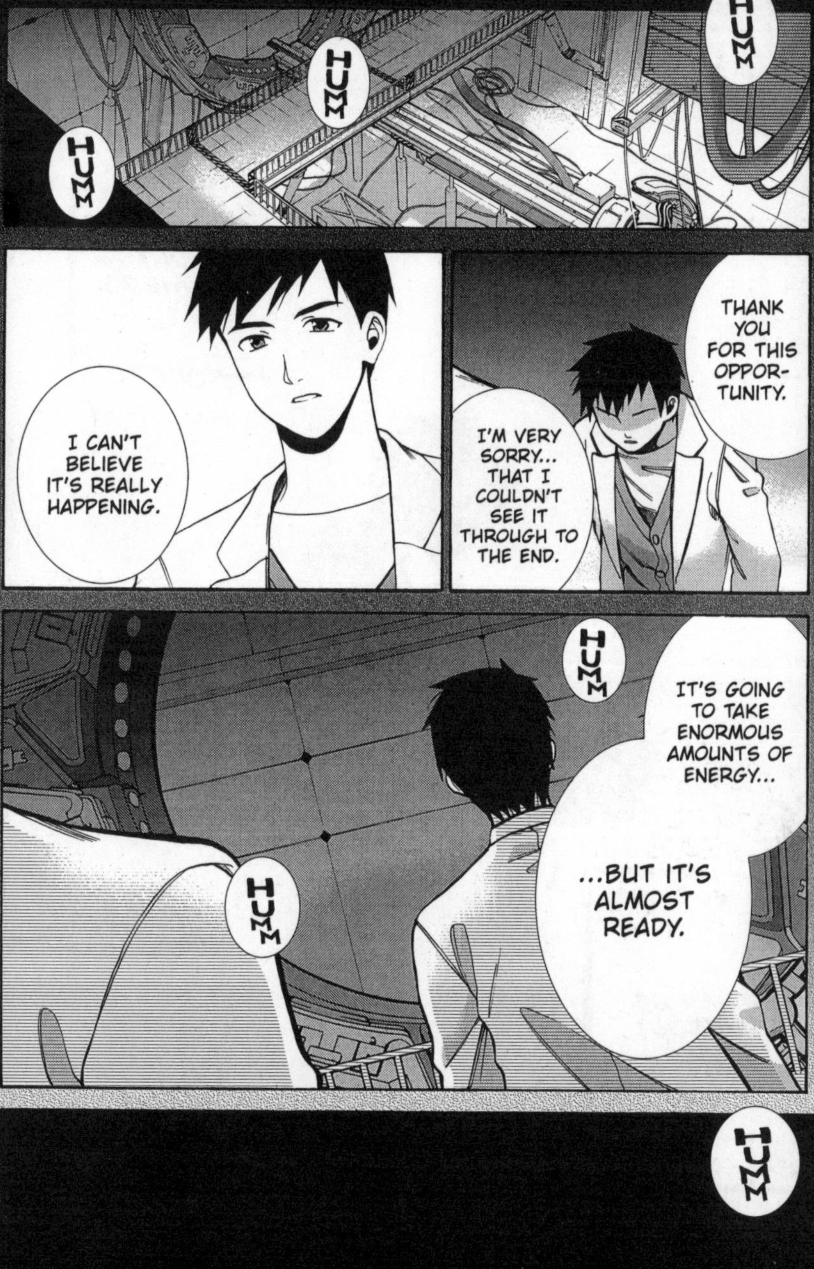
HUMM
HUMM
HUMM
THANK YOU FOR THIS OPPORTUNITY.
I'M VERY SORRY... THAT I COULDN'T SEE IT THROUGH TO THE END.
I CAN'T BELIEVE IT'S REALLY HAPPENING.
IT'S GOING TO TAKE ENORMOUS AMOUNTS OF ENERGY...
HUMM
...BUT IT'S ALMOST READY.
HUMM
HUMM

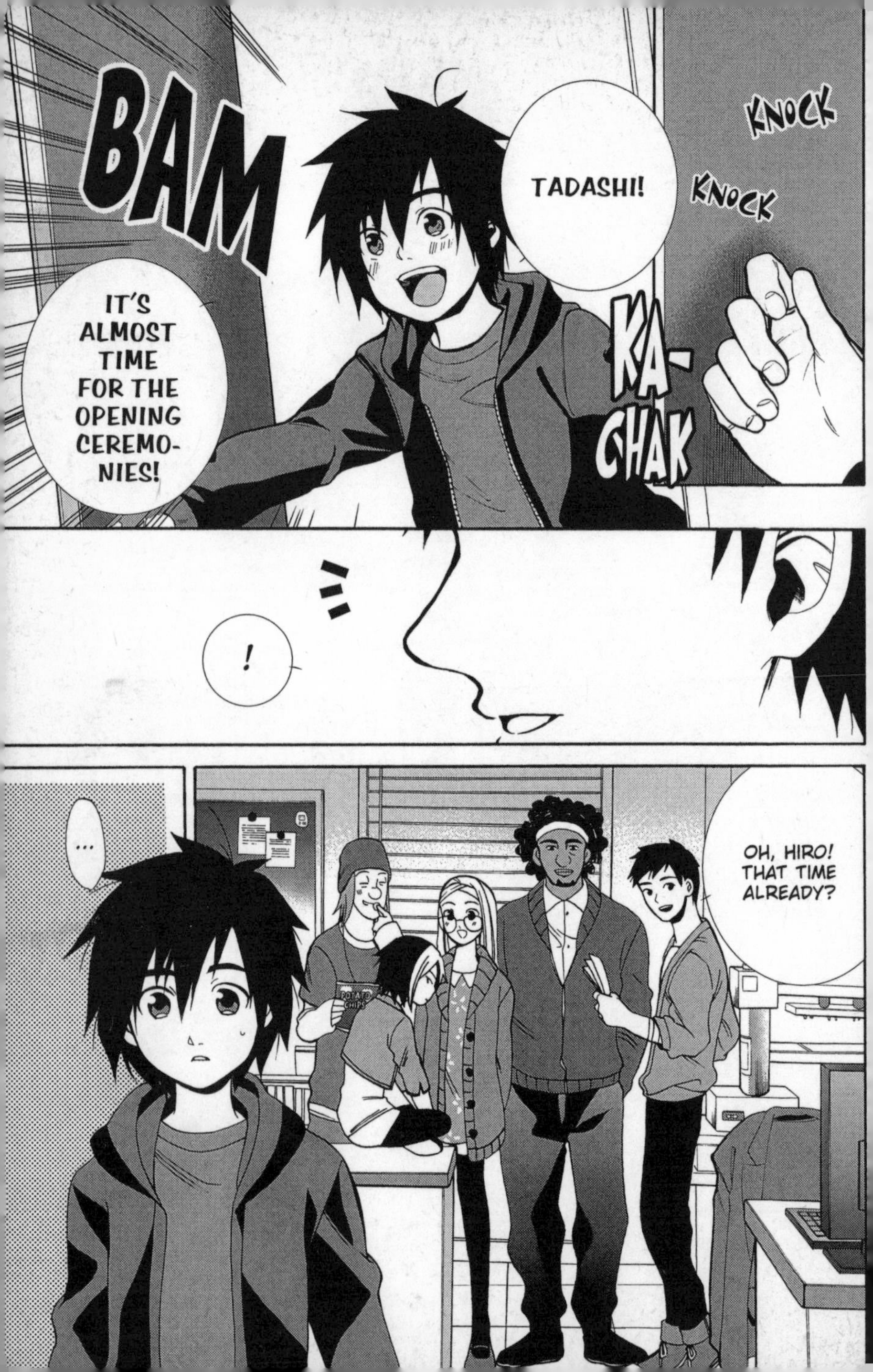
KNOCK
KNOCK
TADASHI!
BAM
KA-CHAK
IT'S ALMOST TIME FOR THE OPENING CEREMO-NIES!
!
OH, HIRO! THAT TIME ALREADY?
...
POTATO CHIPS

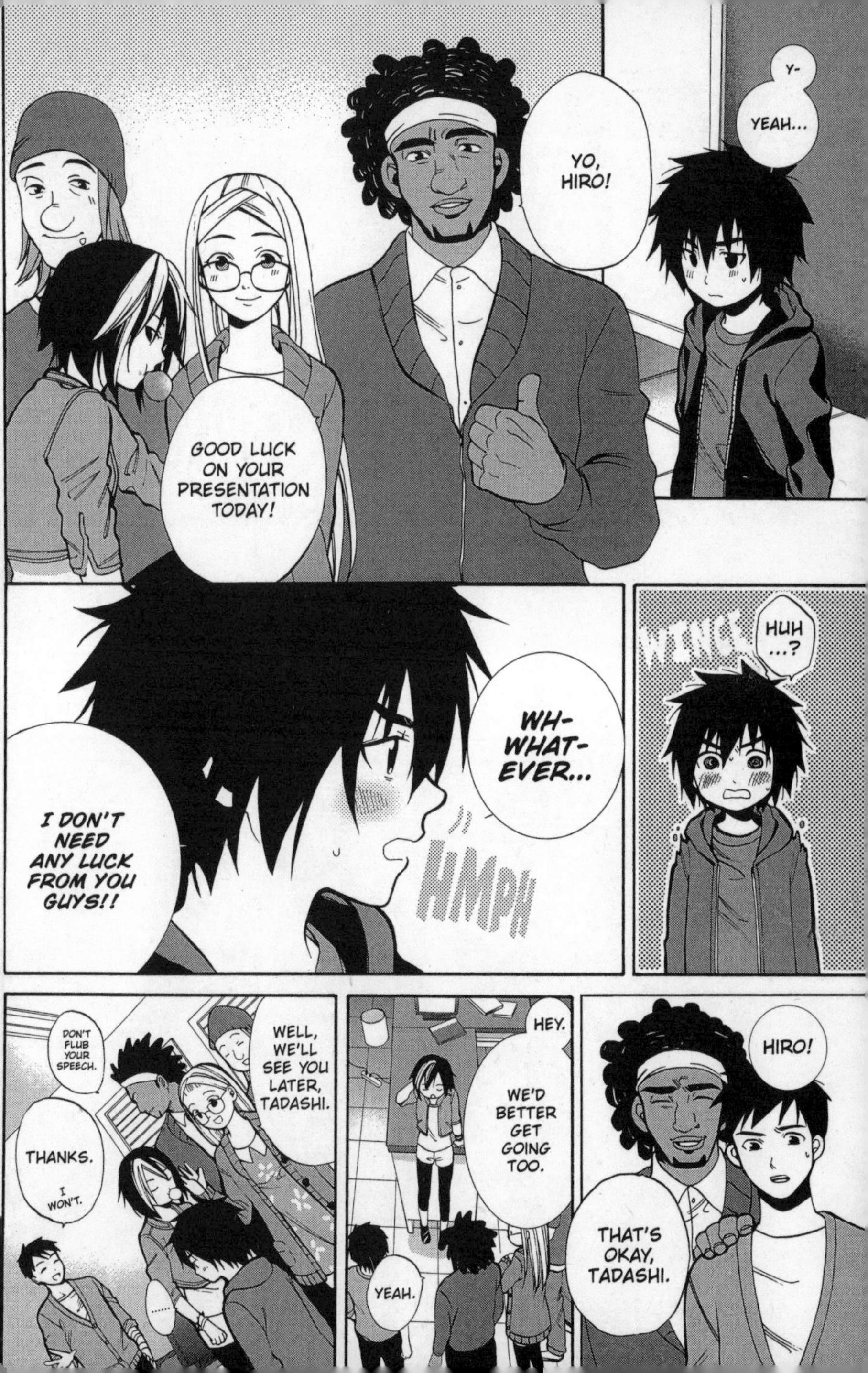
Y-
YEAH...
YO, HIRO!
GOOD LUCK ON YOUR PRESENTATION TODAY!
WINCE
HUH ...?
WH- WHAT- EVER...
HMPH
I DON'T NEED ANY LUCK FROM YOU GUYS!!
HIRO!
THAT'S OKAY, TADASHI.
HEY.
WE'D BETTER GET GOING TOO.
YEAH.
WELL, WE'LL SEE YOU LATER, TADASHI.
DON'T FLUB YOUR SPEECH.
THANKS.
I WON'T.
......

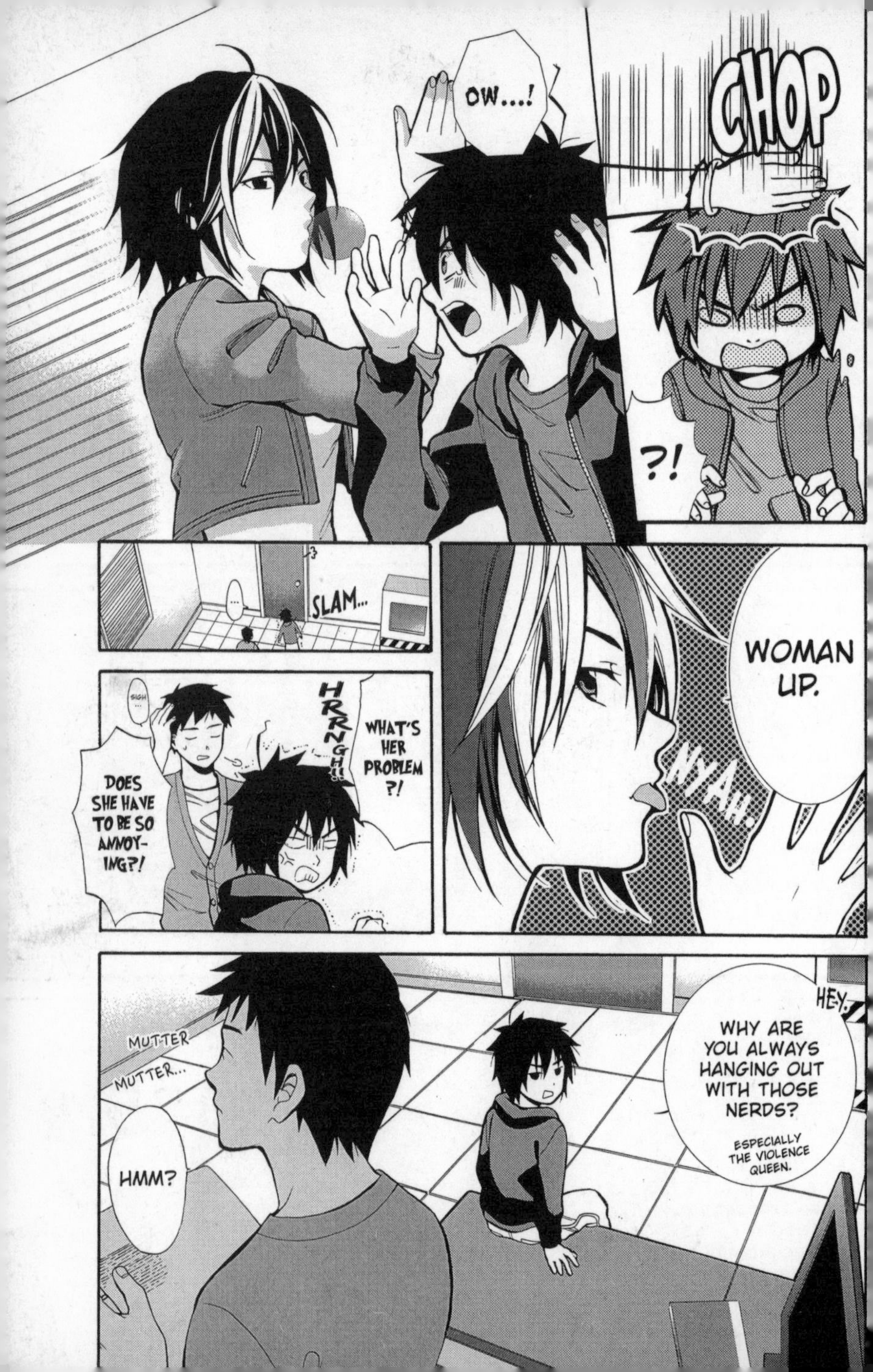
CHOP
?!
OW...!
WOMAN UP.
NYAH.
...
SLAM...
HRRNGH!!
WHAT'S HER PROBLEM?!
SIGH...
DOES SHE HAVE TO BE SO ANNOY-ING?!
HEY.
WHY ARE YOU ALWAYS HANGING OUT WITH THOSE NERDS?
ESPECIALLY THE VIOLENCE QUEEN.
MUTTER MUTTER...
HMM?

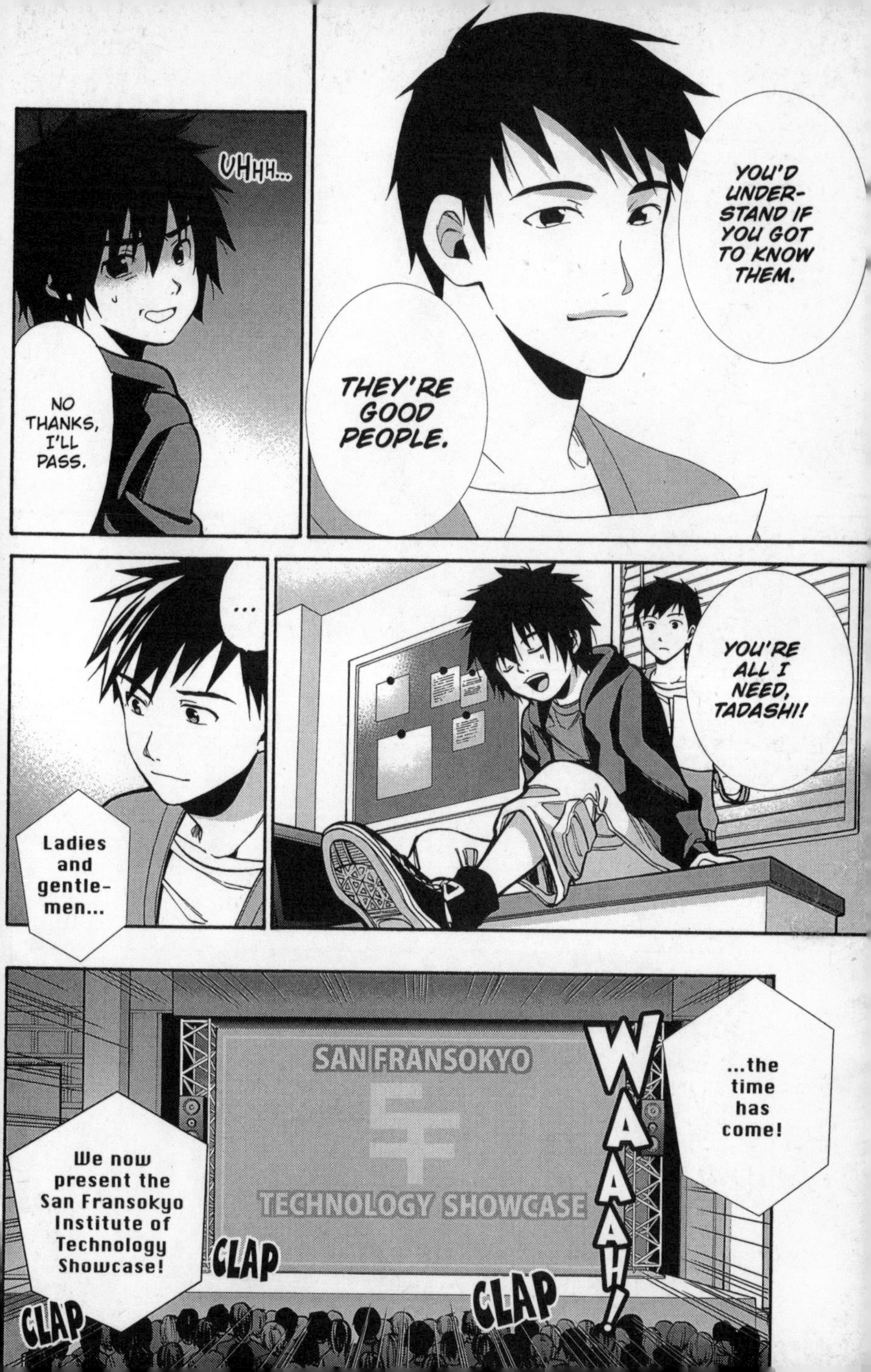
YOU'D UNDERSTAND IF YOU GOT TO KNOW THEM.
THEY'RE GOOD PEOPLE.
UHHH...
NO THANKS, I'LL PASS.
YOU'RE ALL I NEED, TADASHI!
...
Ladies and gentlemen...
...the time has come!
WAAAH!
SAN FRANSOKYO
TECHNOLOGY SHOWCASE
We now present the San Fransokyo Institute of Technology Showcase!
CLAP
CLAP
CLAP

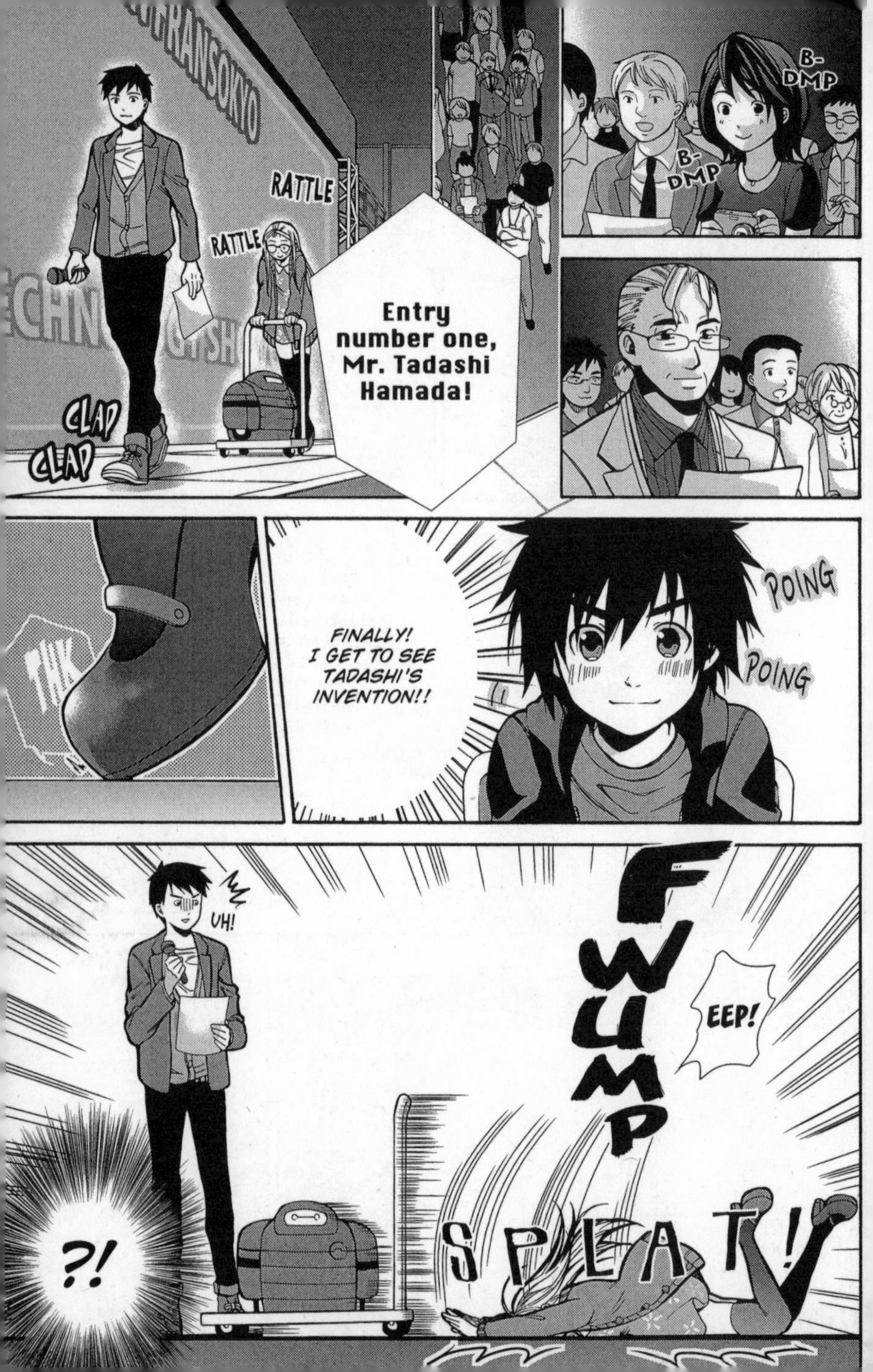
B-DMP
B-DMP
Entry number one, Mr. Tadashi Hamada!
RATTLE
RATTLE
CLAP
CLAP
FINALLY! I GET TO SEE TADASHI'S INVENTION!!
POING
POING
THK
FWUMP
EEP!
UH!
SPLAT!
?!

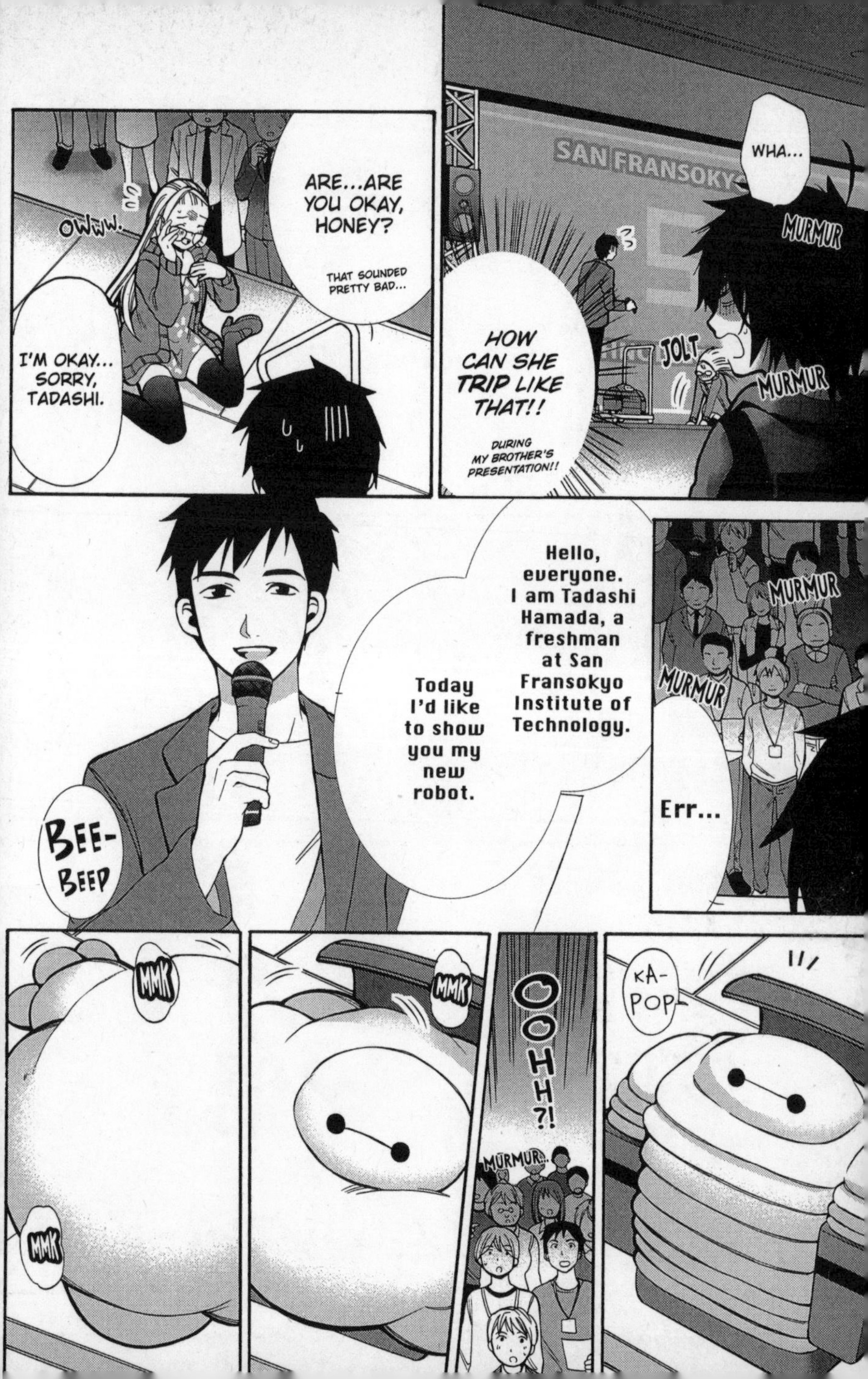
WHA...
MURMUR
SAN FRANSOKY
HOW CAN SHE TRIP LIKE THAT!!
DURING MY BROTHER'S PRESENTATION!!
JOLT
MURMUR
ARE...ARE YOU OKAY, HONEY?
THAT SOUNDED PRETTY BAD...
OWWW.
I'M OKAY... SORRY, TADASHI.
MURMUR
MURMUR
Err...
Hello, everyone. I am Tadashi Hamada, a freshman at San Fransokyo Institute of Technology.
Today I'd like to show you my new robot.
BEE-BEEP
KA-POP
OOOHH?!
MURMUR...
MMK
MMK
MMK

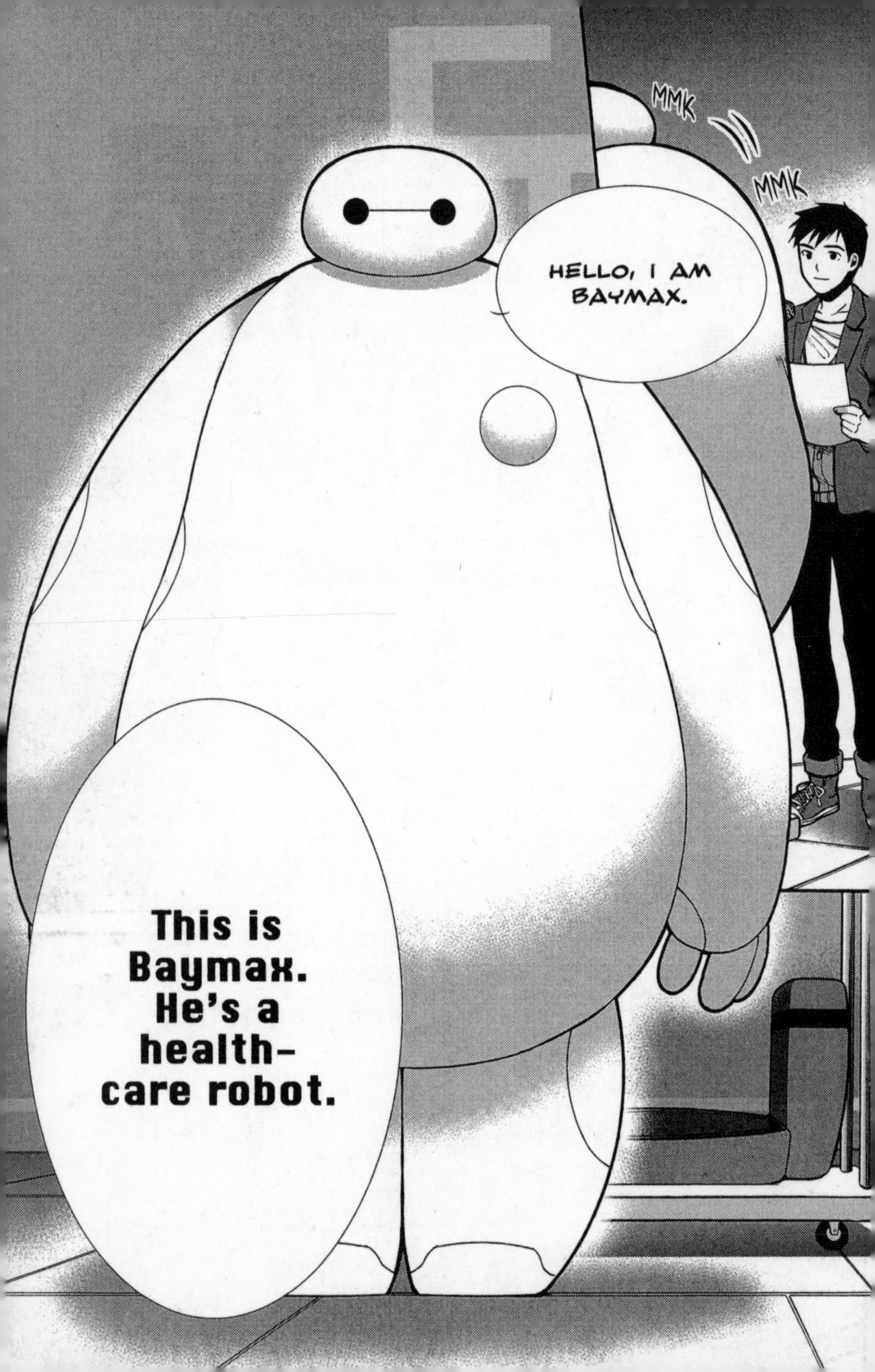
MMK
MMK
HELLO, I AM BAYMAX.
This is Baymax. He's a health-care robot.

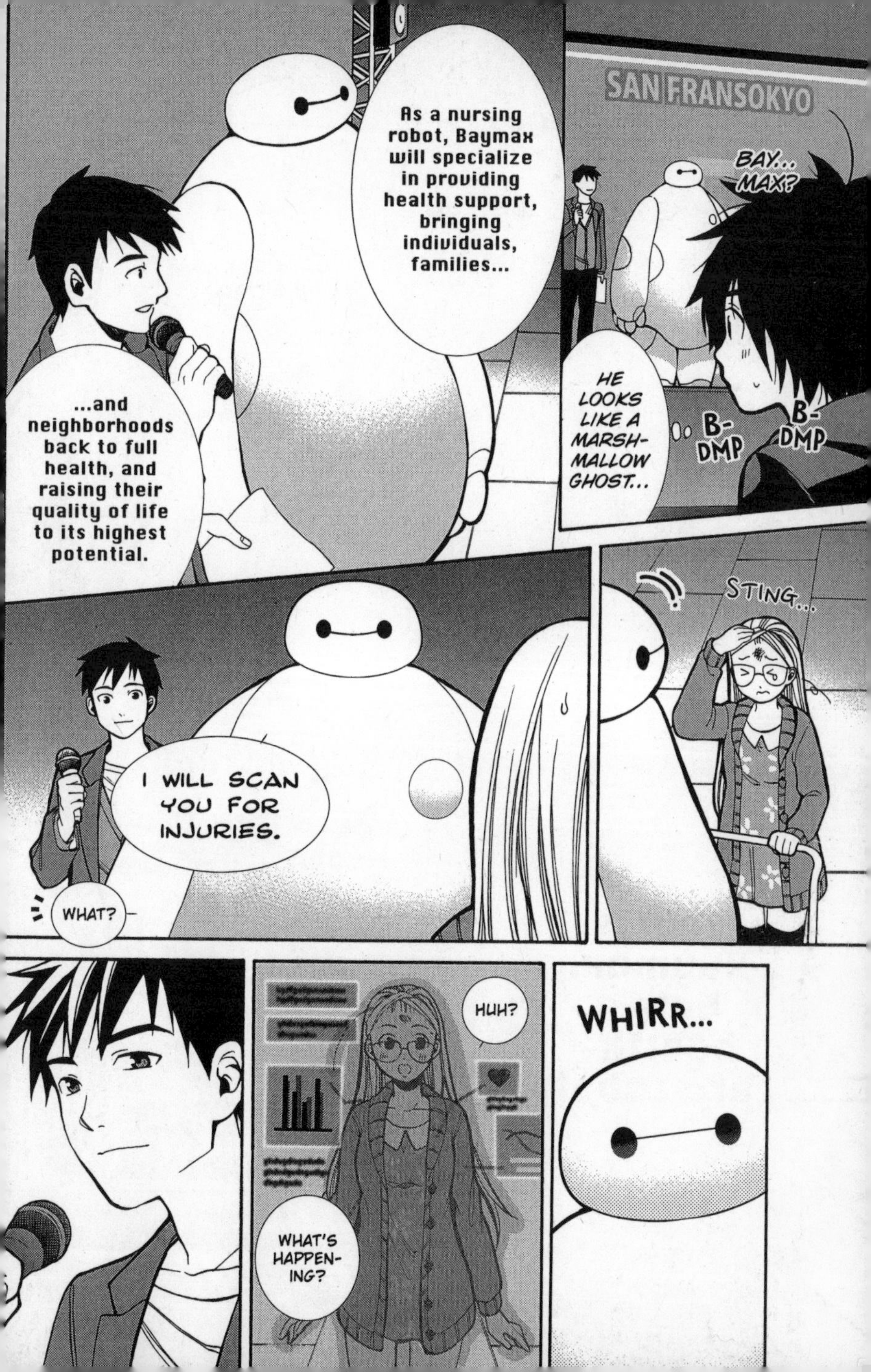
SAN FRANSOKYO
BAY... MAX?
B-DMP
B-DMP
HE LOOKS LIKE A MARSH-MALLOW GHOST...
As a nursing robot, Baymax will specialize in providing health support, bringing individuals, families...
...and neighborhoods back to full health, and raising their quality of life to its highest potential.
STING...
I WILL SCAN YOU FOR INJURIES.
WHAT?
WHIRR...
HUH?
WHAT'S HAPPEN-ING?

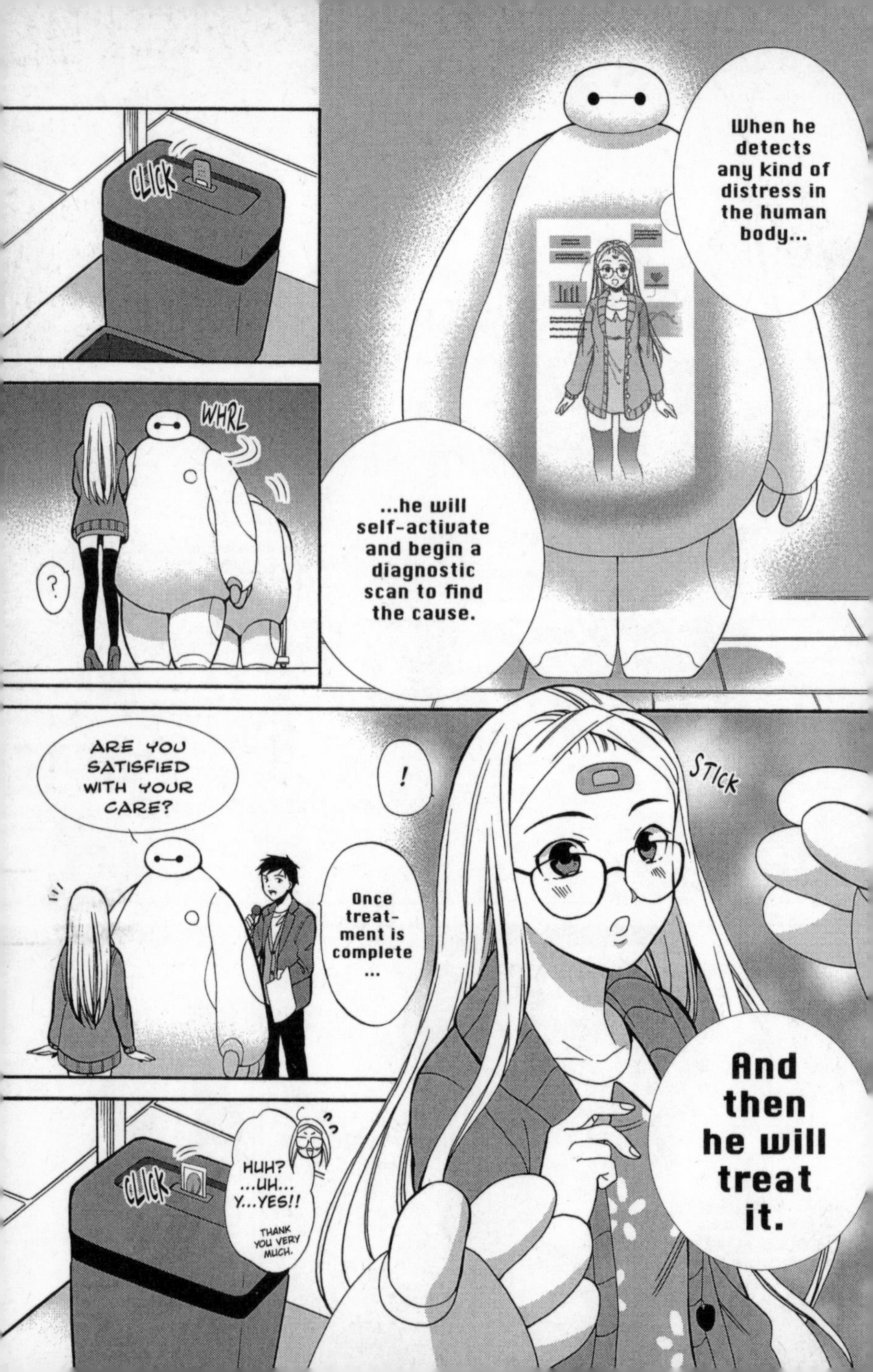
When he detects any kind of distress in the human body...
...he will self-activate and begin a diagnostic scan to find the cause.
CLICK
WHRL
?
STICK
!
And then he will treat it.
Once treatment is complete ...
ARE YOU SATISFIED WITH YOUR CARE?
CLICK
HUH? ...UH... Y...YES!!
THANK YOU VERY MUCH.

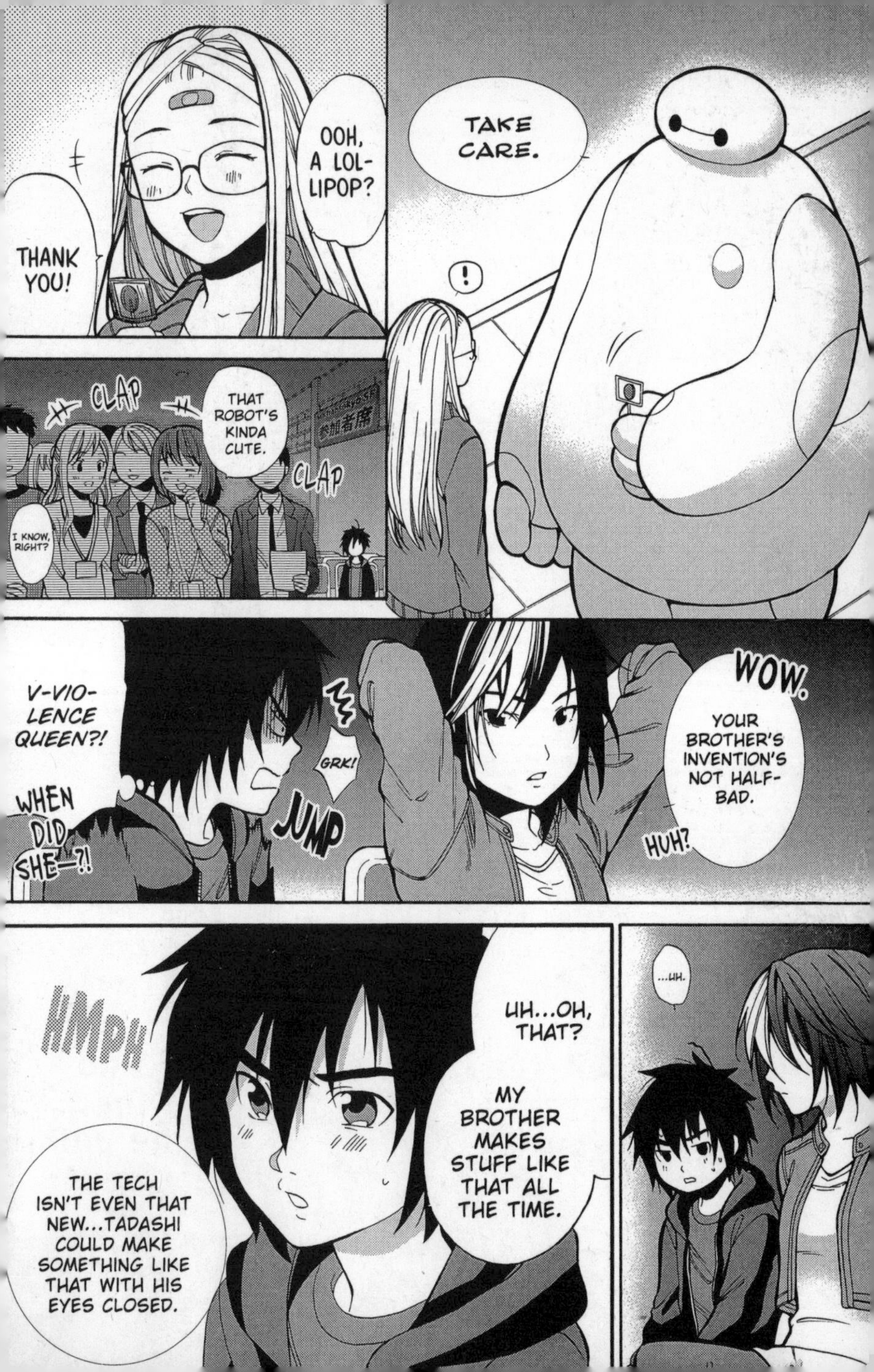
!
TAKE CARE.
OOH, A LOL-LIPOP?
THANK YOU!
CLAP
THAT ROBOT'S KINDA CUTE.
参加者席
CLAP
I KNOW, RIGHT?
WOW.
YOUR BROTHER'S INVENTION'S NOT HALF-BAD.
HUH?
GRK!
JUMP
V-VIO-LENCE QUEEN?!
WHEN DID SHE—?!
...UH.
UH...OH, THAT?
MY BROTHER MAKES STUFF LIKE THAT ALL THE TIME.
HMPH
THE TECH ISN'T EVEN THAT NEW...TADASHI COULD MAKE SOMETHING LIKE THAT WITH HIS EYES CLOSED.

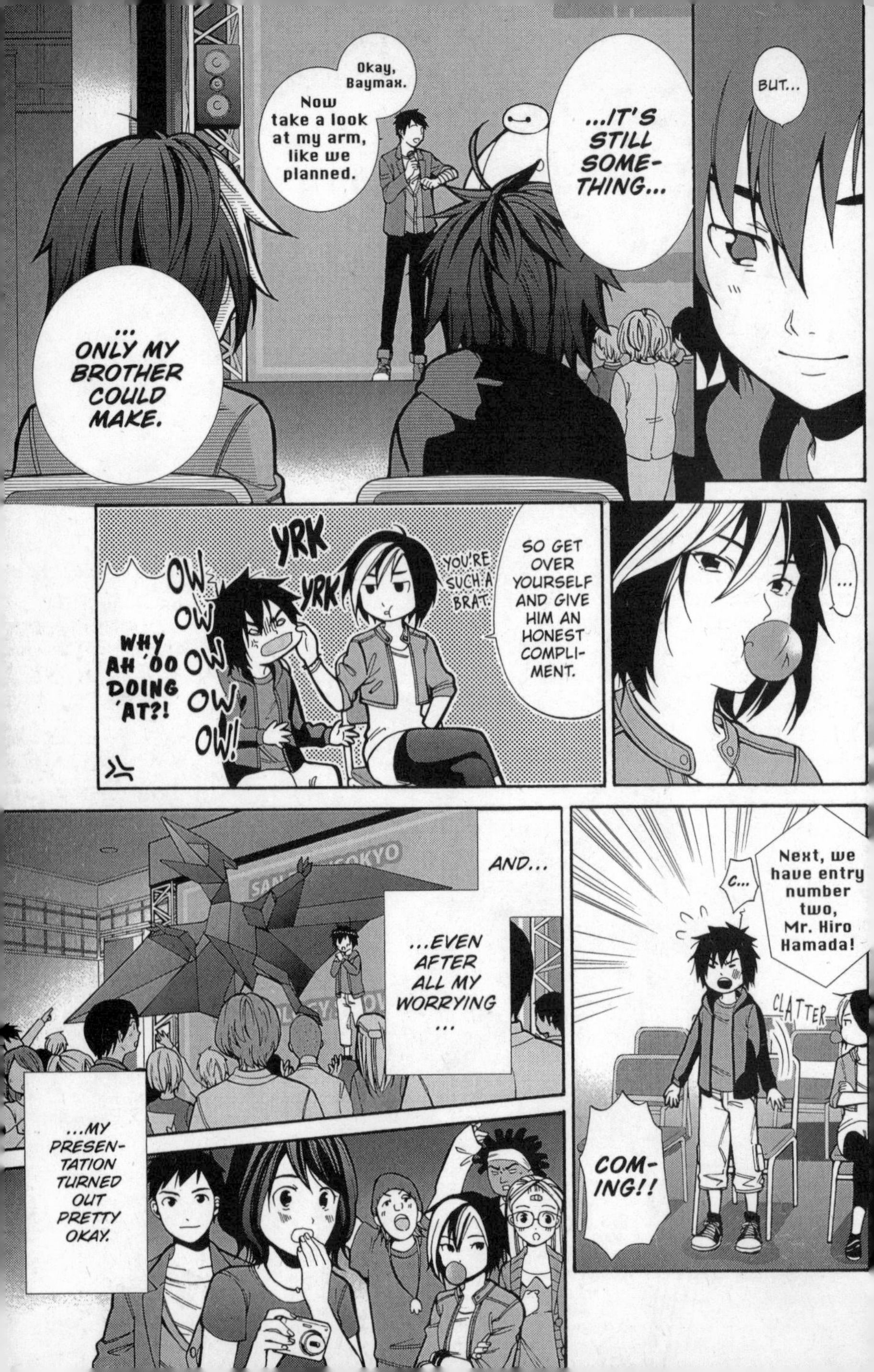
BUT...
...IT'S STILL SOMETHING...
Okay, Baymax. Now take a look at my arm, like we planned.
...ONLY MY BROTHER COULD MAKE.
...
SO GET OVER YOURSELF AND GIVE HIM AN HONEST COMPLIMENT.
YOU'RE SUCH A BRAT.
YRK
YRK
OW OW OW OW OW OW!
WHY AH 'OO DOING 'AT?!
Next, we have entry number two, Mr. Hiro Hamada!
C...
CLATTER
COMING!!
AND...
...EVEN AFTER ALL MY WORRYING...
...MY PRESENTATION TURNED OUT PRETTY OKAY.

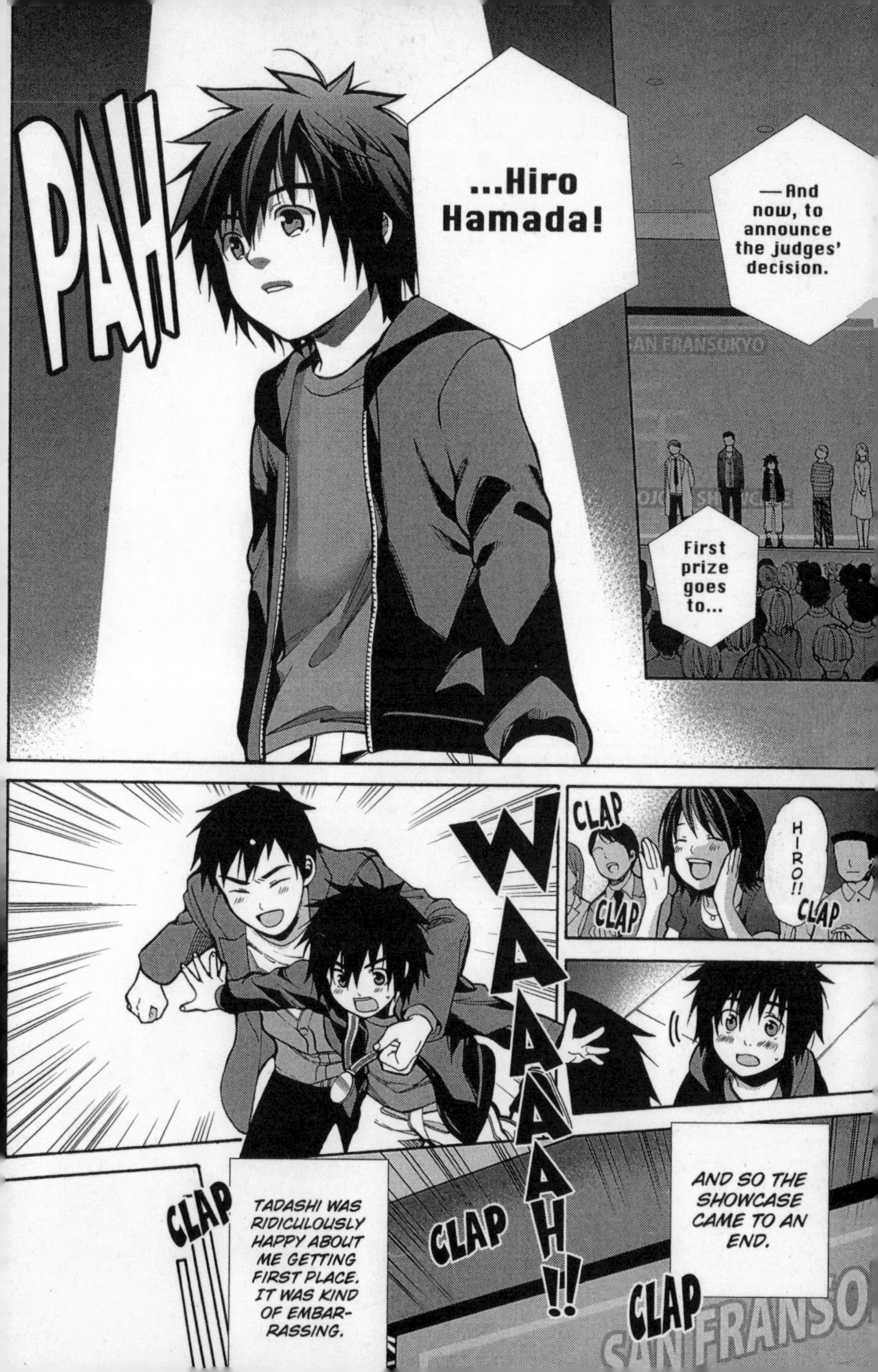
—And now, to announce the judges' decision.
First prize goes to...
PAH
...Hiro Hamada!
CLAP
HIRO!!
CLAP
CLAP
WAAAAAH!!
AND SO THE SHOWCASE CAME TO AN END.
CLAP
CLAP
TADASHI WAS RIDICULOUSLY HAPPY ABOUT ME GETTING FIRST PLACE. IT WAS KIND OF EMBARRASSING.
CLAP
SAN FRANSO

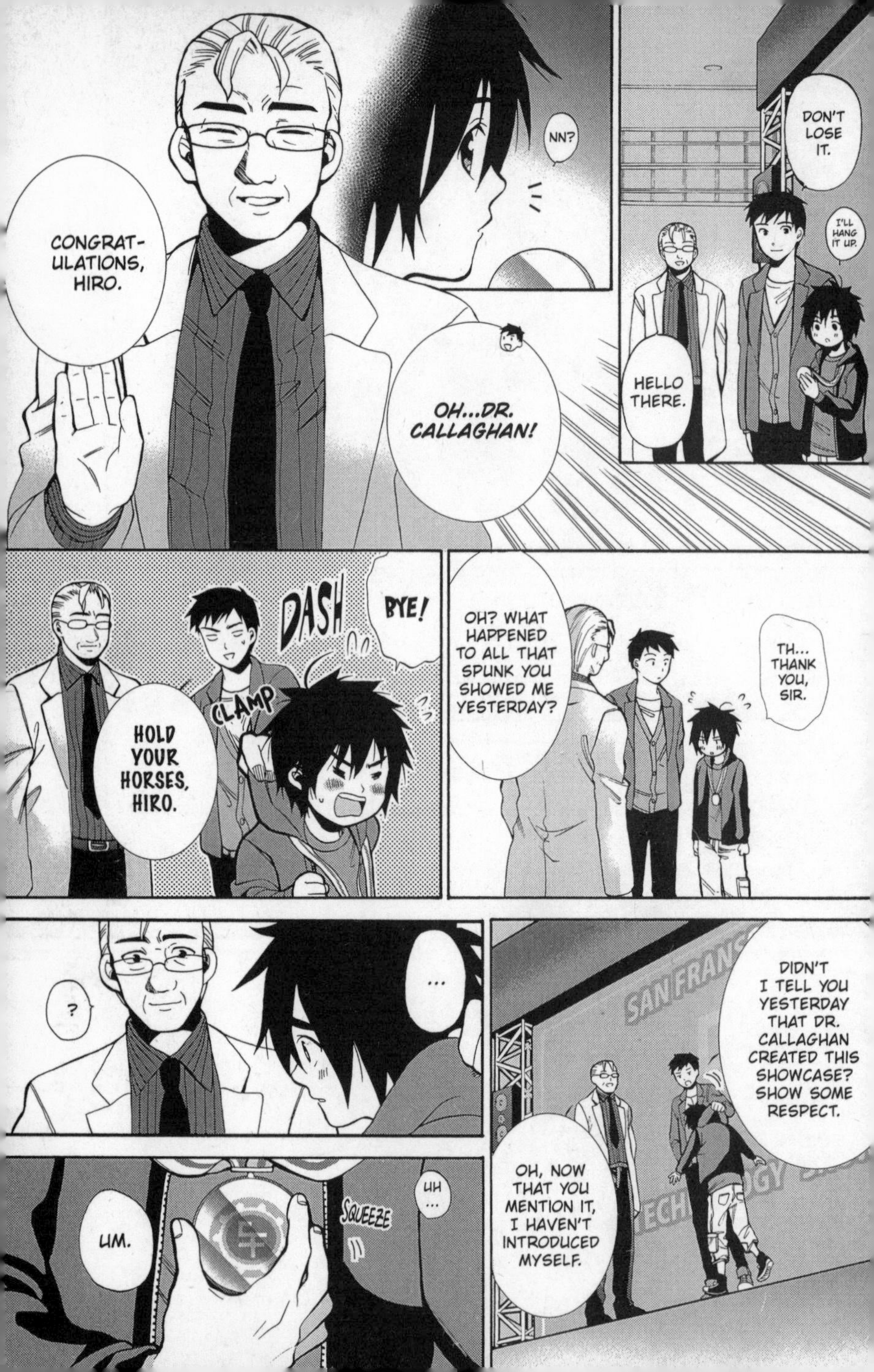
DON'T LOSE IT.
I'LL HANG IT UP.
HELLO THERE.
NN?
CONGRAT-ULATIONS, HIRO.
OH...DR. CALLAGHAN!
TH... THANK YOU, SIR.
OH? WHAT HAPPENED TO ALL THAT SPUNK YOU SHOWED ME YESTERDAY?
BYE!
DASH
CLAMP
HOLD YOUR HORSES, HIRO.
DIDN'T I TELL YOU YESTERDAY THAT DR. CALLAGHAN CREATED THIS SHOWCASE? SHOW SOME RESPECT.
OH, NOW THAT YOU MENTION IT, I HAVEN'T INTRODUCED MYSELF.
...
?
UH ...
SQUEEZE
UM.

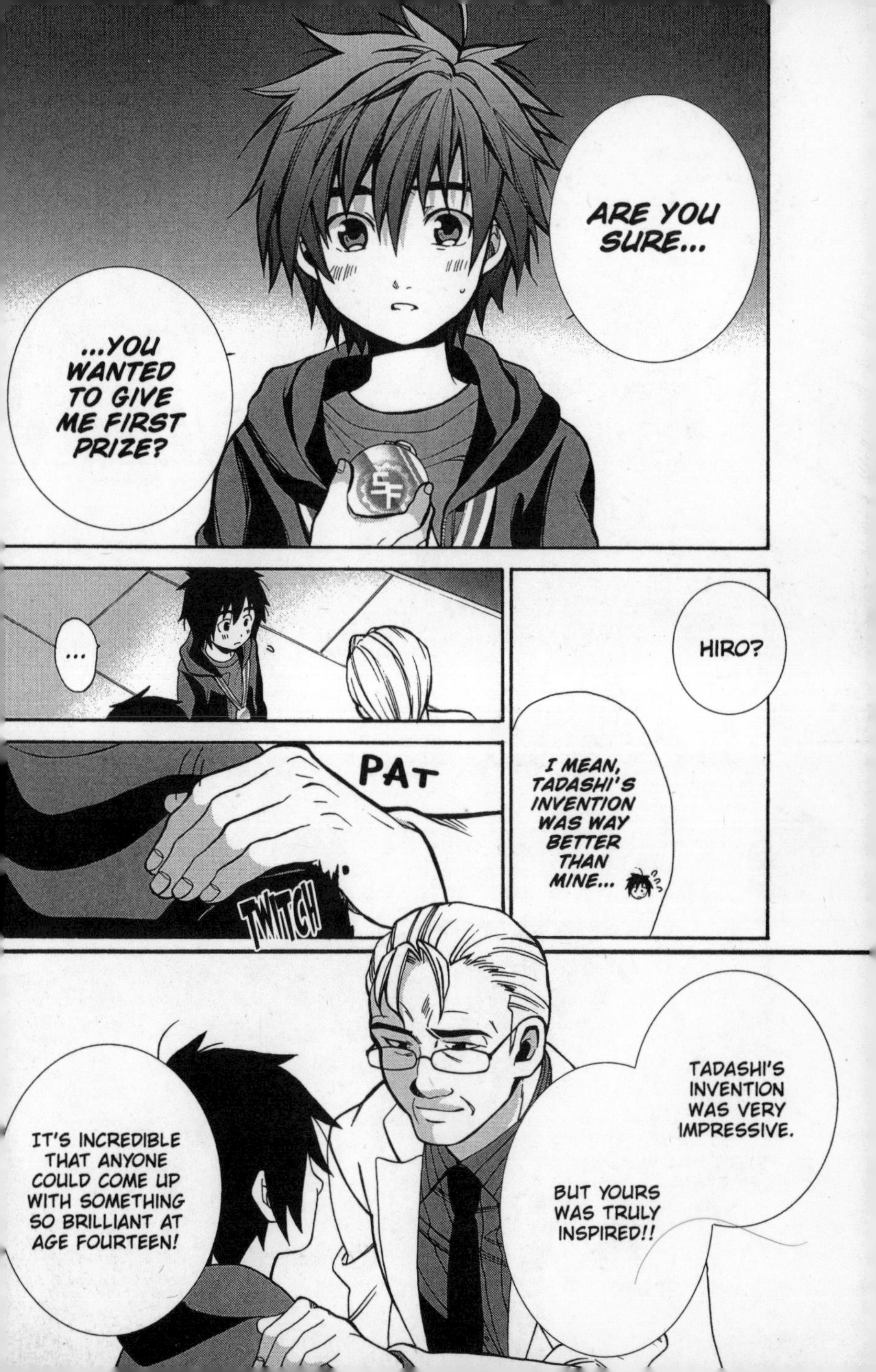
ARE YOU SURE...
...YOU WANTED TO GIVE ME FIRST PRIZE?
HIRO?
I MEAN, TADASHI'S INVENTION WAS WAY BETTER THAN MINE...
...
PAT
TWITCH
TADASHI'S INVENTION WAS VERY IMPRESSIVE.
BUT YOURS WAS TRULY INSPIRED!!
IT'S INCREDIBLE THAT ANYONE COULD COME UP WITH SOMETHING SO BRILLIANT AT AGE FOURTEEN!

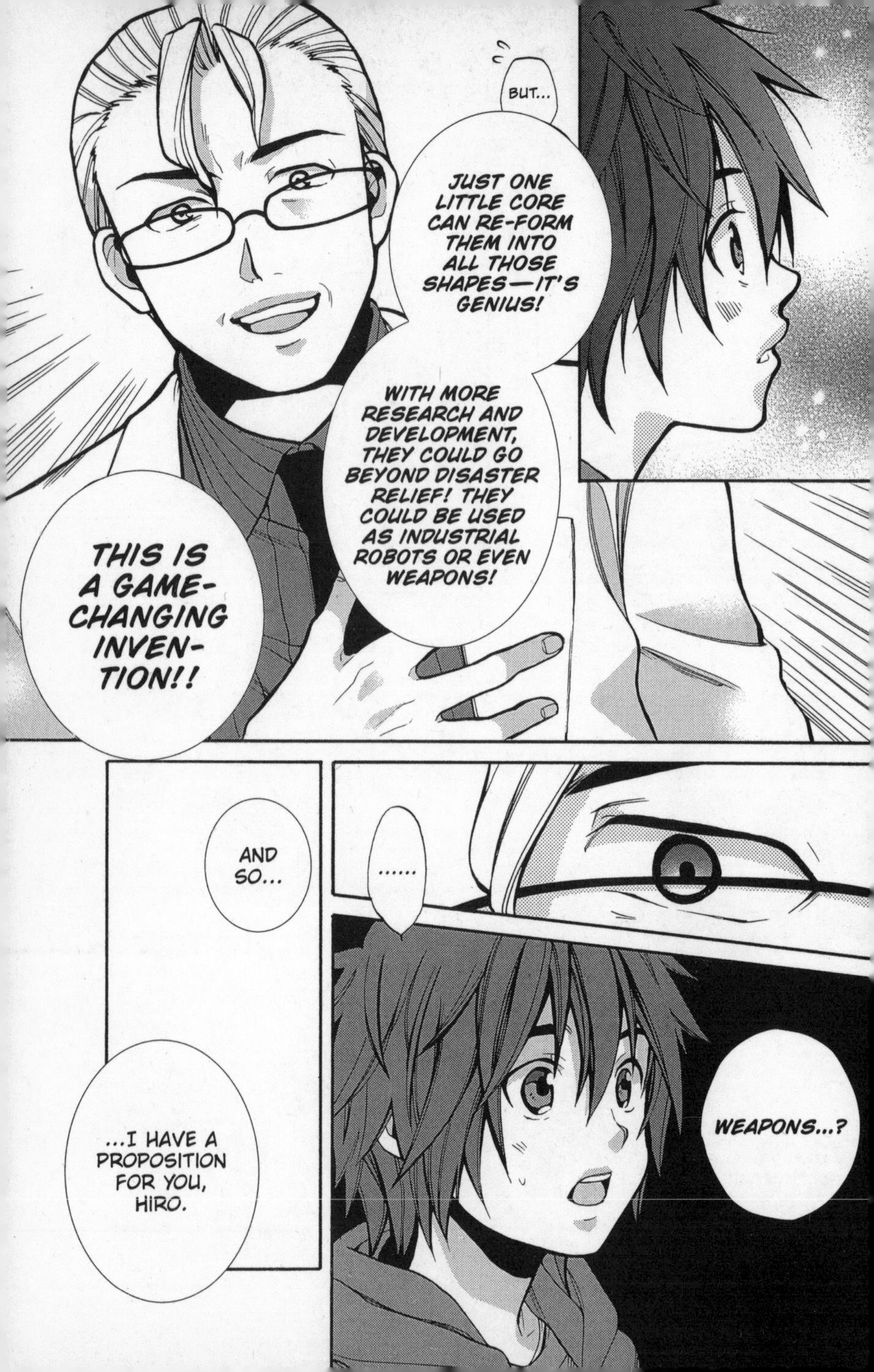
BUT...
JUST ONE LITTLE CORE CAN RE-FORM THEM INTO ALL THOSE SHAPES—IT'S GENIUS!
WITH MORE RESEARCH AND DEVELOPMENT, THEY COULD GO BEYOND DISASTER RELIEF! THEY COULD BE USED AS INDUSTRIAL ROBOTS OR EVEN WEAPONS!
THIS IS A GAME-CHANGING INVEN-TION!!
......
WEAPONS...?
AND SO...
...I HAVE A PROPOSITION FOR YOU, HIRO.

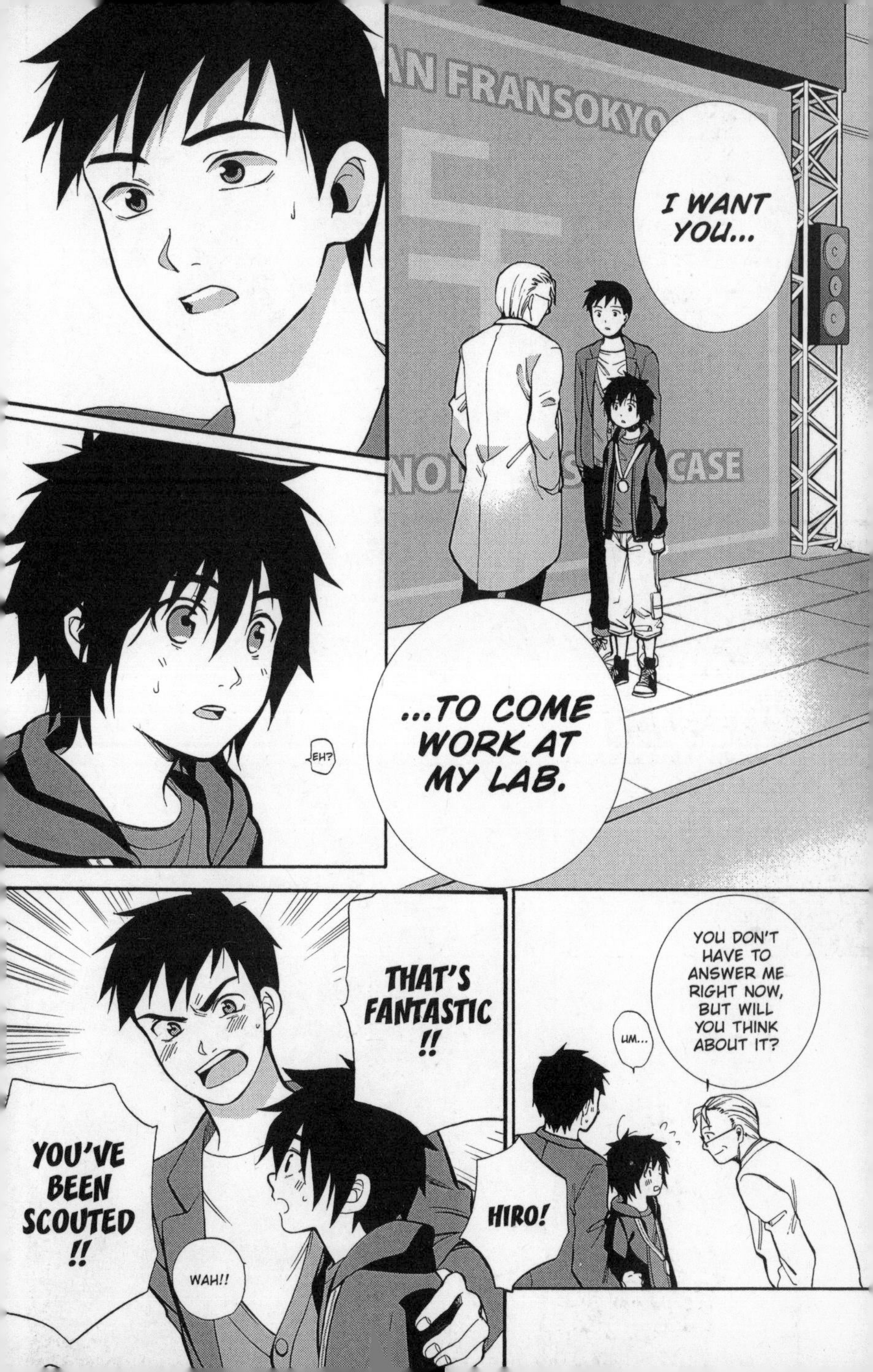
I WANT YOU...
...TO COME WORK AT MY LAB.
EH?
YOU DON'T HAVE TO ANSWER ME RIGHT NOW, BUT WILL YOU THINK ABOUT IT?
UM...
THAT'S FANTASTIC!!
HIRO!
YOU'VE BEEN SCOUTED!!
WAH!!

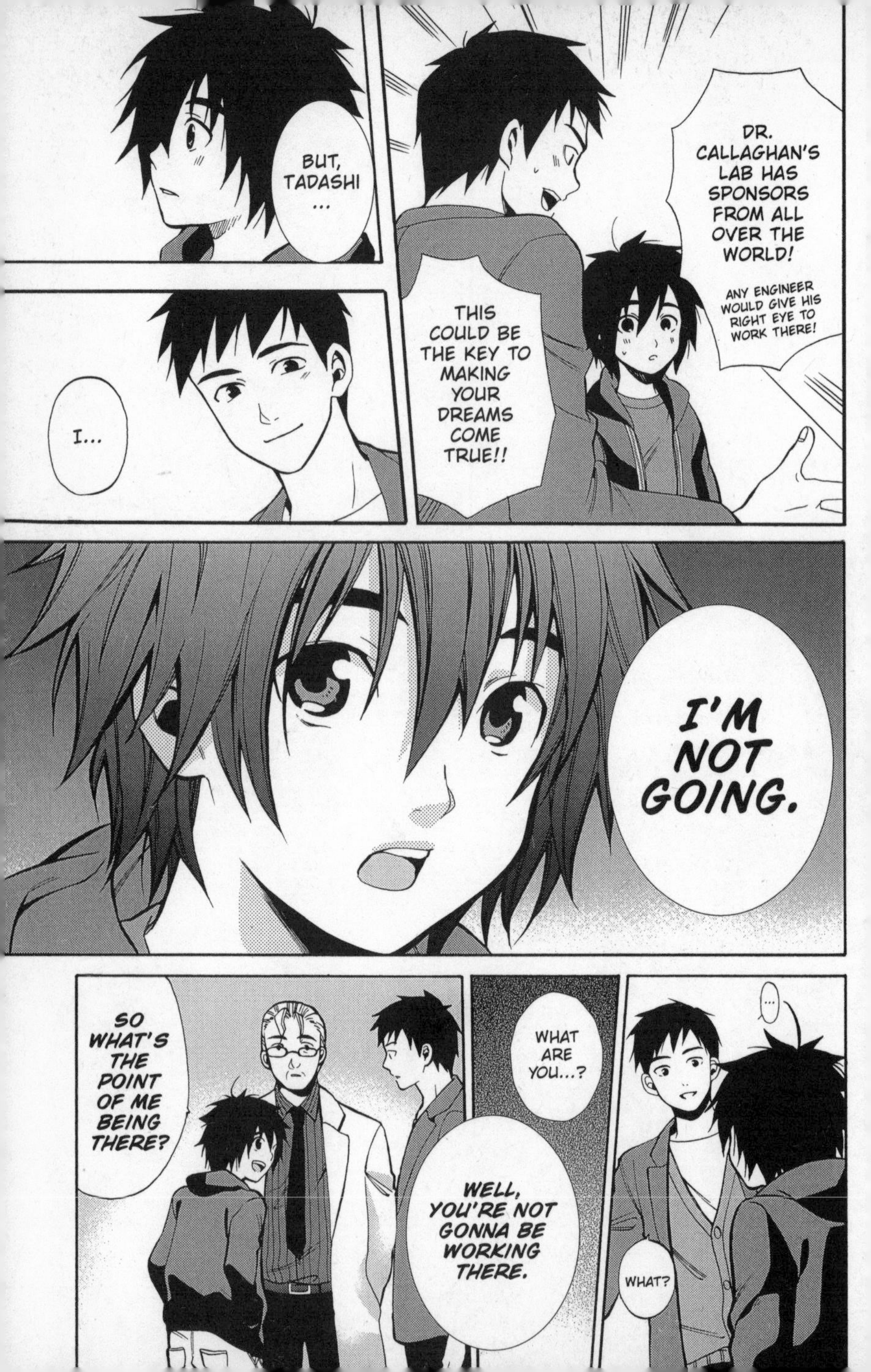
DR. CALLAGHAN'S LAB HAS SPONSORS FROM ALL OVER THE WORLD!
ANY ENGINEER WOULD GIVE HIS RIGHT EYE TO WORK THERE!
THIS COULD BE THE KEY TO MAKING YOUR DREAMS COME TRUE!!
BUT, TADASHI ...
I...
I'M NOT GOING.
...
WHAT?
WHAT ARE YOU...?
WELL, YOU'RE NOT GONNA BE WORKING THERE.
SO WHAT'S THE POINT OF ME BEING THERE?

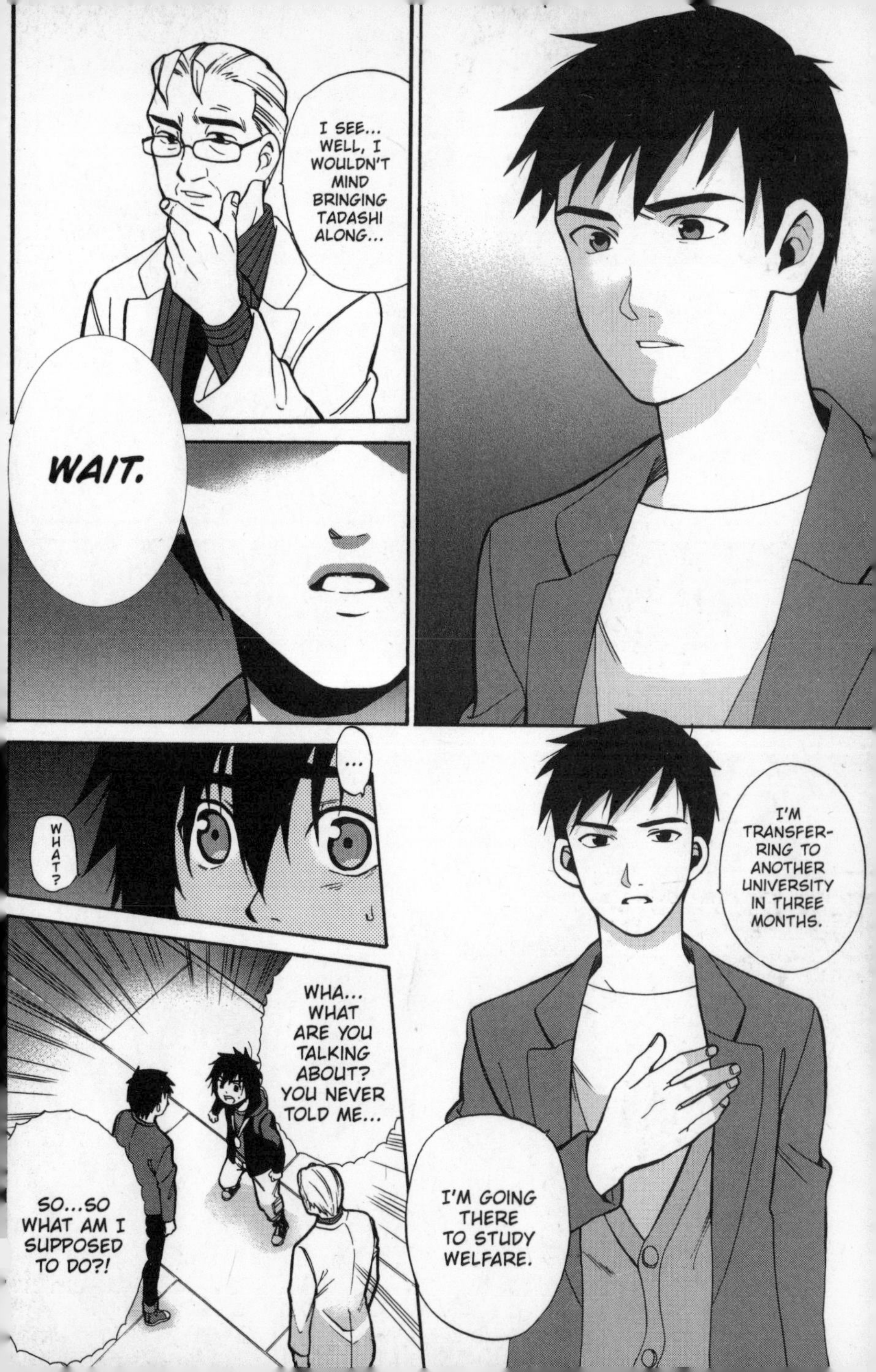
I SEE... WELL, I WOULDN'T MIND BRINGING TADASHI ALONG...
WAIT.
I'M TRANSFER-RING TO ANOTHER UNIVERSITY IN THREE MONTHS.
I'M GOING THERE TO STUDY WELFARE.
...
WHAT?
WHA... WHAT ARE YOU TALKING ABOUT? YOU NEVER TOLD ME...
SO...SO WHAT AM I SUPPOSED TO DO?!

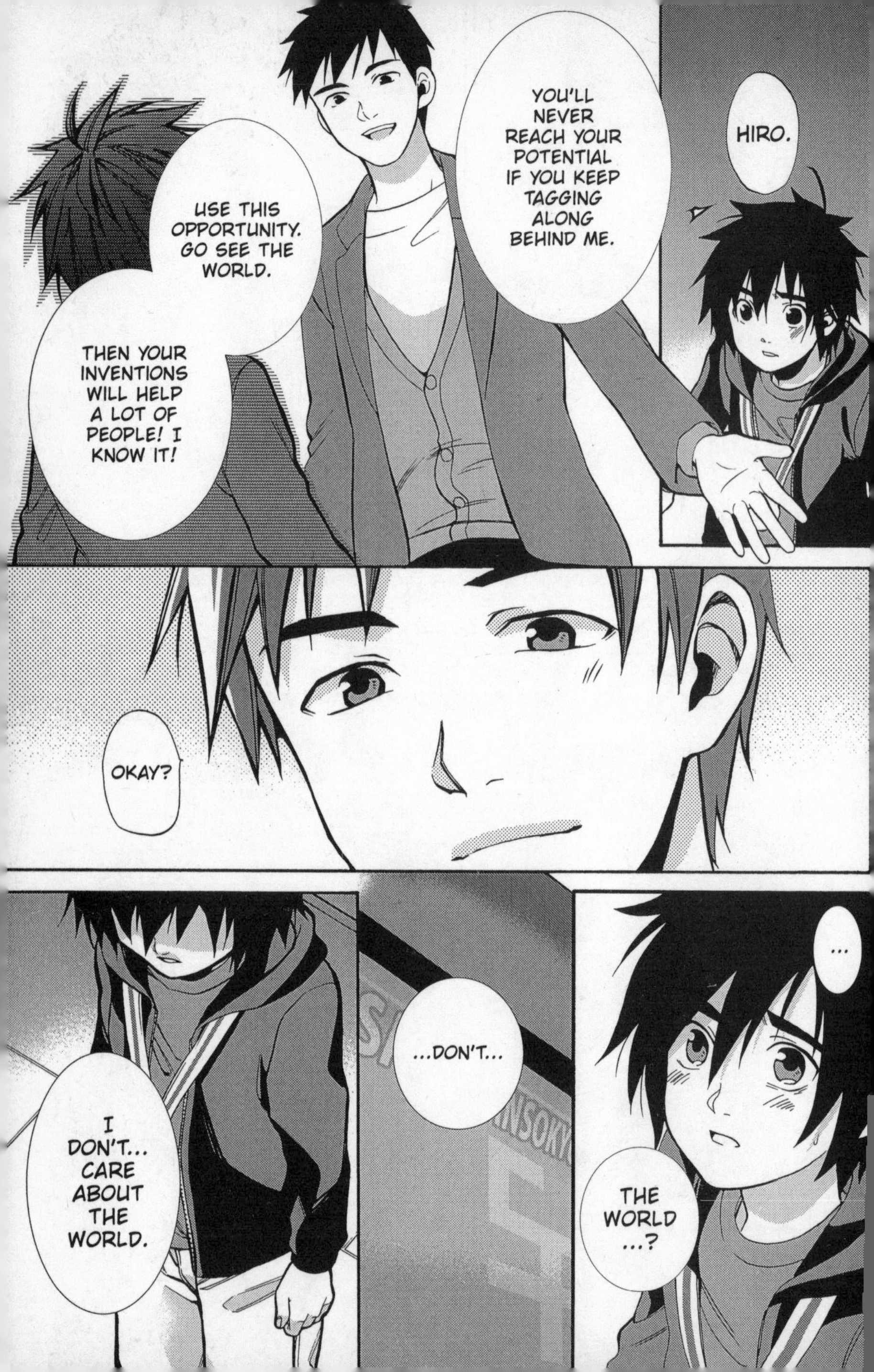
HIRO.
YOU'LL NEVER REACH YOUR POTENTIAL IF YOU KEEP TAGGING ALONG BEHIND ME.
USE THIS OPPORTUNITY. GO SEE THE WORLD.
THEN YOUR INVENTIONS WILL HELP A LOT OF PEOPLE! I KNOW IT!
OKAY?
...
THE WORLD ...?
...DON'T...
I DON'T... CARE ABOUT THE WORLD.

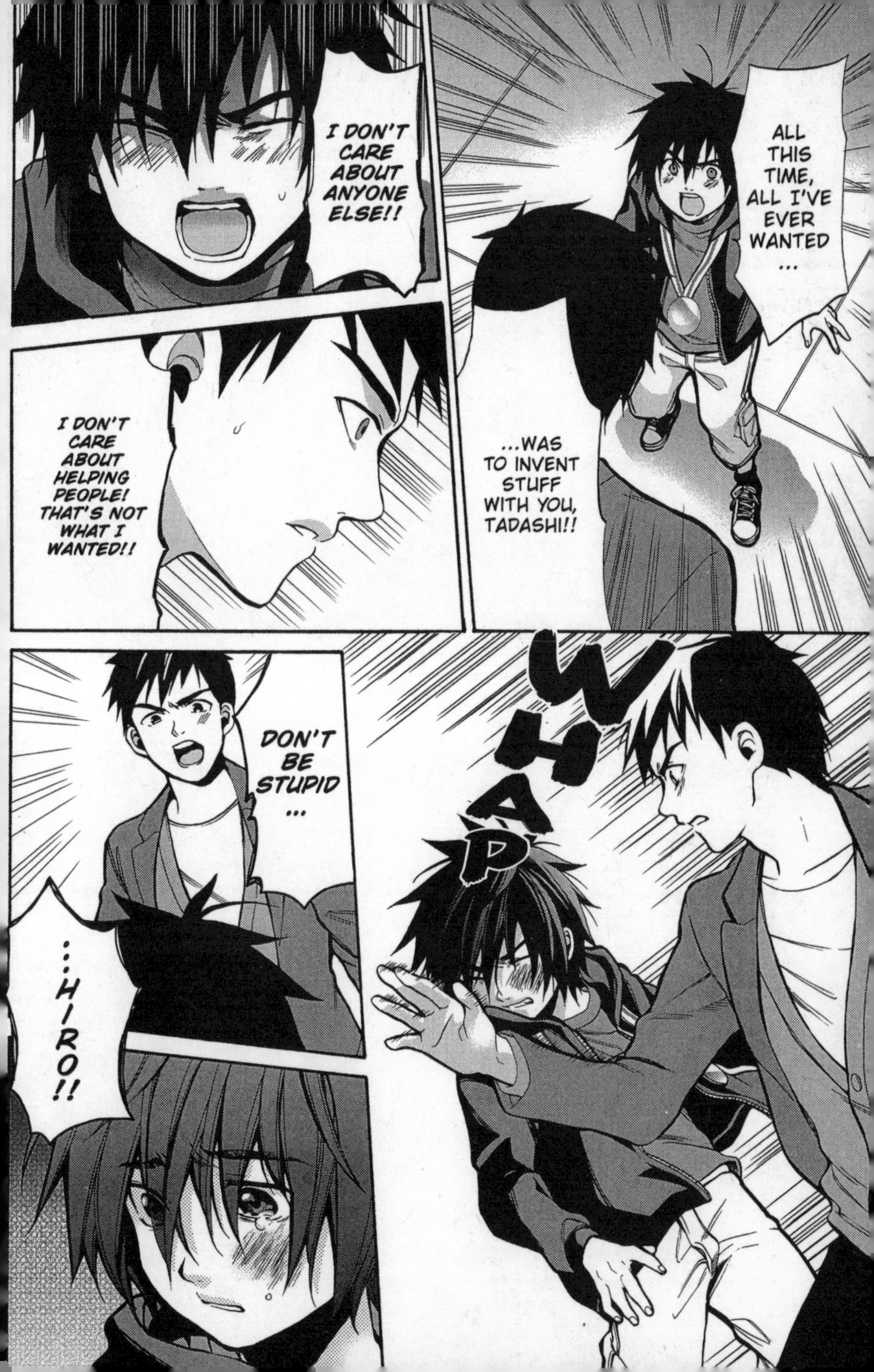
ALL THIS TIME, ALL I'VE EVER WANTED ...
...WAS TO INVENT STUFF WITH YOU, TADASHI!!
I DON'T CARE ABOUT ANYONE ELSE!!
I DON'T CARE ABOUT HELPING PEOPLE! THAT'S NOT WHAT I WANTED!!
WHAP
DON'T BE STUPID ...
...HIRO!!

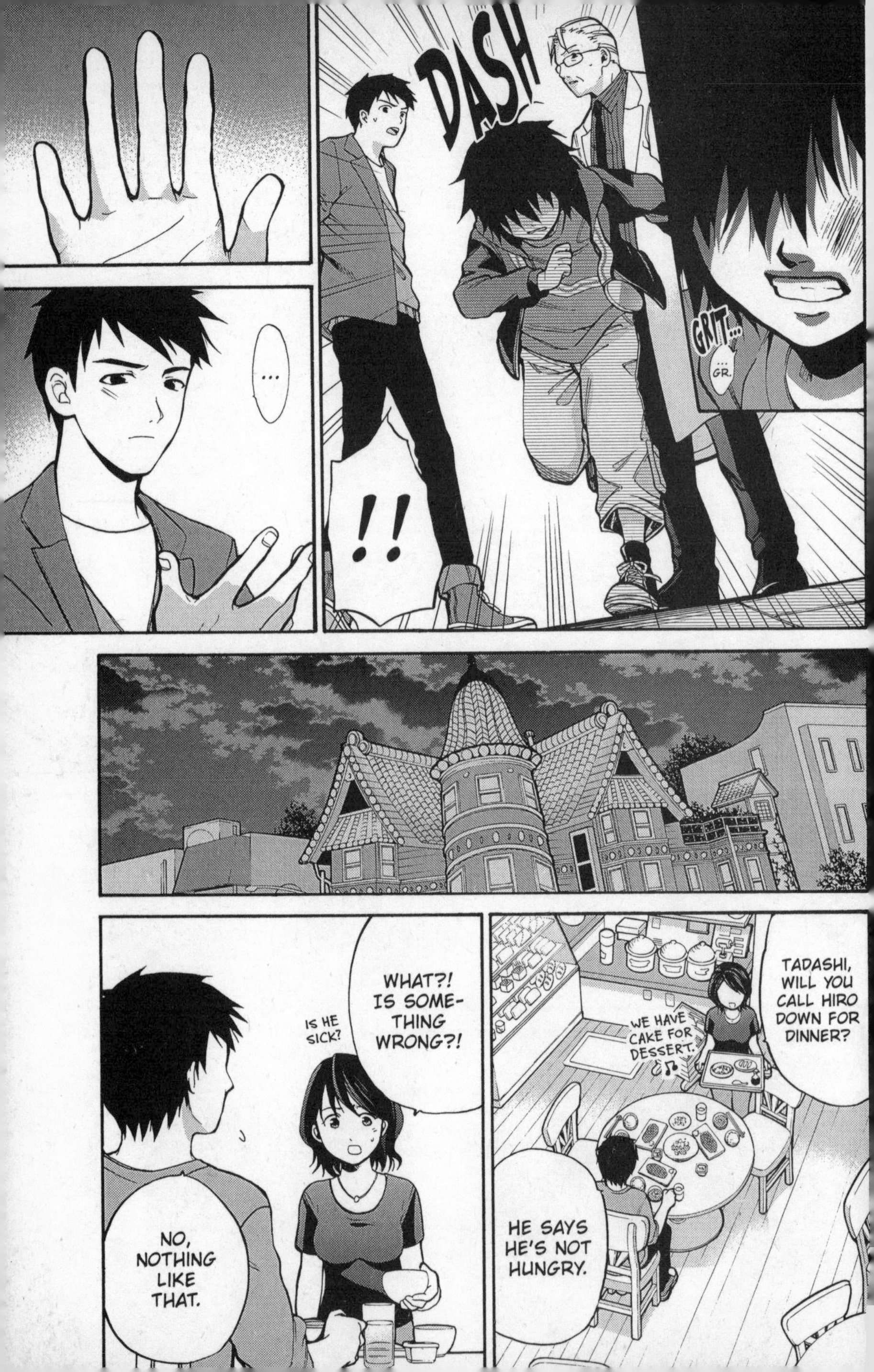
GRIT...
...GR.
DASH
!!
...
TADASHI, WILL YOU CALL HIRO DOWN FOR DINNER?
WE HAVE CAKE FOR DESSERT.
HE SAYS HE'S NOT HUNGRY.
WHAT?! IS SOME-THING WRONG?!
IS HE SICK?
NO, NOTHING LIKE THAT.

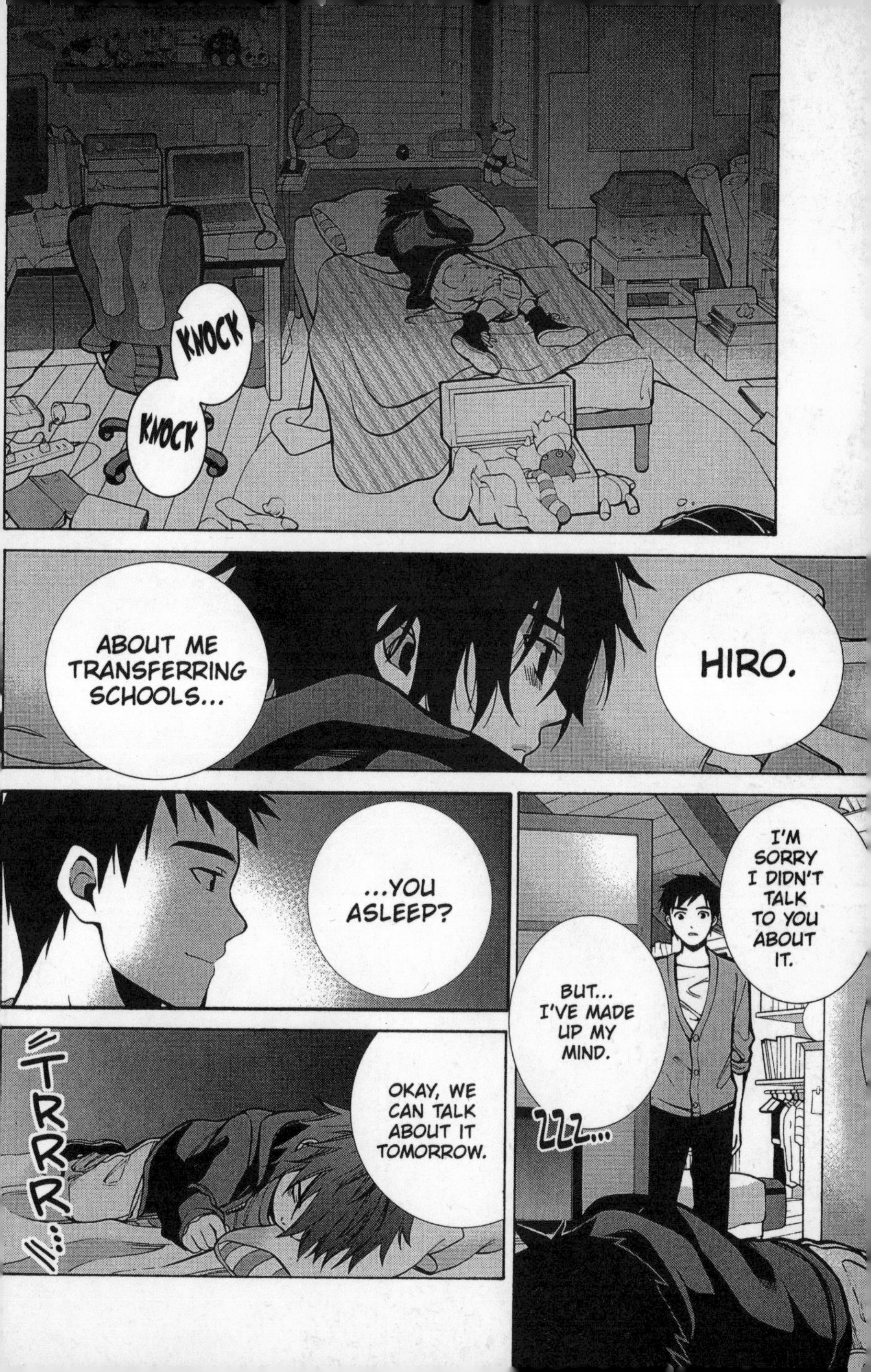
KNOCK
KNOCK
HIRO.
ABOUT ME TRANSFERRING SCHOOLS...
I'M SORRY I DIDN'T TALK TO YOU ABOUT IT.
BUT... I'VE MADE UP MY MIND.
ZZZ...
...YOU ASLEEP?
OKAY, WE CAN TALK ABOUT IT TOMORROW.
TRRR...

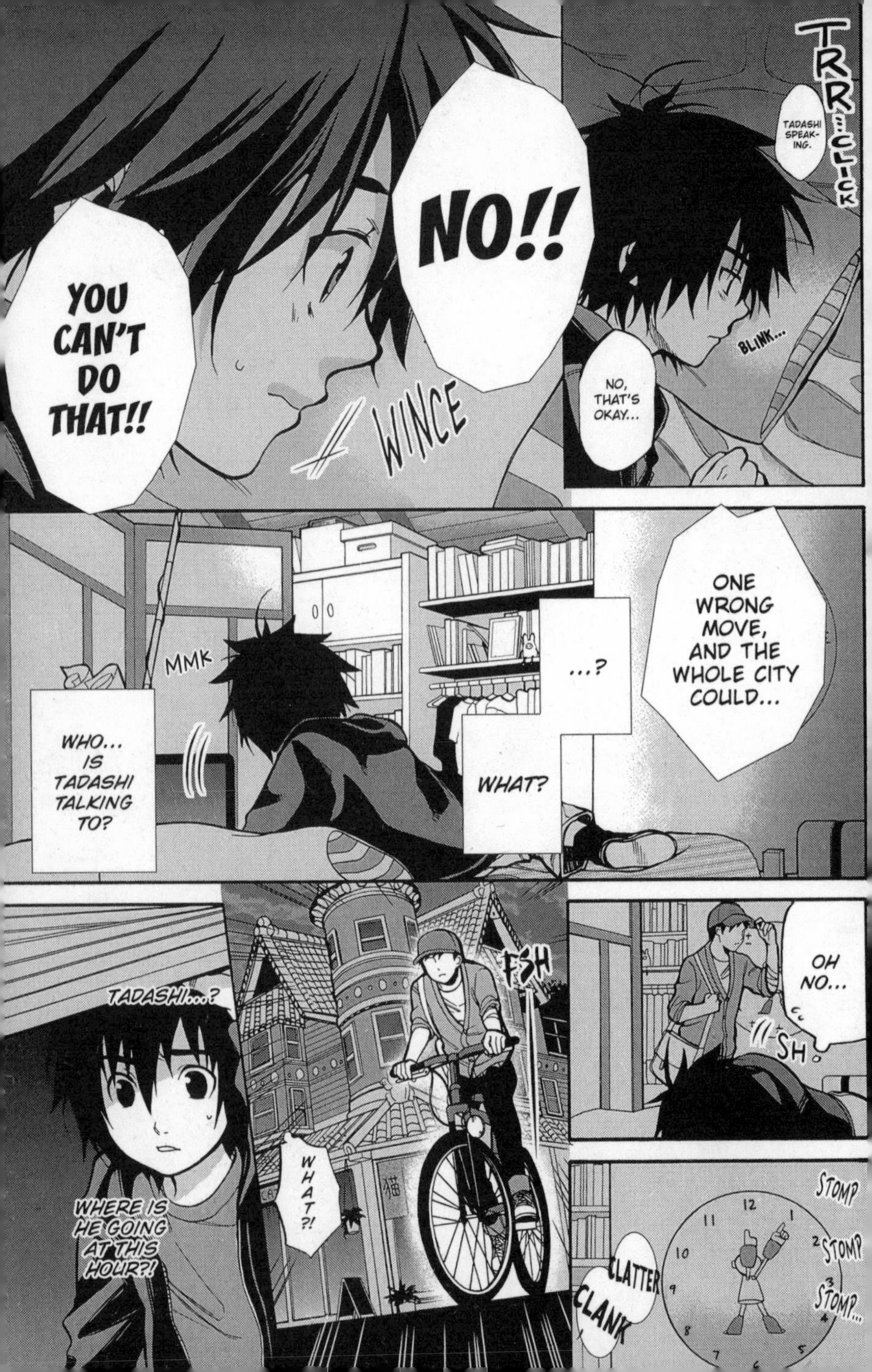
TRR...CLICK
TADASHI SPEAKING.
BLINK...
NO, THAT'S OKAY...
NO!!
YOU CAN'T DO THAT!!
WINCE
ONE WRONG MOVE, AND THE WHOLE CITY COULD...
...?
WHAT?
MMK
WHO... IS TADASHI TALKING TO?
OH NO...
SH
STOMP
STOMP
STOMP...
CLATTER
CLANK
FSH
WHAT?!
TADASHI...?
WHERE IS HE GOING AT THIS HOUR?!

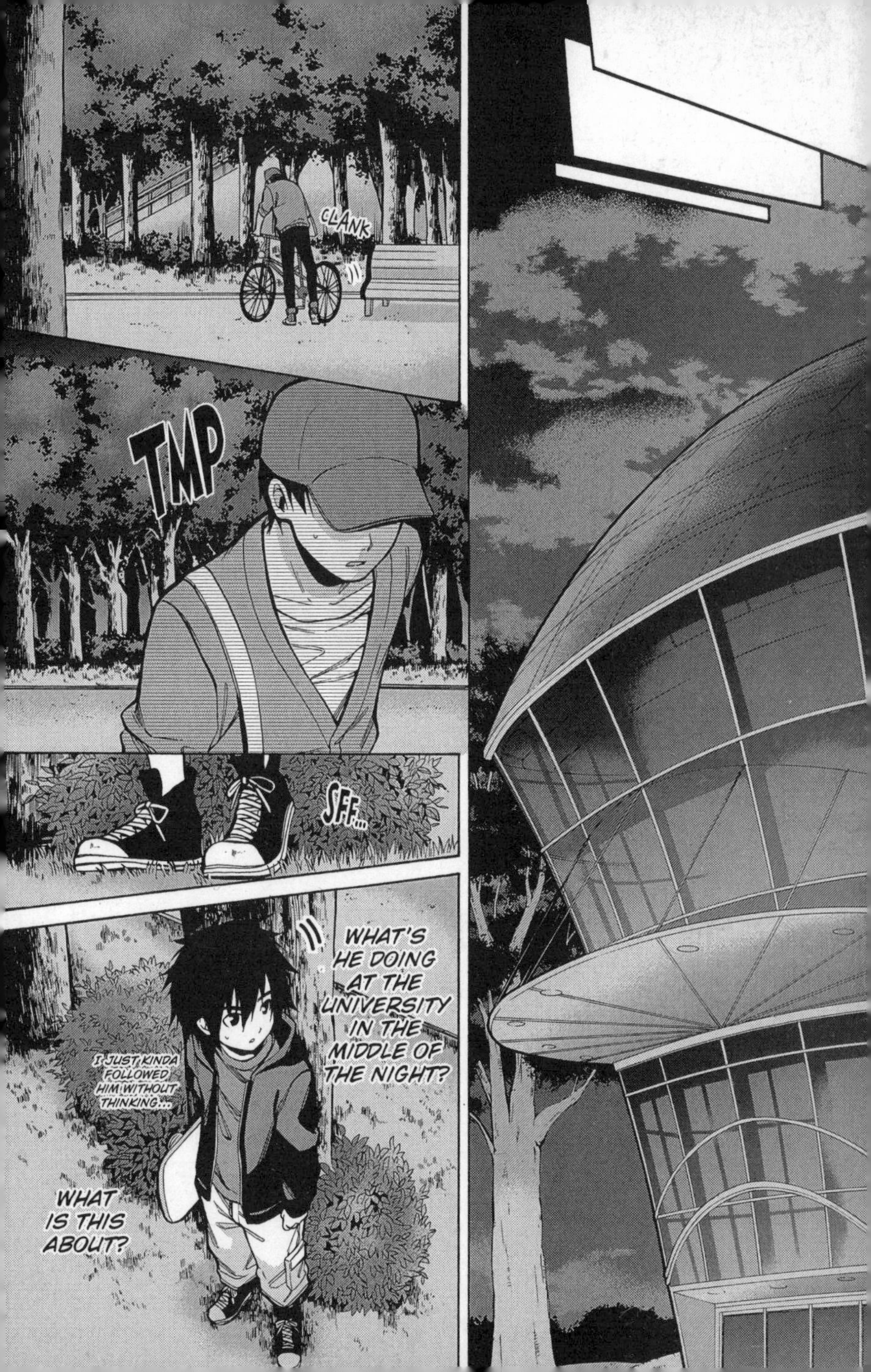
CLANK
TMP
SFF...
WHAT'S HE DOING AT THE UNIVERSITY IN THE MIDDLE OF THE NIGHT?
I JUST KINDA FOLLOWED HIM WITHOUT THINKING...
WHAT IS THIS ABOUT?

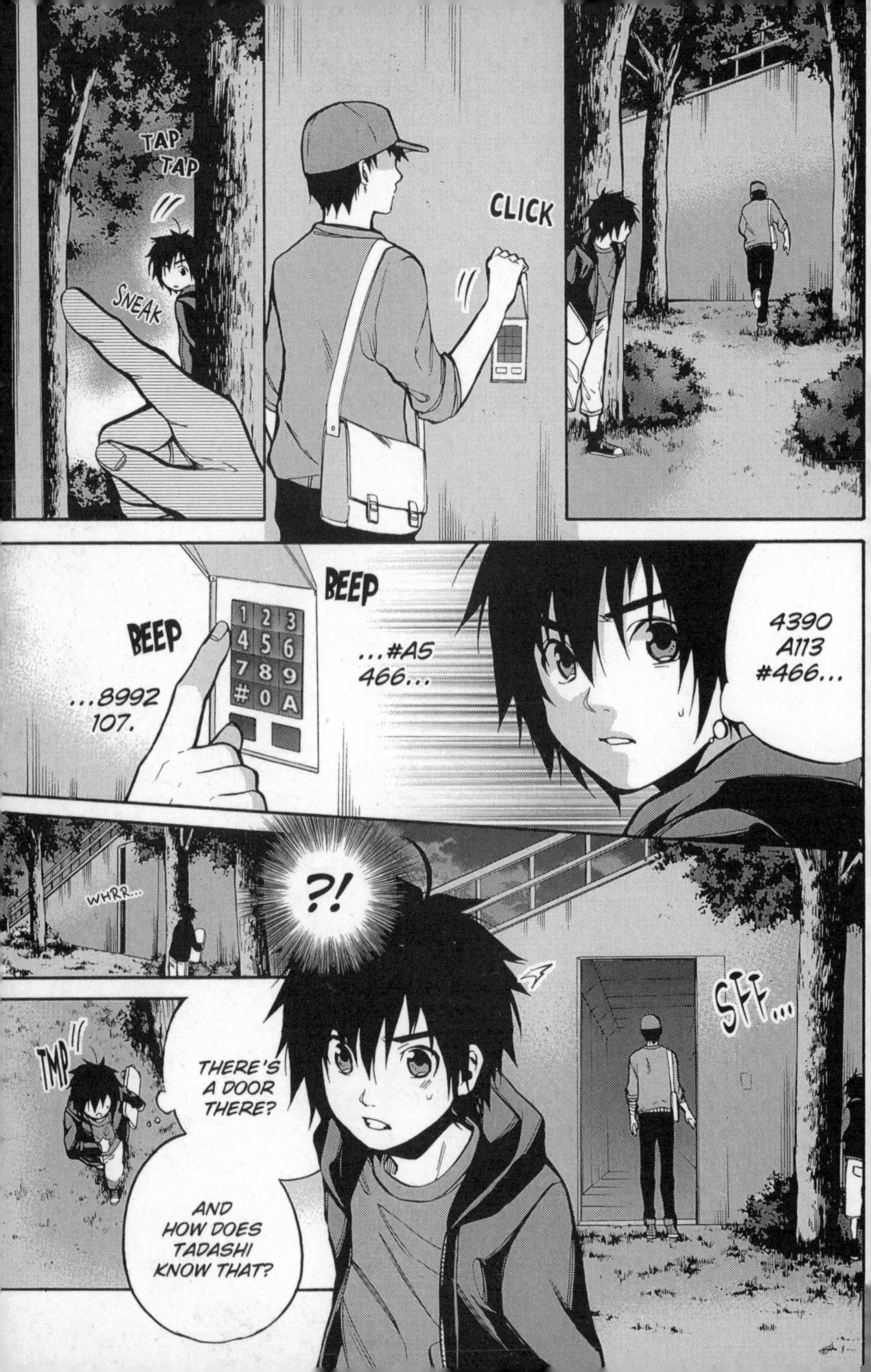
CLICK
TAP TAP
SNEAK
4390
A113
#466...
BEEP
...#A5
466...
BEEP
...8992
107.
?!
SFF...
THERE'S A DOOR THERE?
AND HOW DOES TADASHI KNOW THAT?
WHRR...
TMP

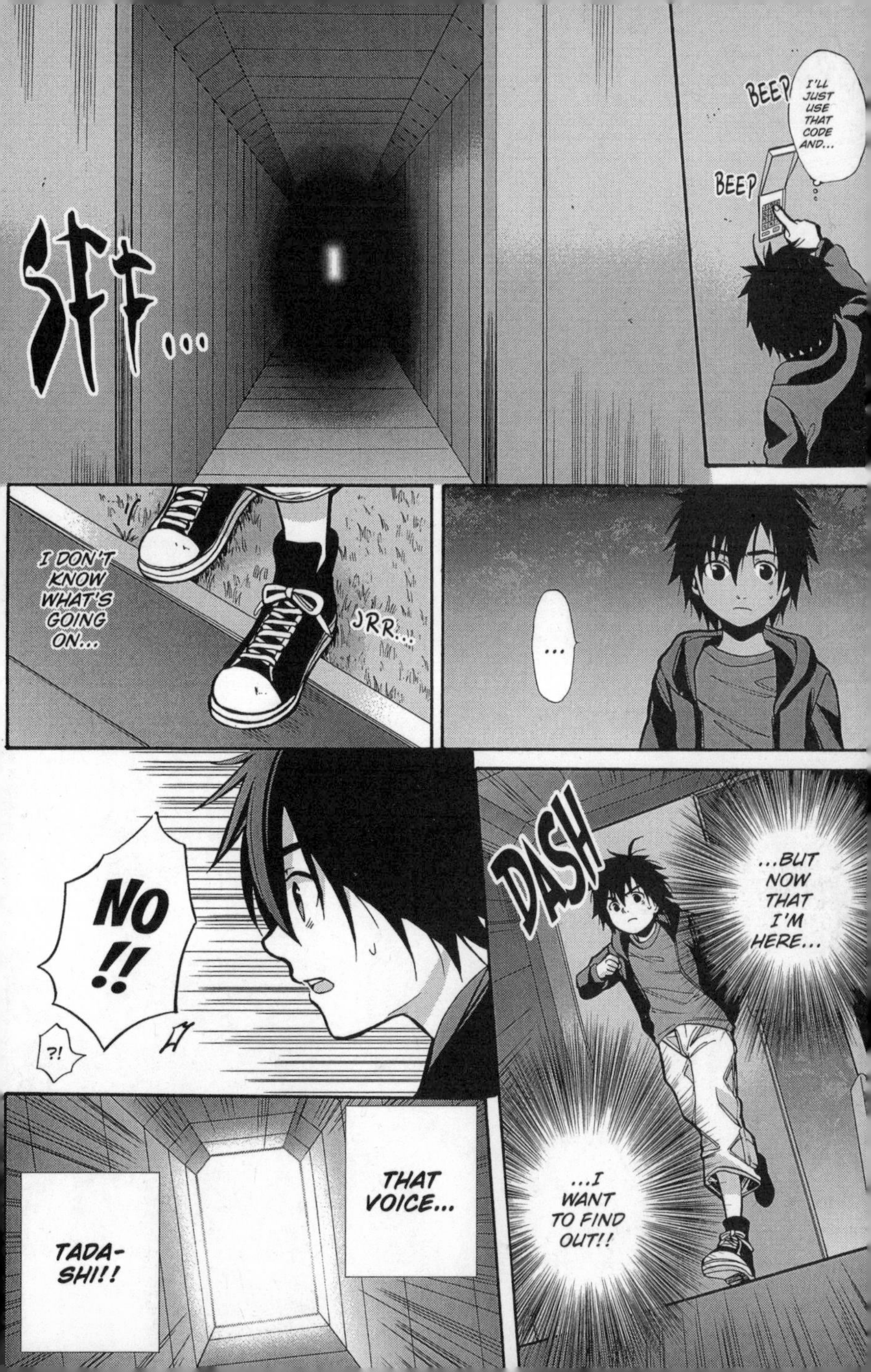

BEEP
I'LL JUST USE THAT CODE AND...
BEEP
...
I DON'T KNOW WHAT'S GOING ON...
JRR...
DASH
...BUT NOW THAT I'M HERE...
...I WANT TO FIND OUT!!
NO!!
?!
THAT VOICE...
TADA-SHI!!

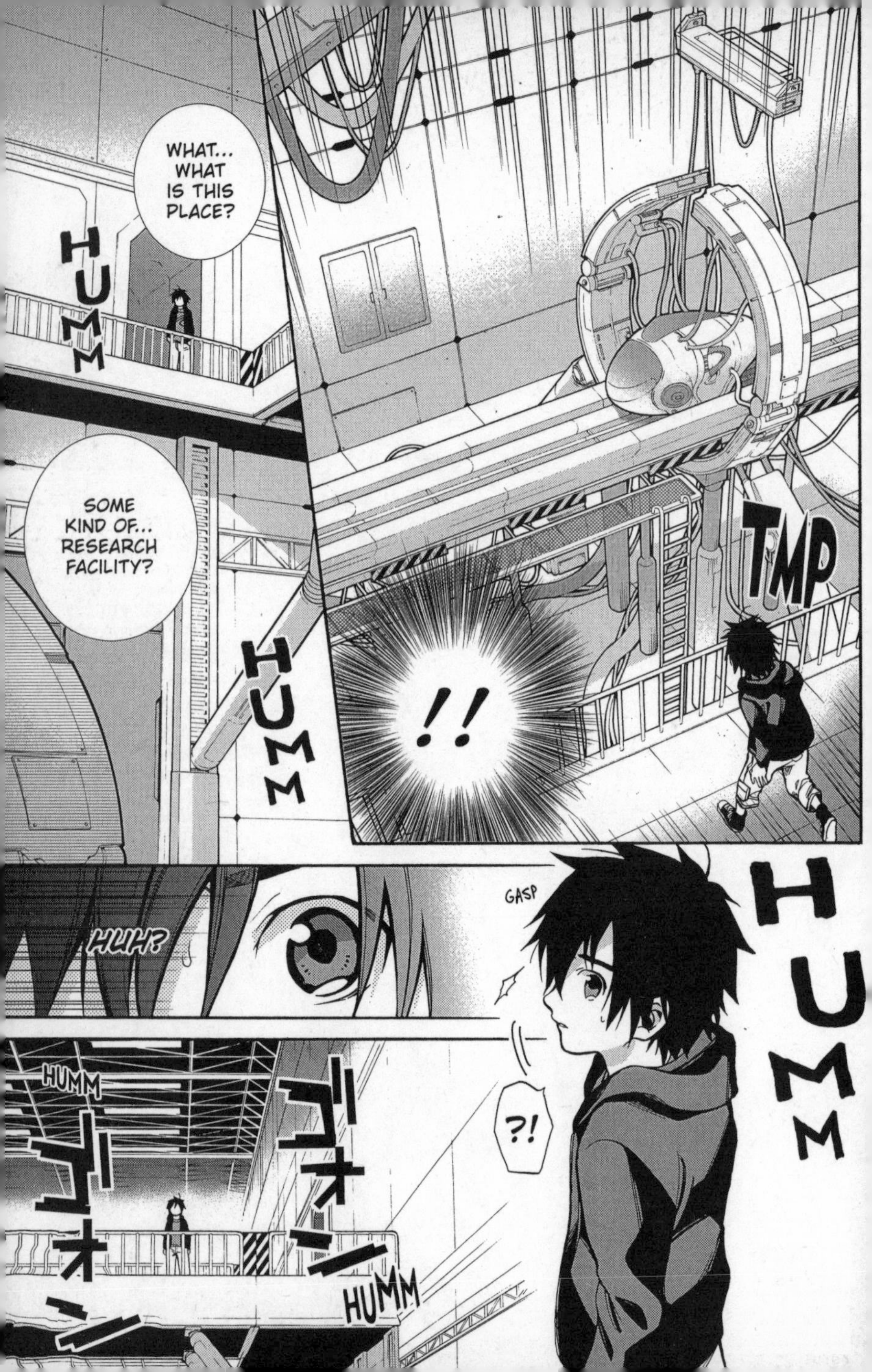
TMP
!!
HUMM
WHAT... WHAT IS THIS PLACE?
HUMM
SOME KIND OF... RESEARCH FACILITY?
HUMM
GASP
?!
HUH?
HUMM
HUMM

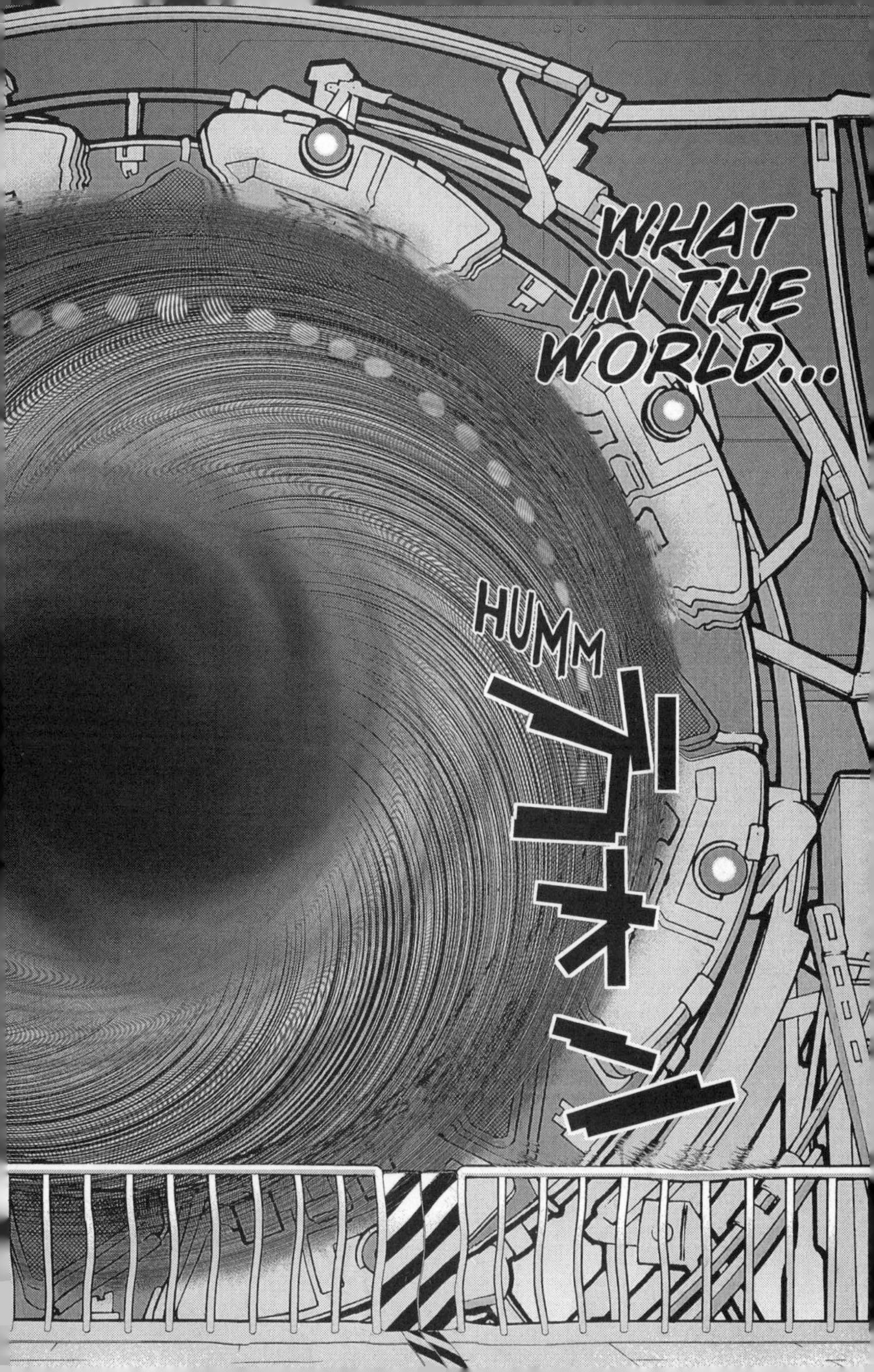
WHAT IN THE WORLD...
HUMM
ブォオォン

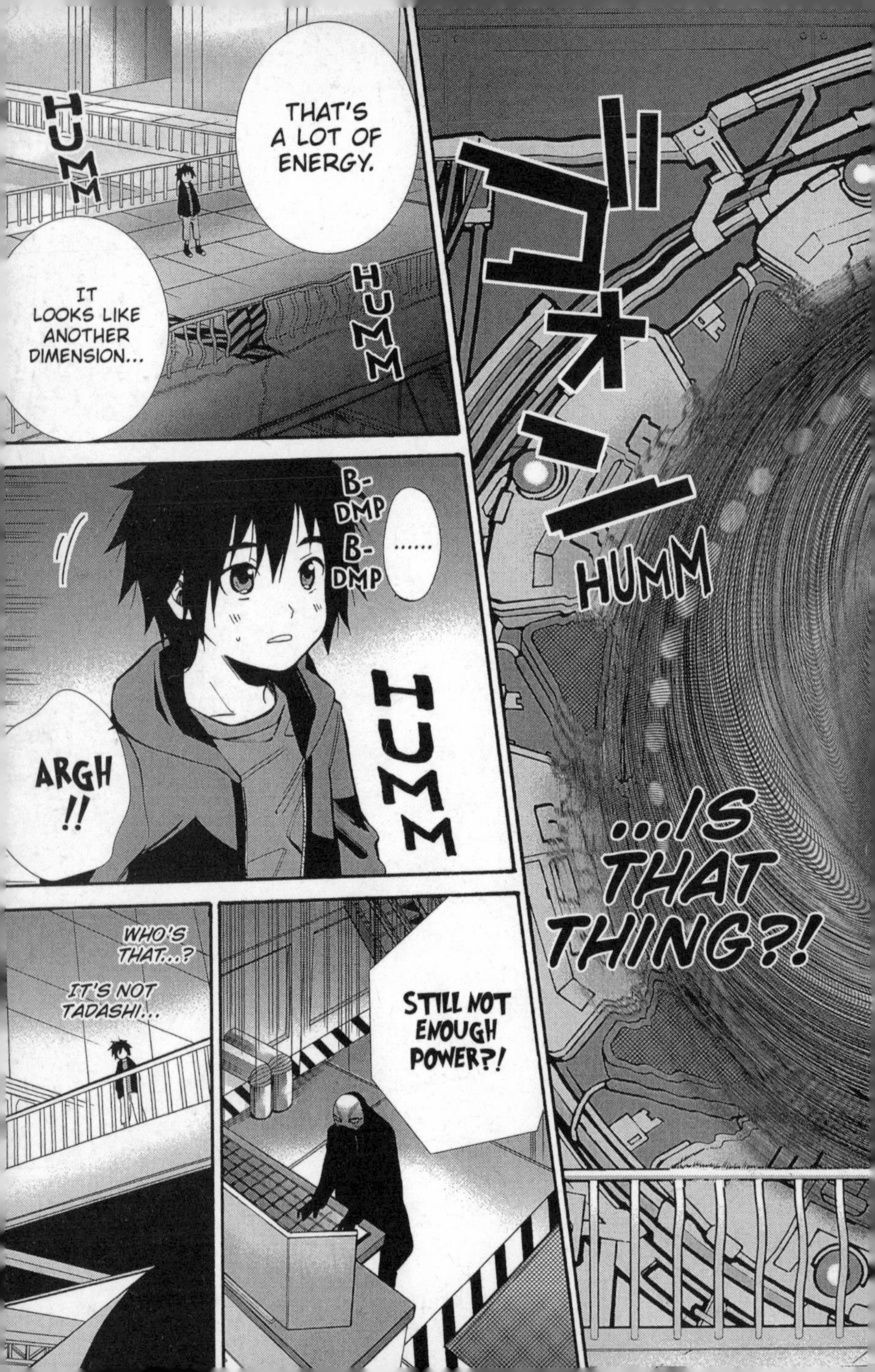
ゴオォー
HUMM
...IS THAT THING?!
THAT'S A LOT OF ENERGY.
HUMM
HUMM
IT LOOKS LIKE ANOTHER DIMENSION...
......
B-DMP B-DMP
HUMM
ARGH!!
STILL NOT ENOUGH POWER?!
WHO'S THAT...?
IT'S NOT TADASHI...

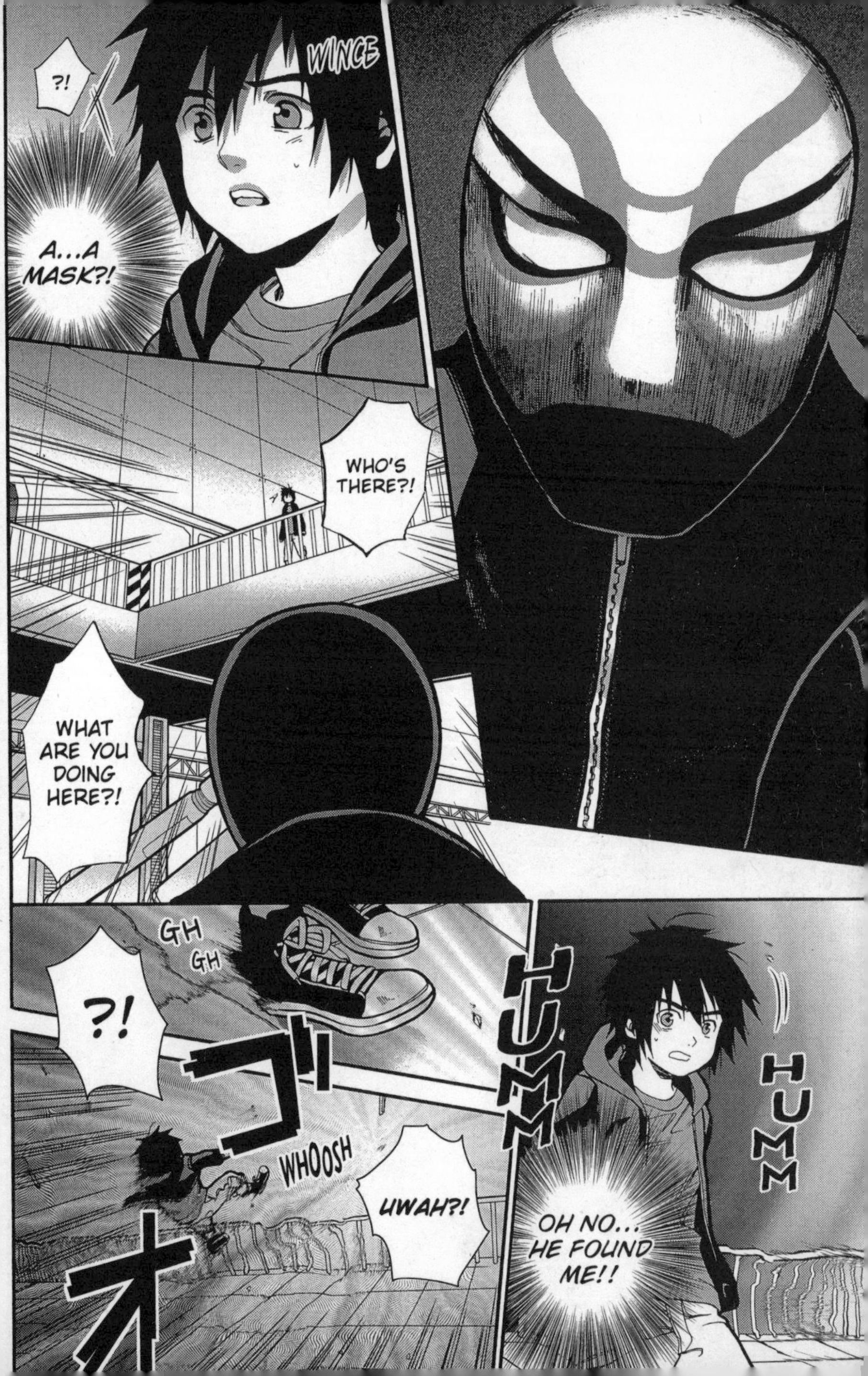
WINCE
?!
A...A MASK?!
WHO'S THERE?!
WHAT ARE YOU DOING HERE?!
HUMM
HUMM
OH NO... HE FOUND ME!!
GH GH
?!
ゴオ
WHOOSH
UWAH?!

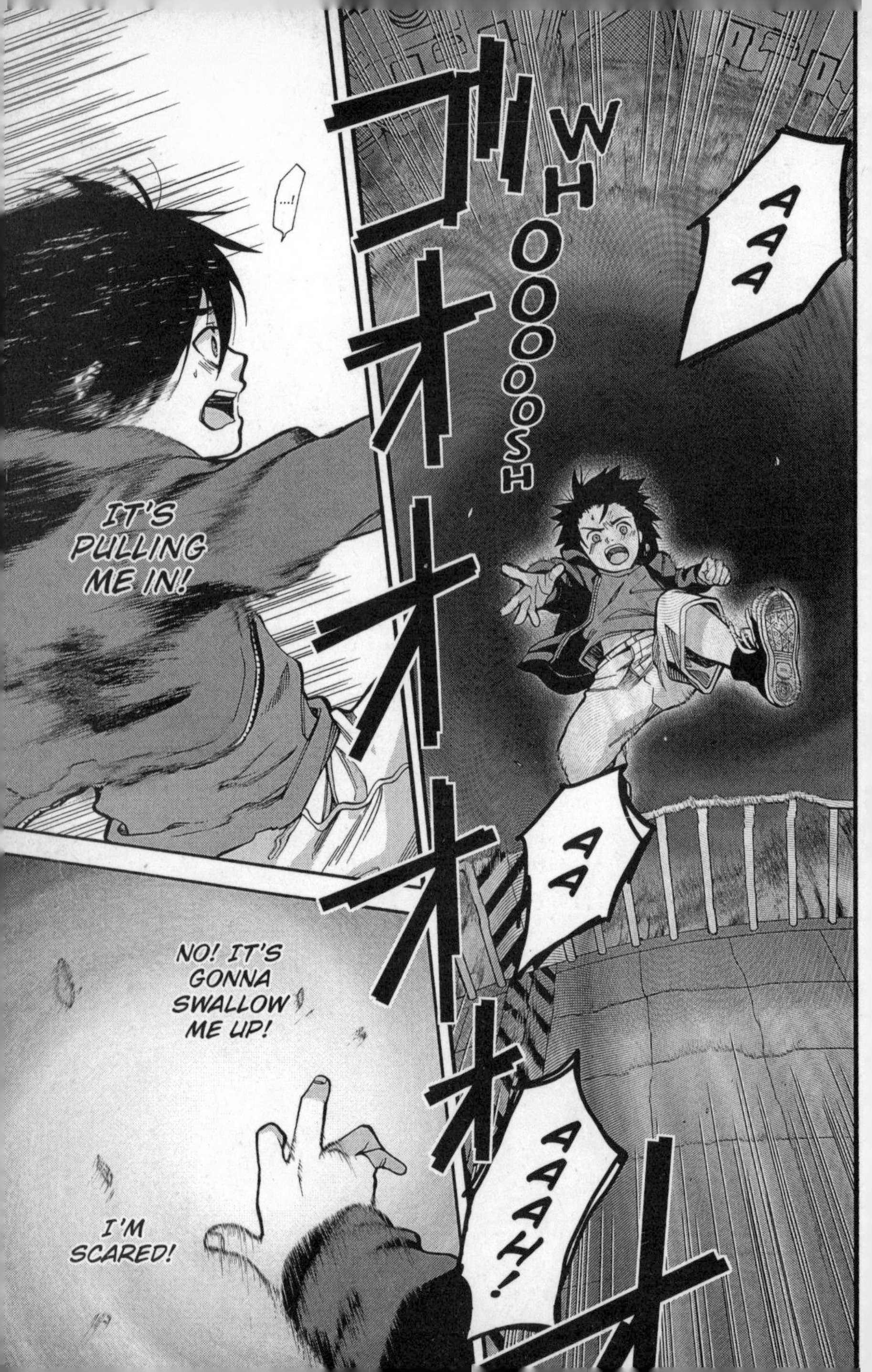
AAA
WHOOOOOOSH
AA
AAAAH!
...!
IT'S PULLING ME IN!
NO! IT'S GONNA SWALLOW ME UP!
I'M SCARED!

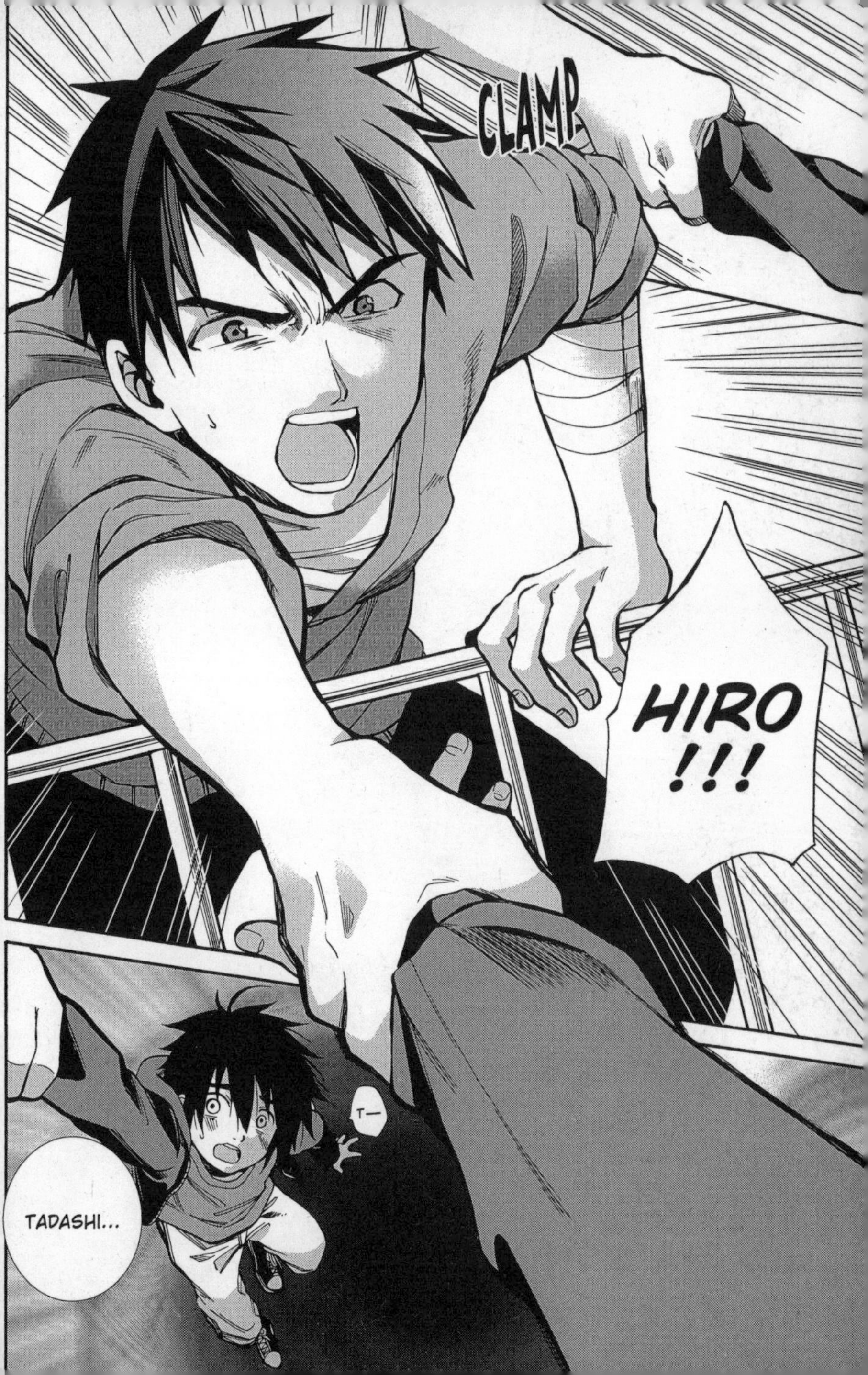
CLAMP
HIRO!!!
T—
TADASHI...

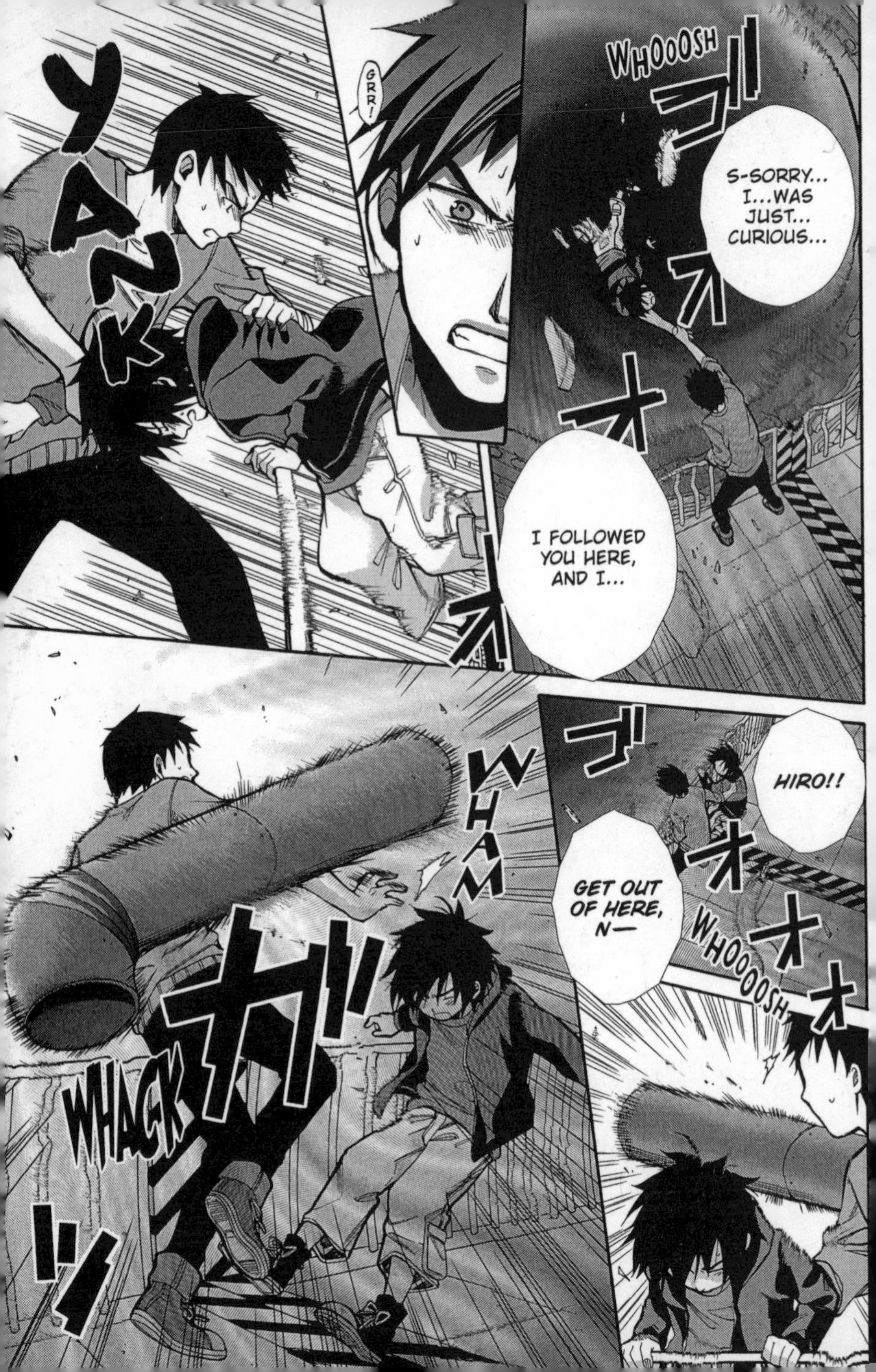
WHOOOSH
S-SORRY... I...WAS JUST... CURIOUS...
I FOLLOWED YOU HERE, AND I...
GRR!
YANK
HIRO!!
GET OUT OF HERE, N—
WHOOOSH
WHAM
WHACK

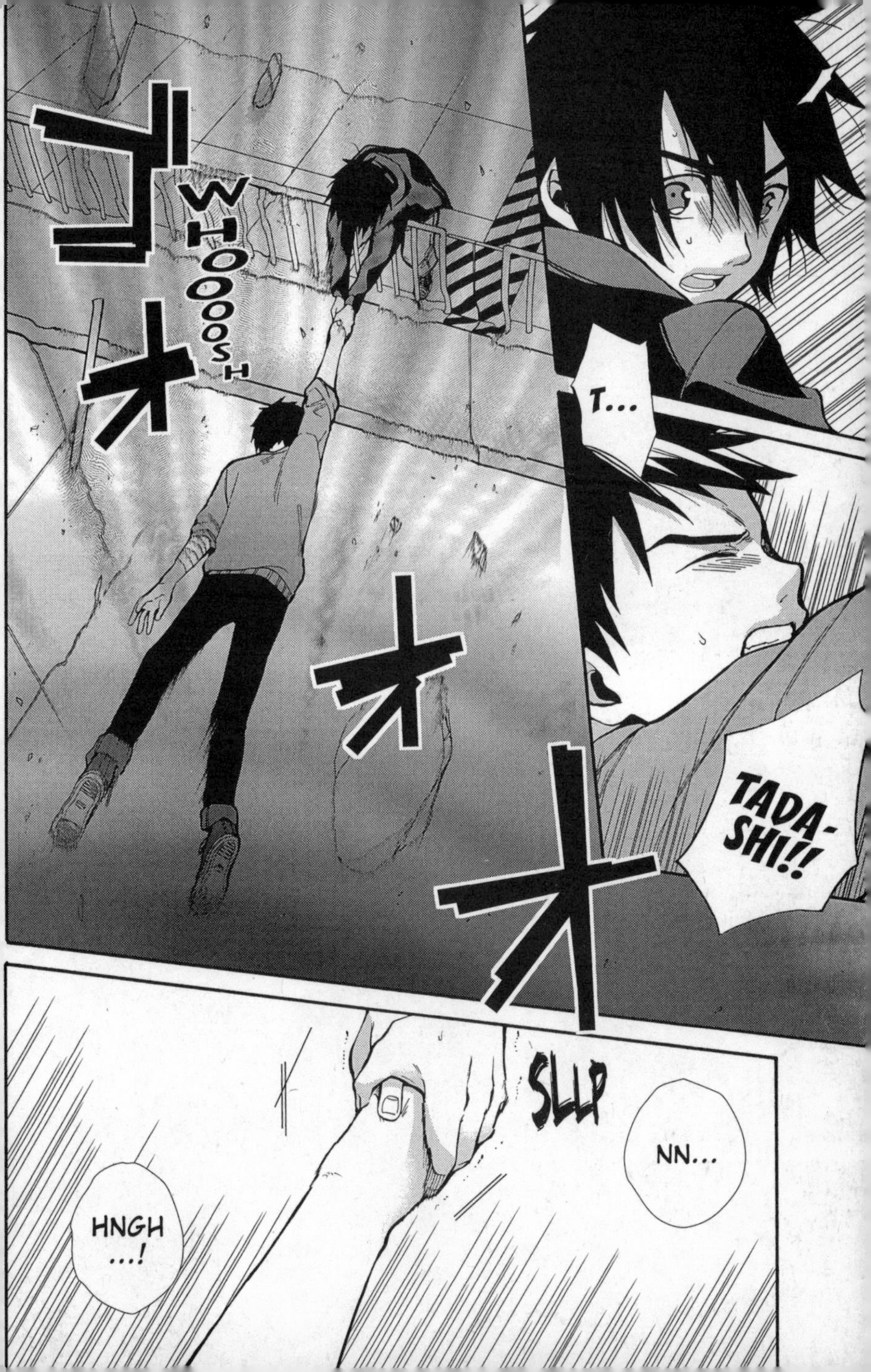
T...
TADASHI!!
WHOOOOSH
SLLP
NN...
HNGH ...!

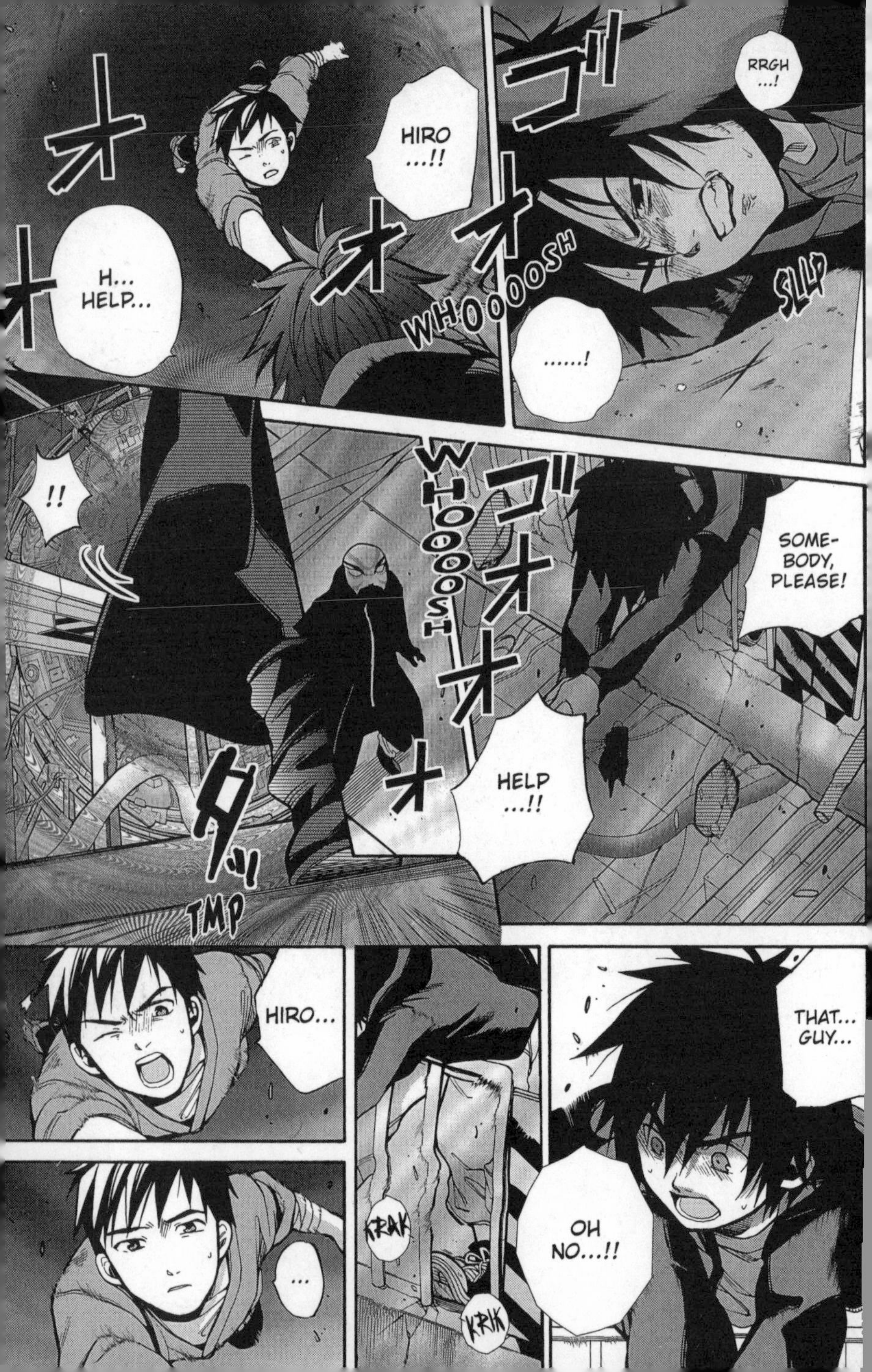
RRGH ...!
SLLP
......!
HIRO ...!!
WHOOOOSH
H... HELP...
SOME-BODY, PLEASE!
HELP ...!!
WHOOOOSH
TMP
!!
THAT... GUY...
OH NO...!!
KRAK
KRIK
HIRO...
...

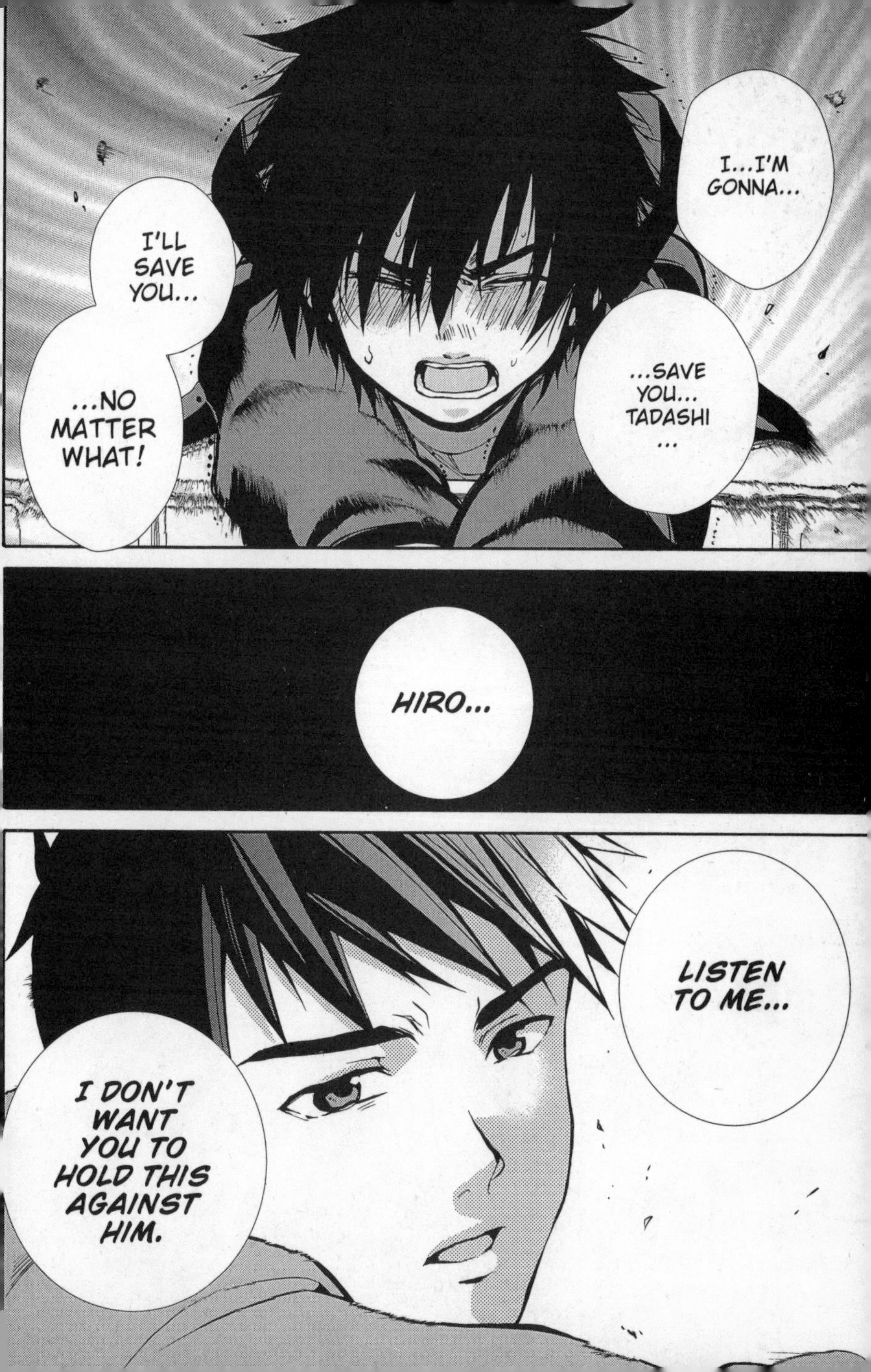
I...I'M GONNA...
...SAVE YOU... TADASHI ...
I'LL SAVE YOU...
...NO MATTER WHAT!
HIRO...
LISTEN TO ME...
I DON'T WANT YOU TO HOLD THIS AGAINST HIM.

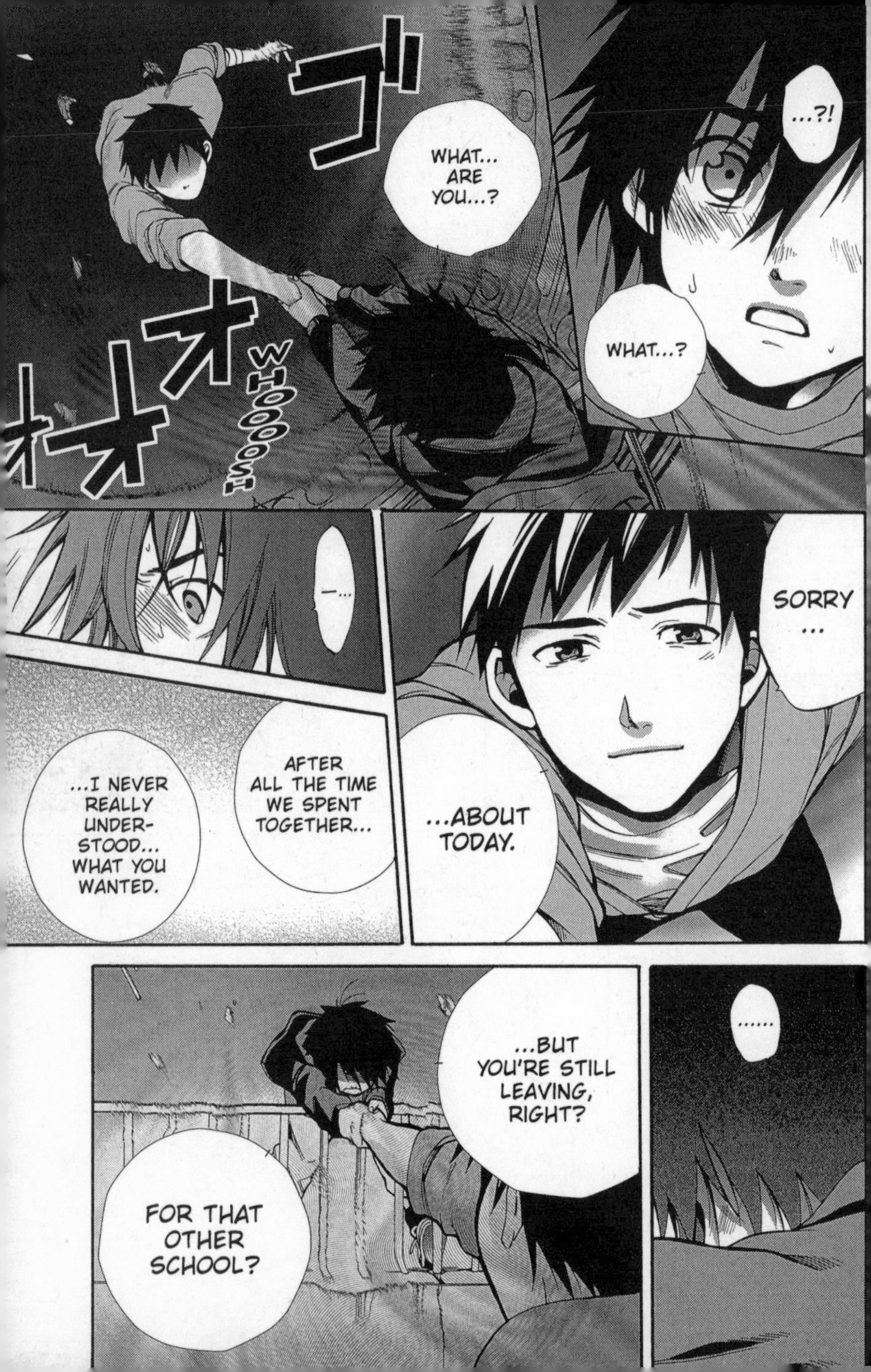
...?!
WHAT...?
WHAT... ARE YOU...?
ゴオオオ
WHOOOOOSH!
SORRY ...
...ABOUT TODAY.
—...
AFTER ALL THE TIME WE SPENT TOGETHER...
...I NEVER REALLY UNDER-STOOD... WHAT YOU WANTED.
......
...BUT YOU'RE STILL LEAVING, RIGHT?
FOR THAT OTHER SCHOOL?

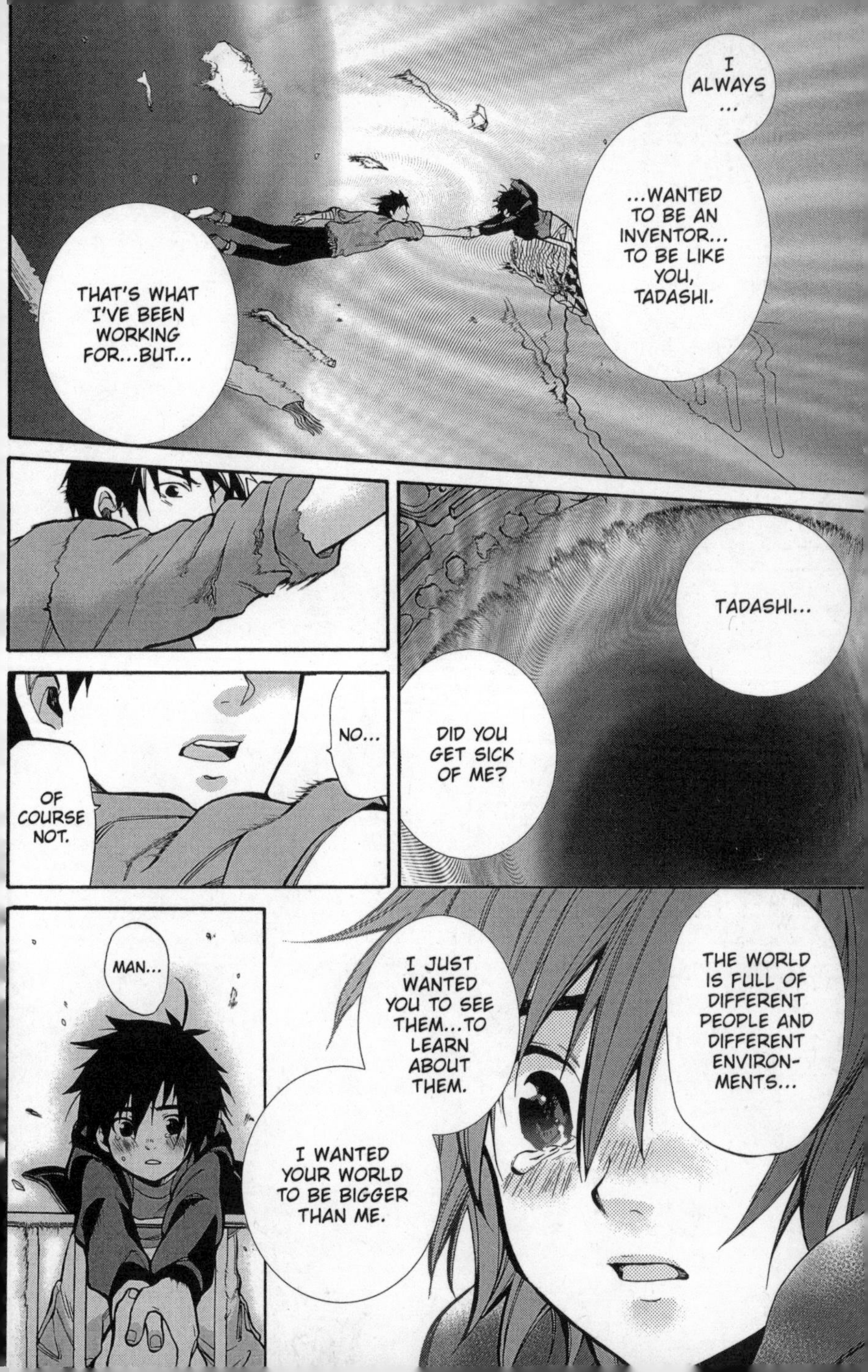
I ALWAYS ...
...WANTED TO BE AN INVENTOR... TO BE LIKE YOU, TADASHI.
THAT'S WHAT I'VE BEEN WORKING FOR...BUT...
TADASHI...
DID YOU GET SICK OF ME?
NO...
OF COURSE NOT.
THE WORLD IS FULL OF DIFFERENT PEOPLE AND DIFFERENT ENVIRON-MENTS...
I JUST WANTED YOU TO SEE THEM...TO LEARN ABOUT THEM.
I WANTED YOUR WORLD TO BE BIGGER THAN ME.
MAN...

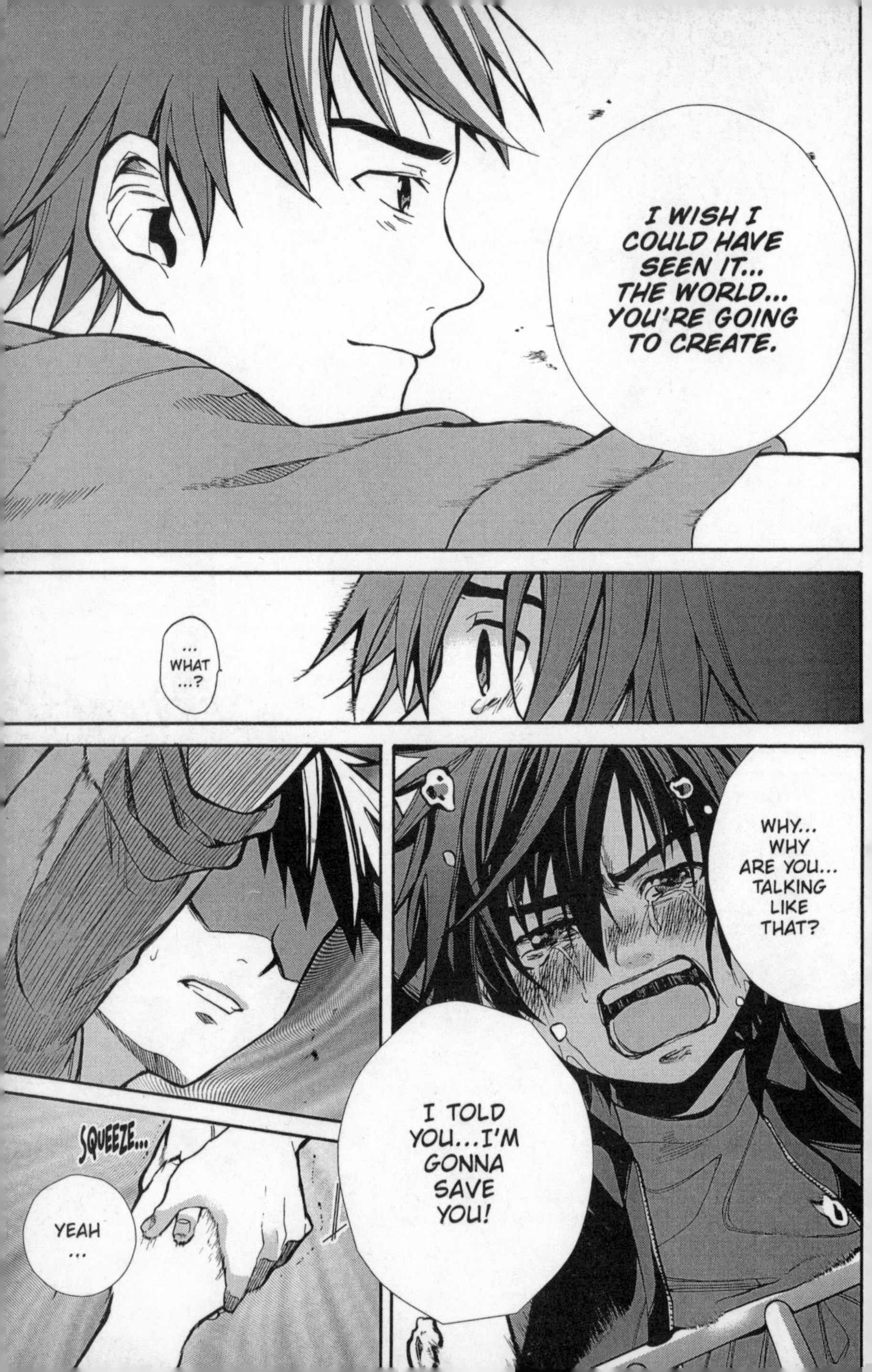
I WISH I COULD HAVE SEEN IT... THE WORLD... YOU'RE GOING TO CREATE.
...WHAT...?
WHY... WHY ARE YOU... TALKING LIKE THAT?
I TOLD YOU...I'M GONNA SAVE YOU!
SQUEEZE...
YEAH...

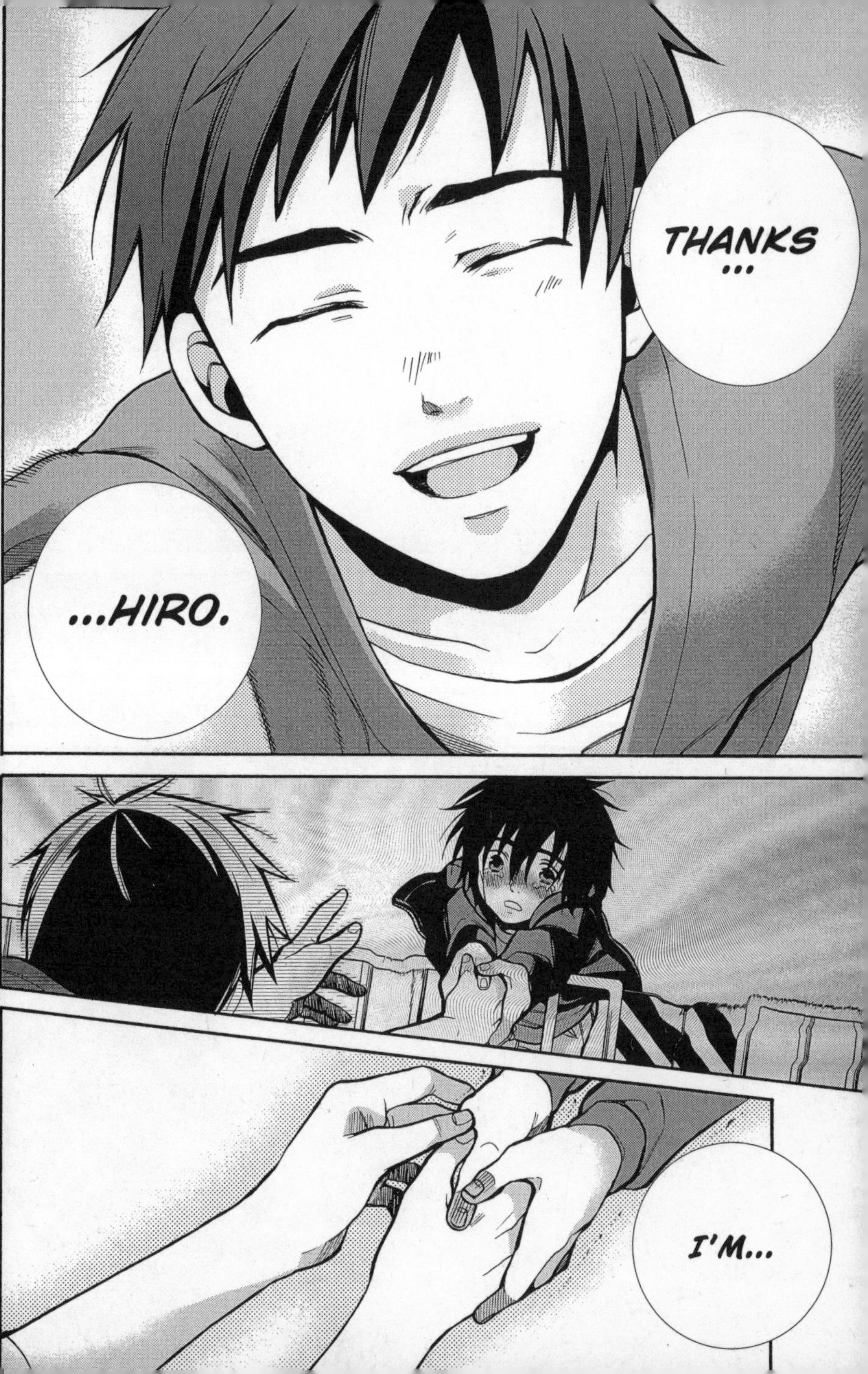
THANKS ...
...HIRO.
I'M...

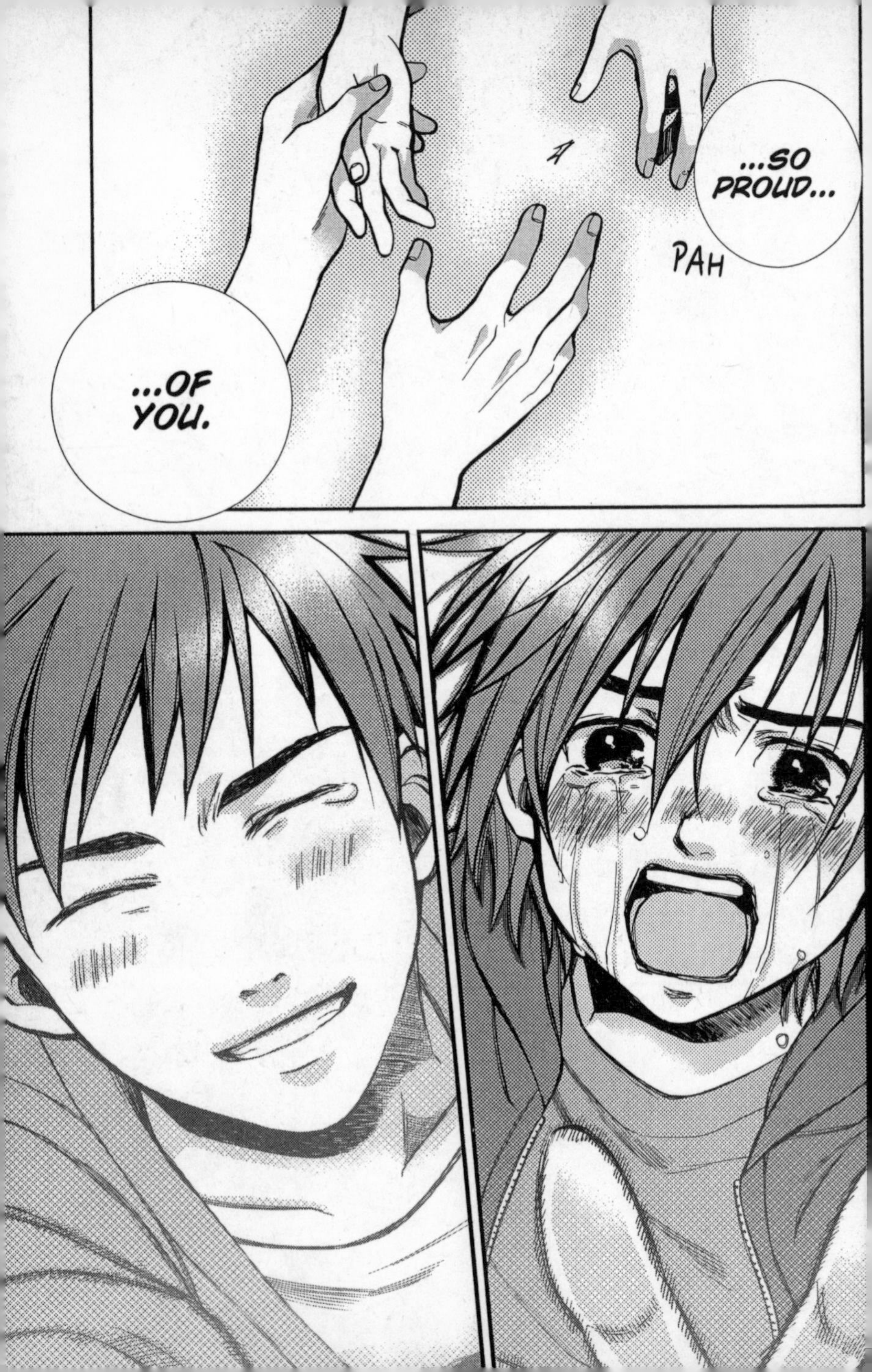
...SO PROUD...
PAH
...OF YOU.

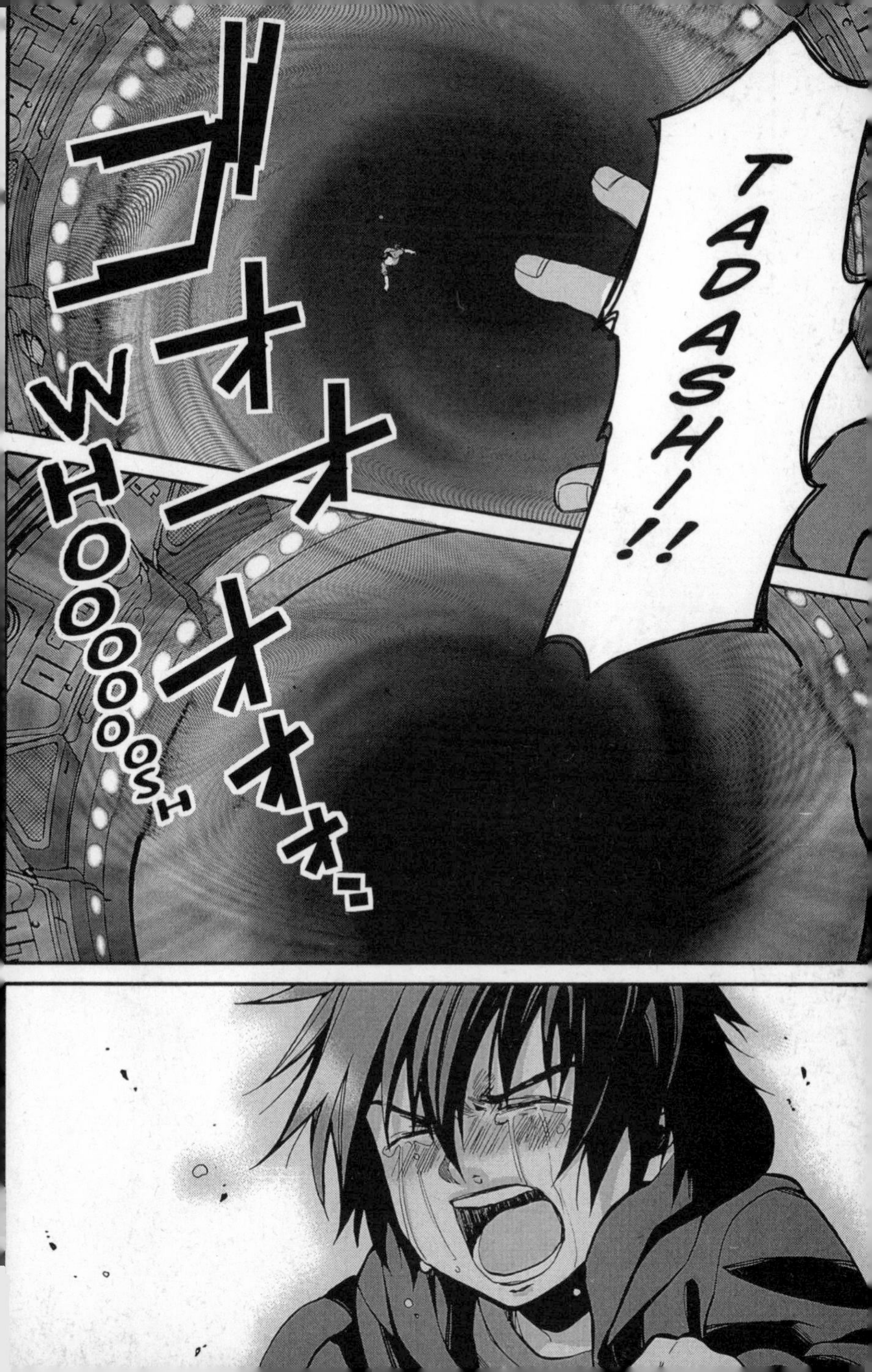
TADASHI!!!
ゴオオオオォ..
WHOOOOOOSH!

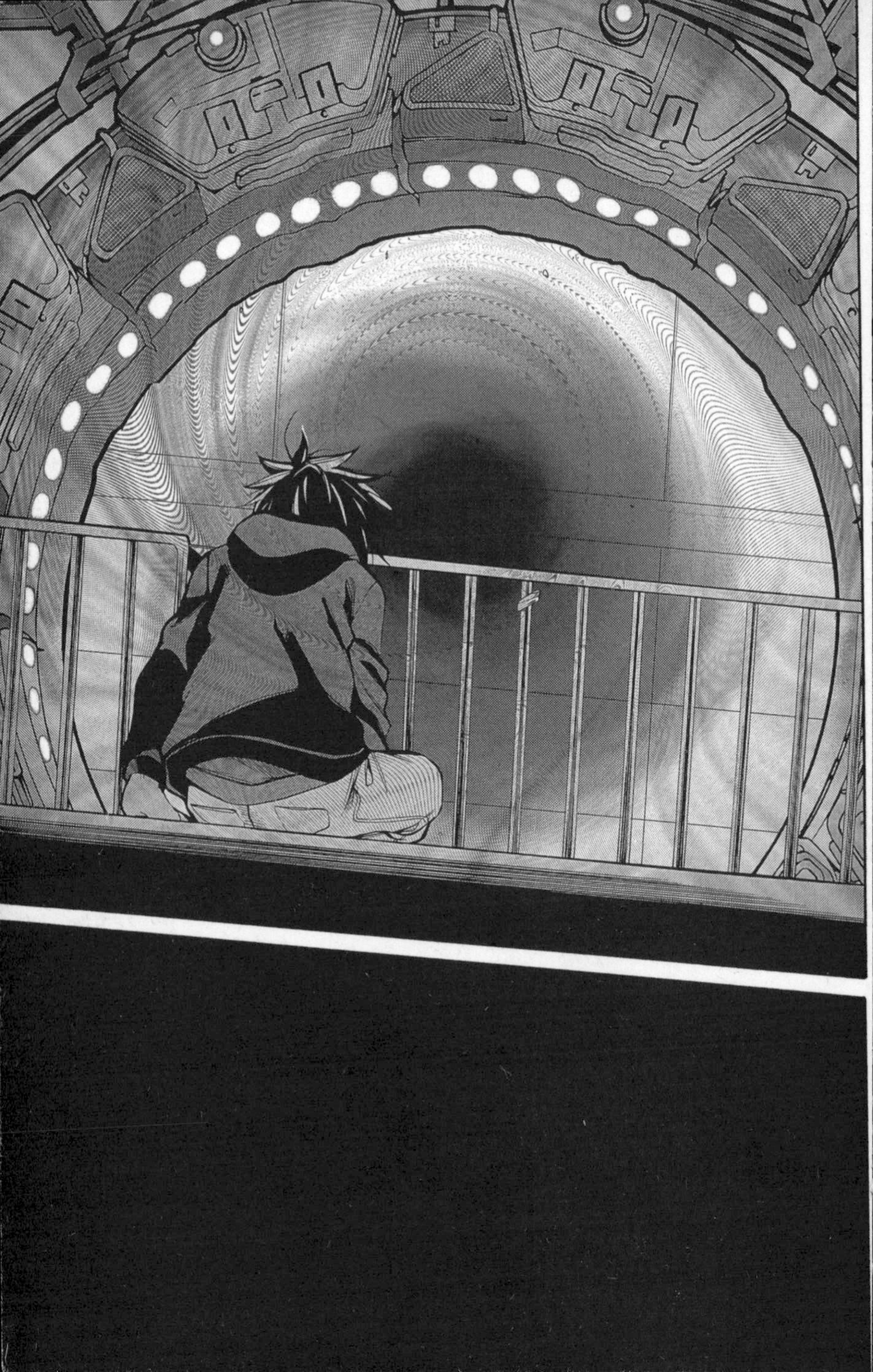

AND
THEN...

...BAYMAX
WAS ALL
THAT WAS
LEFT.

Disney

BIG HERO 6

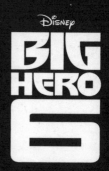

❤ 3: Aunt Cass's Worries

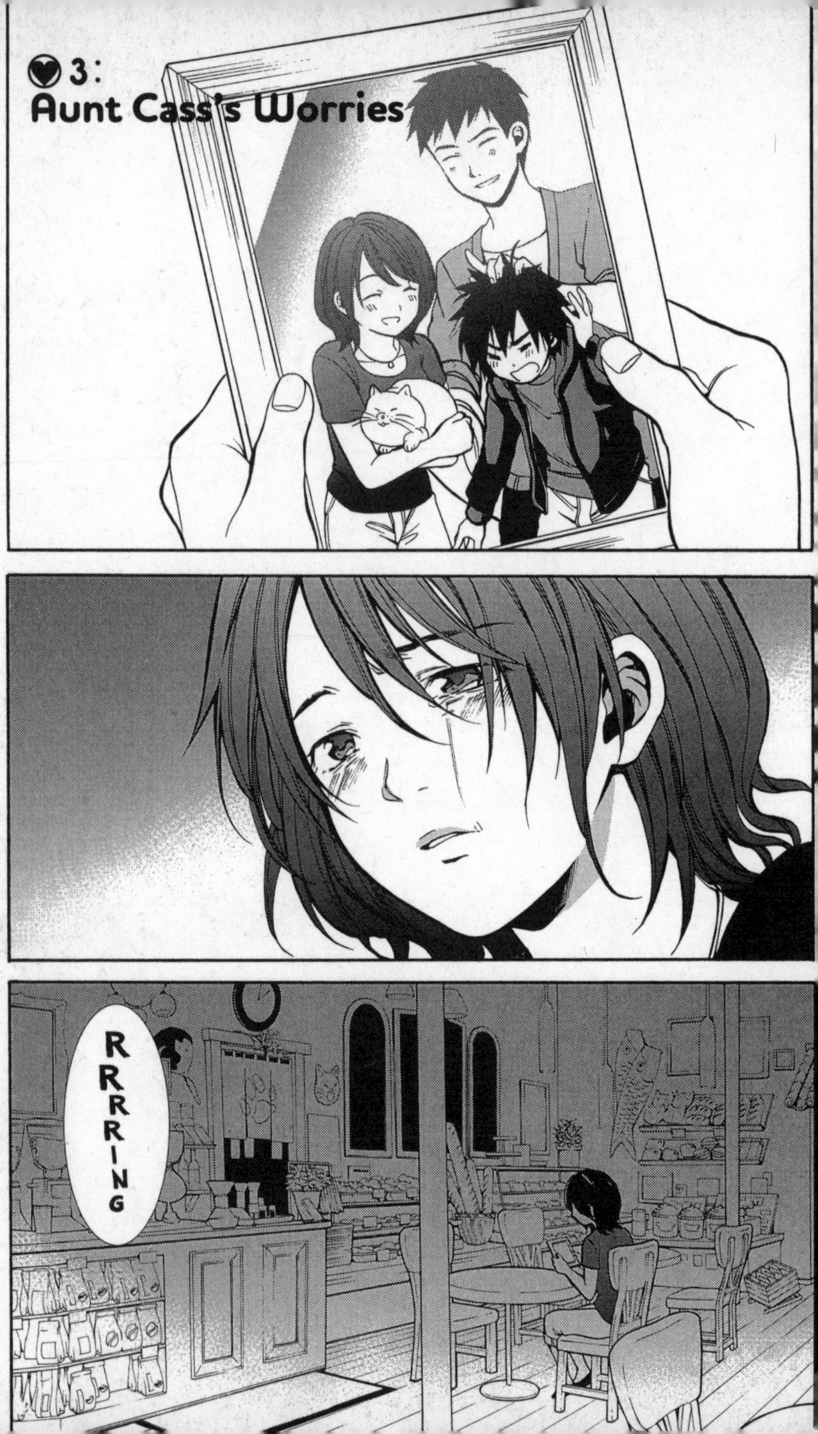
RRRRING

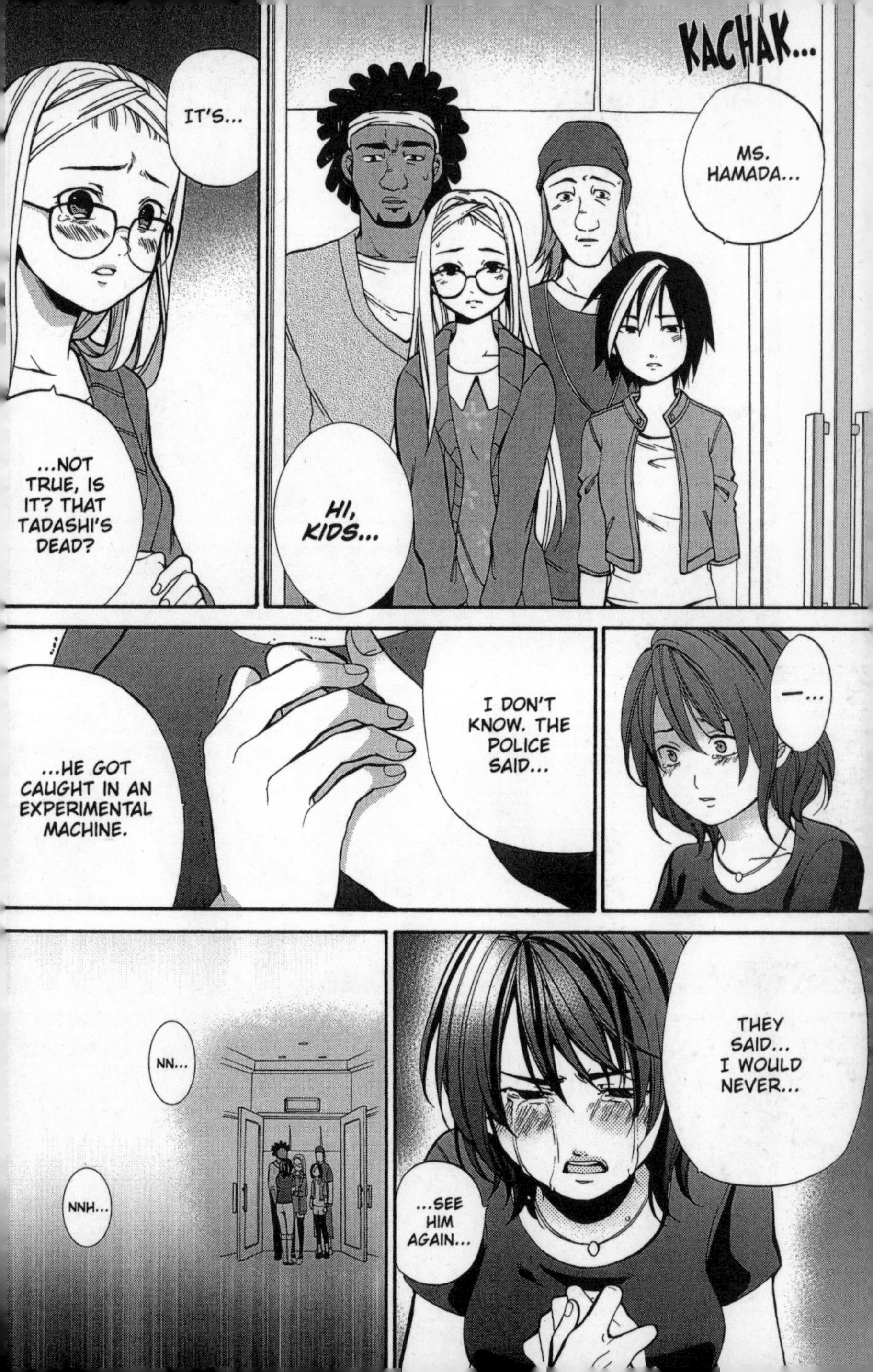
KACHAK...
IT'S...
MS. HAMADA...
...NOT TRUE, IS IT? THAT TADASHI'S DEAD?
HI, KIDS...
...HE GOT CAUGHT IN AN EXPERIMENTAL MACHINE.
I DON'T KNOW. THE POLICE SAID...
—...
NN...
NNH...
THEY SAID... I WOULD NEVER...
...SEE HIM AGAIN...

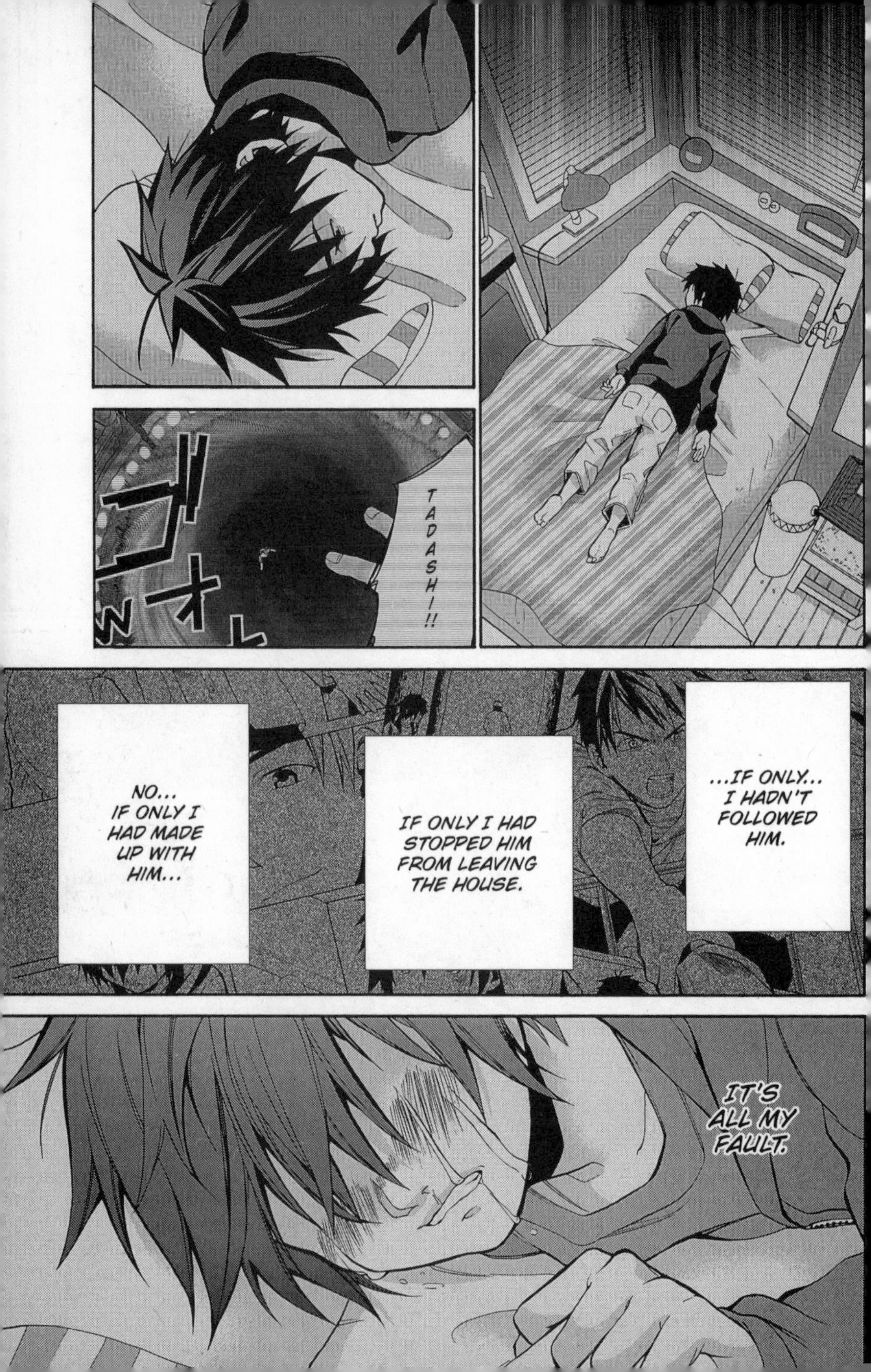
TADASHI!!
...IF ONLY... I HADN'T FOLLOWED HIM.
IF ONLY I HAD STOPPED HIM FROM LEAVING THE HOUSE.
NO... IF ONLY I HAD MADE UP WITH HIM...
IT'S ALL MY FAULT.

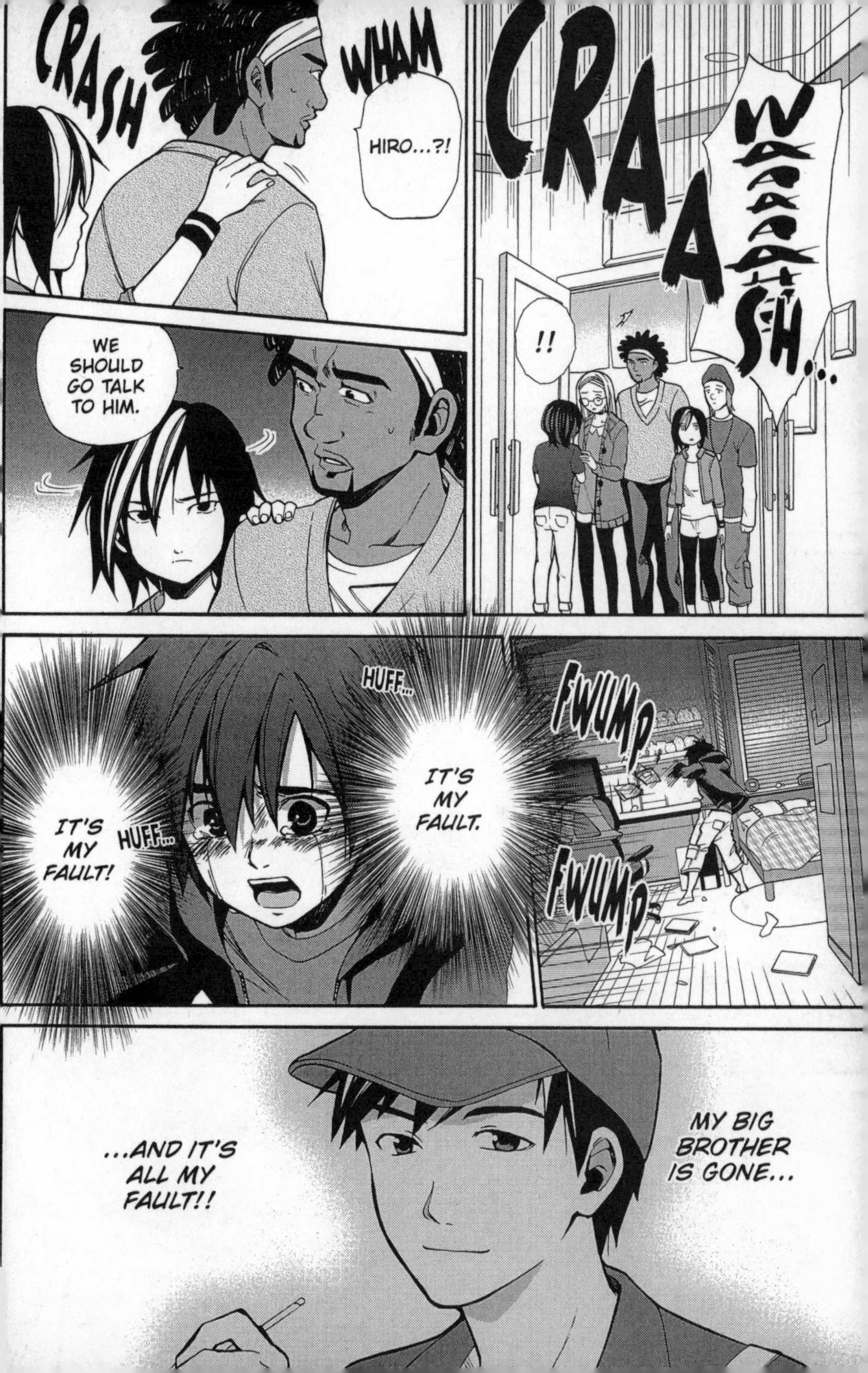
CRAA
WAAAAASH...
!!
CRASH
WHAM
HIRO...?!
WE SHOULD GO TALK TO HIM.
FWUMP
FWUMP
HUFF...
IT'S MY FAULT.
HUFF...
IT'S MY FAULT!
MY BIG BROTHER IS GONE...
...AND IT'S ALL MY FAULT!!

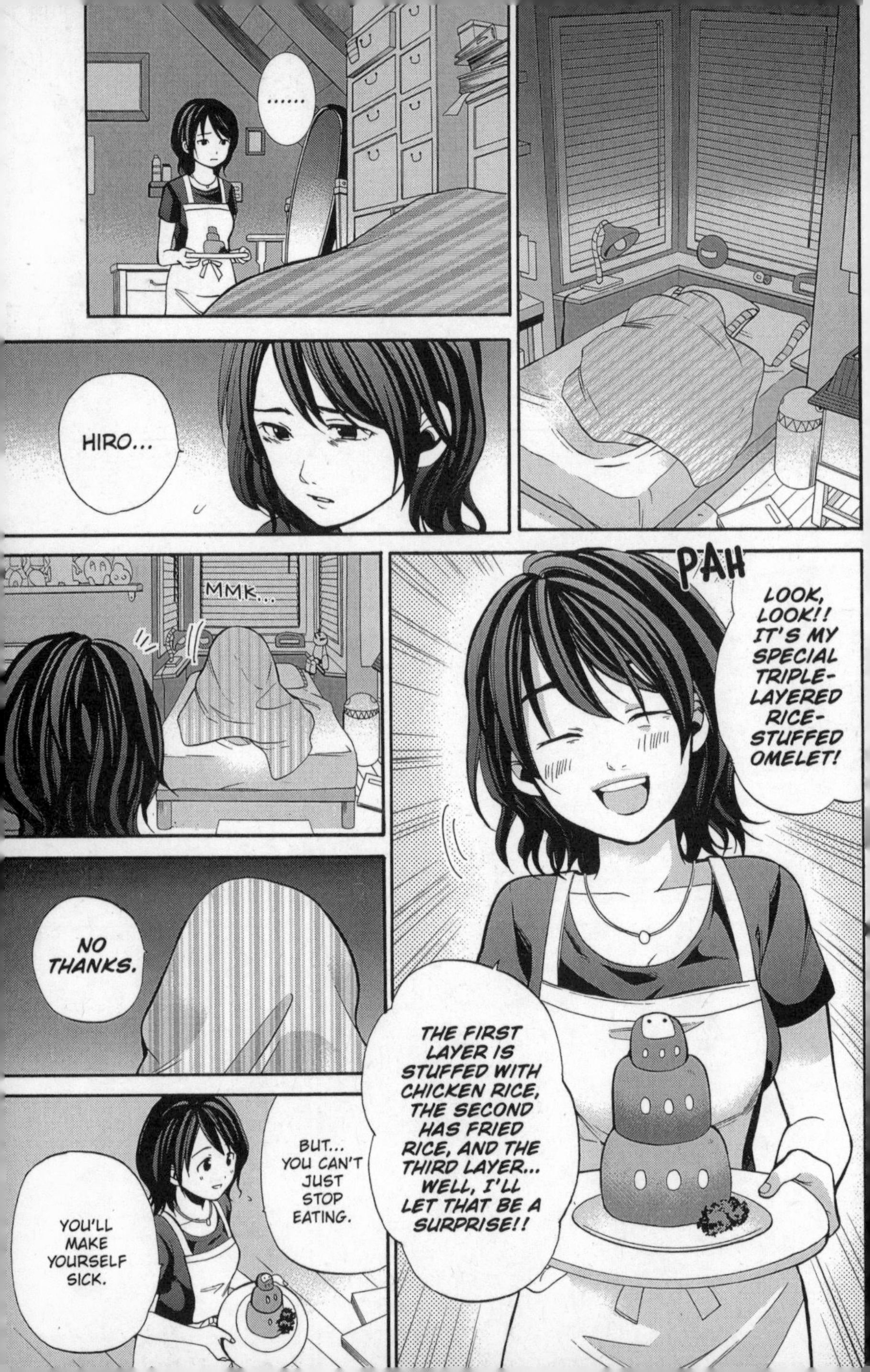
......
HIRO...
PAH
LOOK, LOOK!! IT'S MY SPECIAL TRIPLE-LAYERED RICE-STUFFED OMELET!
THE FIRST LAYER IS STUFFED WITH CHICKEN RICE, THE SECOND HAS FRIED RICE, AND THE THIRD LAYER... WELL, I'LL LET THAT BE A SURPRISE!!
MMK...
NO THANKS.
BUT... YOU CAN'T JUST STOP EATING.
YOU'LL MAKE YOURSELF SICK.

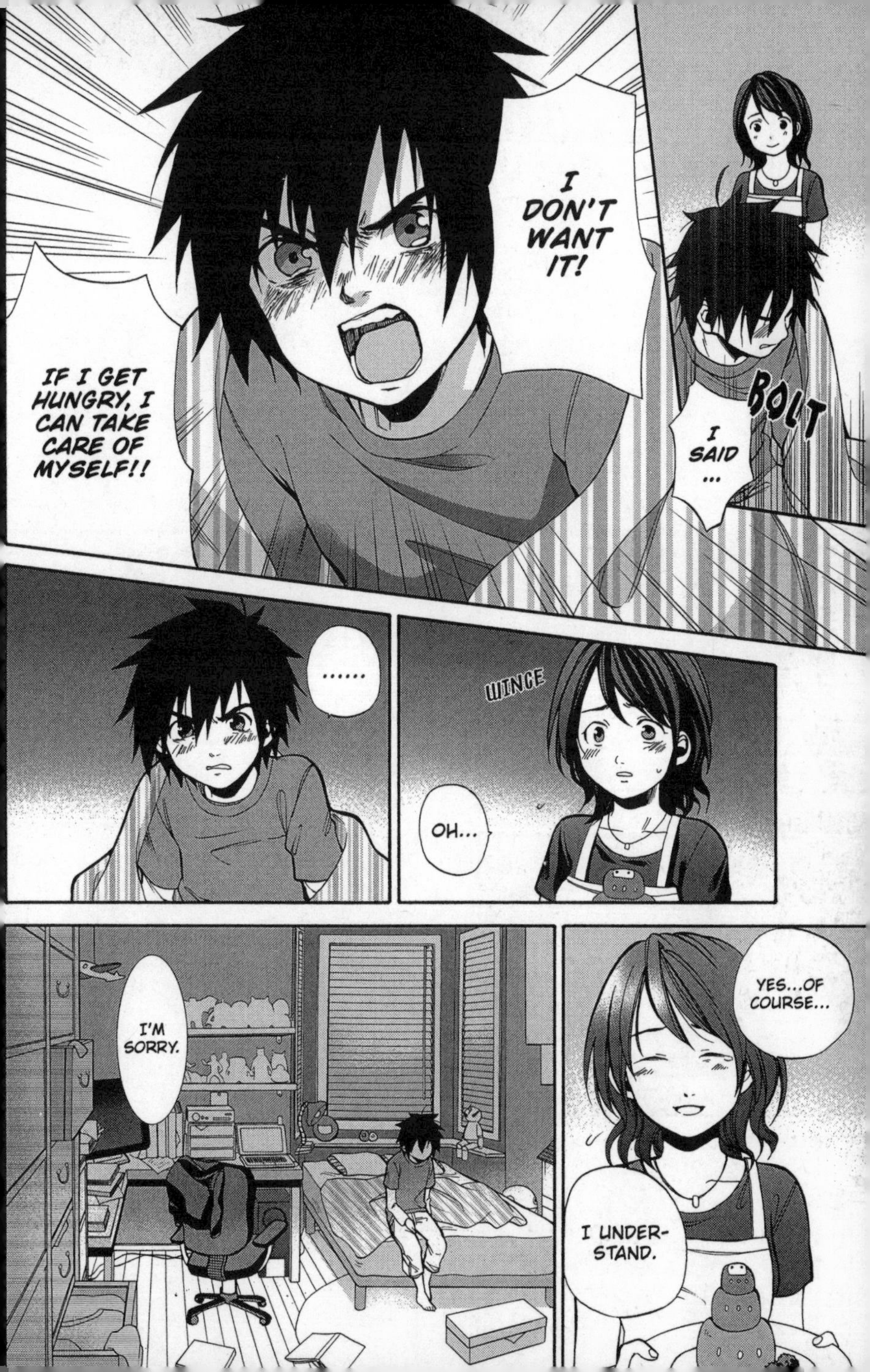
BOLT
I SAID ...
I DON'T WANT IT!
IF I GET HUNGRY, I CAN TAKE CARE OF MYSELF!!
WINCE
OH...
......
YES...OF COURSE...
I UNDER-STAND.
I'M SORRY.

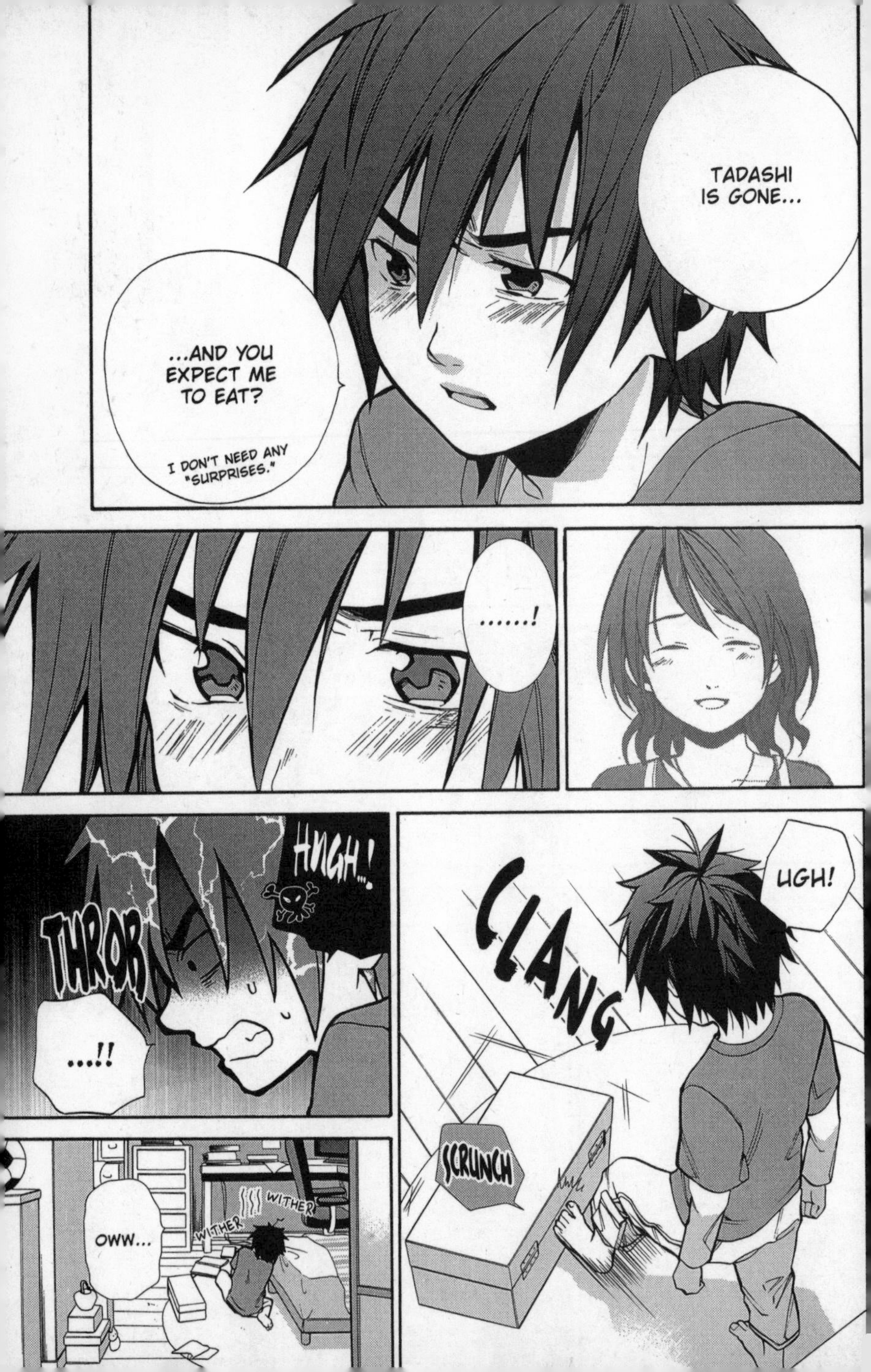
TADASHI IS GONE...
...AND YOU EXPECT ME TO EAT?
I DON'T NEED ANY "SURPRISES."
......!
UGH!
CLANG
SCRUNCH
HNGH...!
THROB
...!!
WITHER
WITHER
OWW...

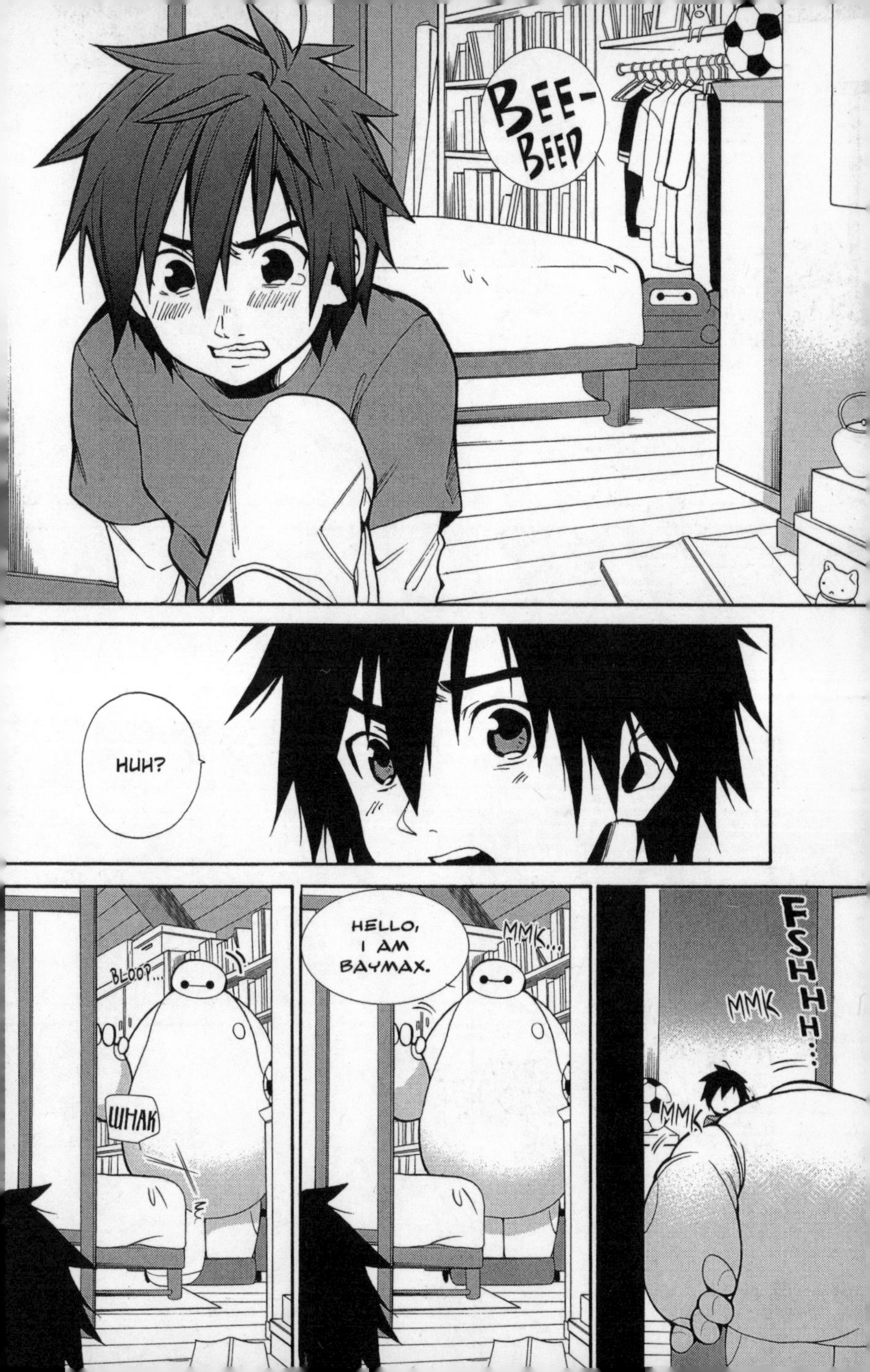
BEE-BEEP
HUH?
FSHHH...
MMK
MMK
MMK...
HELLO, I AM BAYMAX.
BLOOP...
WHAK

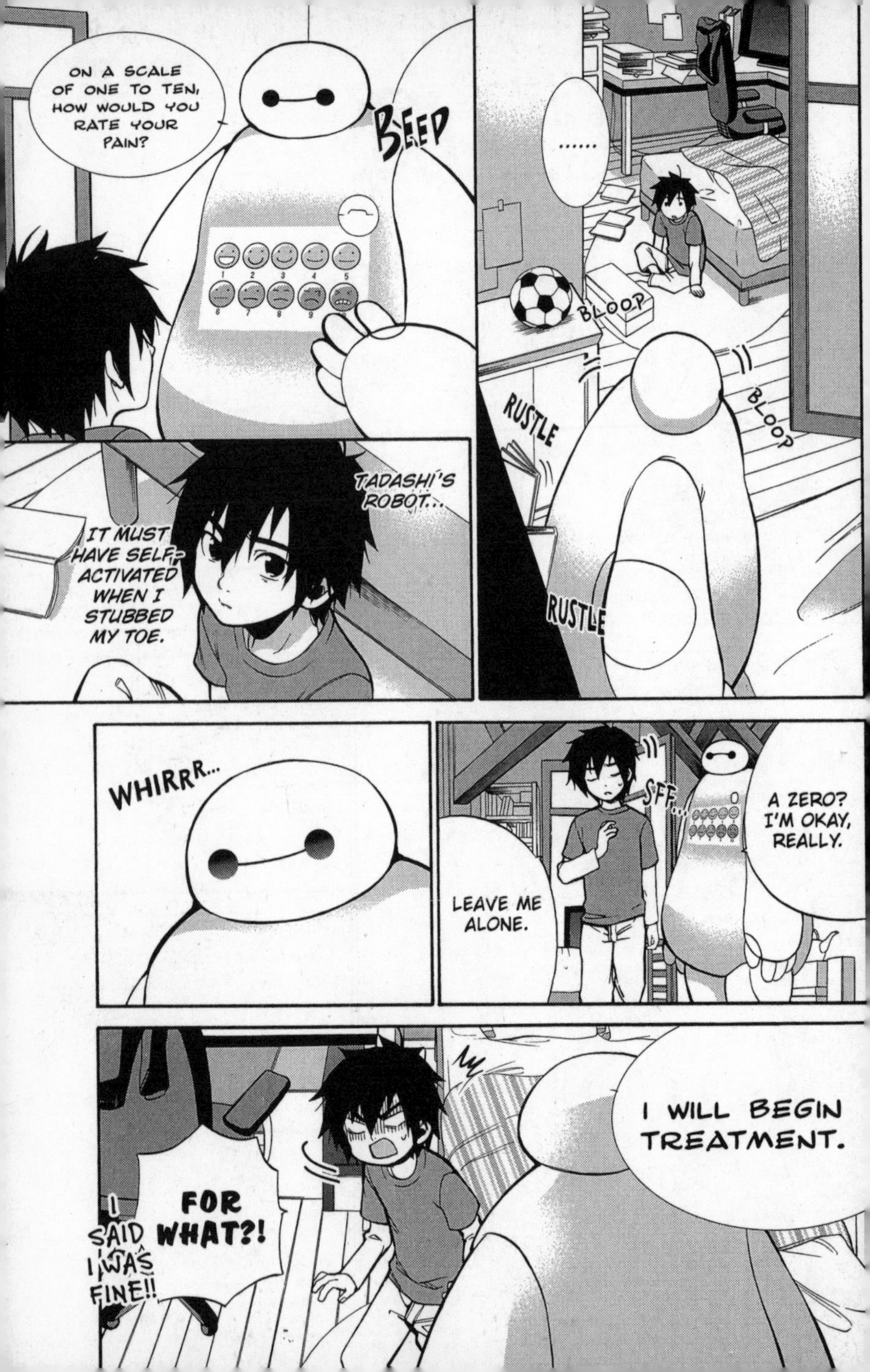
......
BLOOP
RUSTLE
BLOOP
RUSTLE
ON A SCALE OF ONE TO TEN, HOW WOULD YOU RATE YOUR PAIN?
BEEP
TADASHI'S ROBOT...
IT MUST HAVE SELF-ACTIVATED WHEN I STUBBED MY TOE.
A ZERO? I'M OKAY, REALLY.
SFF...
LEAVE ME ALONE.
WHIRRR...
I WILL BEGIN TREATMENT.
FOR WHAT?!
I SAID I WAS FINE!!

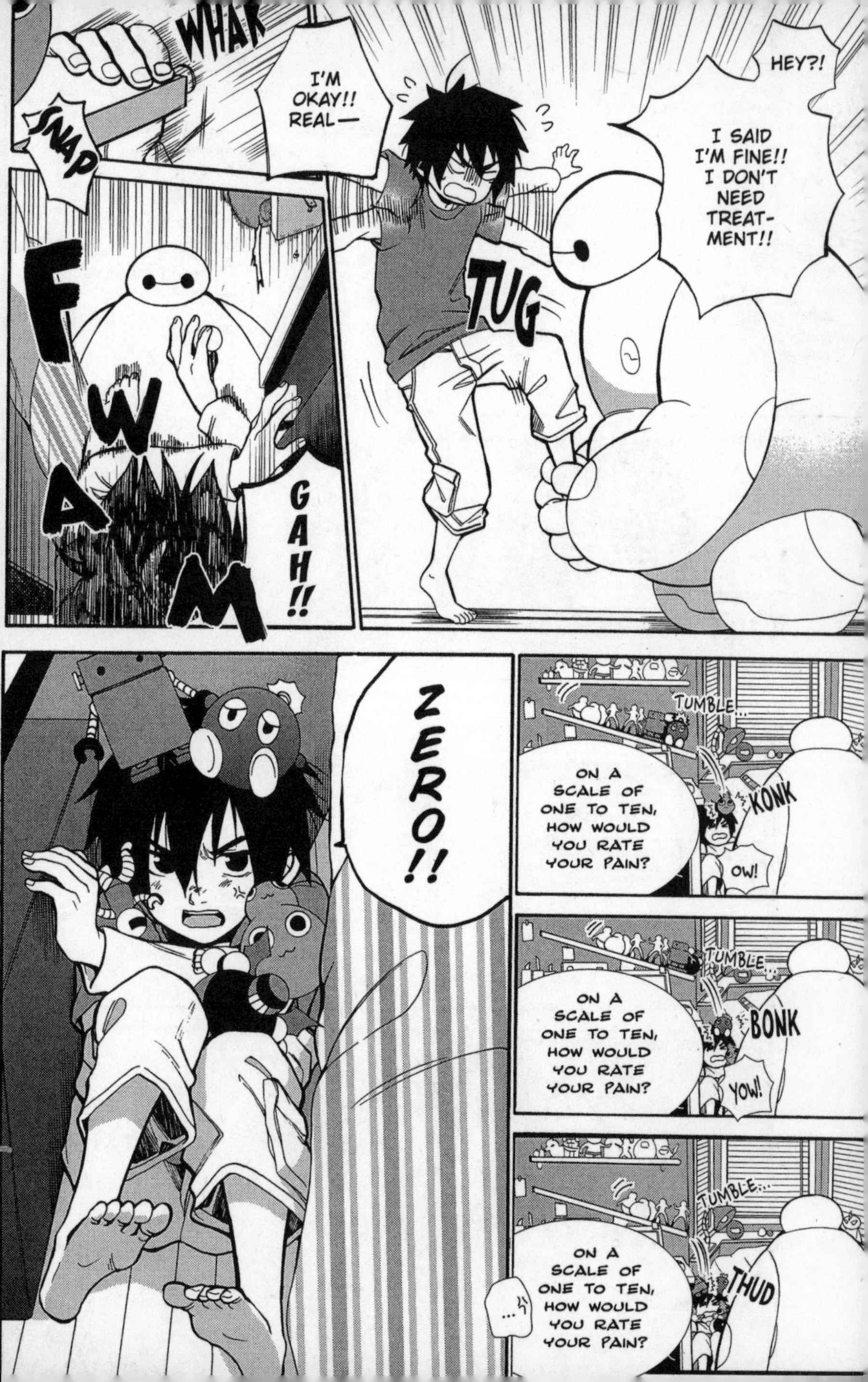
HEY?!
I SAID I'M FINE!! I DON'T NEED TREAT-MENT!!
I'M OKAY!! REAL—
TUG
WHAK
SNAP
FWAM
GAH!!
TUMBLE...
ON A SCALE OF ONE TO TEN, HOW WOULD YOU RATE YOUR PAIN?
KONK
OW!
TUMBLE...
ON A SCALE OF ONE TO TEN, HOW WOULD YOU RATE YOUR PAIN?
BONK
YOW!
TUMBLE...
ON A SCALE OF ONE TO TEN, HOW WOULD YOU RATE YOUR PAIN?
THUD
ZERO!!

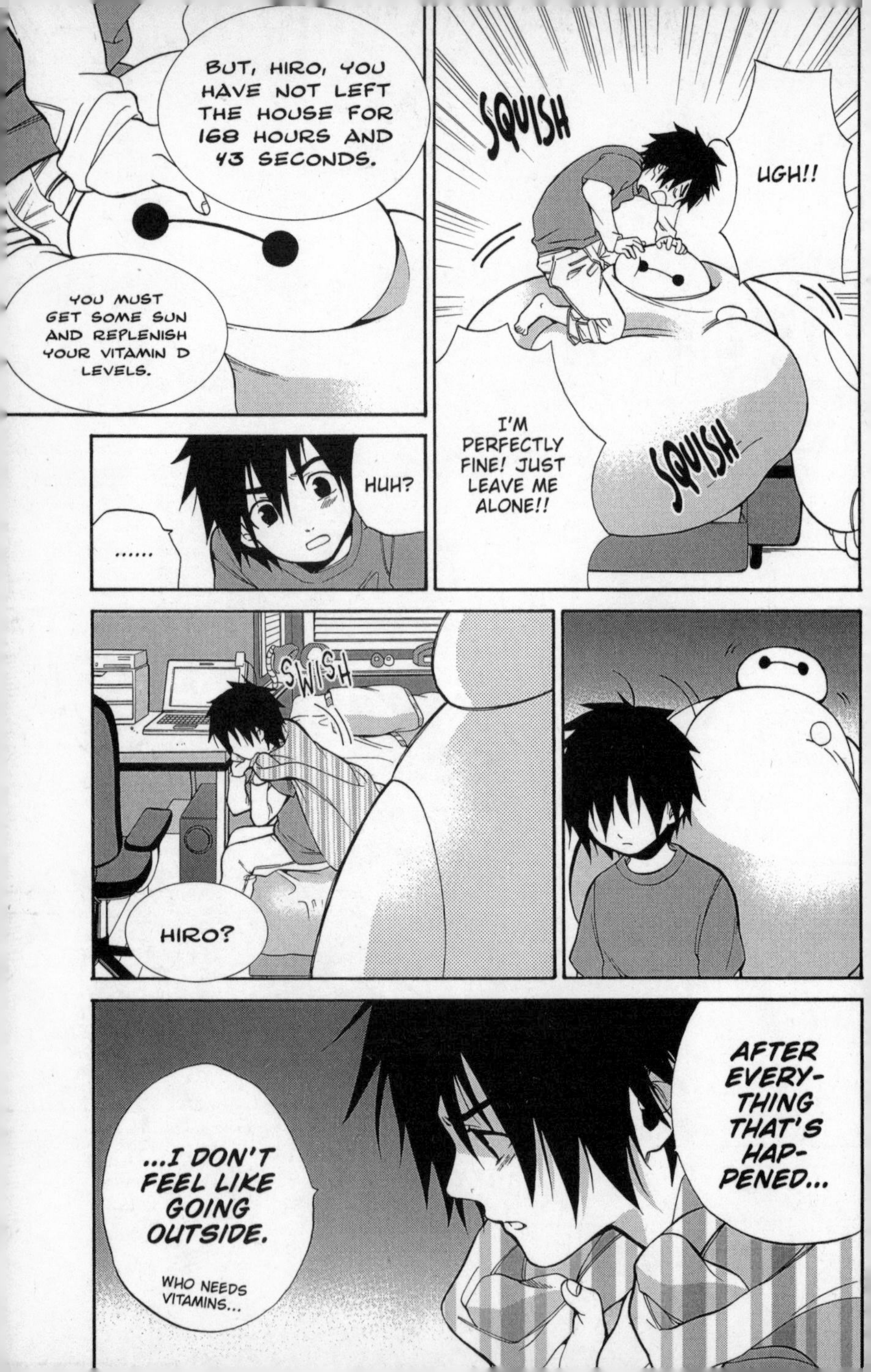
SQUISH
UGH!!
I'M PERFECTLY FINE! JUST LEAVE ME ALONE!!
SQUISH
BUT, HIRO, YOU HAVE NOT LEFT THE HOUSE FOR 168 HOURS AND 43 SECONDS.
YOU MUST GET SOME SUN AND REPLENISH YOUR VITAMIN D LEVELS.
HUH?
......
SWISH
HIRO?
AFTER EVERY-THING THAT'S HAP-PENED...
...I DON'T FEEL LIKE GOING OUTSIDE.
WHO NEEDS VITAMINS...

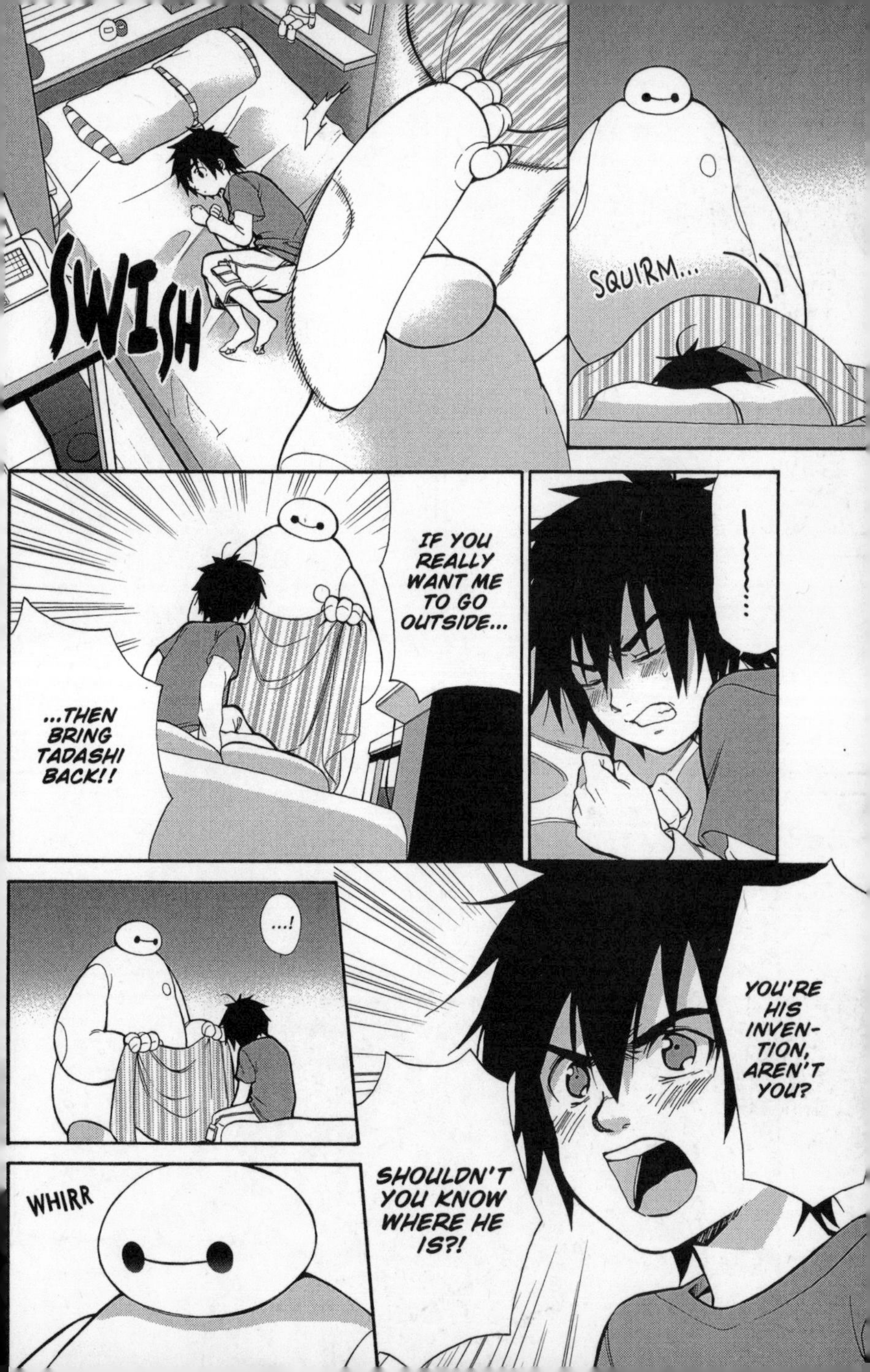

SQUIRM...
SWISH
......!!
IF YOU REALLY WANT ME TO GO OUTSIDE...
...THEN BRING TADASHI BACK!!
YOU'RE HIS INVENTION, AREN'T YOU?
SHOULDN'T YOU KNOW WHERE HE IS?!
...!
WHIRR

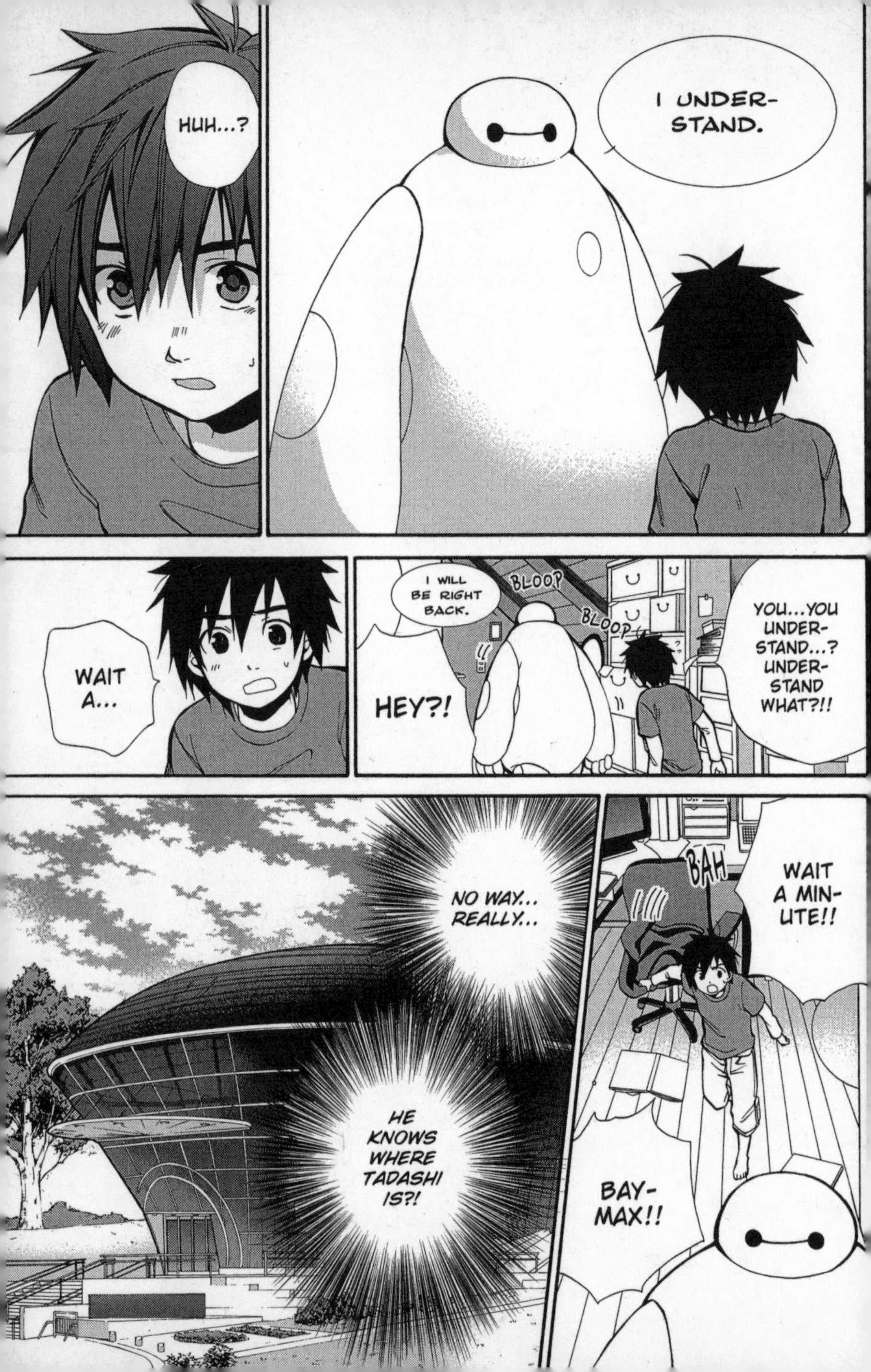
I UNDERSTAND.
HUH...?
YOU...YOU UNDERSTAND...? UNDERSTAND WHAT?!!
I WILL BE RIGHT BACK.
BLOOP
BLOOP
HEY?!
WAIT A...
BAH
WAIT A MINUTE!!
BAYMAX!!
NO WAY... REALLY...
HE KNOWS WHERE TADASHI IS?!

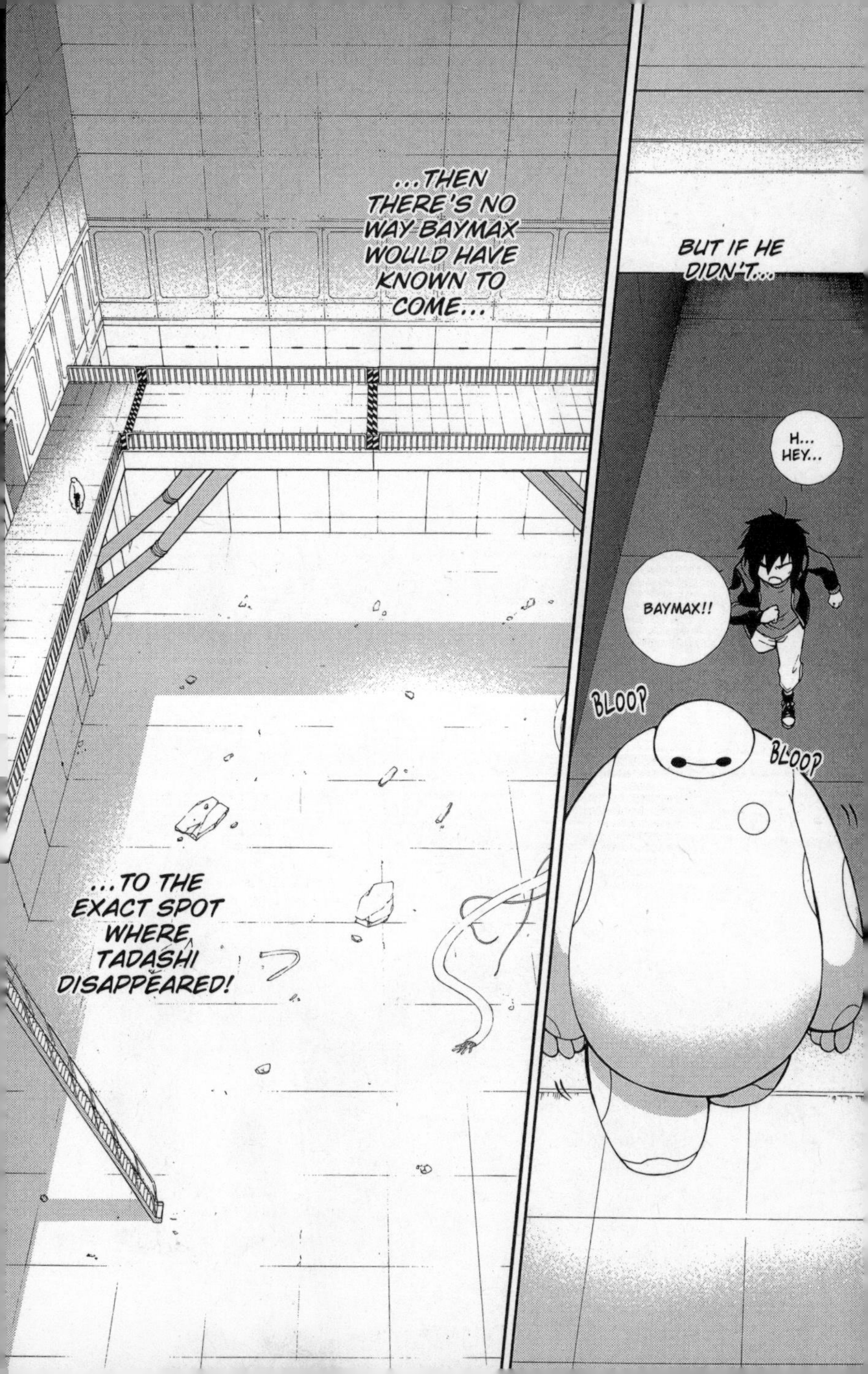
BUT IF HE DIDN'T...
H... HEY...
BAYMAX!!
BLOOP
BLOOP
...THEN THERE'S NO WAY BAYMAX WOULD HAVE KNOWN TO COME...
...TO THE EXACT SPOT WHERE TADASHI DISAPPEARED!

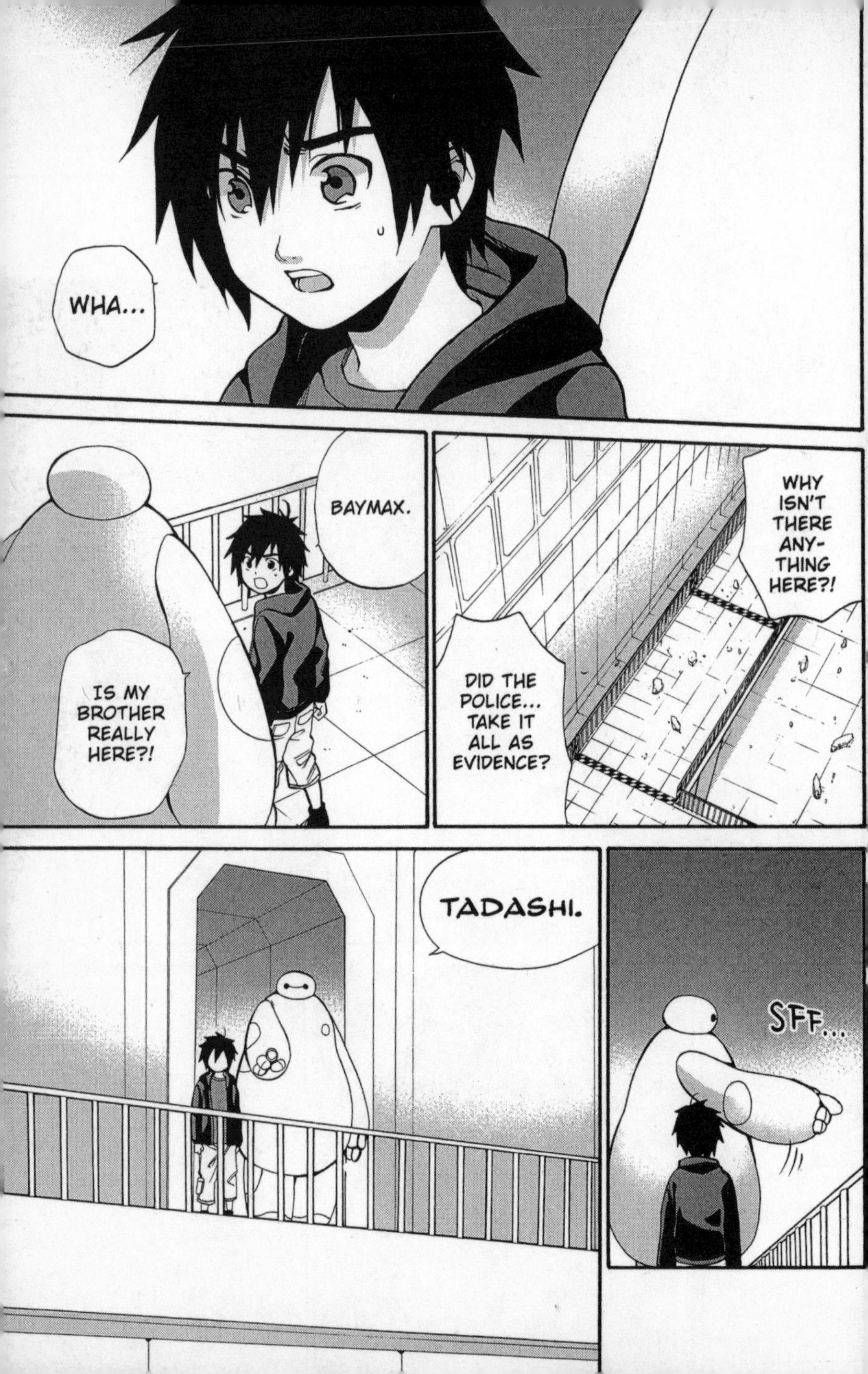
WHA...
WHY ISN'T THERE ANY-THING HERE?!
DID THE POLICE... TAKE IT ALL AS EVIDENCE?
BAYMAX.
IS MY BROTHER REALLY HERE?!
SFF...
TADASHI.

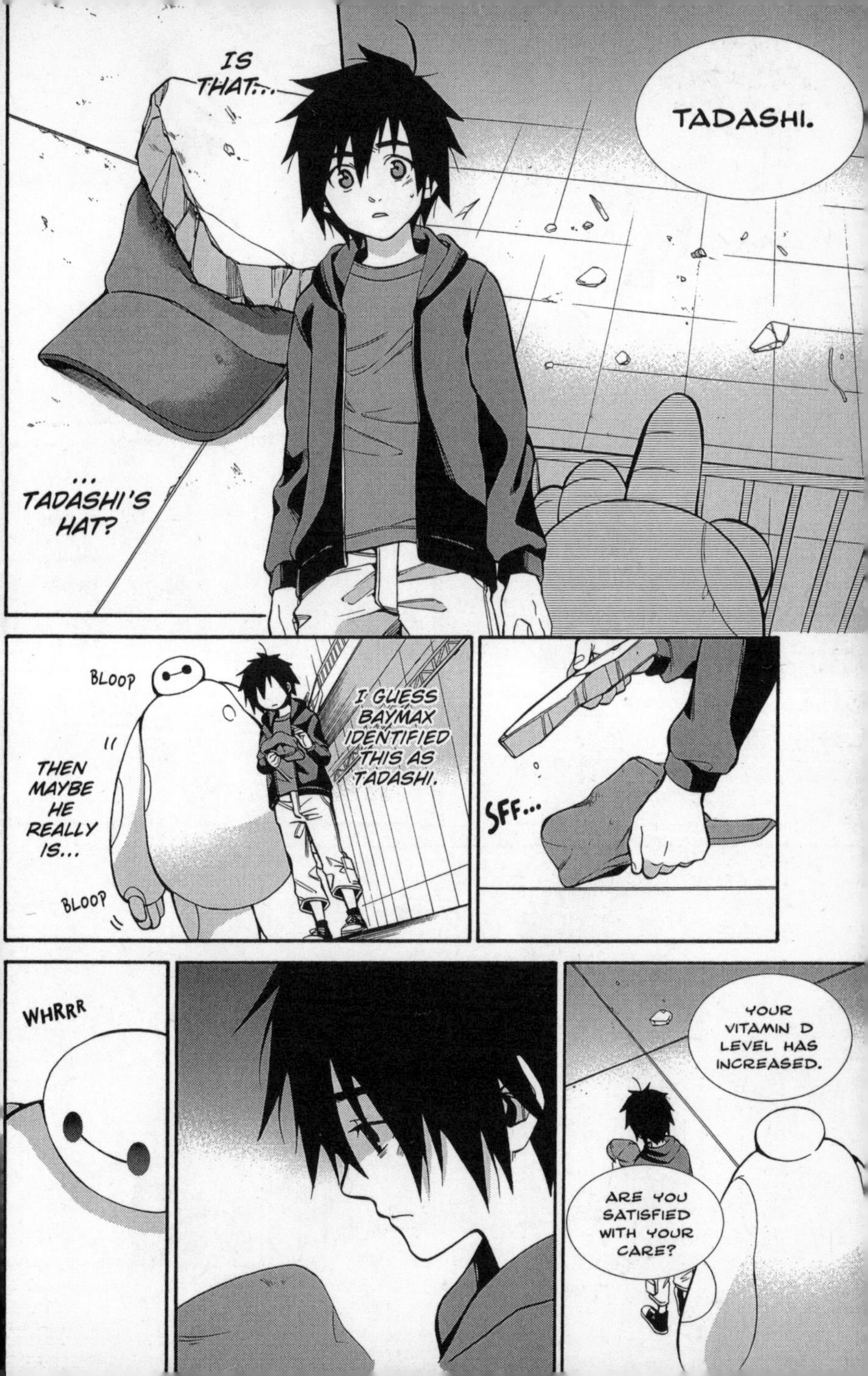
TADASHI.
IS THAT...
...TADASHI'S HAT?
SFF...
I GUESS BAYMAX IDENTIFIED THIS AS TADASHI.
BLOOP
THEN MAYBE HE REALLY IS...
BLOOP
YOUR VITAMIN D LEVEL HAS INCREASED.
ARE YOU SATISFIED WITH YOUR CARE?
WHRRR

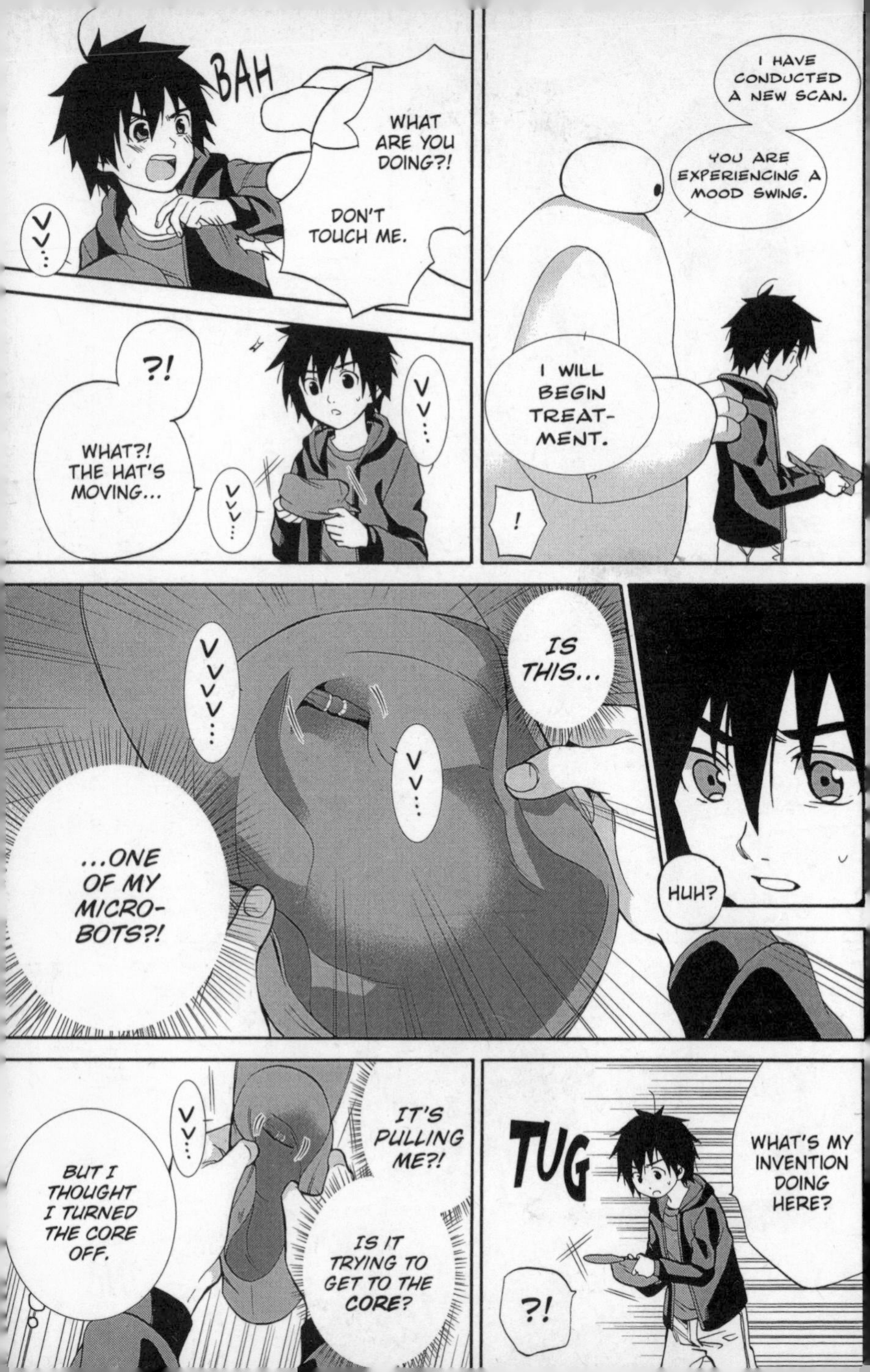
I HAVE CONDUCTED A NEW SCAN.
YOU ARE EXPERIENCING A MOOD SWING.
I WILL BEGIN TREATMENT.
!
BAH
WHAT ARE YOU DOING?!
DON'T TOUCH ME.
VV...
?!
VVV...
WHAT?! THE HAT'S MOVING...
VVV...
IS THIS...
HUH?
VVVVV...
VVV...
...ONE OF MY MICRO-BOTS?!
WHAT'S MY INVENTION DOING HERE?
TUG
?!
IT'S PULLING ME?!
VVV...
BUT I THOUGHT I TURNED THE CORE OFF.
IS IT TRYING TO GET TO THE CORE?

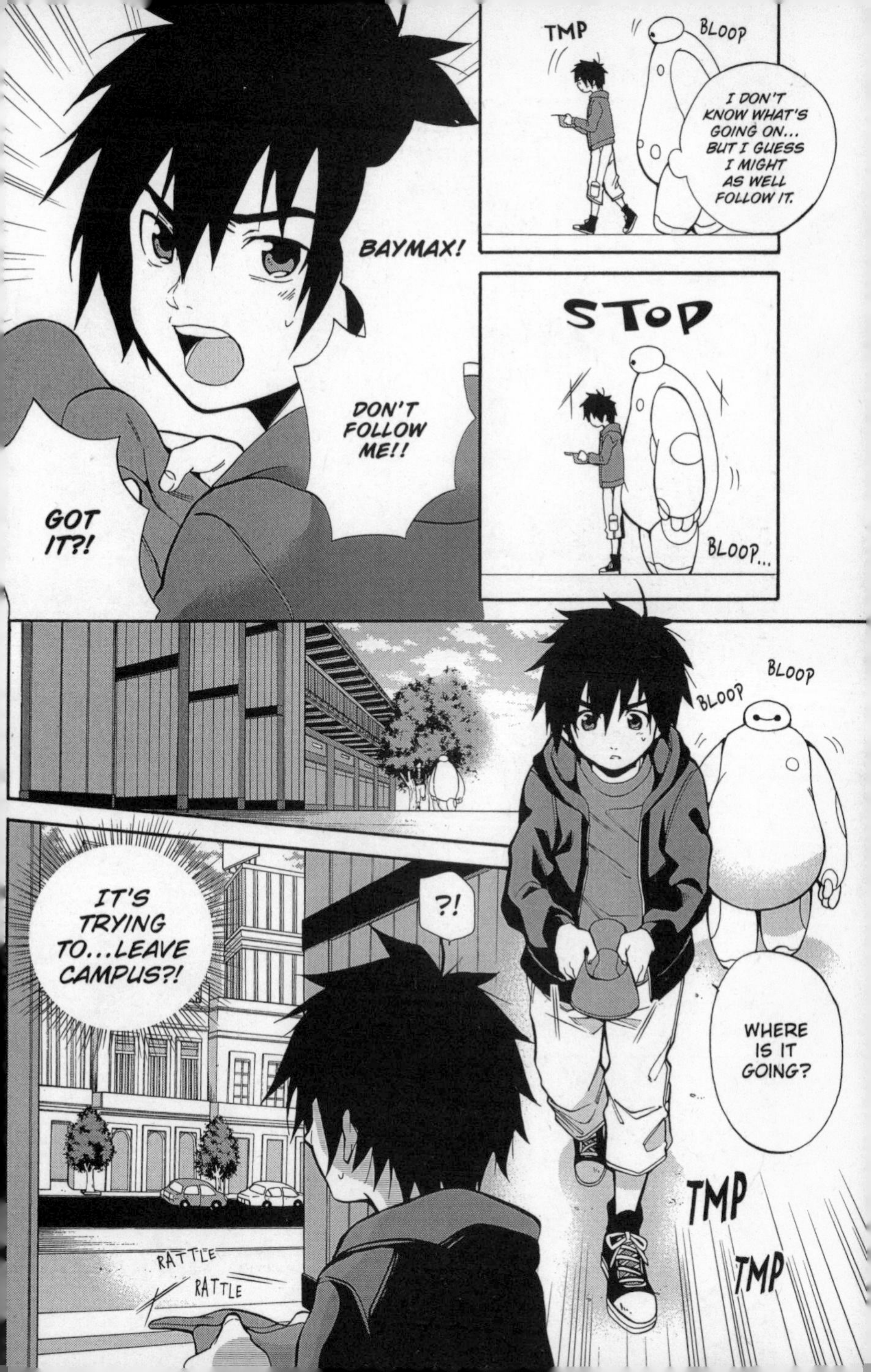
TMP
BLOOP
I DON'T KNOW WHAT'S GOING ON... BUT I GUESS I MIGHT AS WELL FOLLOW IT.
STOP
BLOOP...
BAYMAX!
DON'T FOLLOW ME!!
GOT IT?!
BLOOP
BLOOP
WHERE IS IT GOING?
TMP
TMP
?!
IT'S TRYING TO...LEAVE CAMPUS?!
RATTLE
RATTLE

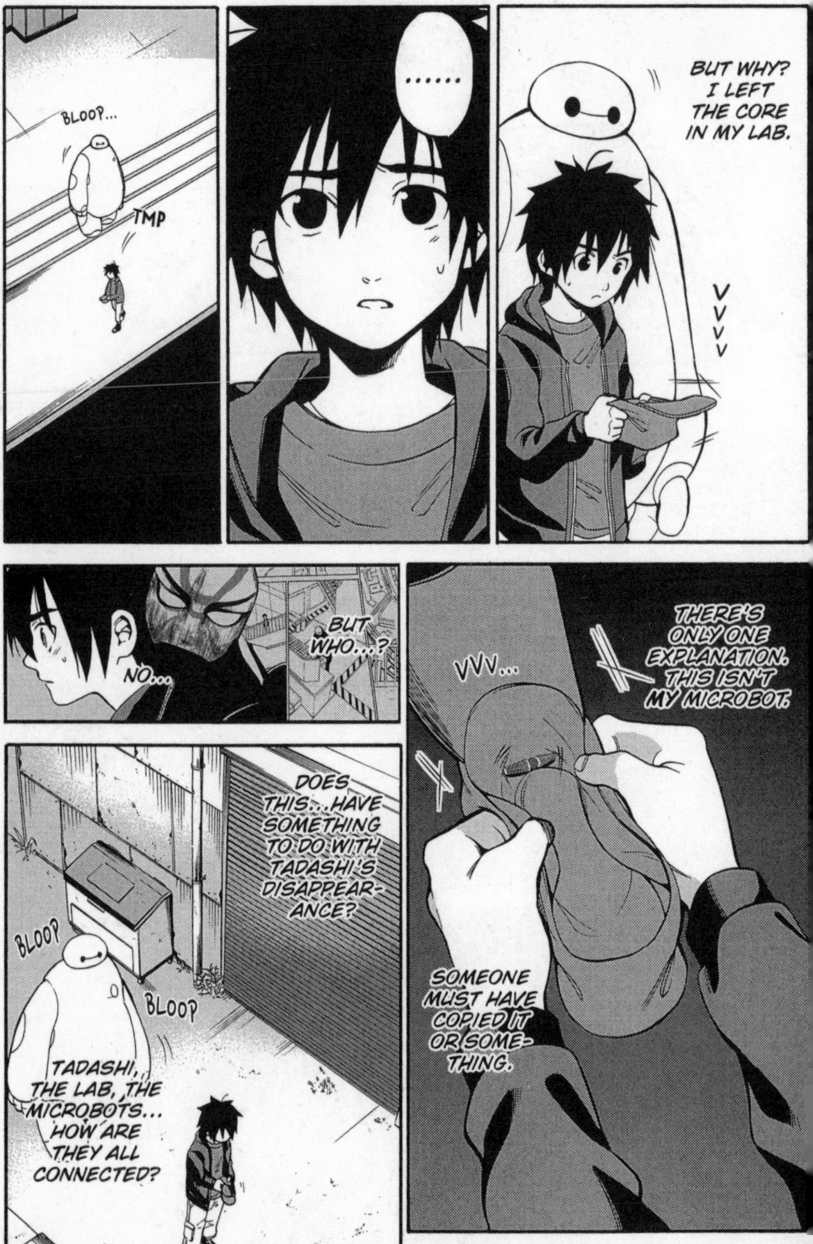
BUT WHY? I LEFT THE CORE IN MY LAB.
VVVV
......
BLOOP...
TMP
THERE'S ONLY ONE EXPLANATION. THIS ISN'T MY MICROBOT.
VVV...
SOMEONE MUST HAVE COPIED IT OR SOME-THING.
BUT WHO...?
NO...
DOES THIS...HAVE SOMETHING TO DO WITH TADASHI'S DISAPPEAR-ANCE?
BLOOP
BLOOP
TADASHI, THE LAB, THE MICROBOTS... HOW ARE THEY ALL CONNECTED?

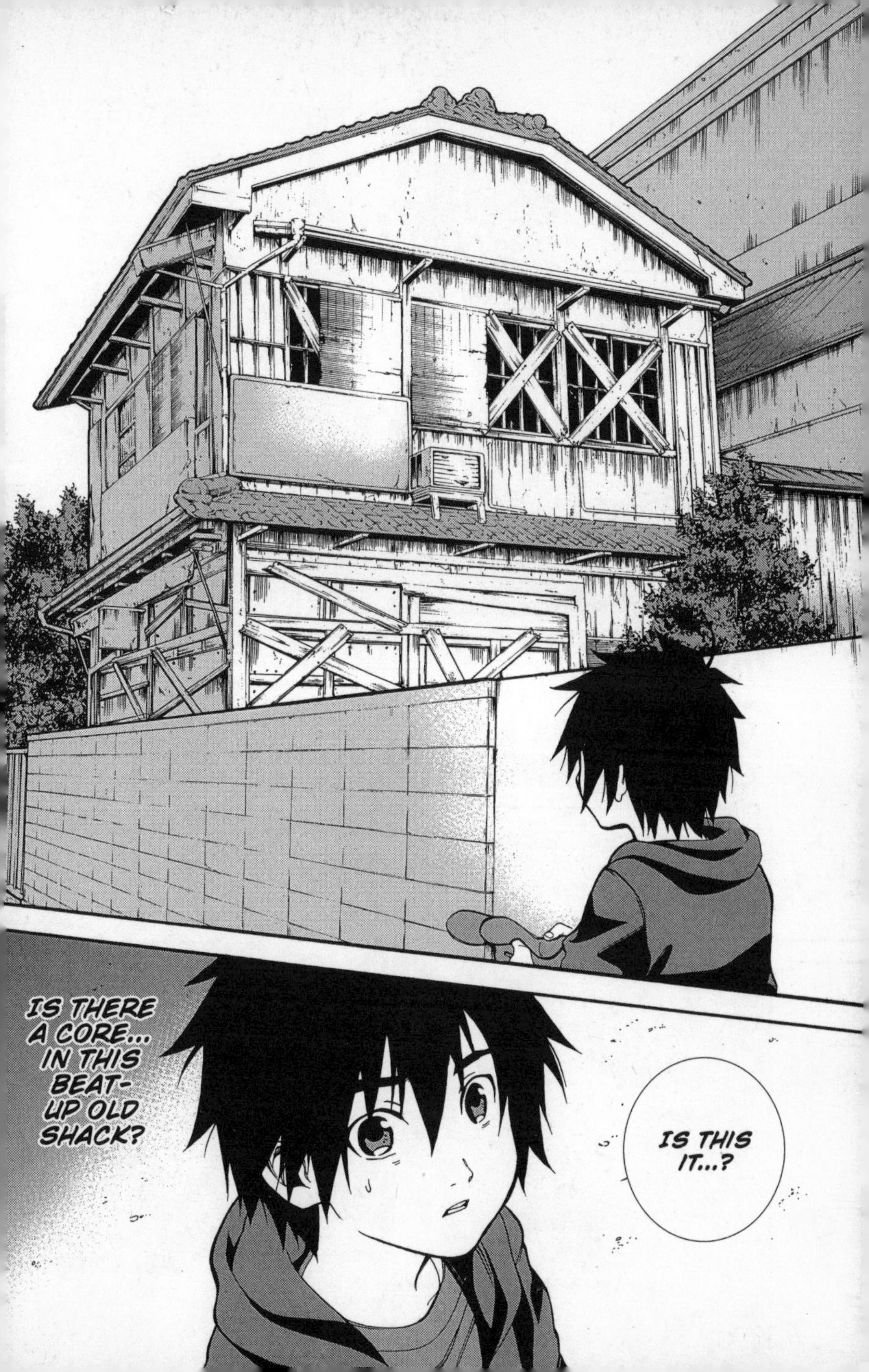
IS THIS IT...?
IS THERE A CORE... IN THIS BEAT-UP OLD SHACK?

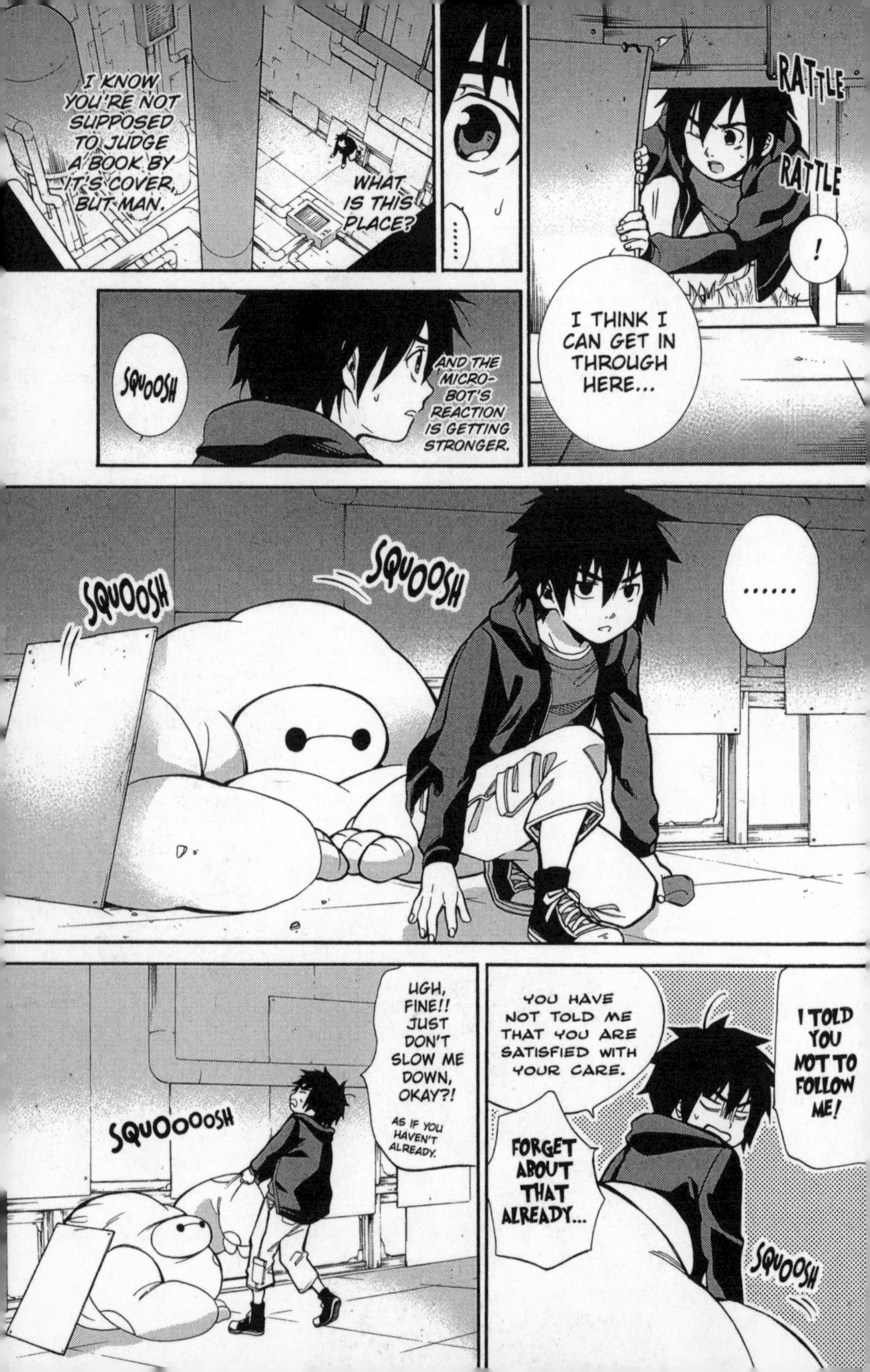
RATTLE
RATTLE
!
I THINK I CAN GET IN THROUGH HERE...
......
I KNOW YOU'RE NOT SUPPOSED TO JUDGE A BOOK BY IT'S COVER, BUT MAN.
WHAT IS THIS PLACE?
AND THE MICRO-BOT'S REACTION IS GETTING STRONGER.
SQUOOSH
......
SQUOOSH
SQUOOSH
I TOLD YOU NOT TO FOLLOW ME!
YOU HAVE NOT TOLD ME THAT YOU ARE SATISFIED WITH YOUR CARE.
FORGET ABOUT THAT ALREADY...
SQUOOSH
UGH, FINE!! JUST DON'T SLOW ME DOWN, OKAY?!
AS IF YOU HAVEN'T ALREADY.
SQUOOOOSH

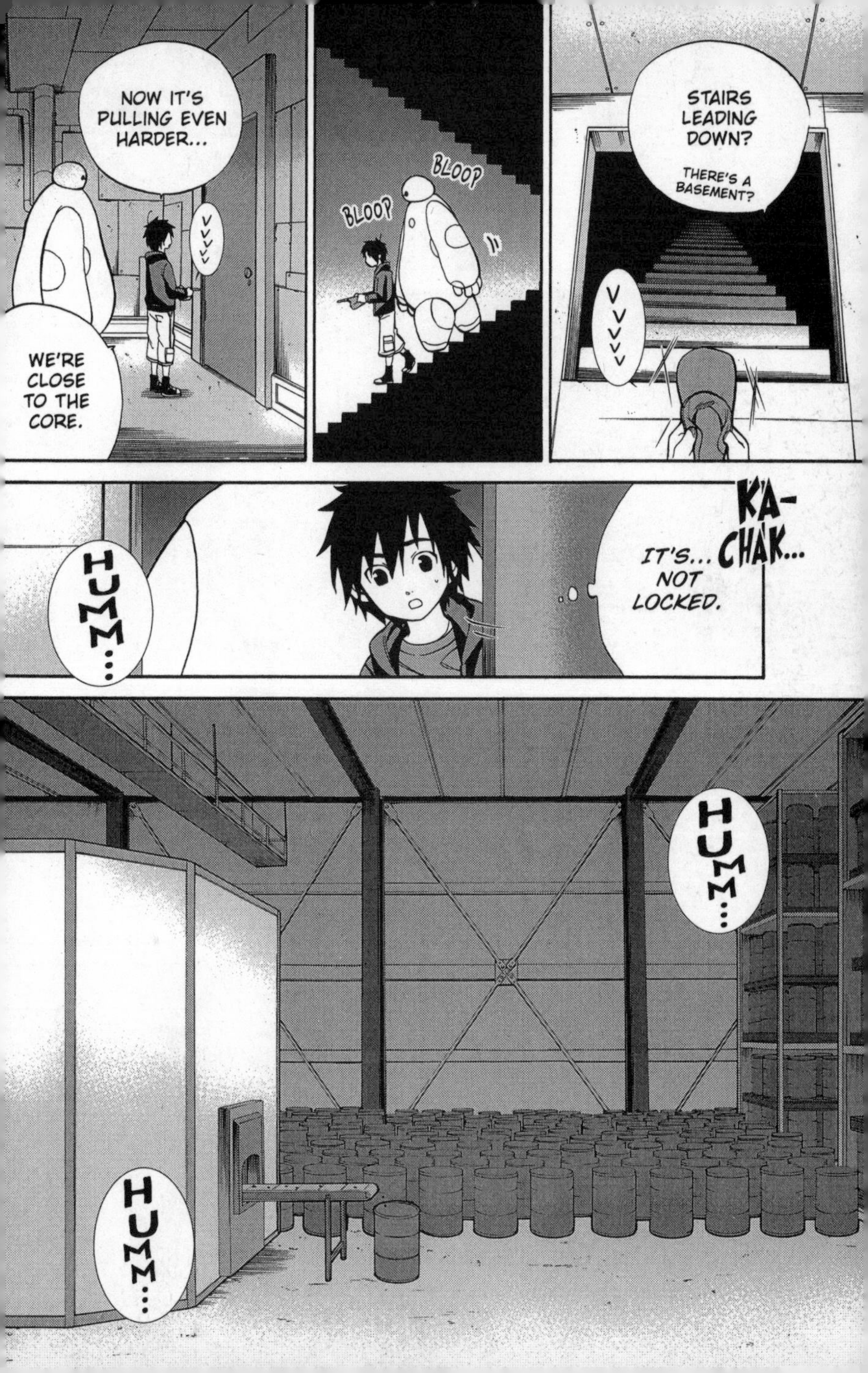
STAIRS LEADING DOWN?
THERE'S A BASEMENT?
VVVVV
BLOOP
BLOOP
NOW IT'S PULLING EVEN HARDER...
VVVVV
WE'RE CLOSE TO THE CORE.
KA-CHAK...
IT'S... NOT LOCKED.
HUMM...
HUMM...
HUMM...

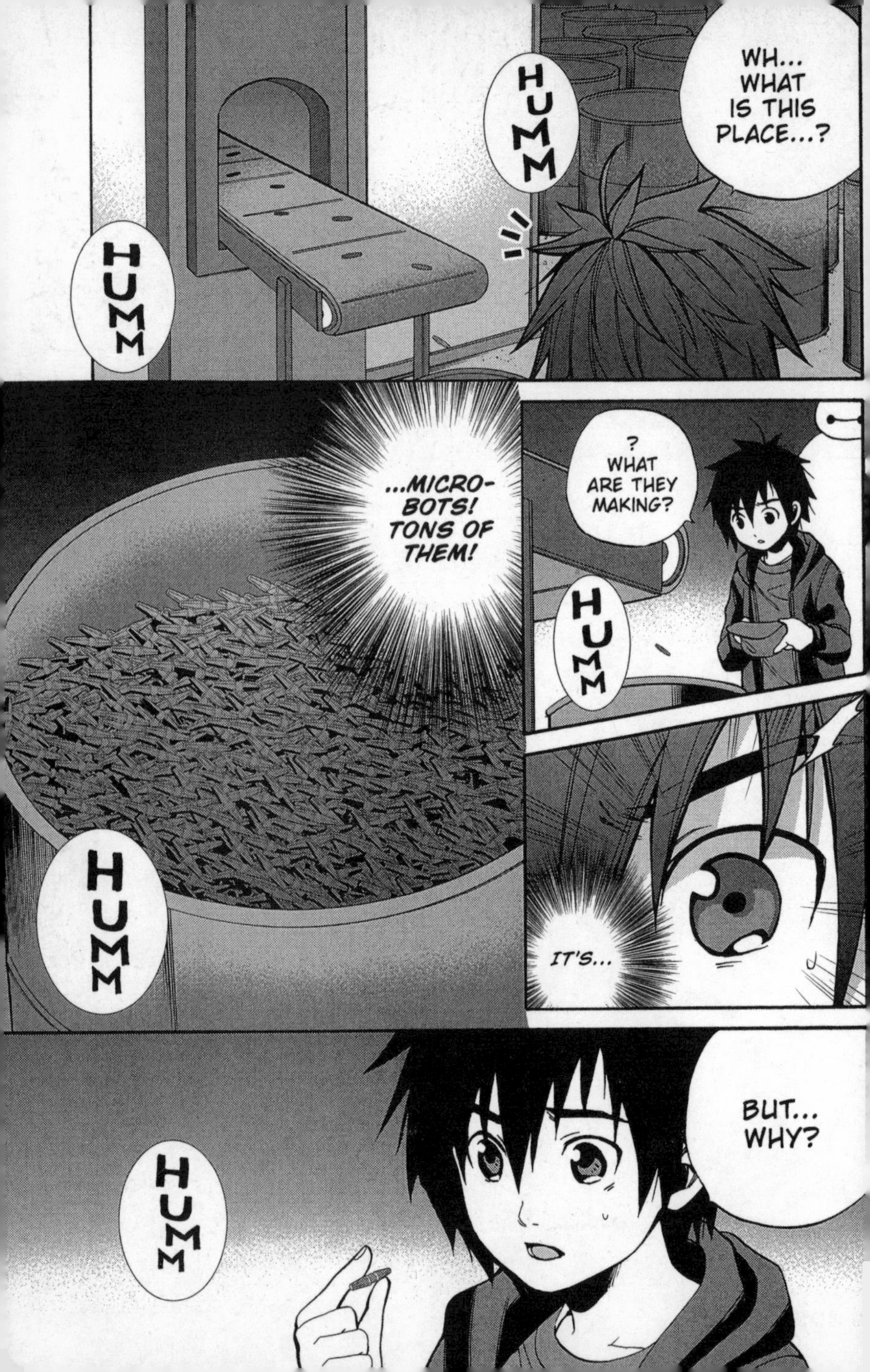

WH... WHAT IS THIS PLACE...?
HUMM
HUMM
? WHAT ARE THEY MAKING?
HUMM
IT'S...
...MICRO-BOTS! TONS OF THEM!
HUMM
BUT... WHY?
HUMM

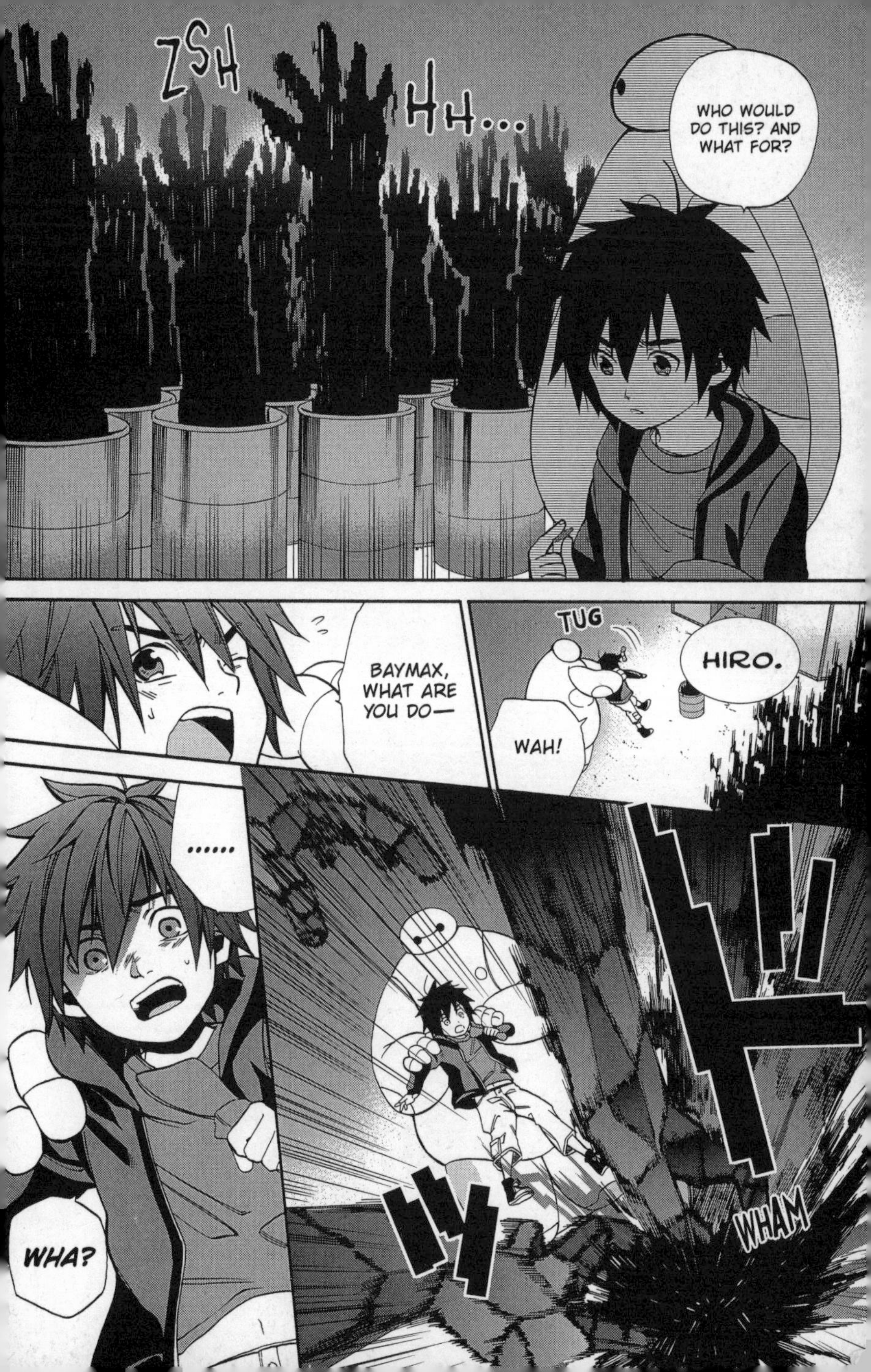

WHO WOULD DO THIS? AND WHAT FOR?
ZSH HH...
HIRO.
TUG
WAH!
BAYMAX, WHAT ARE YOU DO—
WHAM
......
WHA?

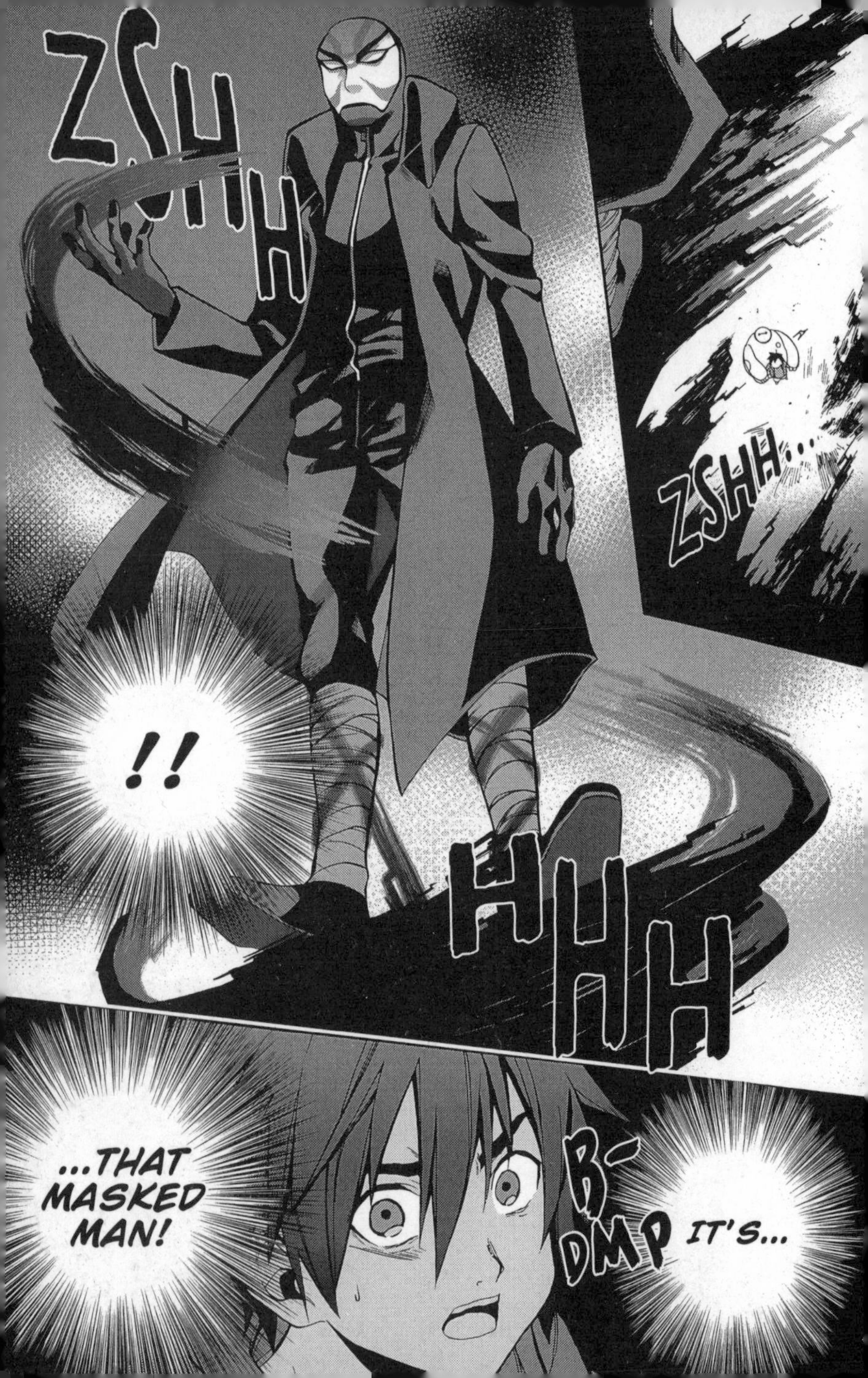
ZSHH...
ZSHHH
!!
HHHH
B-DMP
IT'S...
...THAT MASKED MAN!

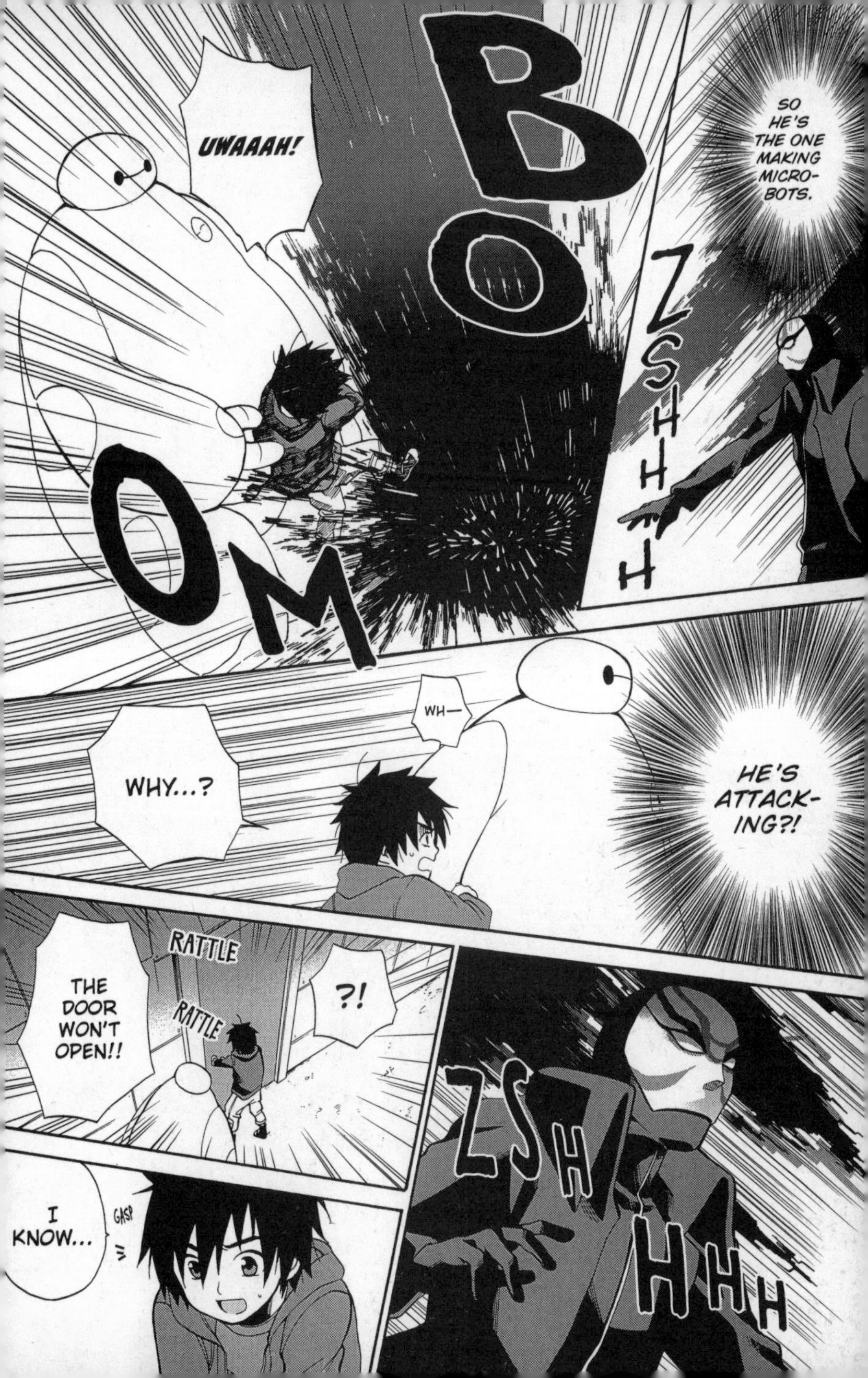
SO HE'S THE ONE MAKING MICRO-BOTS.
ZSHHHH
BOOM
UWAAAH!
HE'S ATTACKING?!
WH—
WHY...?
ZSHHHH
?!
RATTLE
RATTLE
THE DOOR WON'T OPEN!!
GASP
I KNOW...

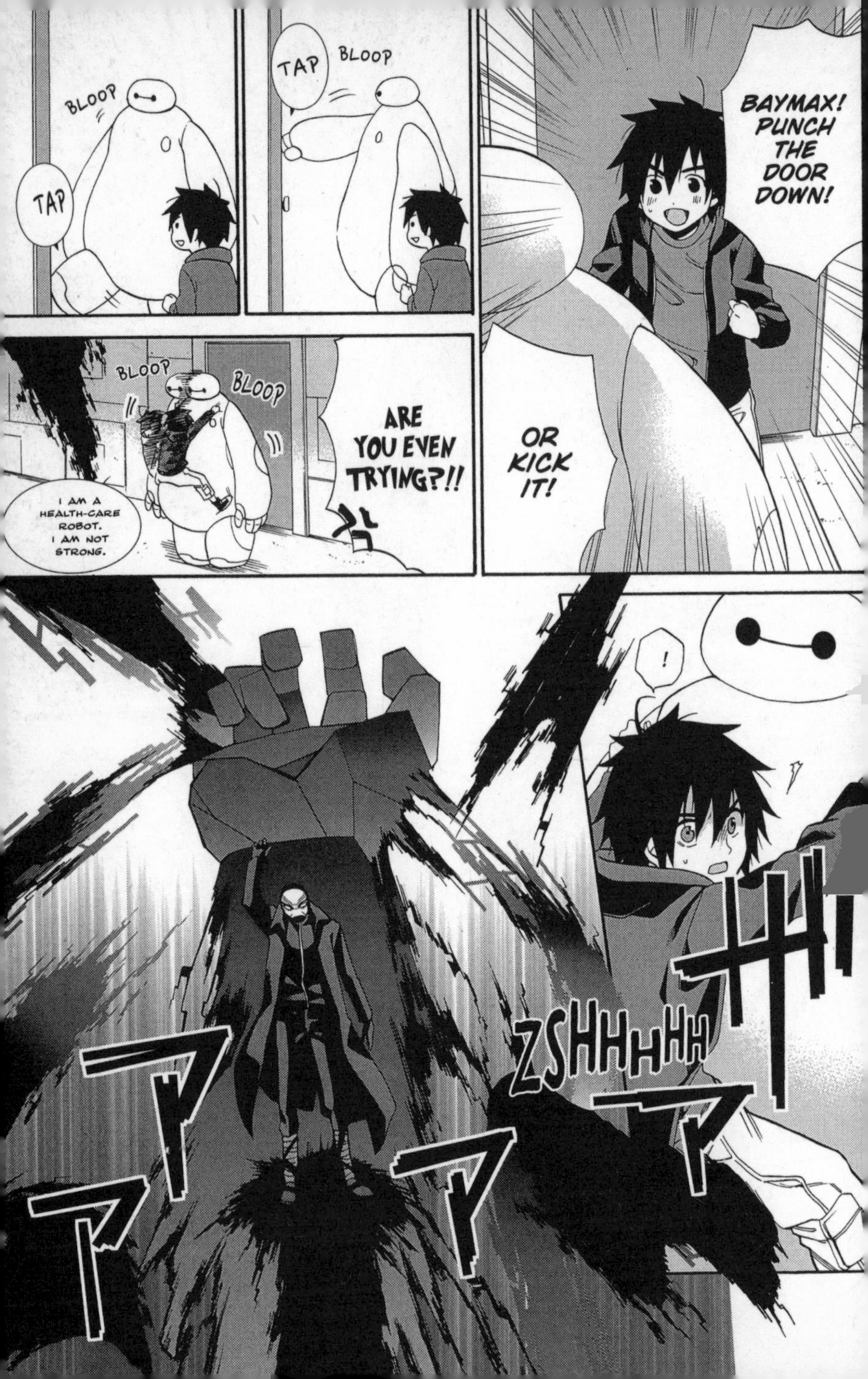

BAYMAX! PUNCH THE DOOR DOWN!
OR KICK IT!
TAP
BLOOP
BLOOP
TAP
ARE YOU EVEN TRYING?!!
BLOOP
BLOOP
I AM A HEALTH-CARE ROBOT. I AM NOT STRONG.
!
ZSHHHHH

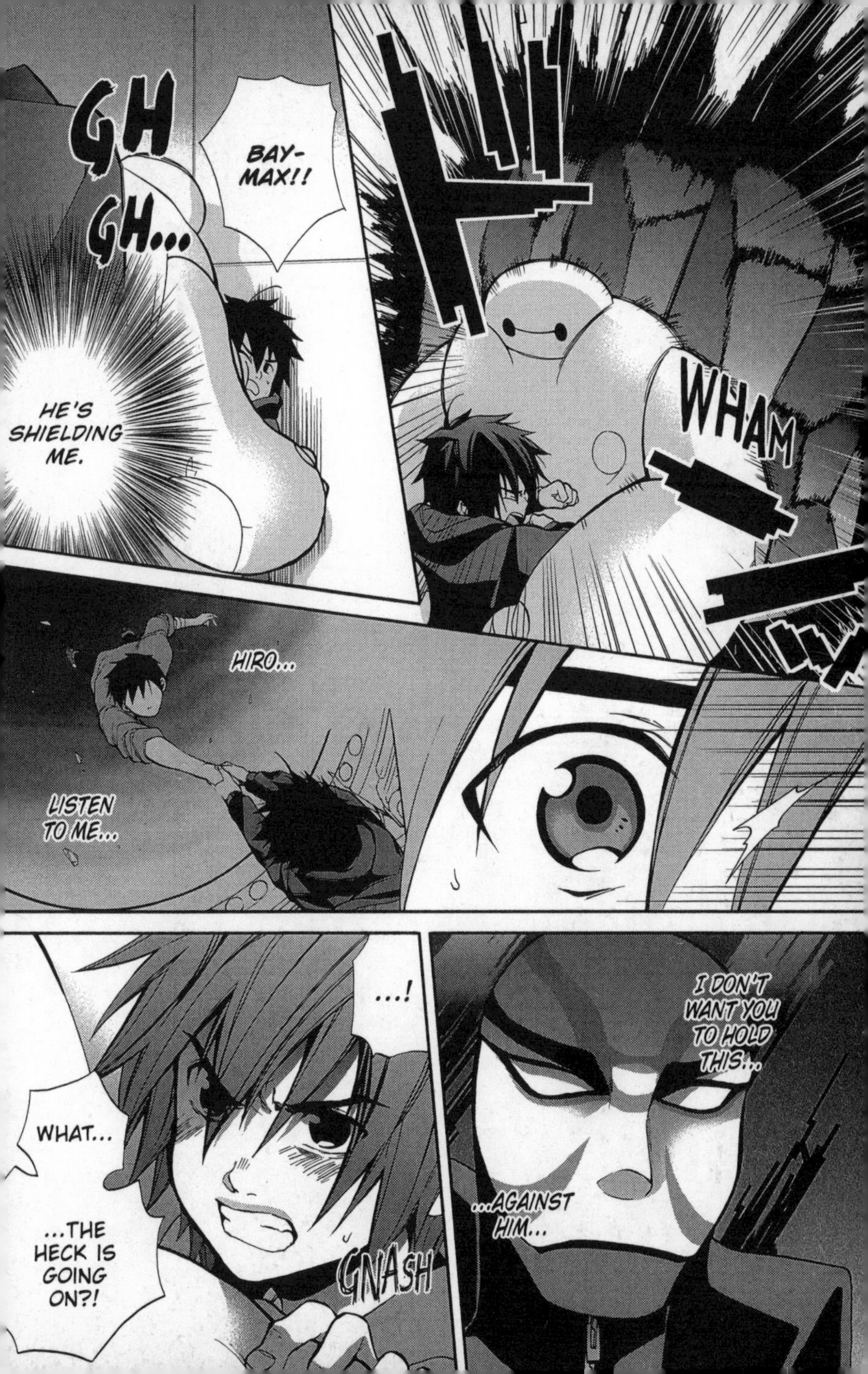
WHAM
BAY-MAX!!
GH GH...
HE'S SHIELDING ME.
HIRO...
LISTEN TO ME...
I DON'T WANT YOU TO HOLD THIS...
...AGAINST HIM...
...!
WHAT...
...THE HECK IS GOING ON?!
GNASH

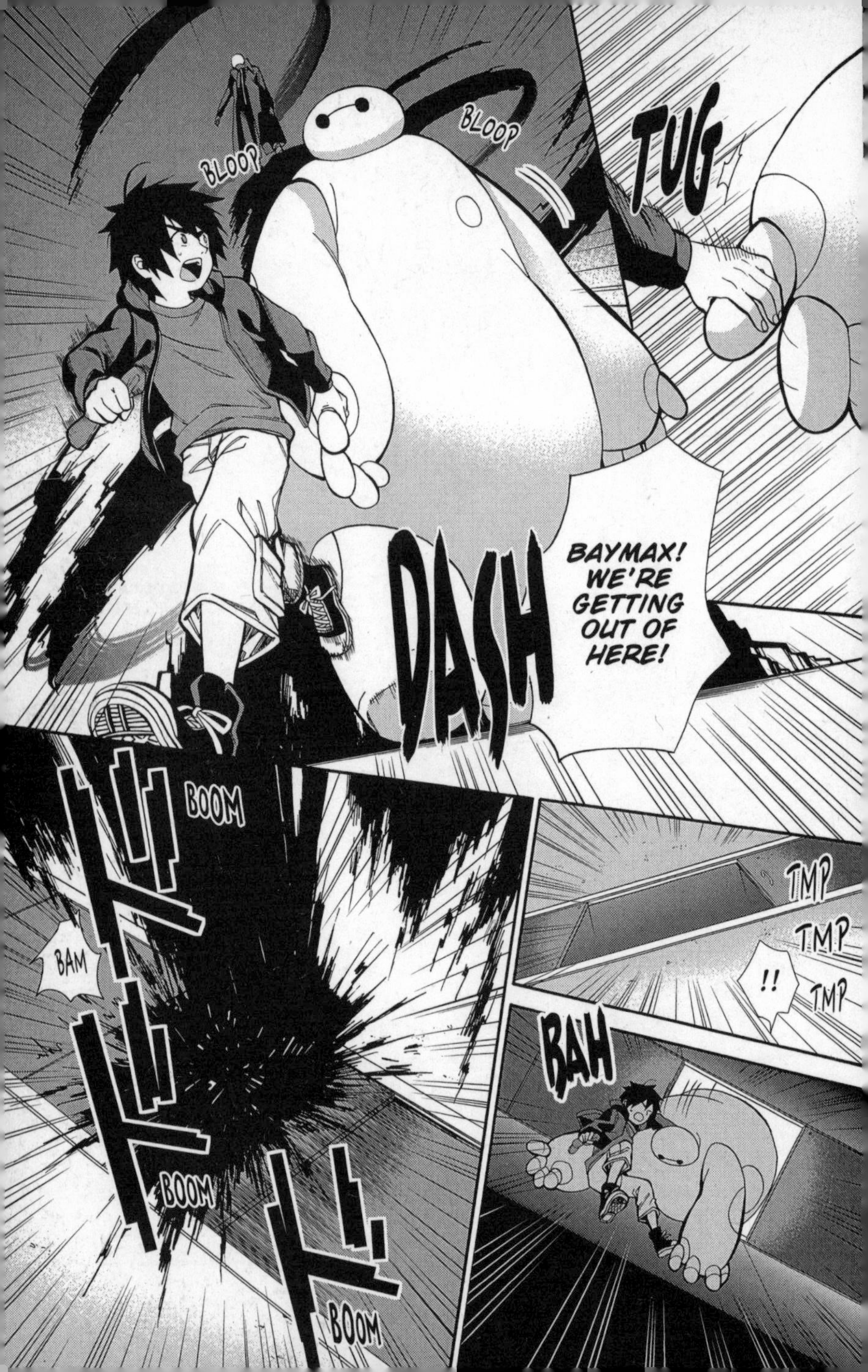
TUG
BLOOP
BLOOP
BAYMAX! WE'RE GETTING OUT OF HERE!
DASH
TMP
TMP
TMP
!!
BAH
BOOM
BAM
BOOM
BOOM

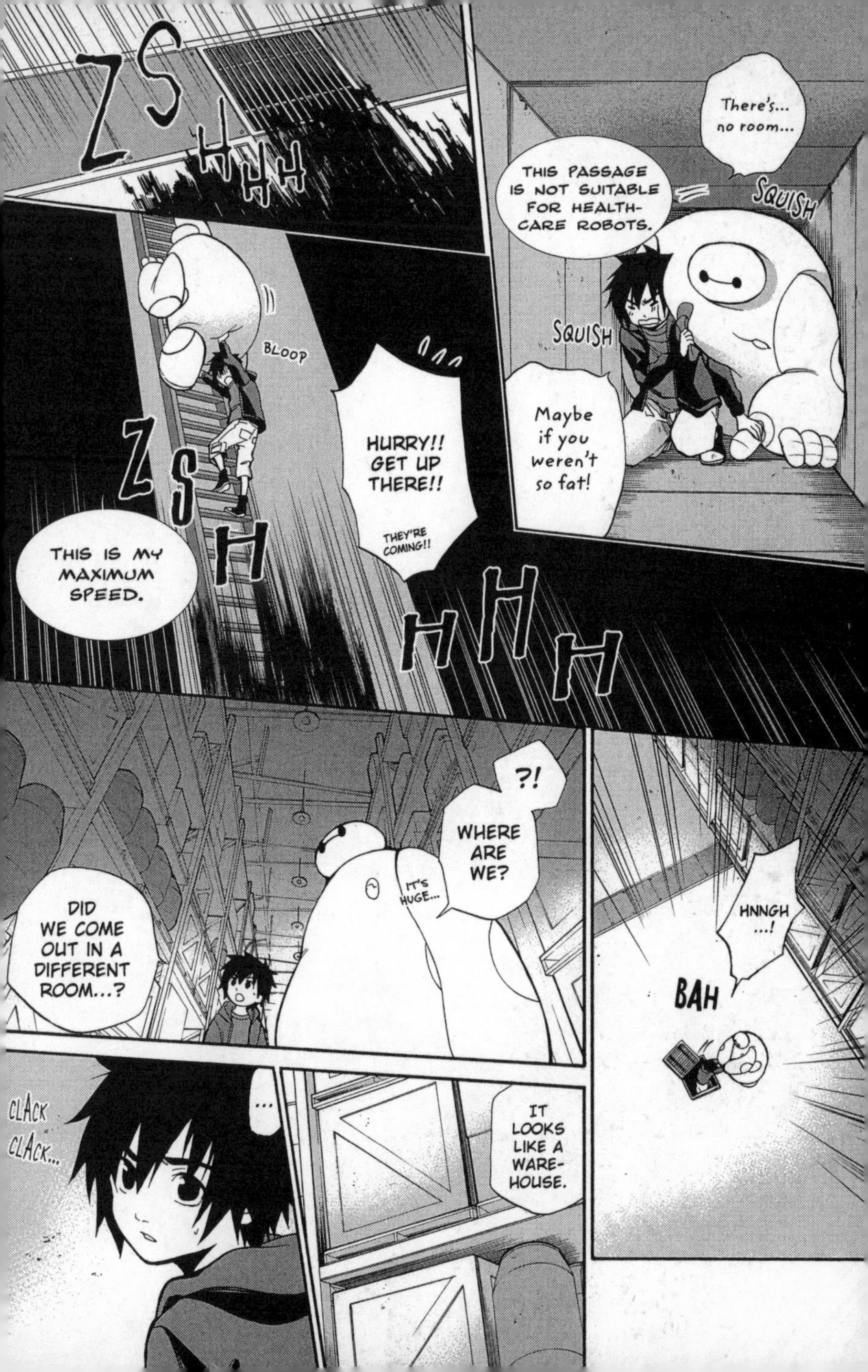
There's... no room...
THIS PASSAGE IS NOT SUITABLE FOR HEALTH-CARE ROBOTS.
SQUISH
SQUISH
Maybe if you weren't so fat!
ZSHHH
HURRY!! GET UP THERE!!
THEY'RE COMING!!
BLOOP
THIS IS MY MAXIMUM SPEED.
ZSHHHHH
HNNGH ...!
BAH
?!
WHERE ARE WE?
IT'S HUGE...
DID WE COME OUT IN A DIFFERENT ROOM...?
IT LOOKS LIKE A WARE-HOUSE.
...
CLACK CLACK...

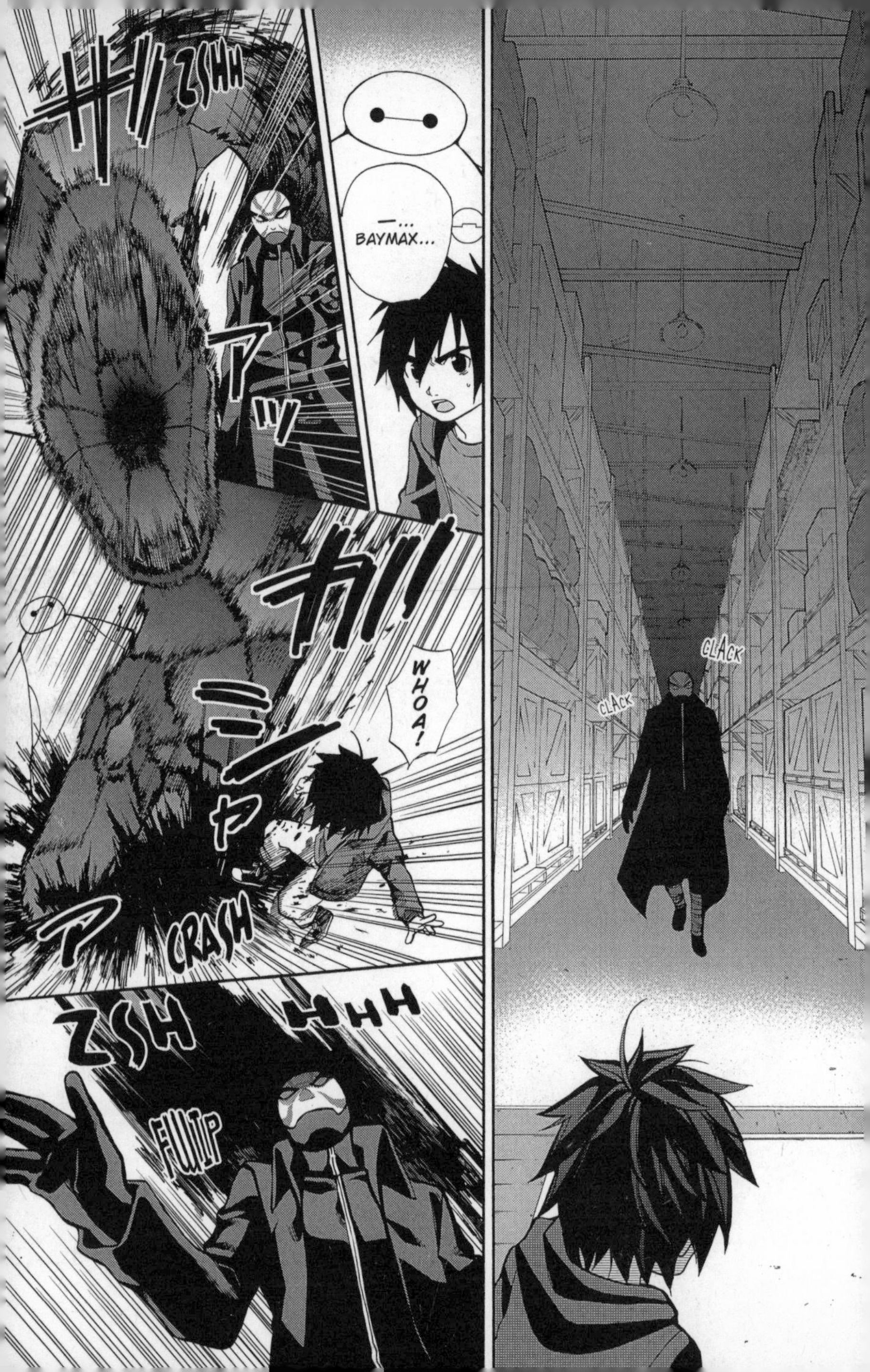
CLACK
CLACK
—... BAYMAX...
ZSHH
WHOA!
CRASH
ZSH HHH
FWIP

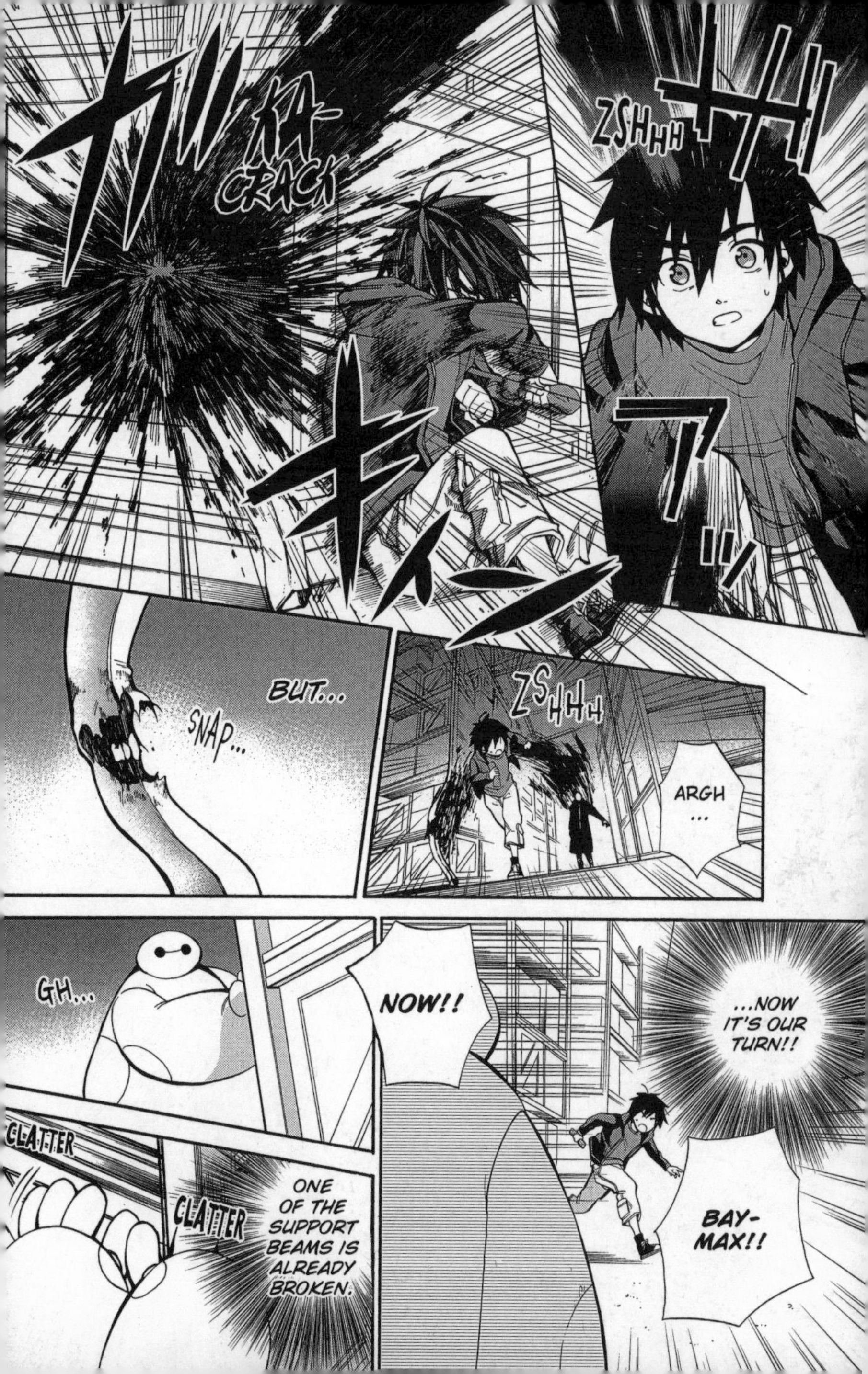
ZSHHH
KA-CRACK
ZSHHH
ARGH
...
BUT...
SNAP...
...NOW IT'S OUR TURN!!
NOW!!
BAY-MAX!!
GH...
CLATTER
CLATTER
ONE OF THE SUPPORT BEAMS IS ALREADY BROKEN.

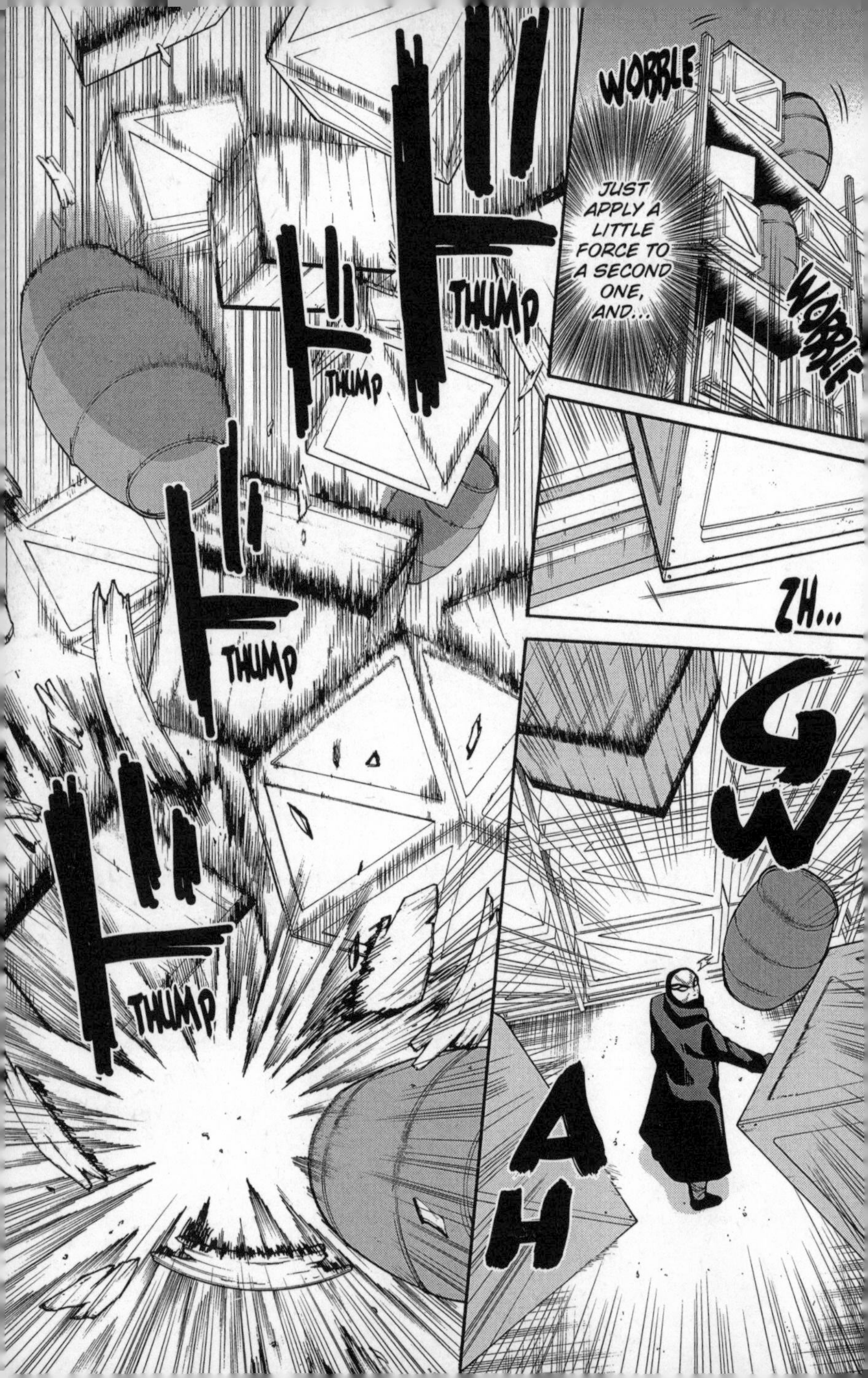
WOBBLE
JUST APPLY A LITTLE FORCE TO A SECOND ONE, AND...
WOBBLE
ZH...
GW
AH
THUMP
THUMP
THUMP
THUMP

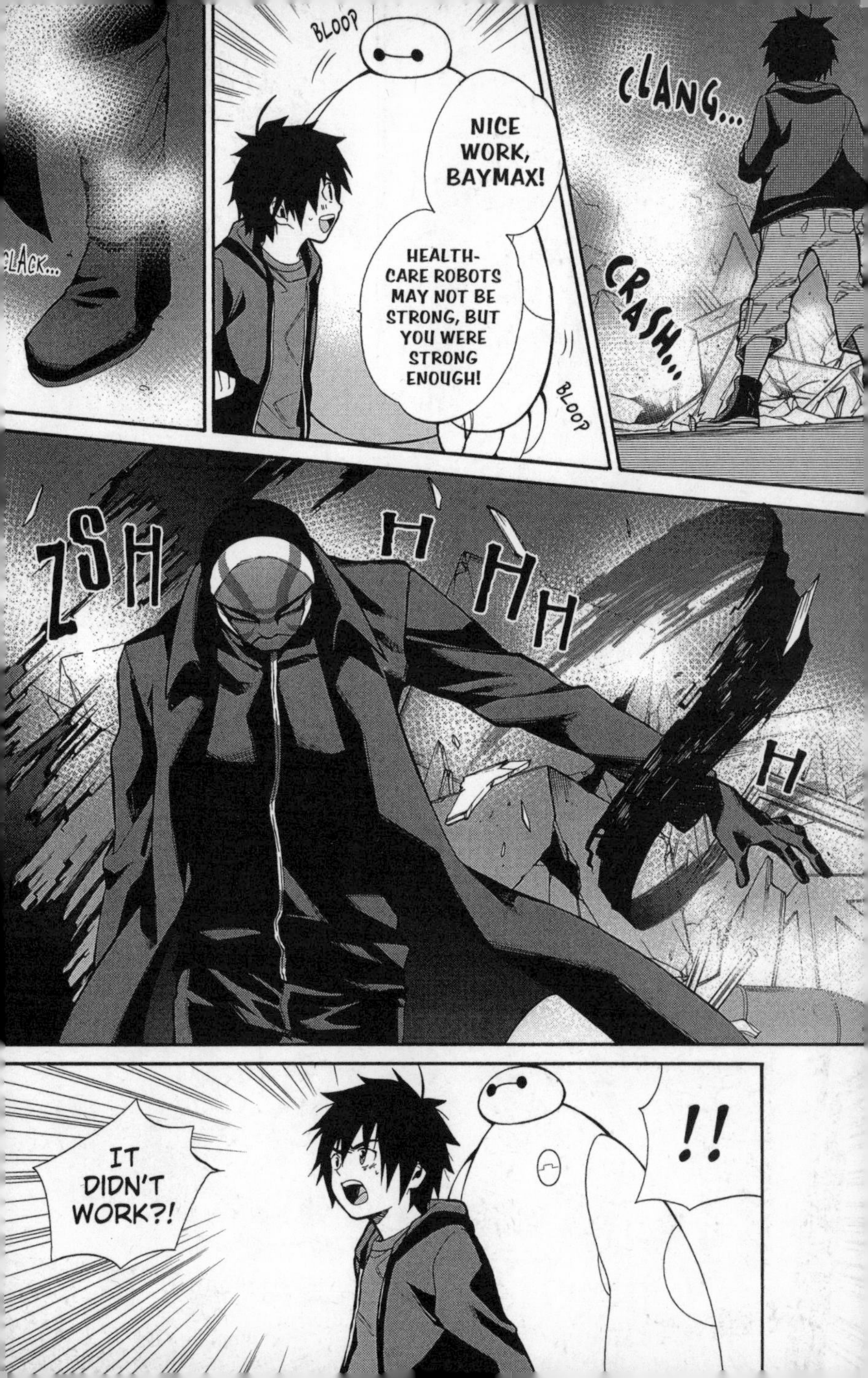
CLANG...
CRASH...
BLOOP
NICE WORK, BAYMAX!
HEALTH-CARE ROBOTS MAY NOT BE STRONG, BUT YOU WERE STRONG ENOUGH!
BLOOP
LACK...
ZSH
HHHH
!!
IT DIDN'T WORK?!

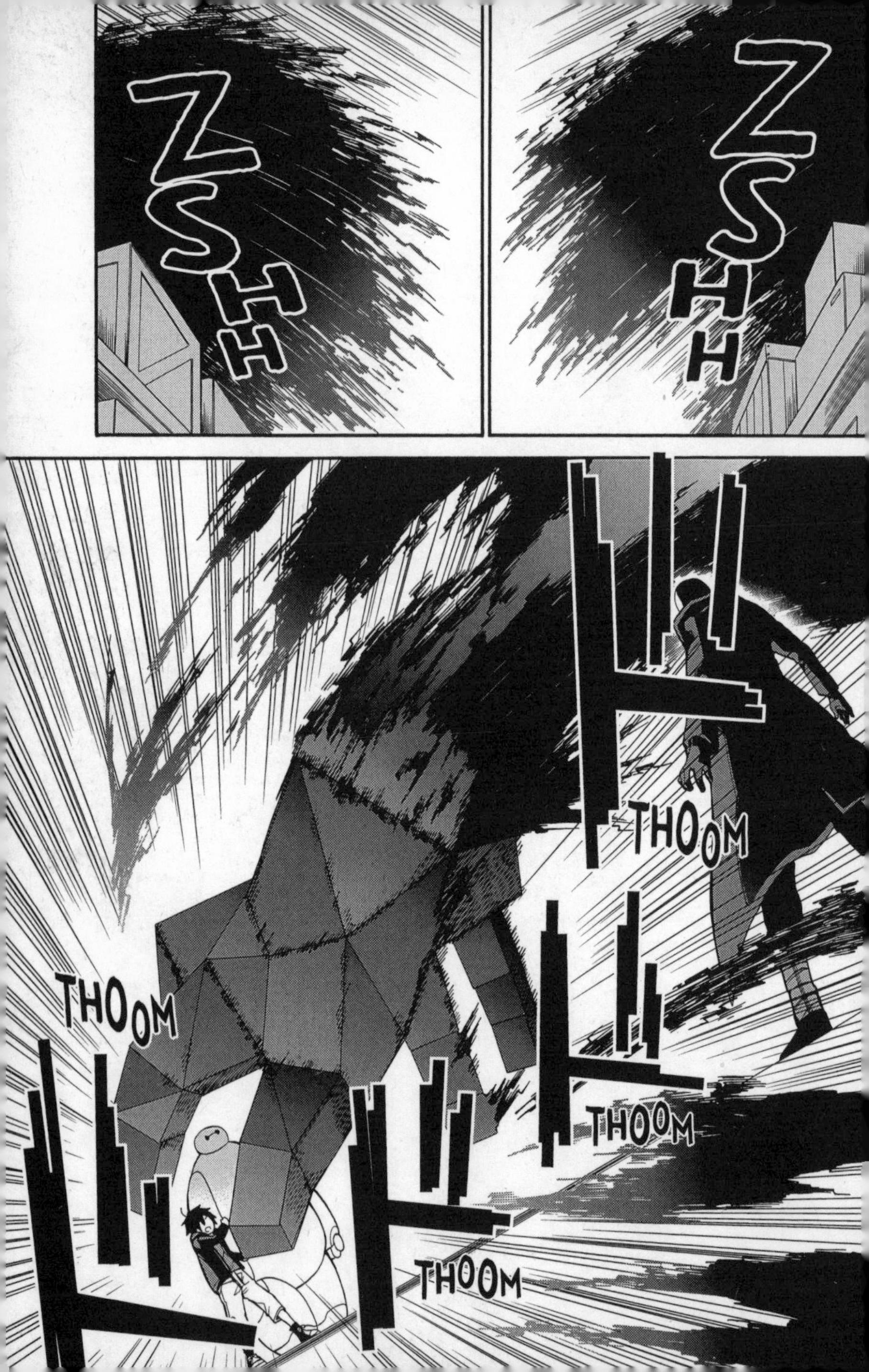
ZSHHH
ZSHHH
THOOM
THOOM
THOOM
THOOM

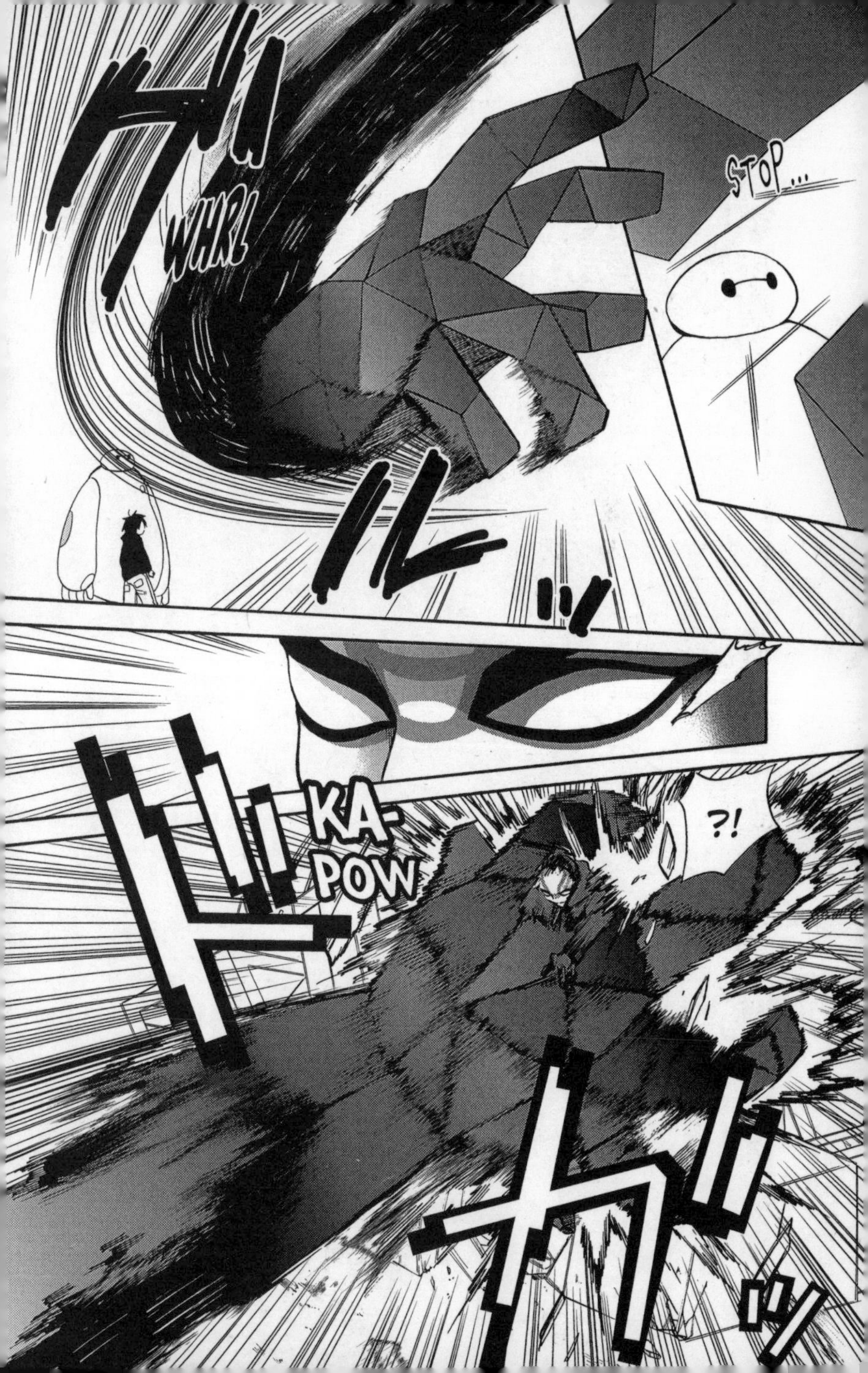
STOP...
WHRL
?!
KA-
POW

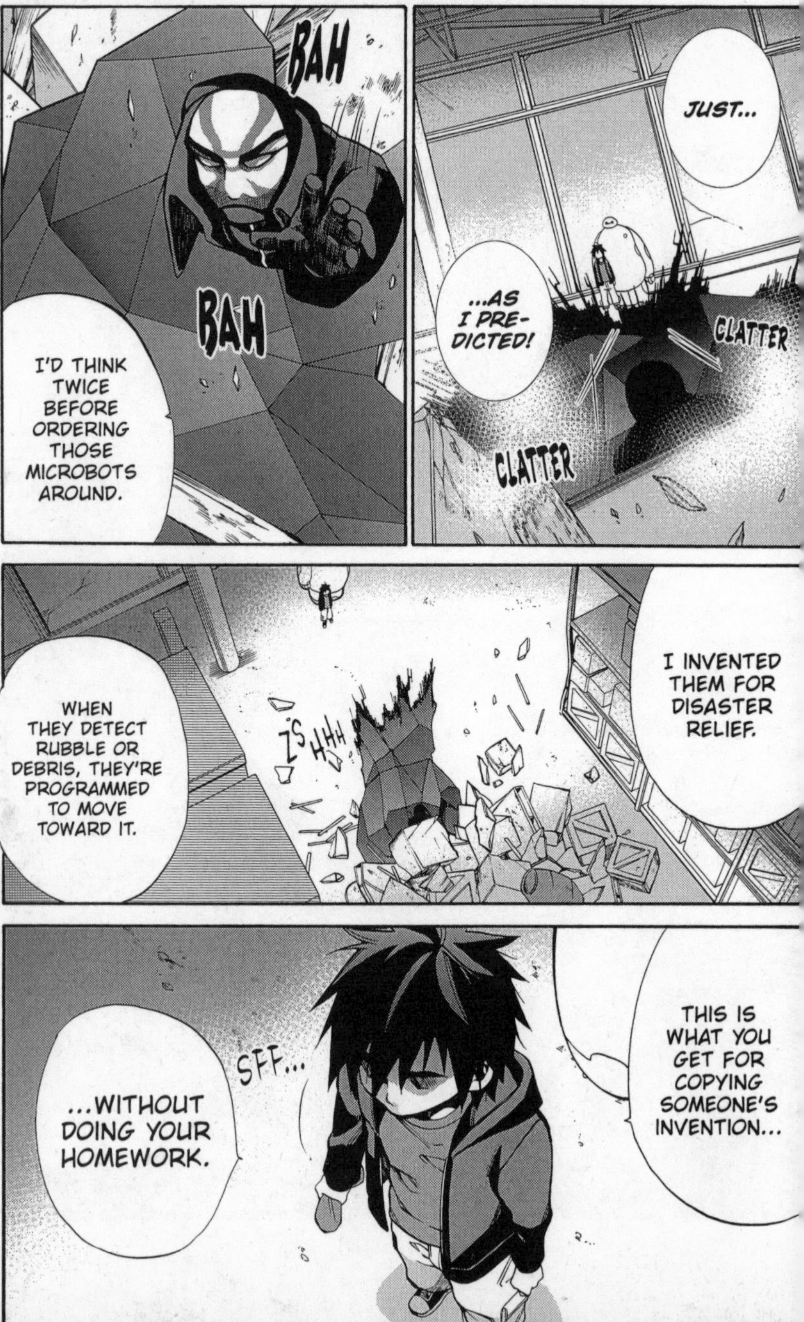
JUST...
...AS I PREDICTED!
CLATTER
CLATTER
BAH
BAH
I'D THINK TWICE BEFORE ORDERING THOSE MICROBOTS AROUND.
I INVENTED THEM FOR DISASTER RELIEF.
ZSHHH
WHEN THEY DETECT RUBBLE OR DEBRIS, THEY'RE PROGRAMMED TO MOVE TOWARD IT.
THIS IS WHAT YOU GET FOR COPYING SOMEONE'S INVENTION...
SFF...
...WITHOUT DOING YOUR HOMEWORK.

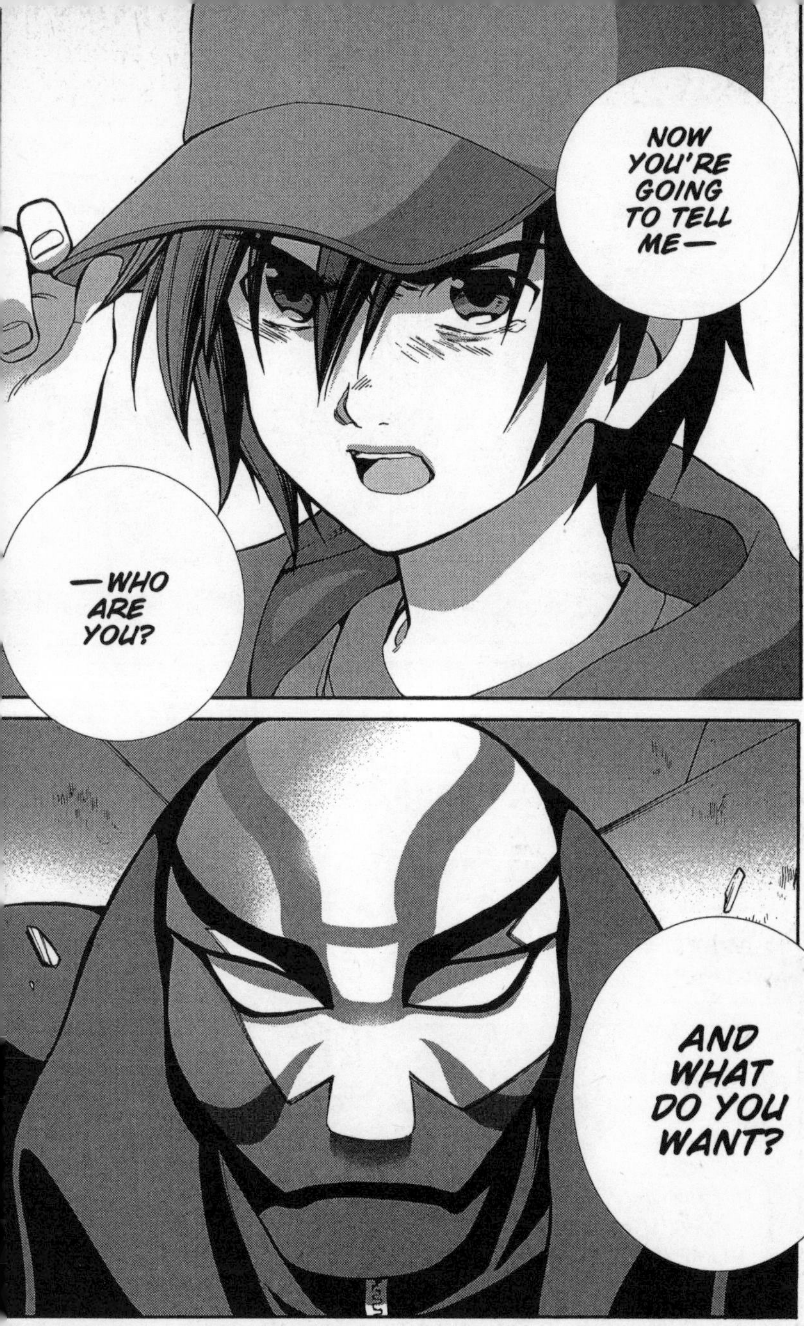
NOW YOU'RE GOING TO TELL ME—
—WHO ARE YOU?
AND WHAT DO YOU WANT?

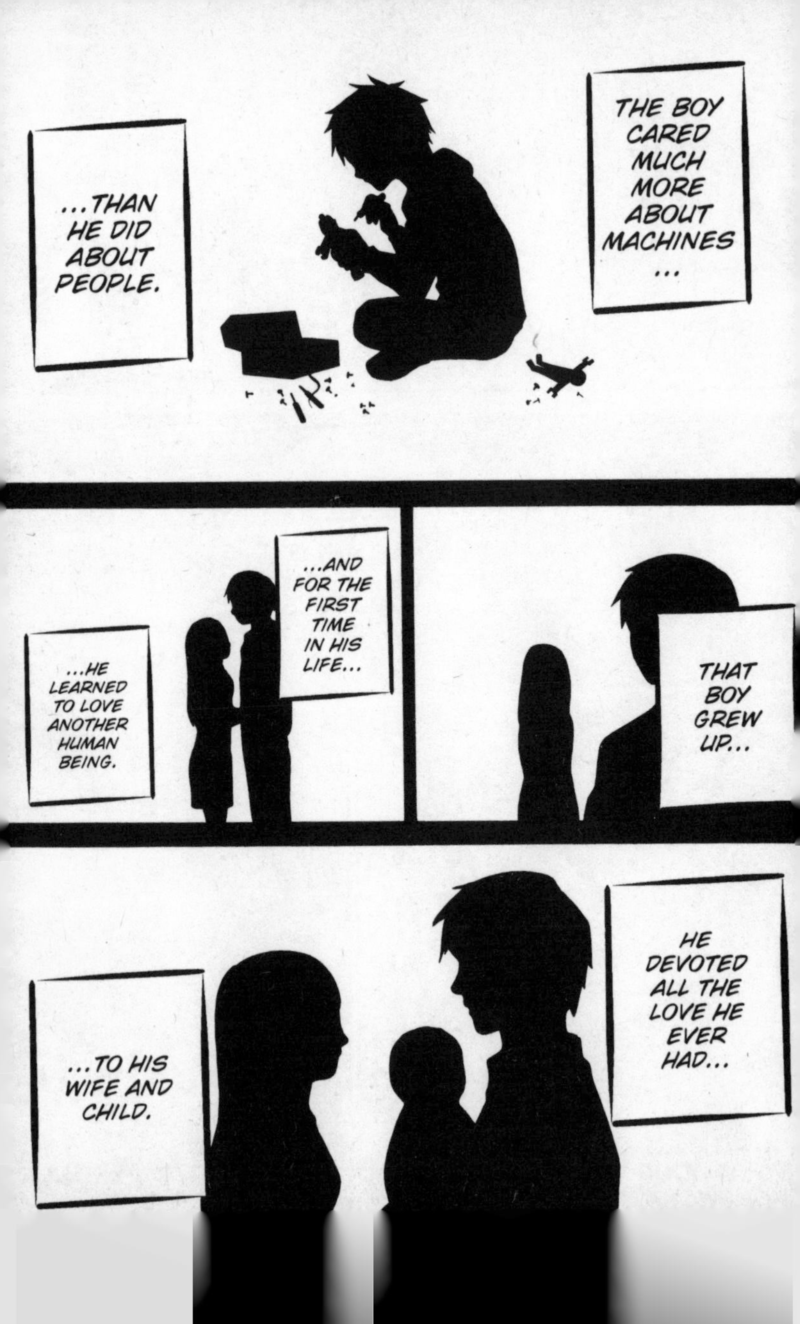
THE BOY CARED MUCH MORE ABOUT MACHINES ...
...THAN HE DID ABOUT PEOPLE.
THAT BOY GREW UP...
...AND FOR THE FIRST TIME IN HIS LIFE...
...HE LEARNED TO LOVE ANOTHER HUMAN BEING.
HE DEVOTED ALL THE LOVE HE EVER HAD...
...TO HIS WIFE AND CHILD.

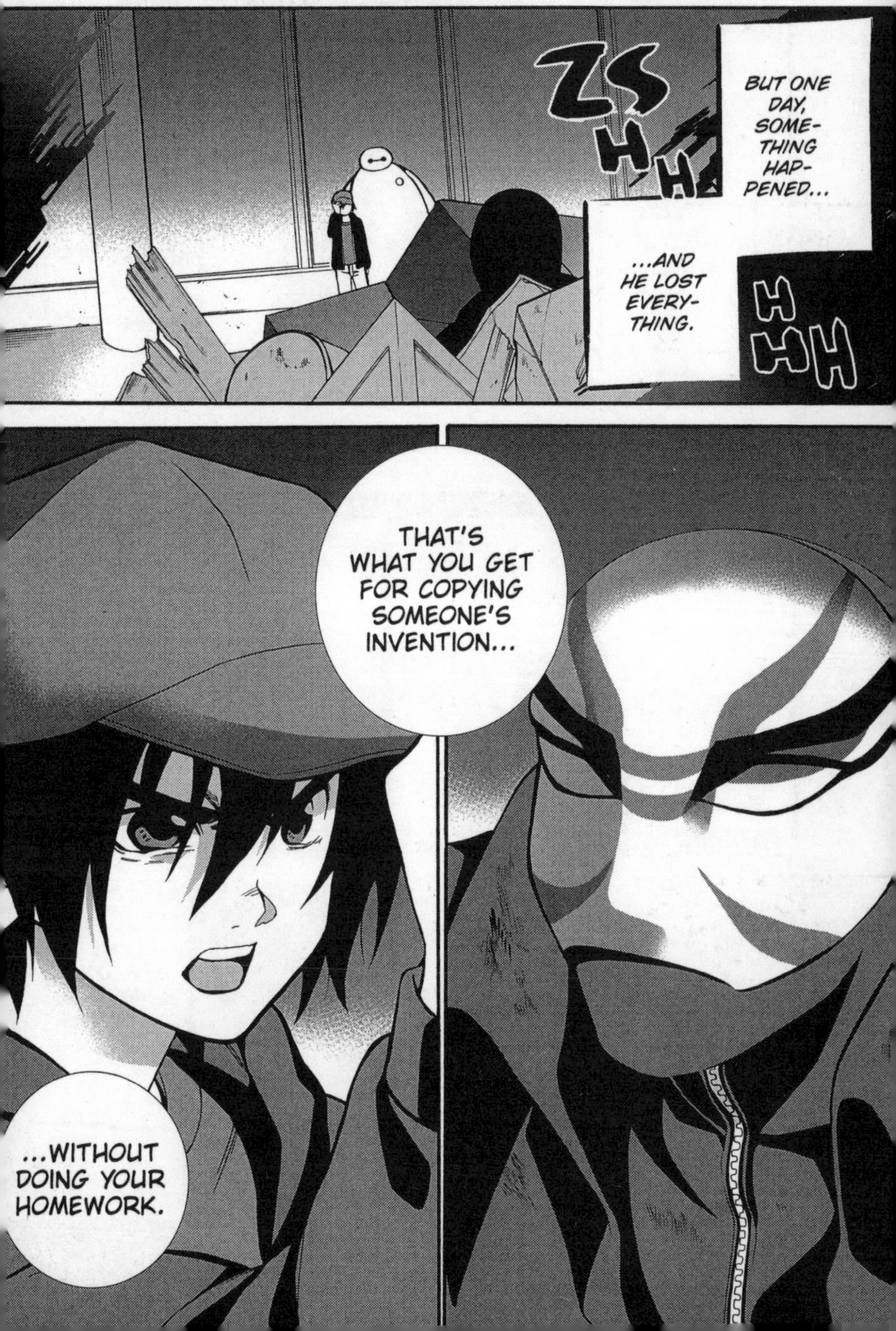
BUT ONE DAY, SOMETHING HAPPENED...
ZSHHH
...AND HE LOST EVERYTHING.
HHHH
THAT'S WHAT YOU GET FOR COPYING SOMEONE'S INVENTION...
...WITHOUT DOING YOUR HOMEWORK.

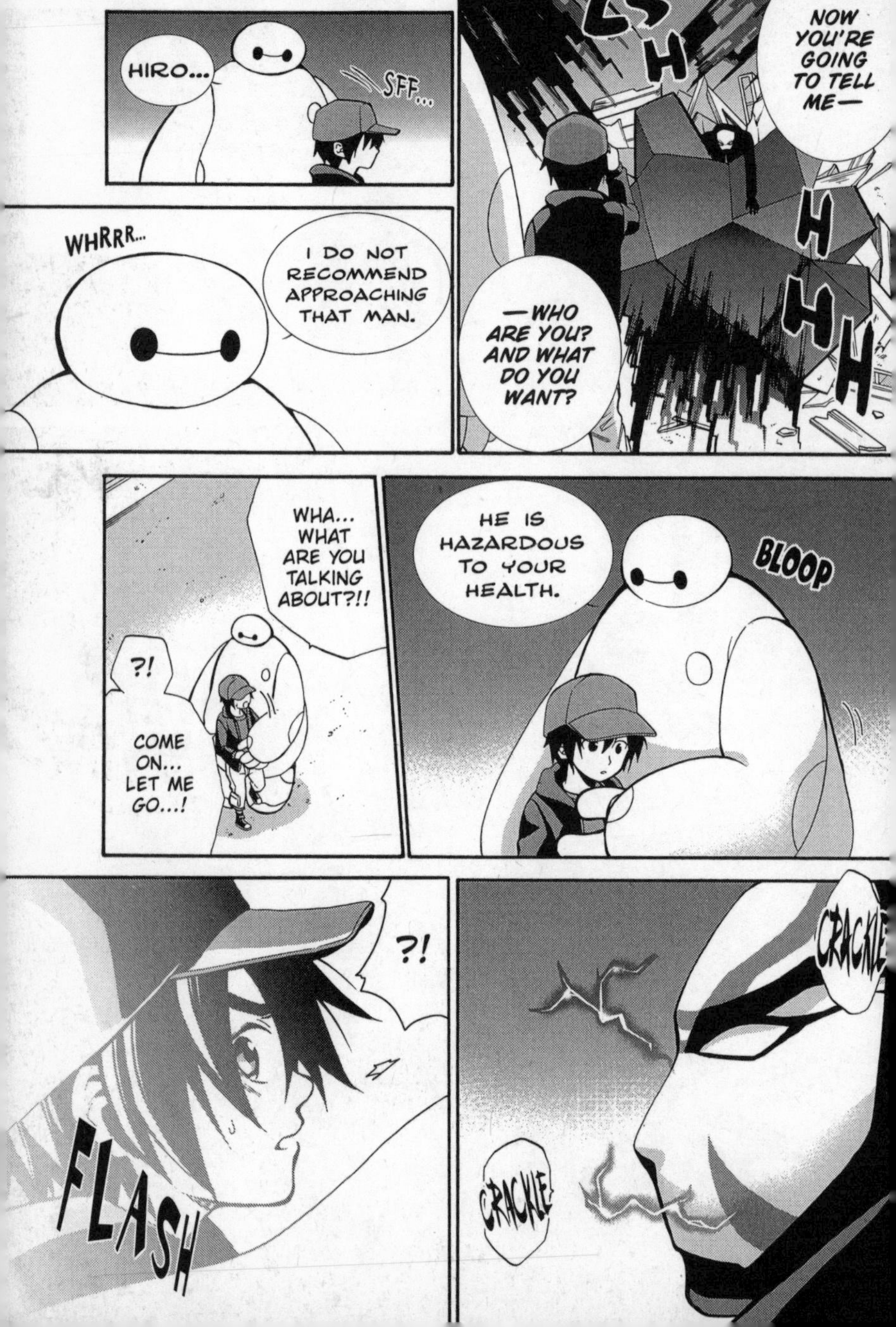
ZSHHHHH
NOW YOU'RE GOING TO TELL ME—
—WHO ARE YOU? AND WHAT DO YOU WANT?
HIRO...
SFF...
WHRRR...
I DO NOT RECOMMEND APPROACHING THAT MAN.
HE IS HAZARDOUS TO YOUR HEALTH.
BLOOP
WHA... WHAT ARE YOU TALKING ABOUT?!!
?!
COME ON... LET ME GO...!
CRACKLE
CRACKLE
?!
FLASH

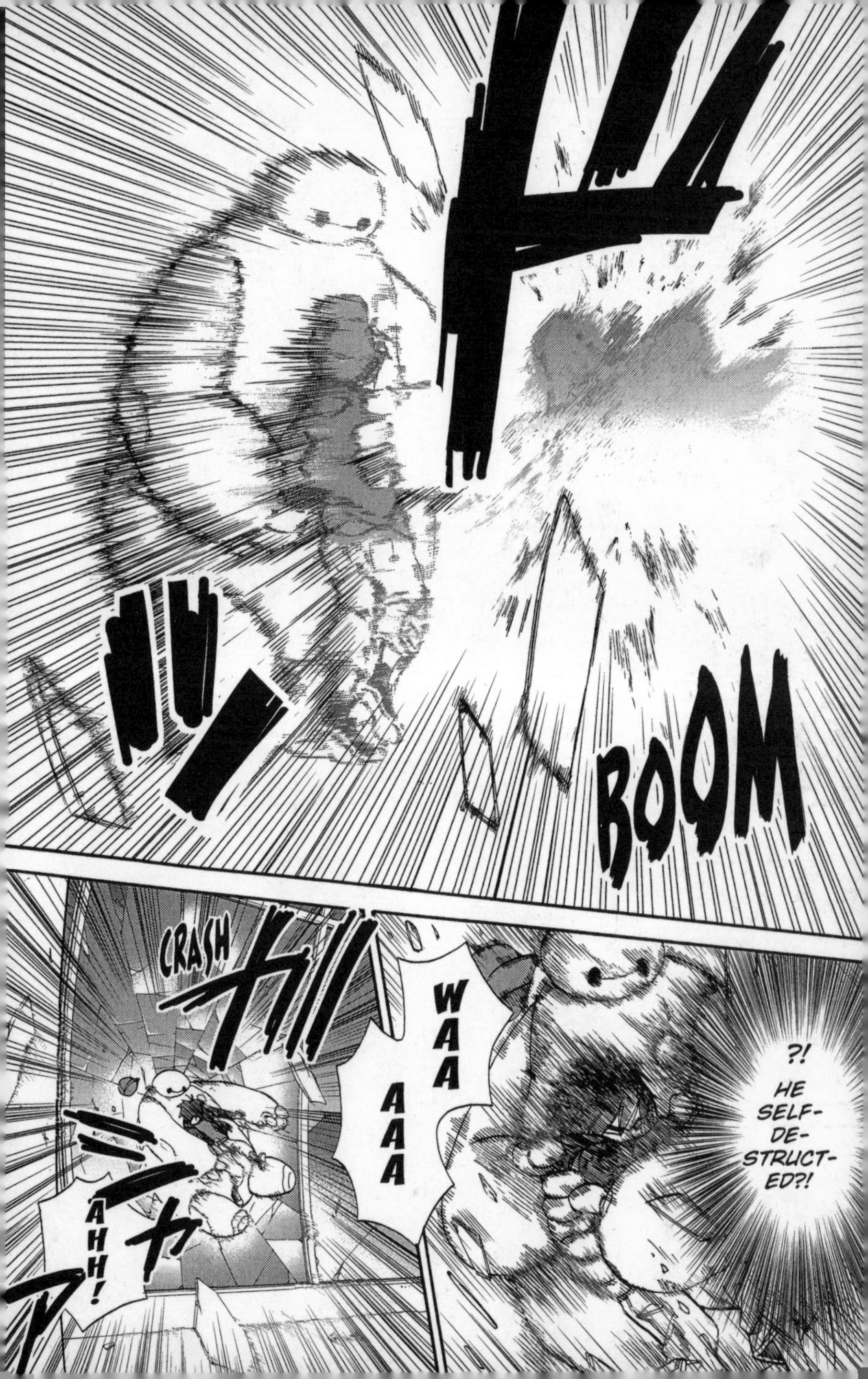
BOOM
?! HE SELF-DESTRUCTED?!
WAAAAAAA
CRASH
AHH!

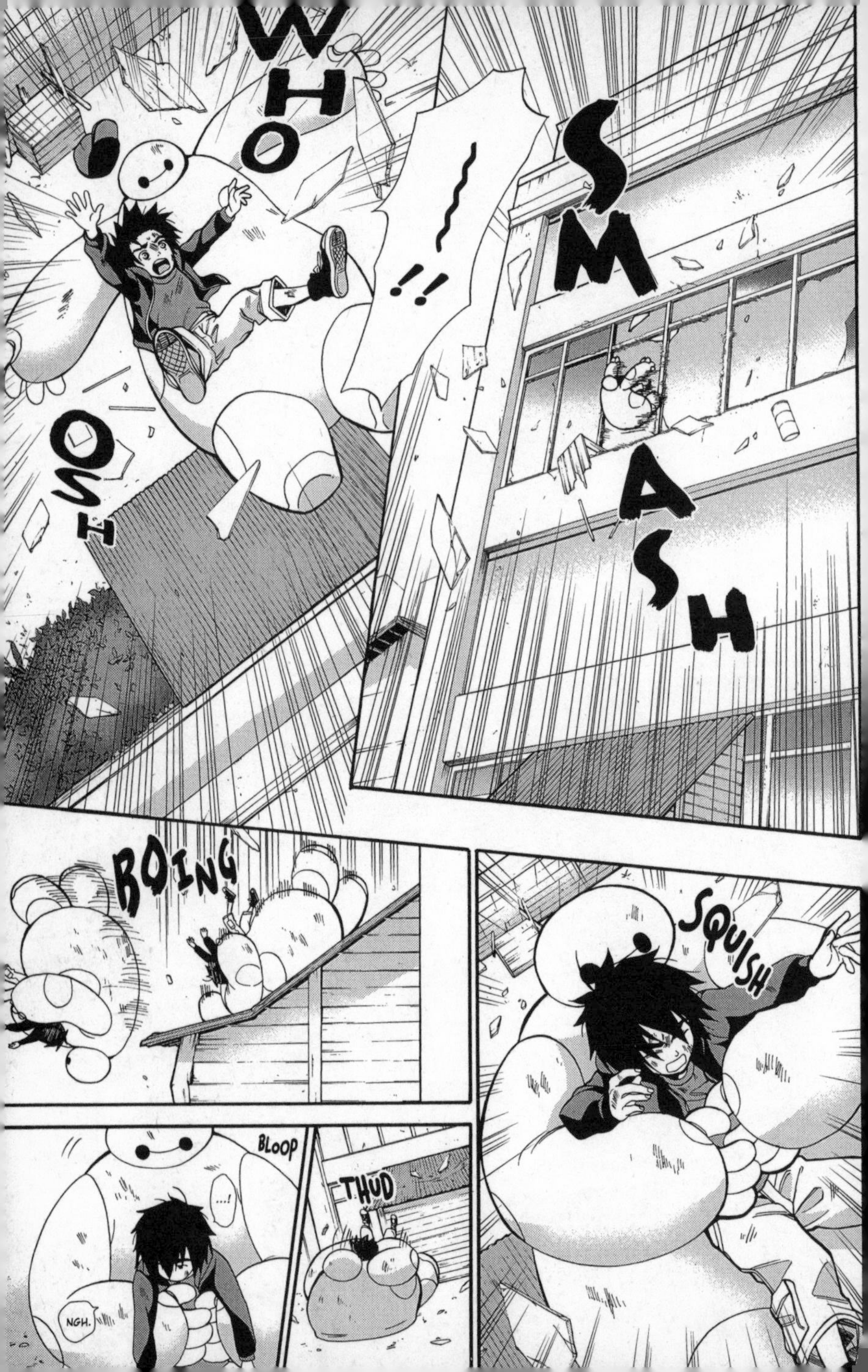
SMASH
—!!
WHOOSH
SQUISH
BOING
THUD
BLOOP
...!
NGH.

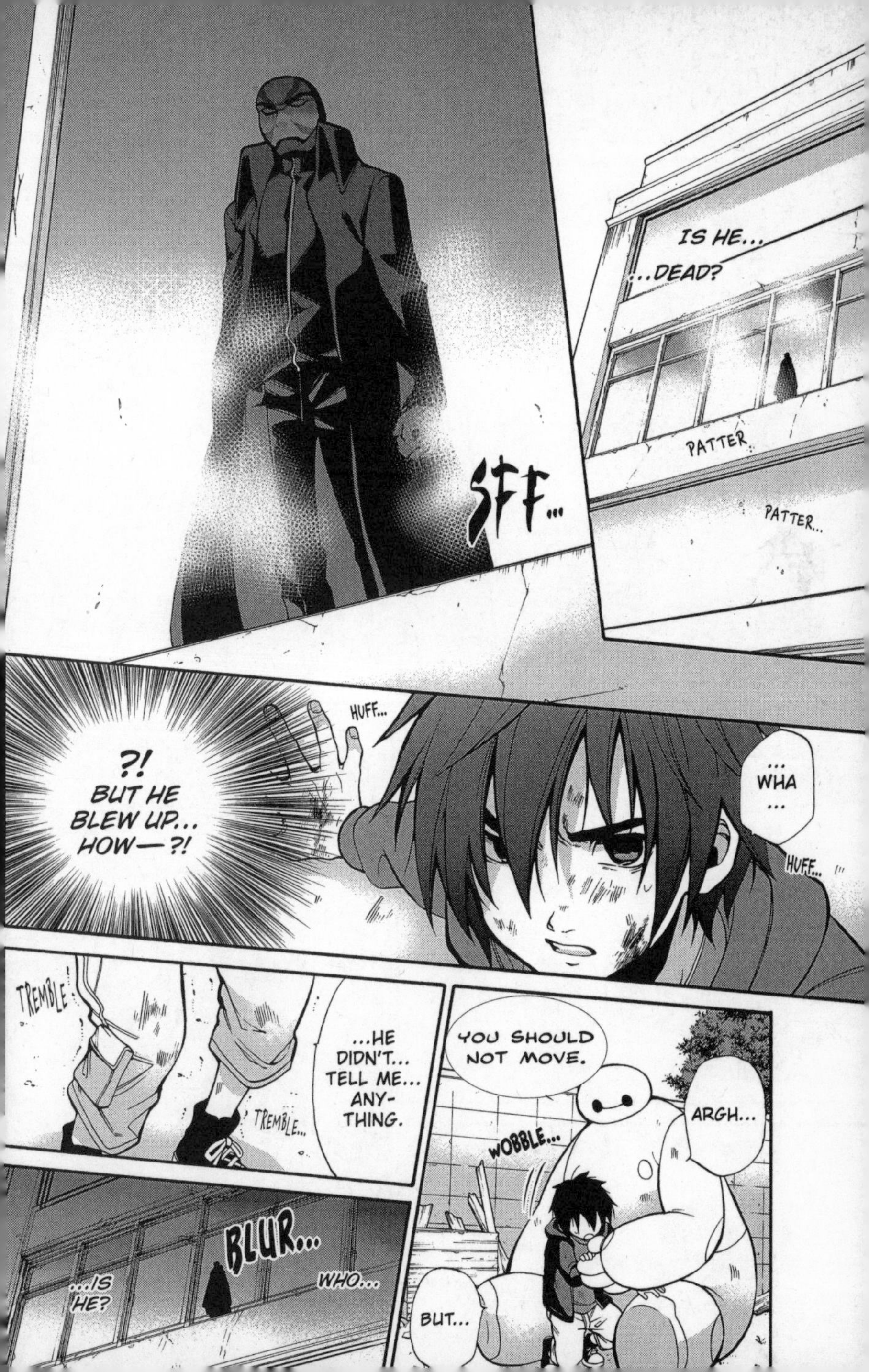
IS HE...
...DEAD?
PATTER
PATTER...
SFF...
... WHA ...
HUFF...
HUFF...
?! BUT HE BLEW UP... HOW—?!
ARGH...
YOU SHOULD NOT MOVE.
WOBBLE...
BUT...
TREMBLE
...HE DIDN'T... TELL ME... ANYTHING.
TREMBLE...
BLUR...
WHO...
...IS HE?

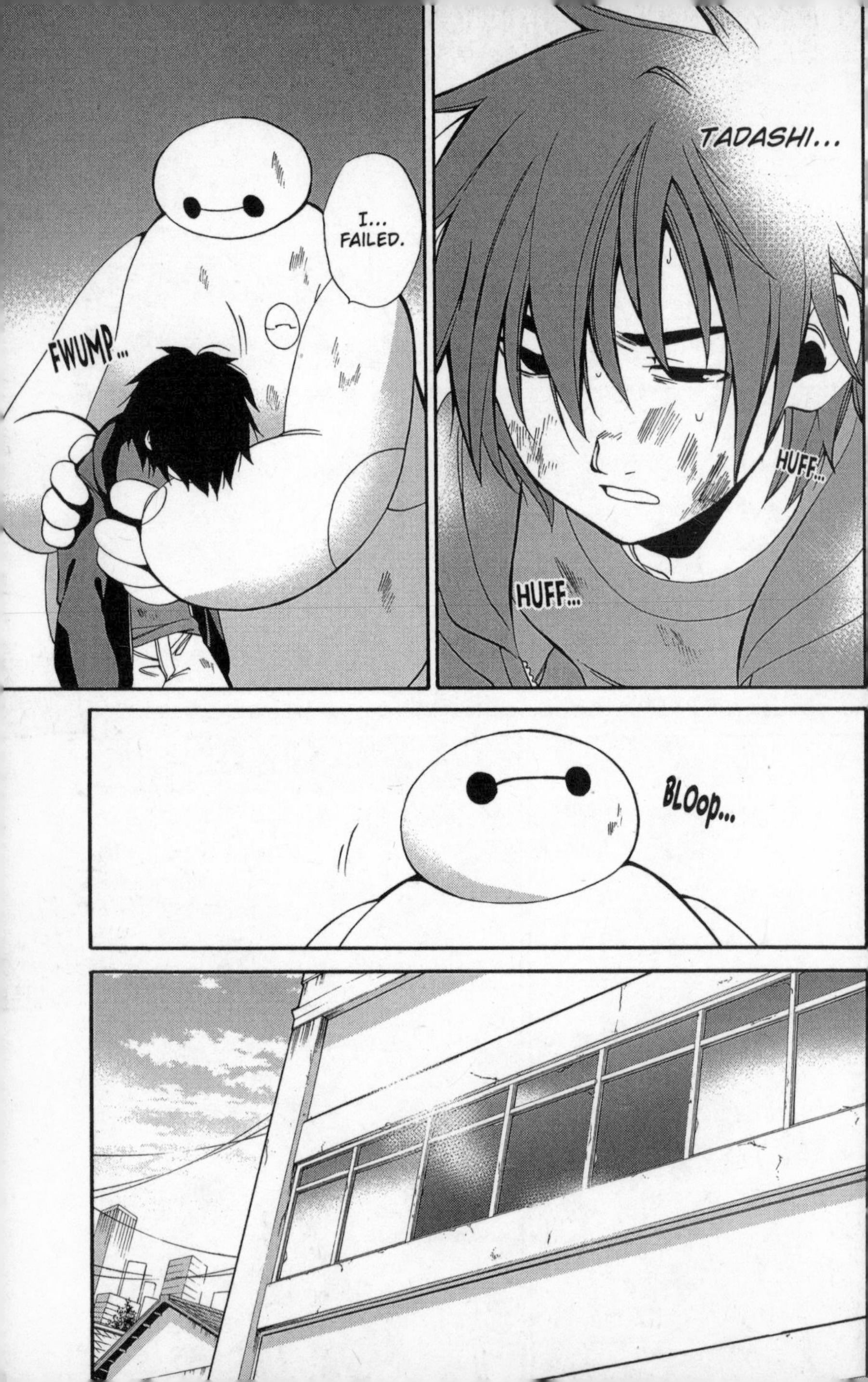
TADASHI...
HUFF...
HUFF...
I... FAILED.
FWUMP...
BLOOP...

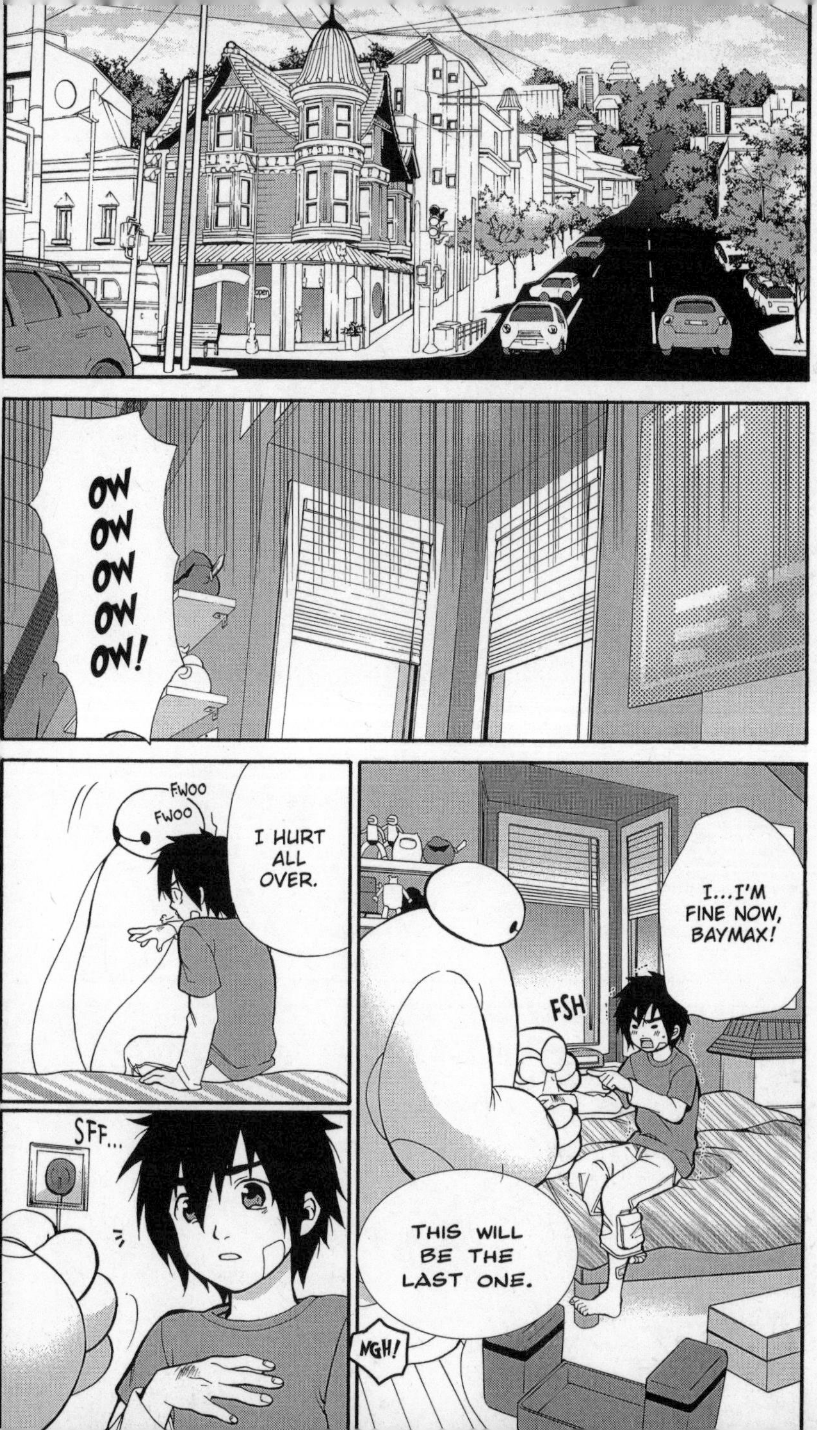
OW OW OW OW OW!
I...I'M FINE NOW, BAYMAX!
FSH
THIS WILL BE THE LAST ONE.
NGH!
FWOO
FWOO
I HURT ALL OVER.
SFF...

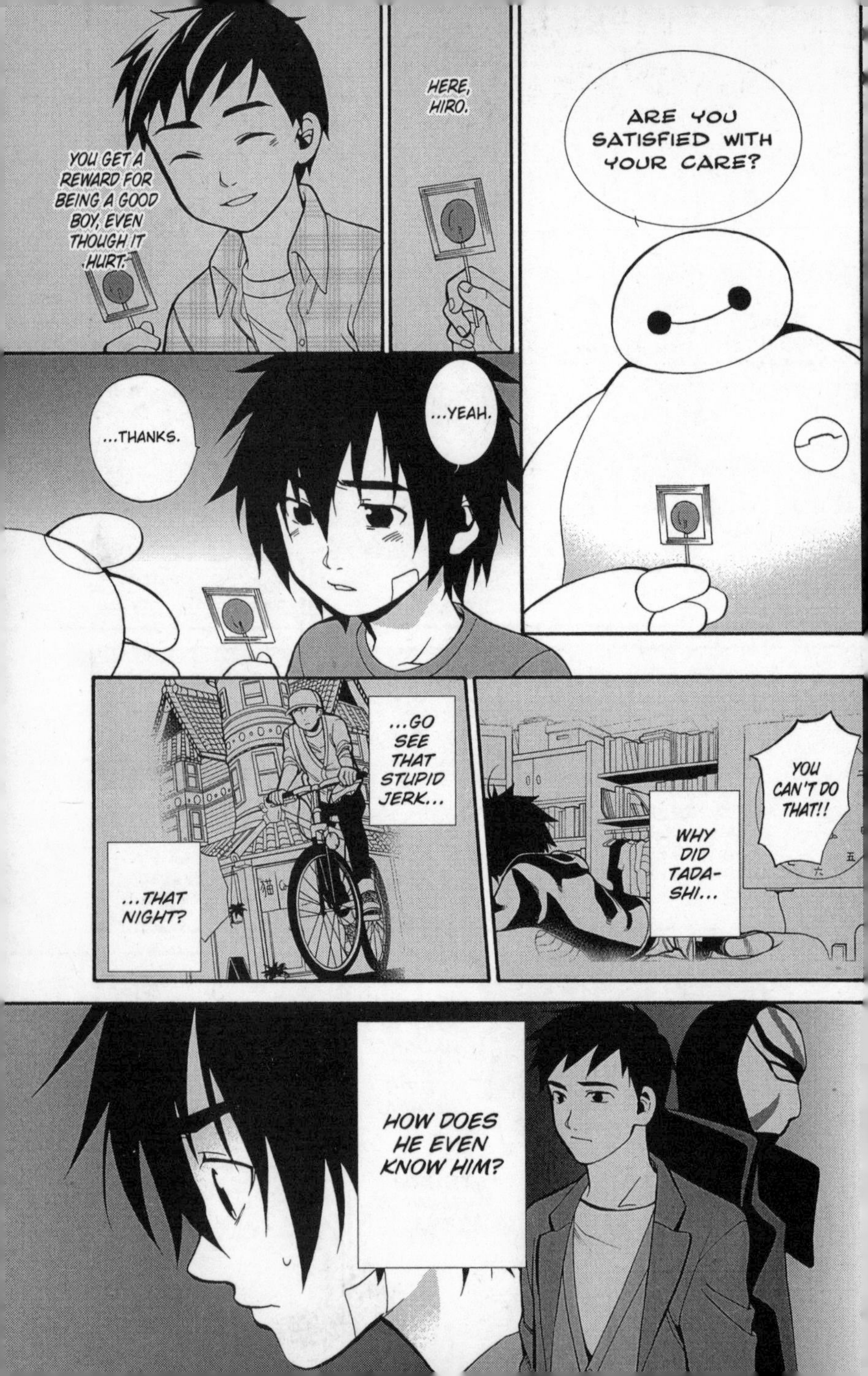

ARE YOU SATISFIED WITH YOUR CARE?
HERE, HIRO.
YOU GET A REWARD FOR BEING A GOOD BOY, EVEN THOUGH IT HURT.
...YEAH.
...THANKS.
YOU CAN'T DO THAT!!
WHY DID TADA-SHI...
...GO SEE THAT STUPID JERK...
...THAT NIGHT?
HOW DOES HE EVEN KNOW HIM?

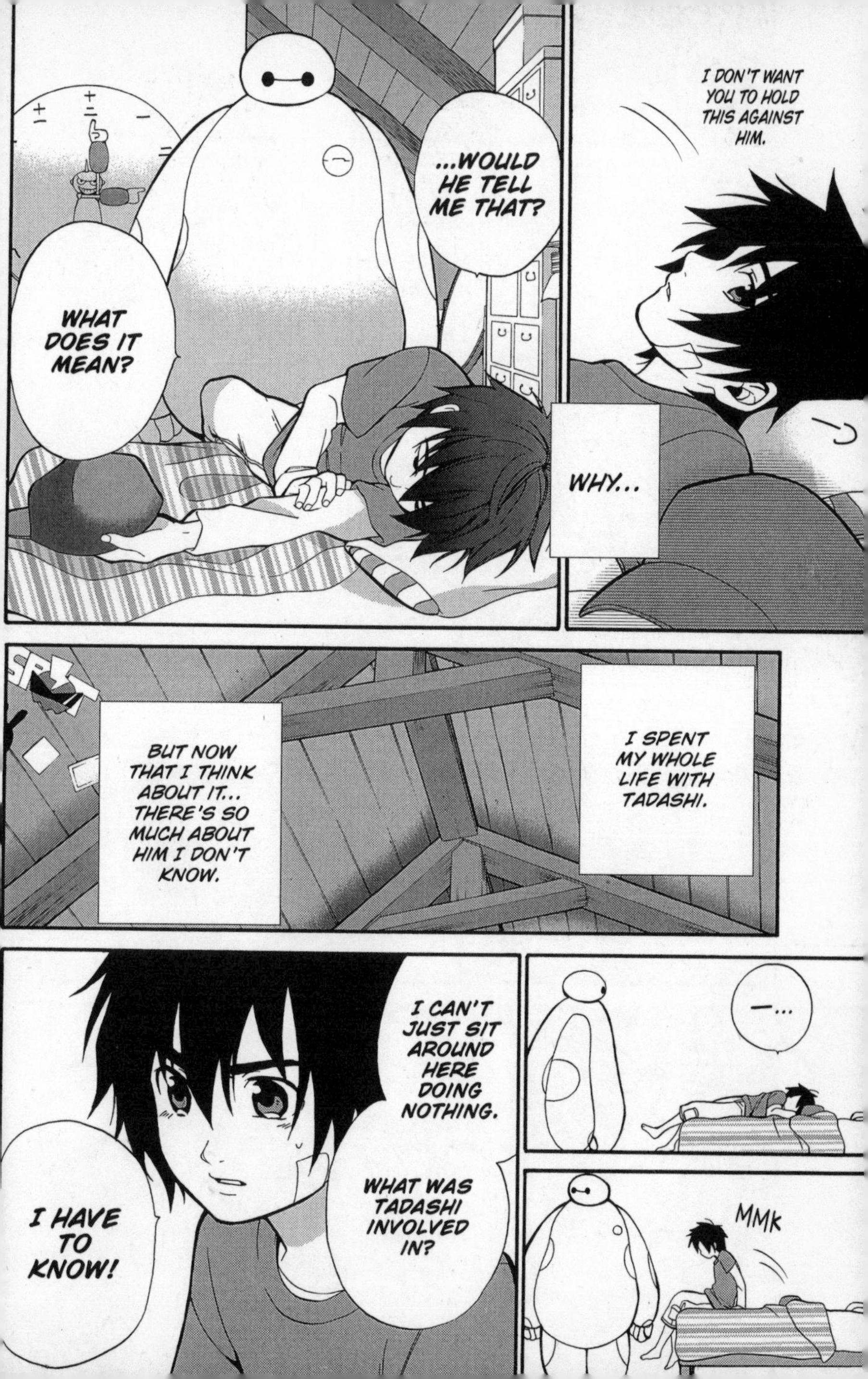
I DON'T WANT YOU TO HOLD THIS AGAINST HIM.
WHY...
...WOULD HE TELL ME THAT?
WHAT DOES IT MEAN?
I SPENT MY WHOLE LIFE WITH TADASHI.
BUT NOW THAT I THINK ABOUT IT... THERE'S SO MUCH ABOUT HIM I DON'T KNOW.
—...
MMK
I CAN'T JUST SIT AROUND HERE DOING NOTHING.
WHAT WAS TADASHI INVOLVED IN?
I HAVE TO KNOW!

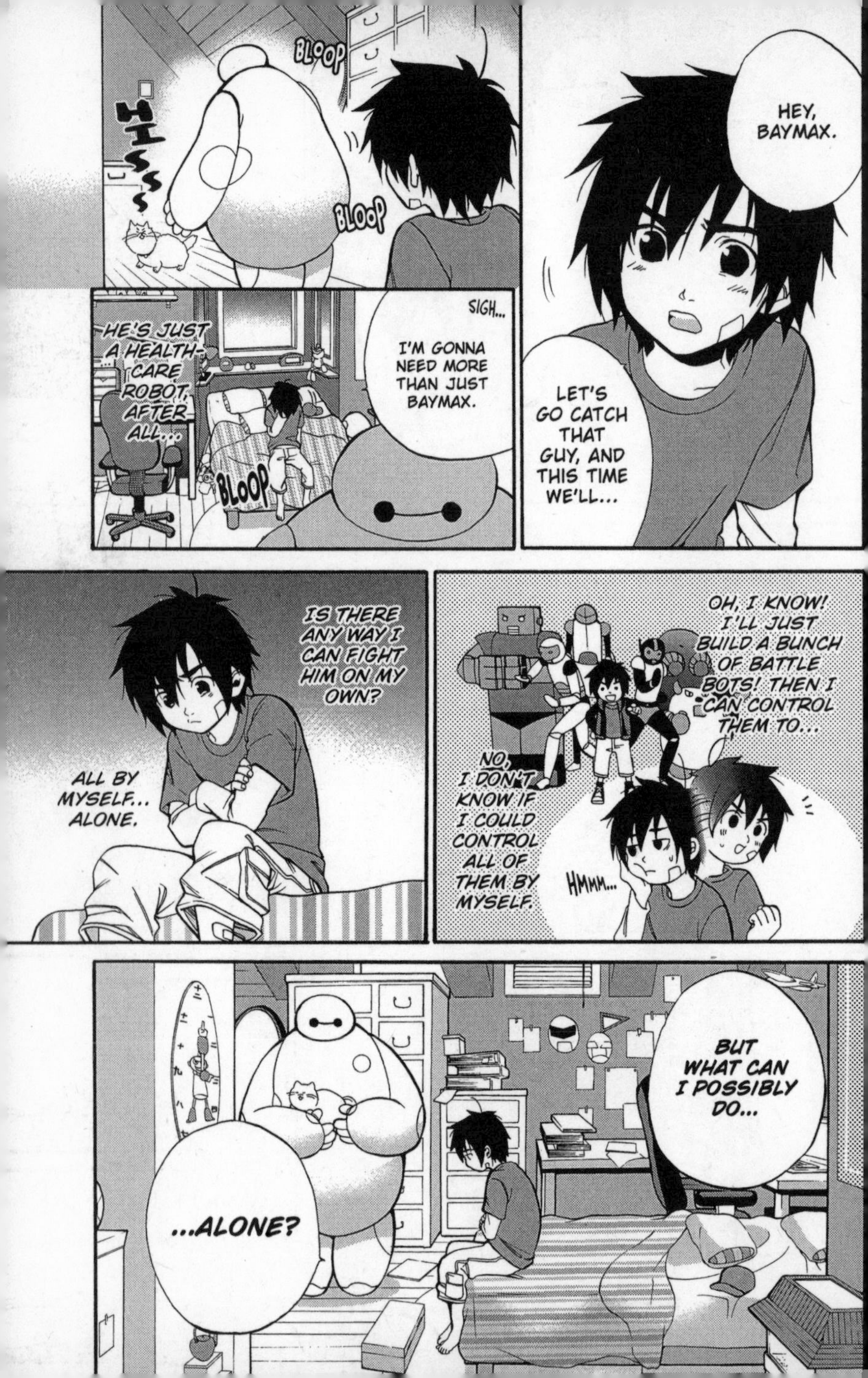
HEY, BAYMAX.
LET'S GO CATCH THAT GUY, AND THIS TIME WE'LL...
BLOOP
HISSS
BLOOP
SIGH...
I'M GONNA NEED MORE THAN JUST BAYMAX.
HE'S JUST A HEALTH-CARE ROBOT, AFTER ALL...
BLOOP
OH, I KNOW! I'LL JUST BUILD A BUNCH OF BATTLE BOTS! THEN I CAN CONTROL THEM TO...
HMMM...
NO, I DON'T KNOW IF I COULD CONTROL ALL OF THEM BY MYSELF.
IS THERE ANY WAY I CAN FIGHT HIM ON MY OWN?
ALL BY MYSELF... ALONE.
BUT WHAT CAN I POSSIBLY DO...
...ALONE?

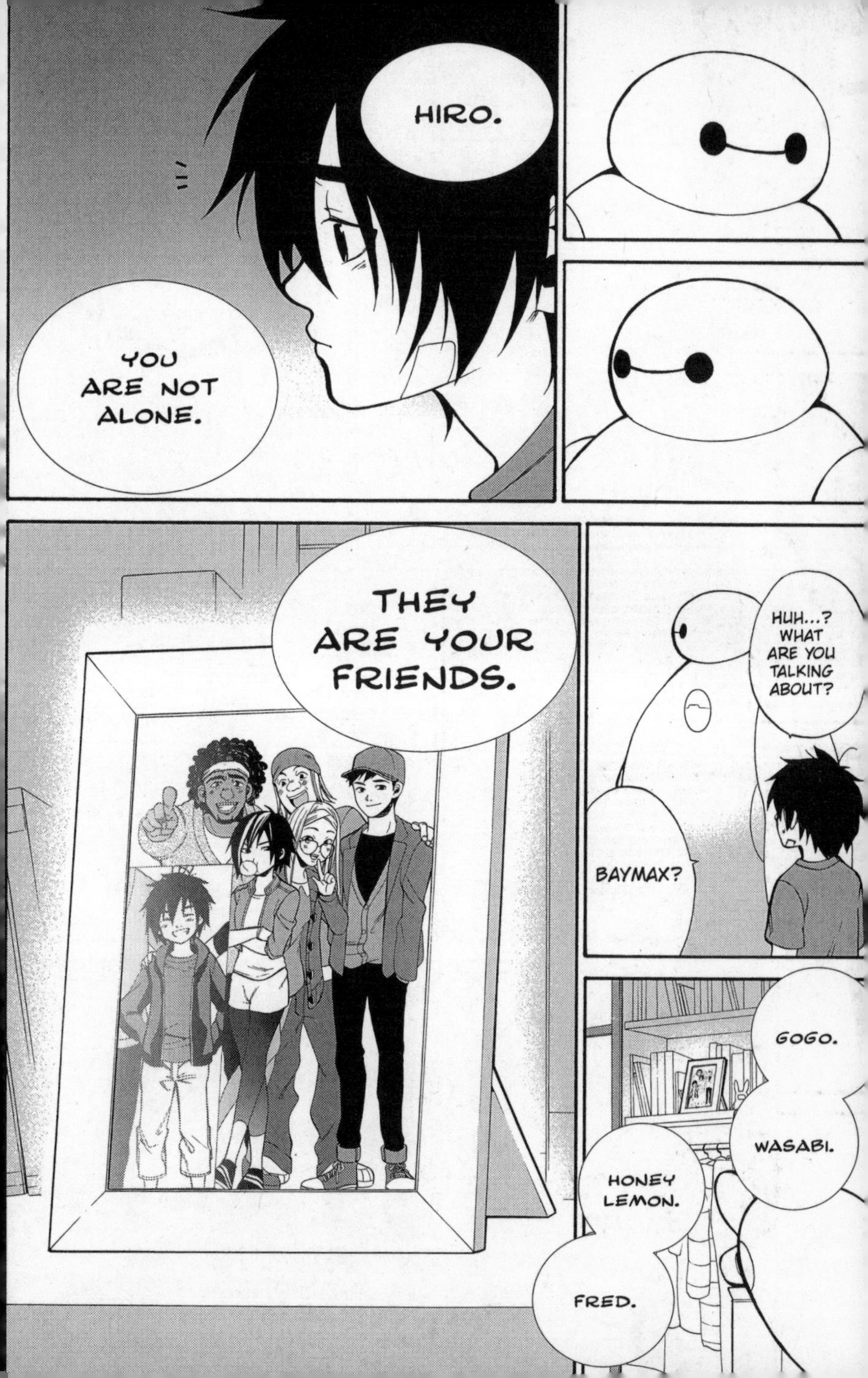
HIRO.
YOU ARE NOT ALONE.
HUH...? WHAT ARE YOU TALKING ABOUT?
BAYMAX?
GOGO.
WASABI.
HONEY LEMON.
FRED.
THEY ARE YOUR FRIENDS.

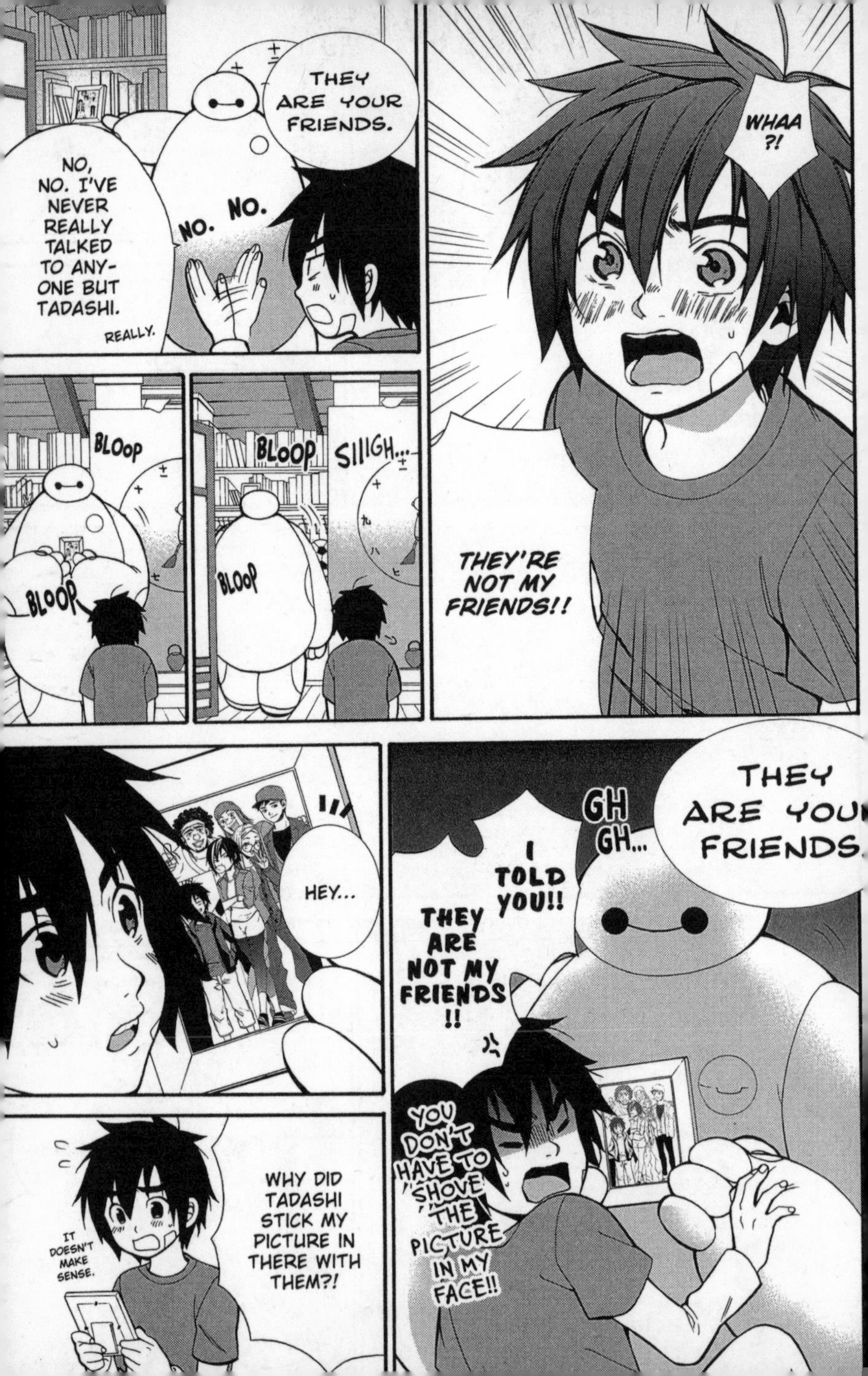
WHAA ?!
THEY'RE NOT MY FRIENDS!!
THEY ARE YOUR FRIENDS.
NO. NO.
NO, NO. I'VE NEVER REALLY TALKED TO ANY-ONE BUT TADASHI.
REALLY.
SIIIGH...
BLOOP
BLOOP
BLOOP
BLOOP
THEY ARE YOUR FRIENDS.
GH GH...
I TOLD YOU!!
THEY ARE NOT MY FRIENDS!!
YOU DON'T HAVE TO "SHOVE" THE PICTURE IN MY FACE!!
HEY...
WHY DID TADASHI STICK MY PICTURE IN THERE WITH THEM?!
IT DOESN'T MAKE SENSE.

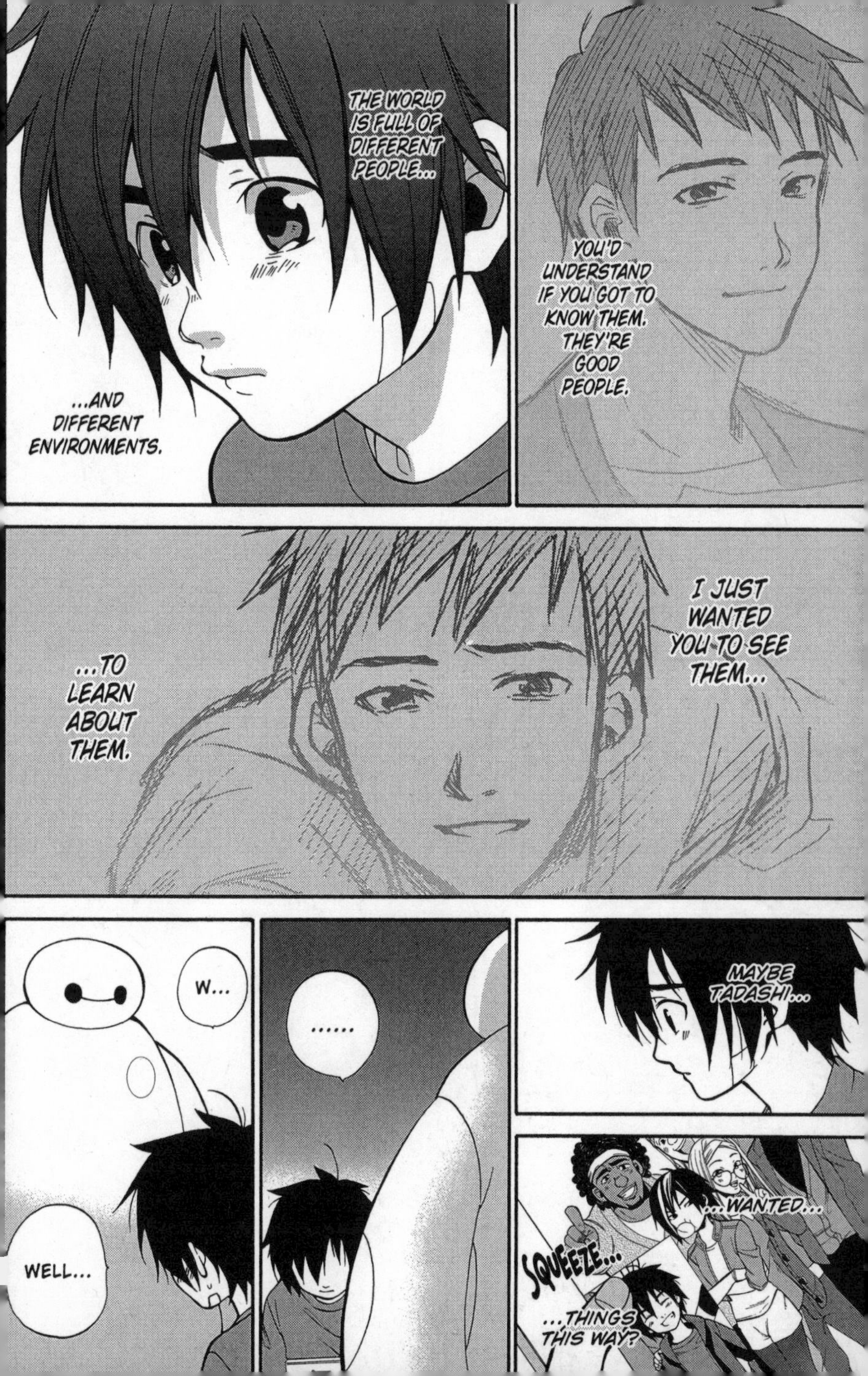
YOU'D UNDERSTAND IF YOU GOT TO KNOW THEM. THEY'RE GOOD PEOPLE.
THE WORLD IS FULL OF DIFFERENT PEOPLE...
...AND DIFFERENT ENVIRONMENTS.
I JUST WANTED YOU TO SEE THEM...
...TO LEARN ABOUT THEM.
MAYBE TADASHI...
...WANTED...
SQUEEZE...
...THINGS THIS WAY?
......
W...
WELL...

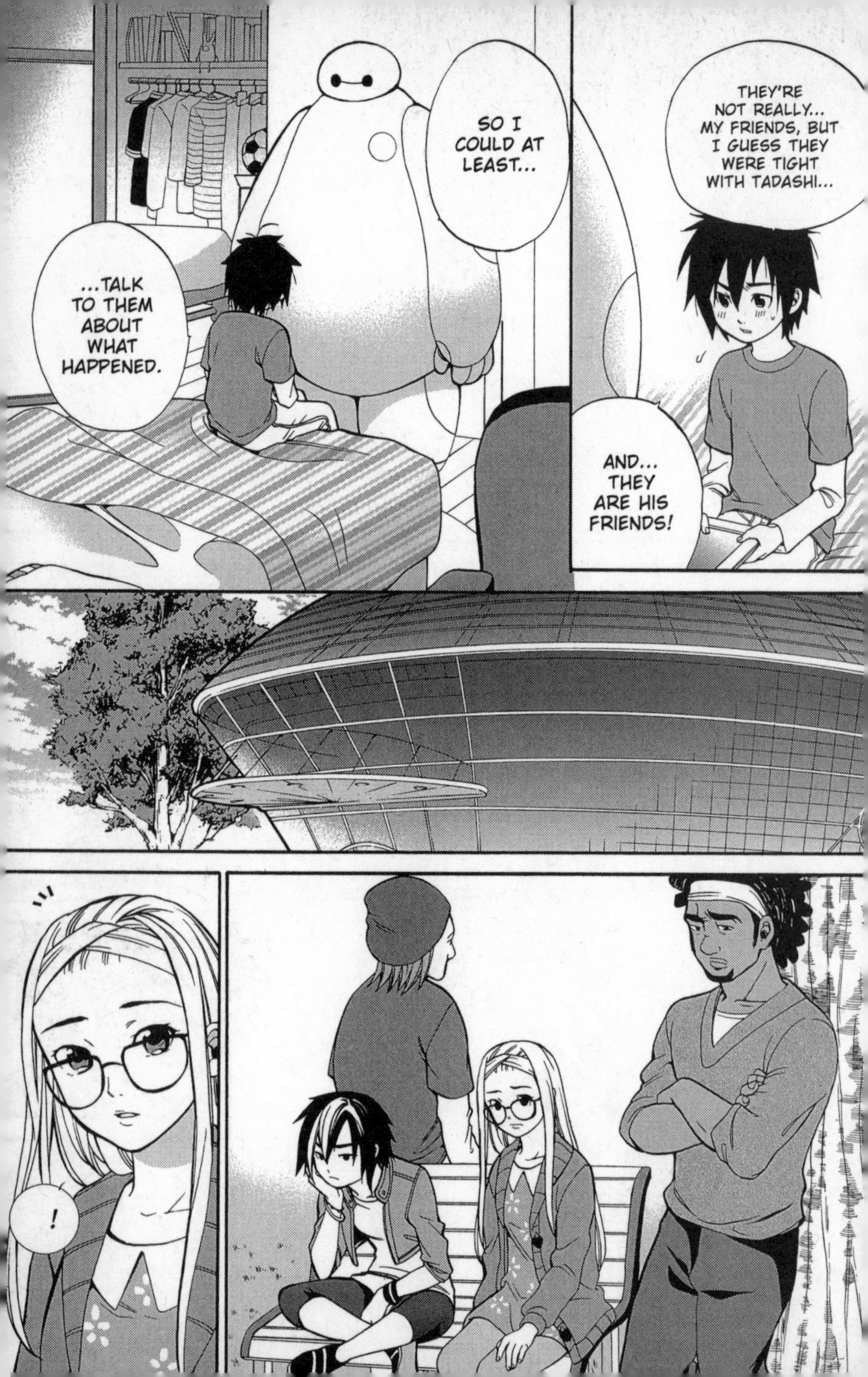
THEY'RE NOT REALLY... MY FRIENDS, BUT I GUESS THEY WERE TIGHT WITH TADASHI...
AND... THEY ARE HIS FRIENDS!
SO I COULD AT LEAST...
...TALK TO THEM ABOUT WHAT HAPPENED.
!

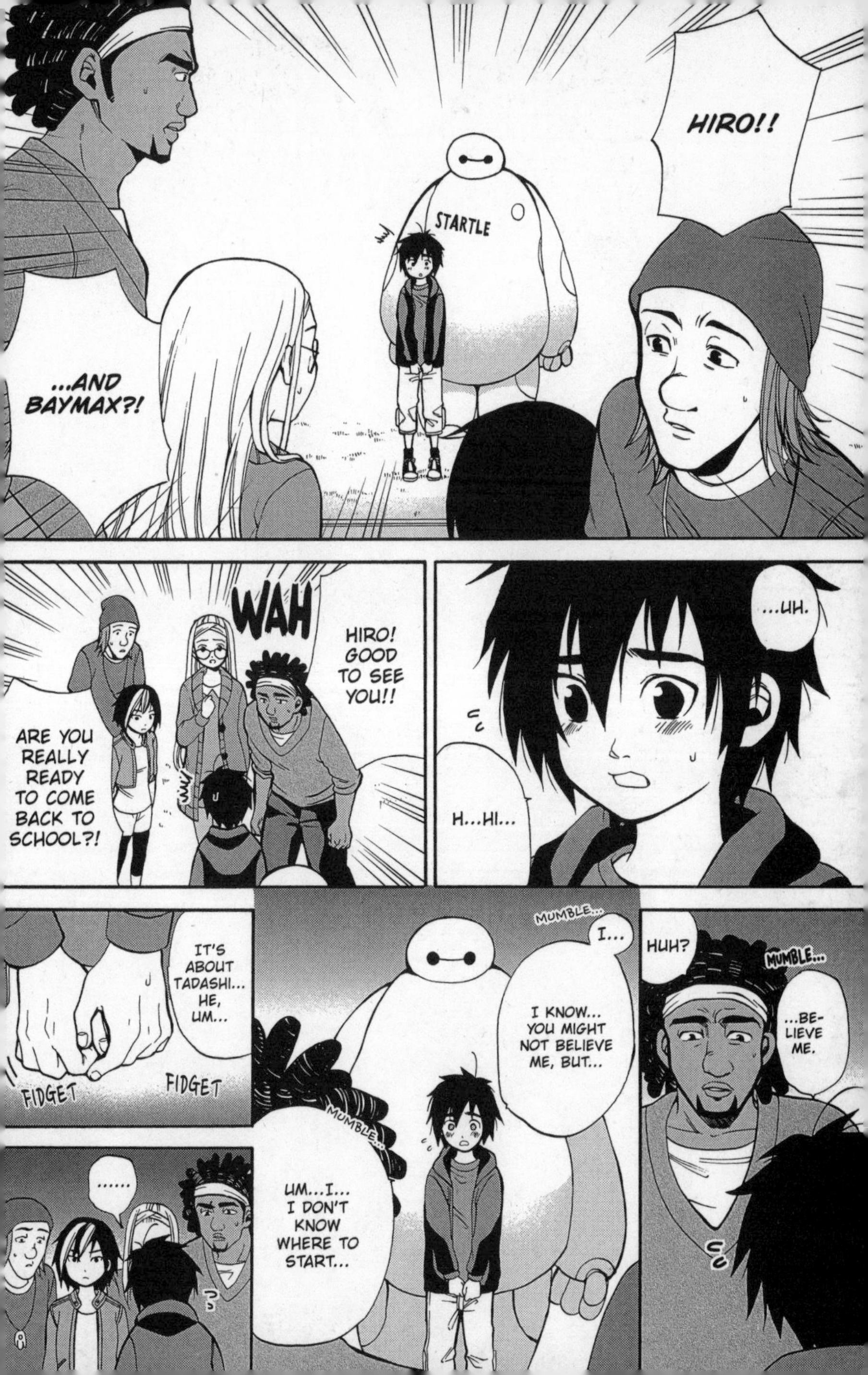
HIRO!!
STARTLE
...AND BAYMAX?!
...UH.
H...HI...
WAH
HIRO! GOOD TO SEE YOU!!
ARE YOU REALLY READY TO COME BACK TO SCHOOL?!
HUH?
MUMBLE...
...BE-LIEVE ME.
MUMBLE...
I...
I KNOW... YOU MIGHT NOT BELIEVE ME, BUT...
MUMBLE...
UM...I... I DON'T KNOW WHERE TO START...
IT'S ABOUT TADASHI... HE, UM...
FIDGET
FIDGET
......

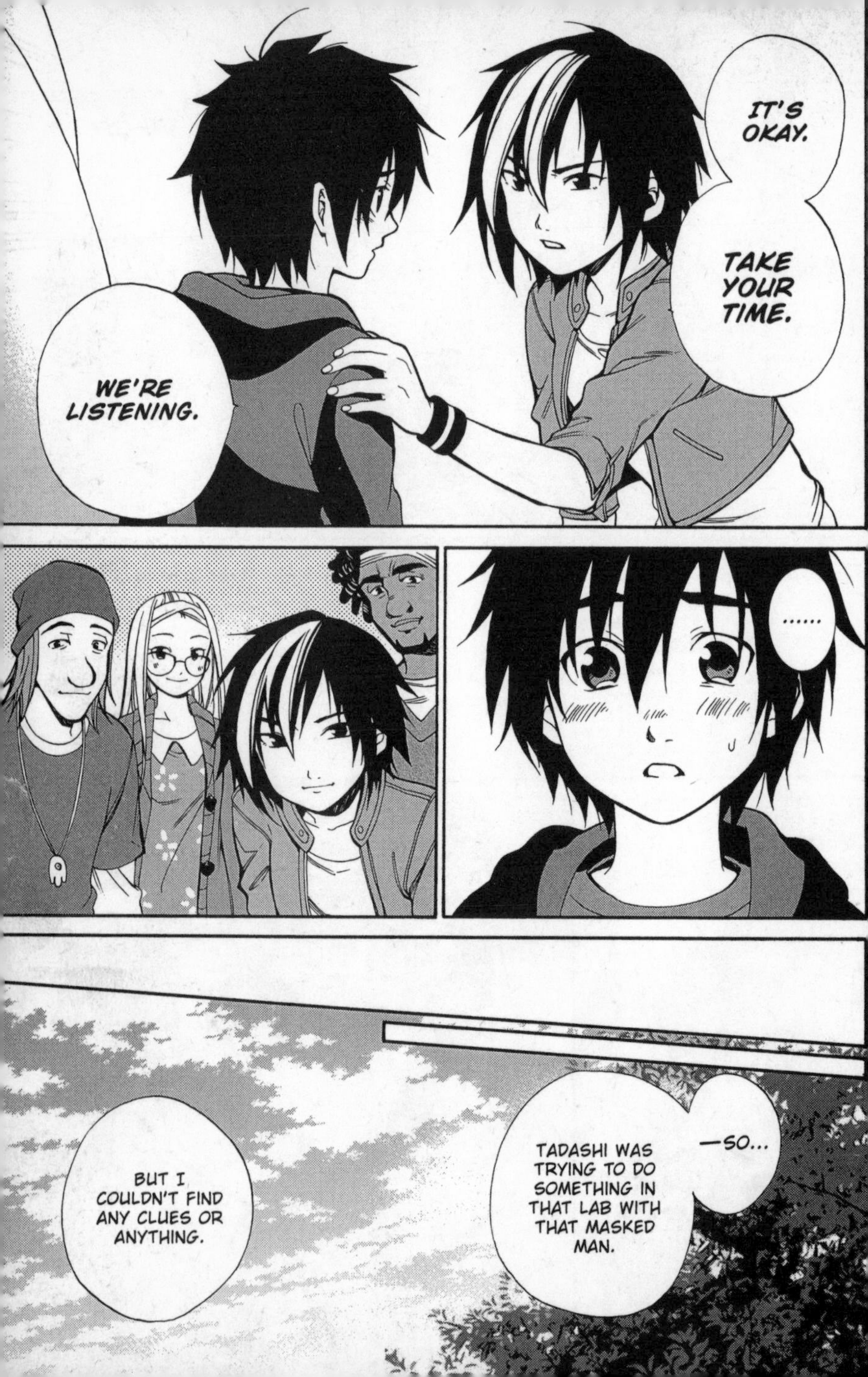
IT'S OKAY.
TAKE YOUR TIME.
WE'RE LISTENING.
......
—SO...
TADASHI WAS TRYING TO DO SOMETHING IN THAT LAB WITH THAT MASKED MAN.
BUT I COULDN'T FIND ANY CLUES OR ANYTHING.

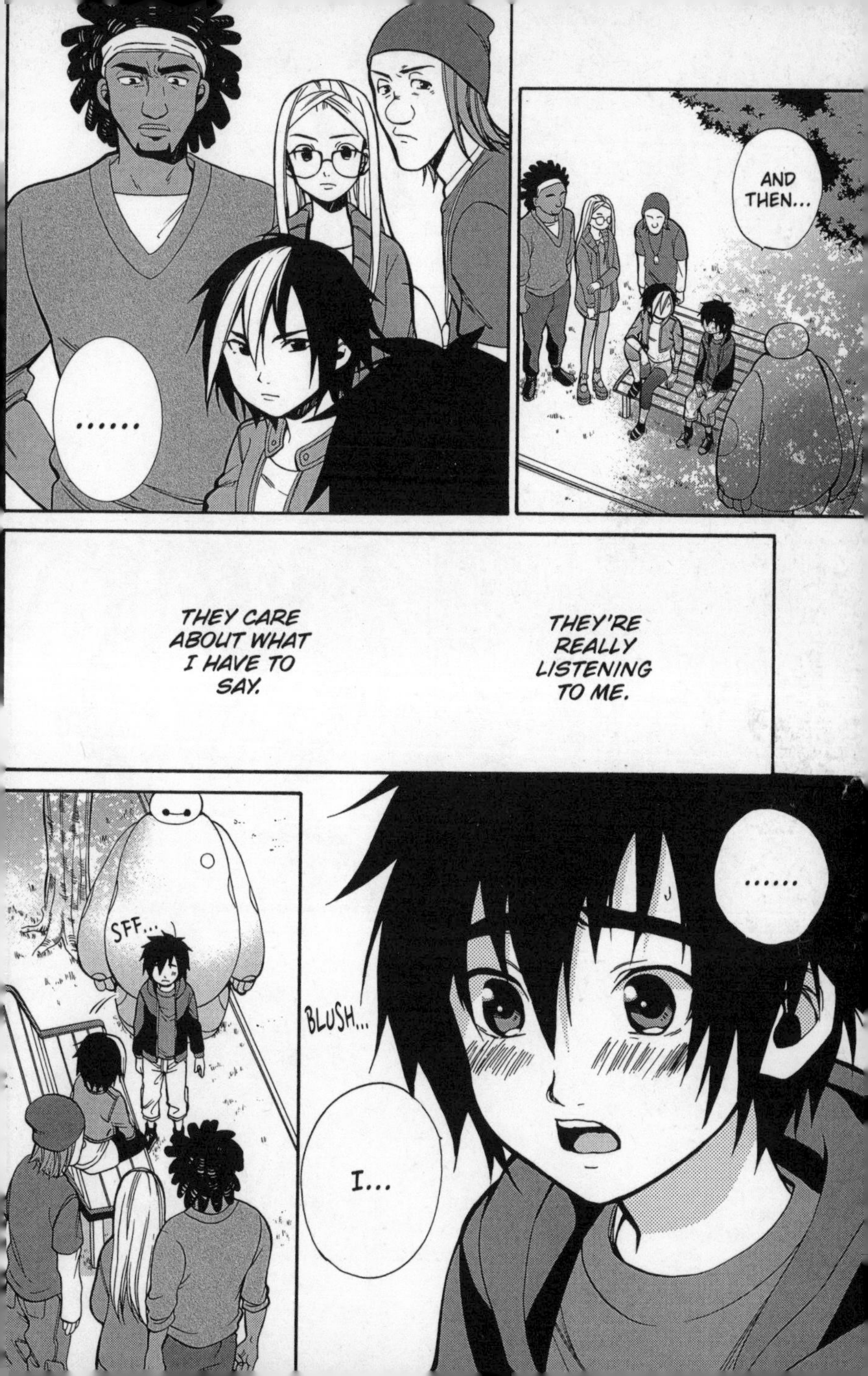
AND THEN...
......
THEY'RE REALLY LISTENING TO ME.
THEY CARE ABOUT WHAT I HAVE TO SAY.
......
BLUSH...
I...
SFF...

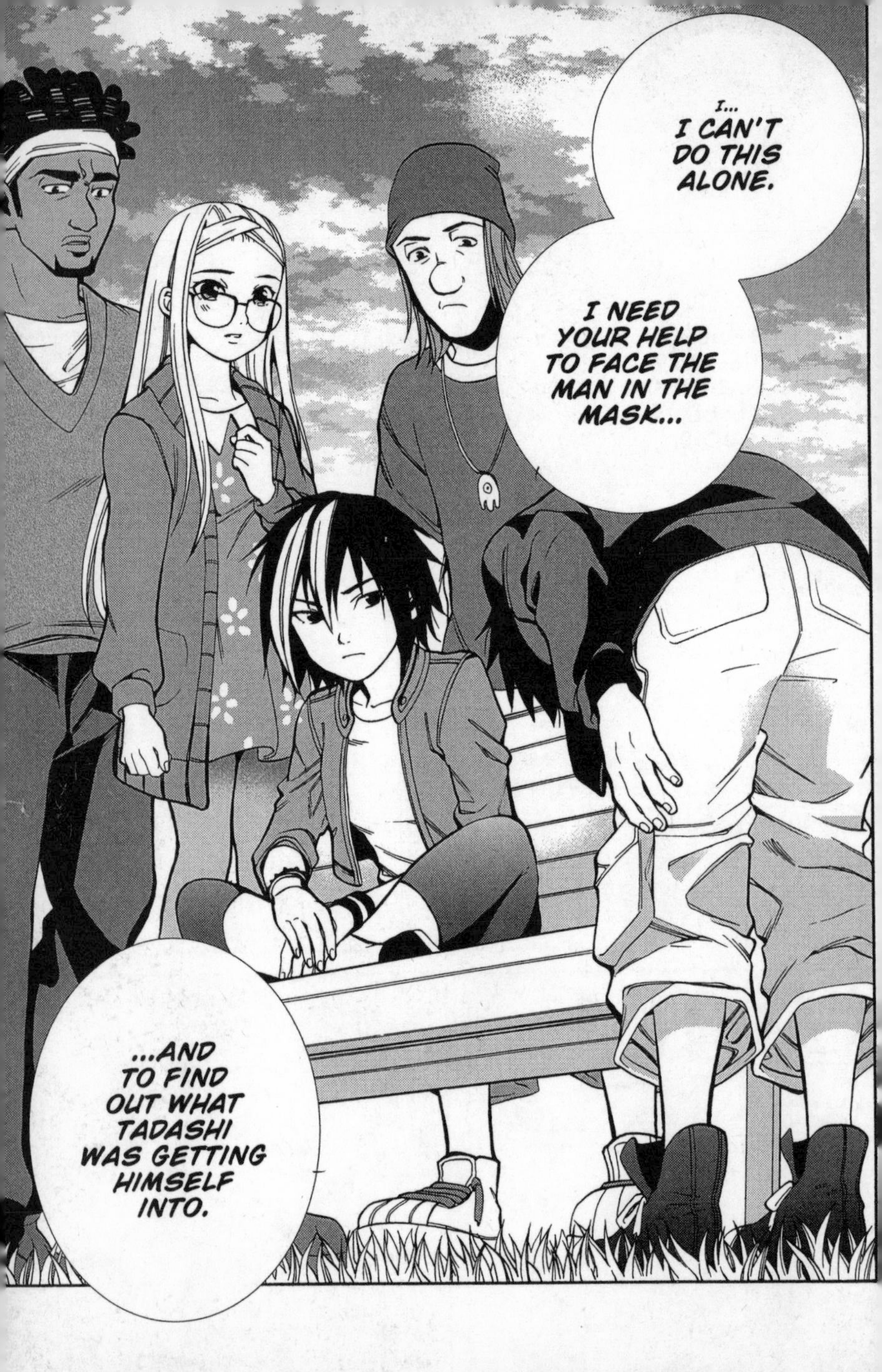
I... I CAN'T DO THIS ALONE.
I NEED YOUR HELP TO FACE THE MAN IN THE MASK...
...AND TO FIND OUT WHAT TADASHI WAS GETTING HIMSELF INTO.

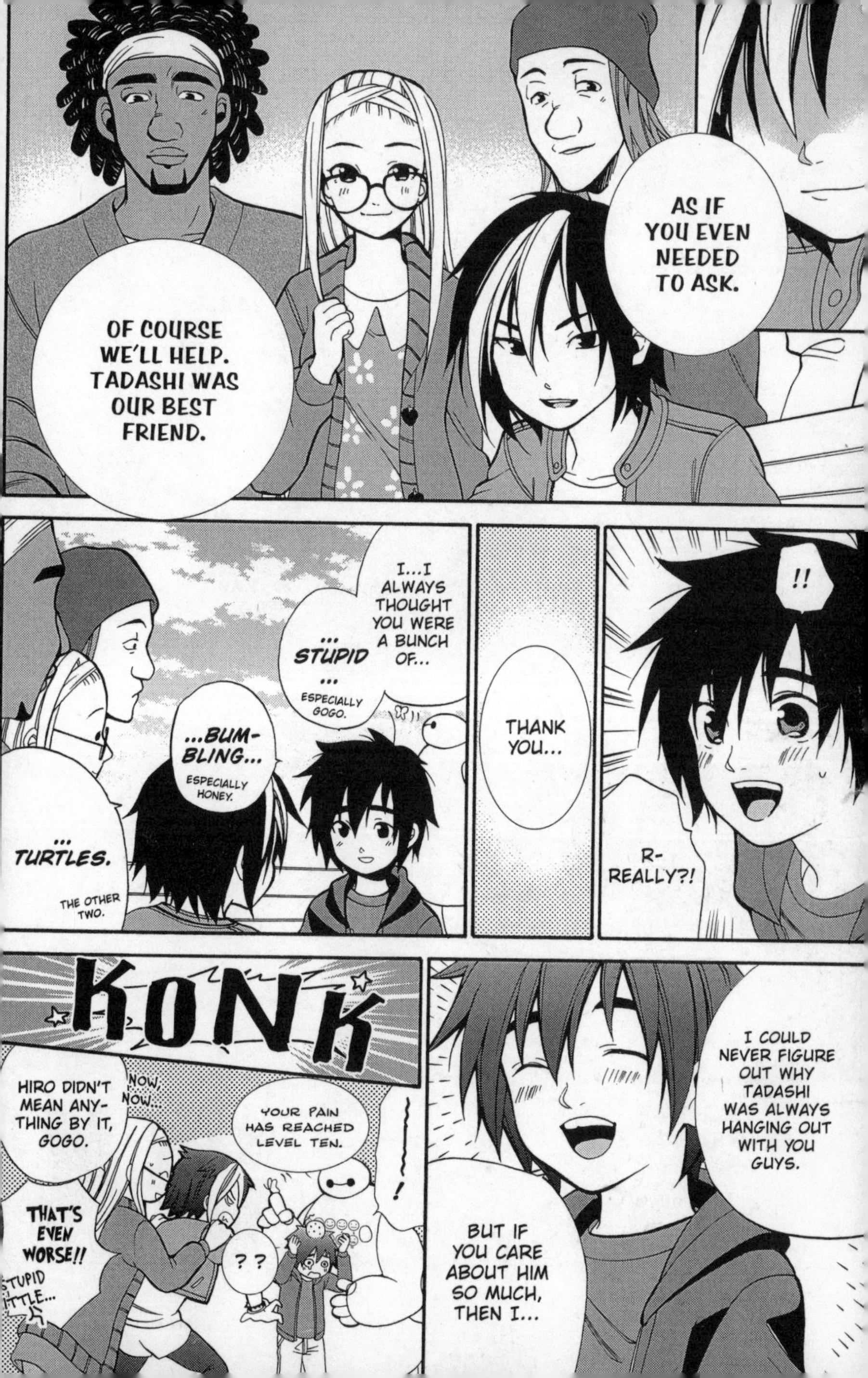
AS IF YOU EVEN NEEDED TO ASK.
OF COURSE WE'LL HELP. TADASHI WAS OUR BEST FRIEND.
!!
R-REALLY?!
THANK YOU...
I...I ALWAYS THOUGHT YOU WERE A BUNCH OF...
...STUPID...
ESPECIALLY GOGO.
...BUMBLING...
ESPECIALLY HONEY.
...TURTLES.
THE OTHER TWO.
I COULD NEVER FIGURE OUT WHY TADASHI WAS ALWAYS HANGING OUT WITH YOU GUYS.
BUT IF YOU CARE ABOUT HIM SO MUCH, THEN I...
KONK
~~~!
YOUR PAIN HAS REACHED LEVEL TEN.
NOW, NOW.
HIRO DIDN'T MEAN ANYTHING BY IT, GOGO.
??
THAT'S EVEN WORSE!!
STUPID LITTLE...
~~~

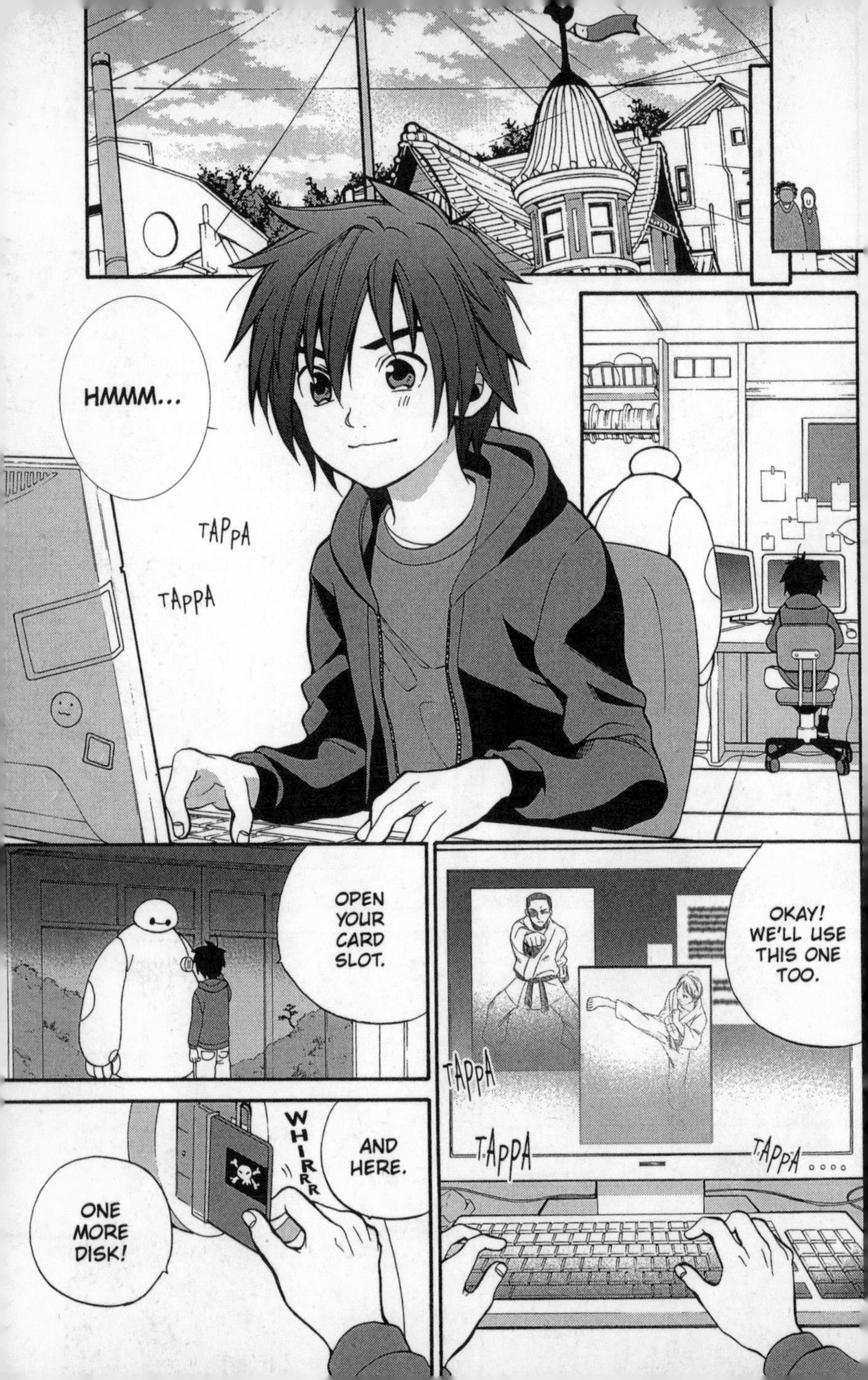
HMMM...
TAPPA
TAPPA
OKAY! WE'LL USE THIS ONE TOO.
TAPPA
TAPPA
TAPPA
OPEN YOUR CARD SLOT.
AND HERE.
WHIRRR
ONE MORE DISK!

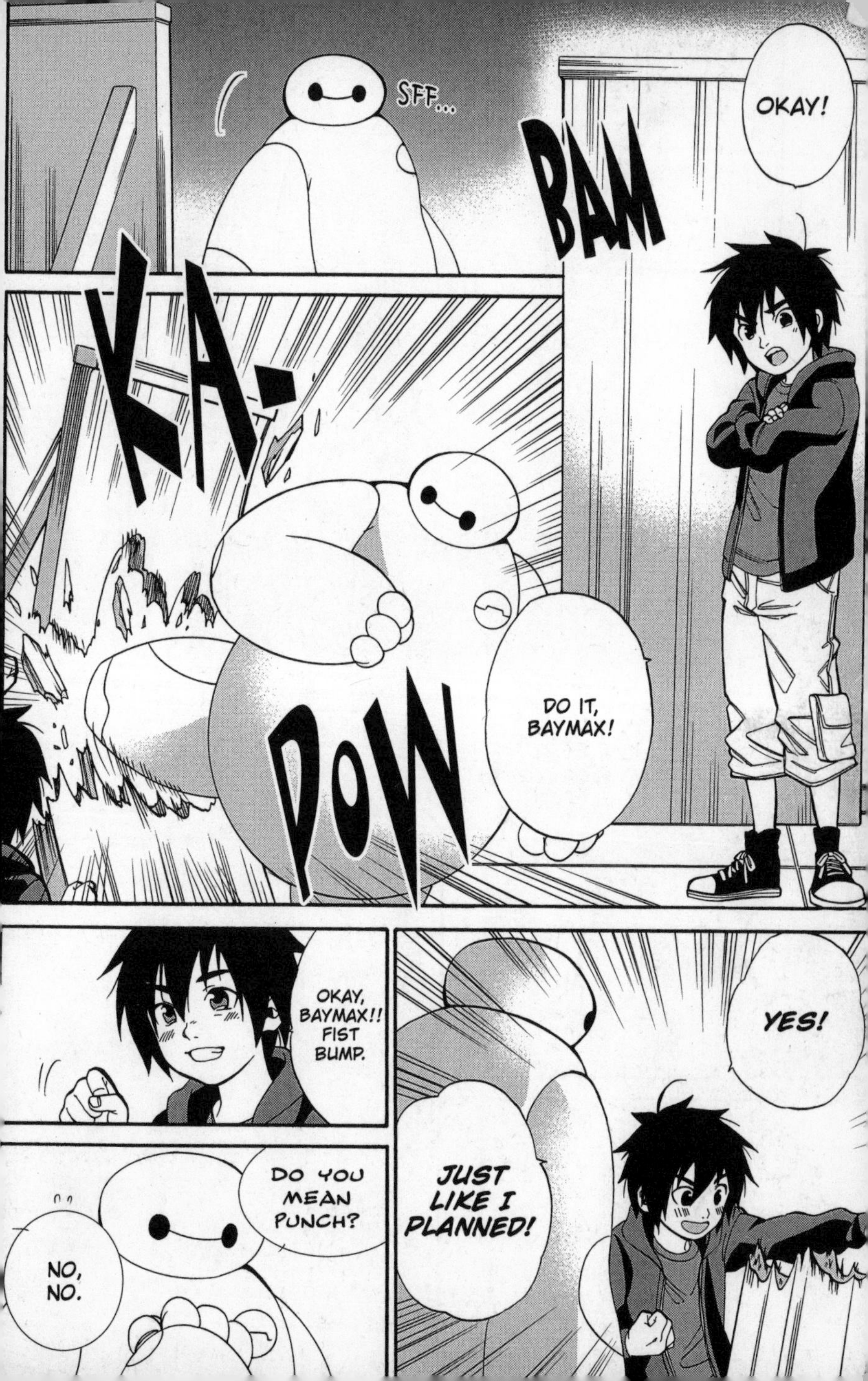
OKAY!
BAM
SFF...
KA-
POW
DO IT, BAYMAX!
YES!
JUST LIKE I PLANNED!
OKAY, BAYMAX!! FIST BUMP.
DO YOU MEAN PUNCH?
NO, NO.

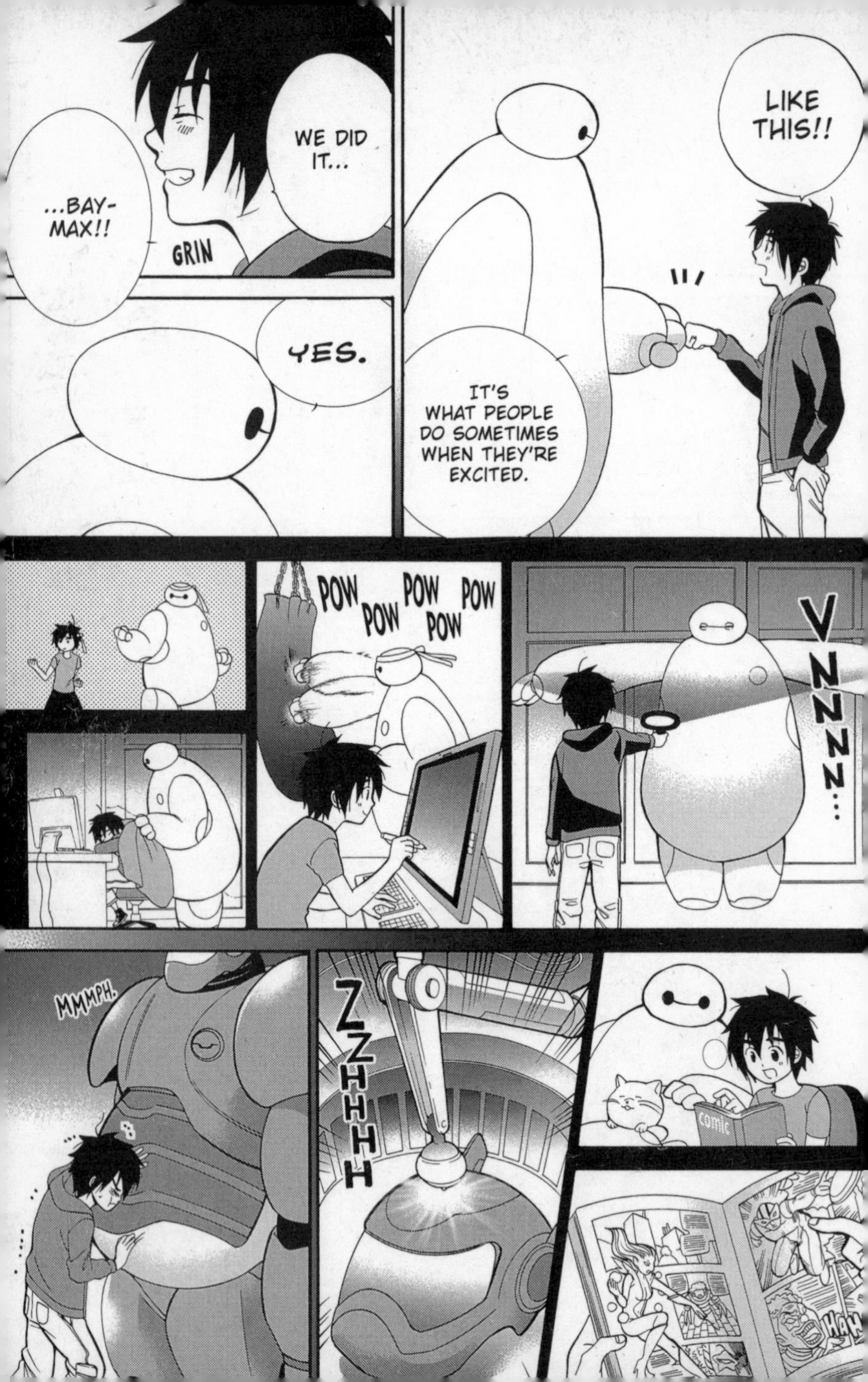
LIKE THIS!!
IT'S WHAT PEOPLE DO SOMETIMES WHEN THEY'RE EXCITED.
WE DID IT...
...BAY-MAX!!
GRIN
YES.
VNNNN...
POW POW POW POW POW POW
comic
ZZHHHHH
MMMPH.

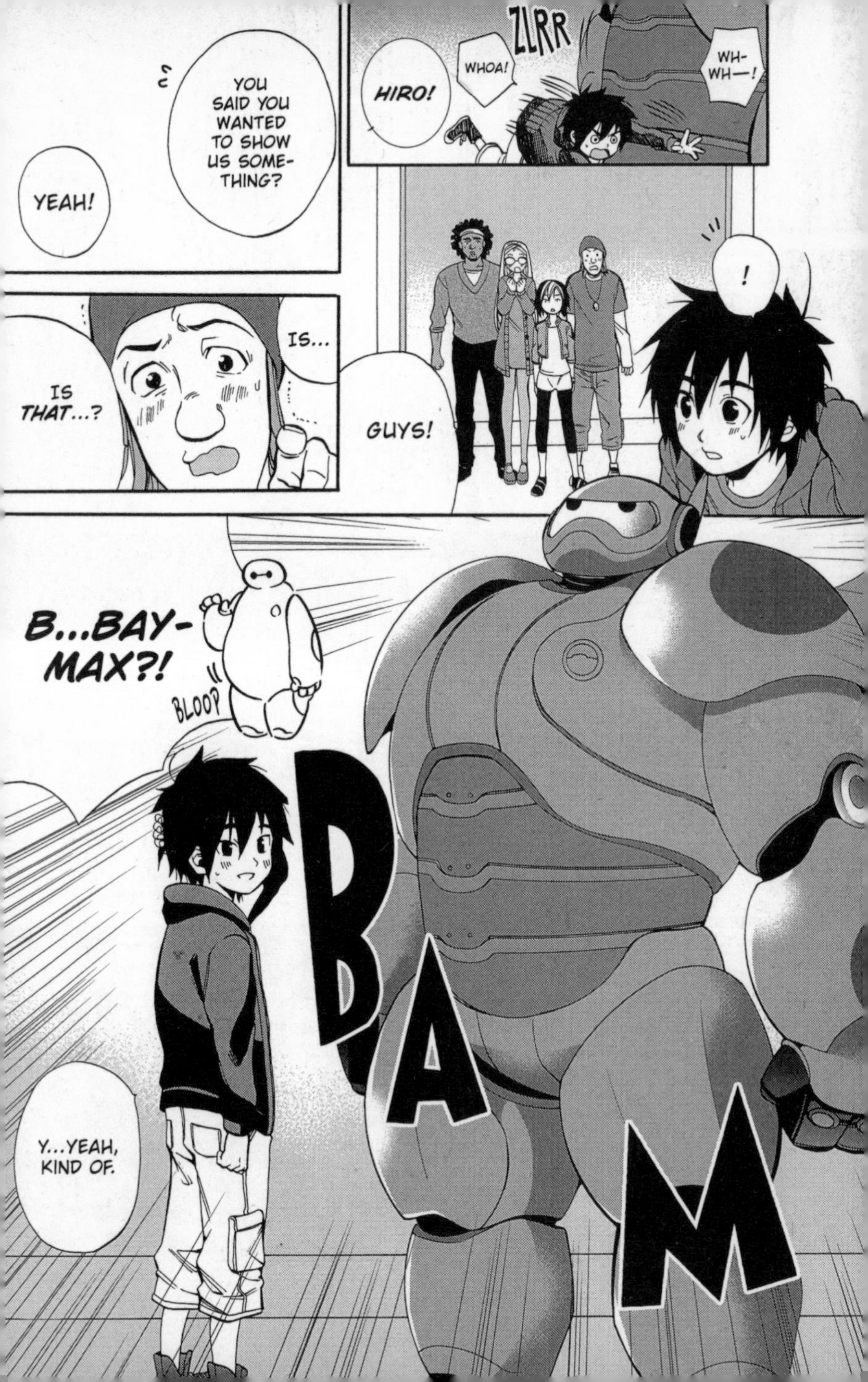
WH-
WH—!
ZLRR
WHOA!
HIRO!
YOU SAID YOU WANTED TO SHOW US SOME-THING?
YEAH!
!
GUYS!
IS...
IS THAT...?
B...BAY-MAX?!
BLOOP
BAM
Y...YEAH, KIND OF.

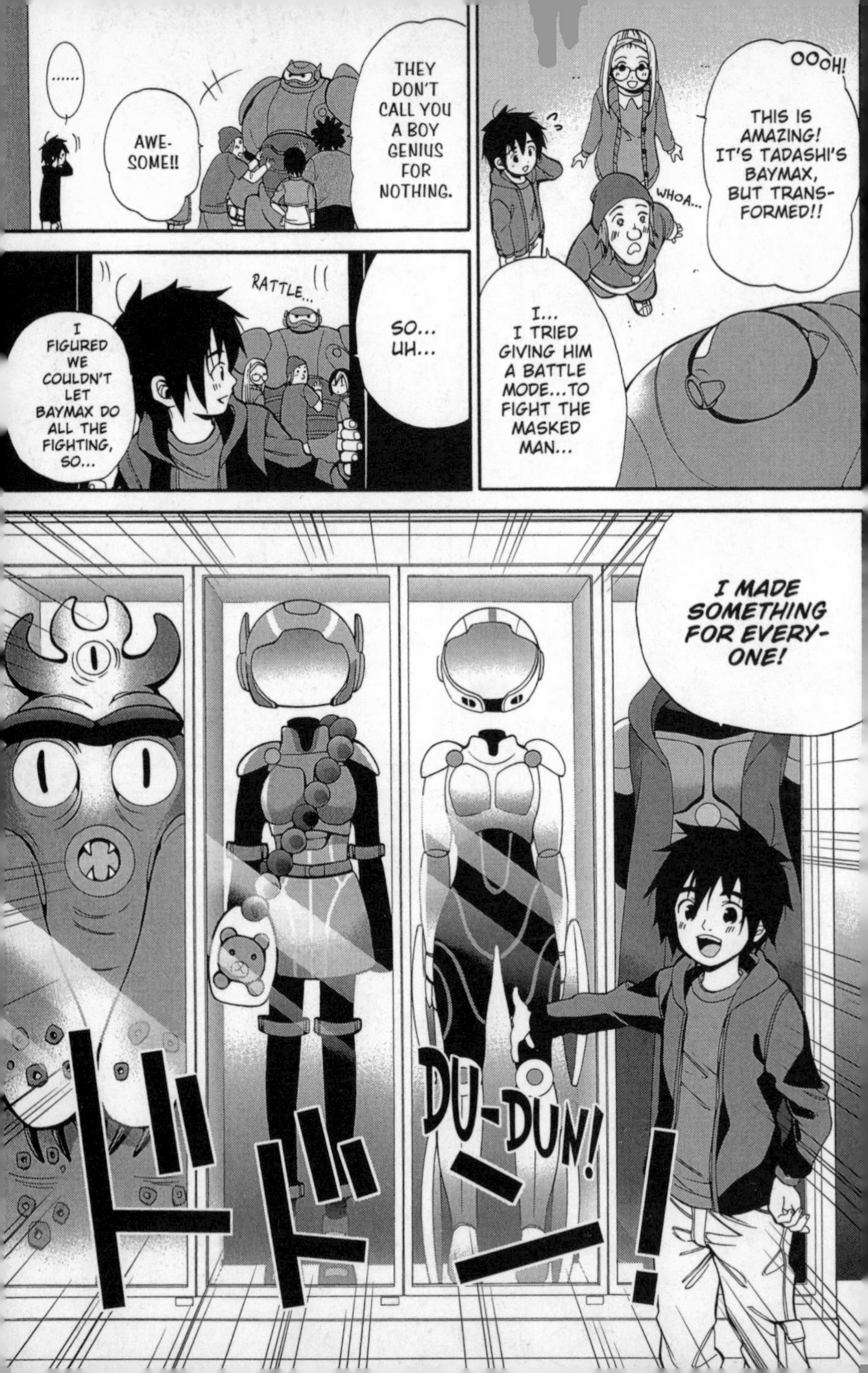
OOOH!
THIS IS AMAZING! IT'S TADASHI'S BAYMAX, BUT TRANS-FORMED!!
WHOA...
I... I TRIED GIVING HIM A BATTLE MODE...TO FIGHT THE MASKED MAN...
THEY DON'T CALL YOU A BOY GENIUS FOR NOTHING.
AWE-SOME!!
......
RATTLE...
SO... UH...
I FIGURED WE COULDN'T LET BAYMAX DO ALL THE FIGHTING, SO...
I MADE SOMETHING FOR EVERY-ONE!
DU-DUN!
ドドドーン!

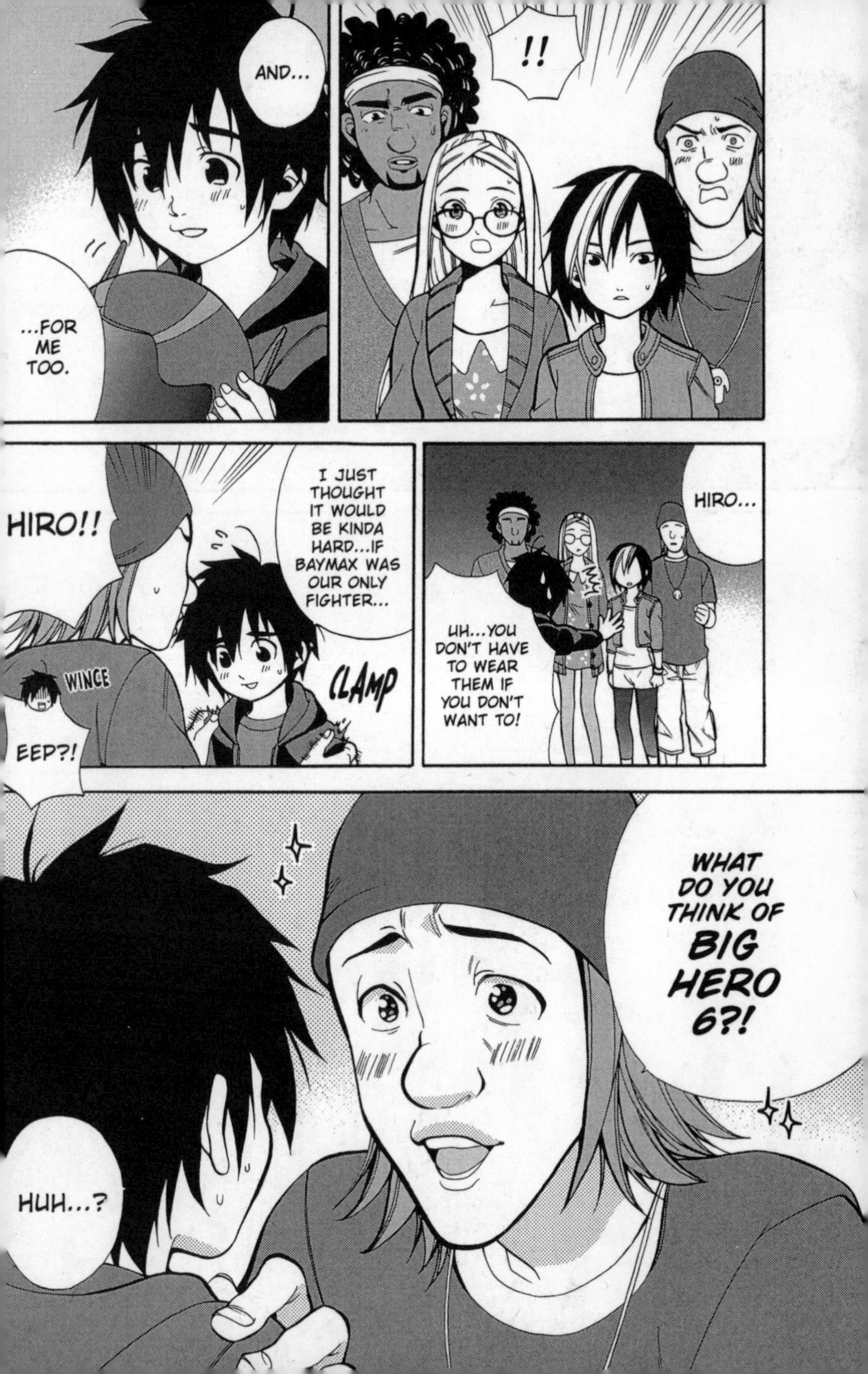
!!
AND...
...FOR ME TOO.
HIRO...
UH...YOU DON'T HAVE TO WEAR THEM IF YOU DON'T WANT TO!
I JUST THOUGHT IT WOULD BE KINDA HARD...IF BAYMAX WAS OUR ONLY FIGHTER...
CLAMP
HIRO!!
WINCE
EEP?!
WHAT DO YOU THINK OF BIG HERO 6?!
HUH...?

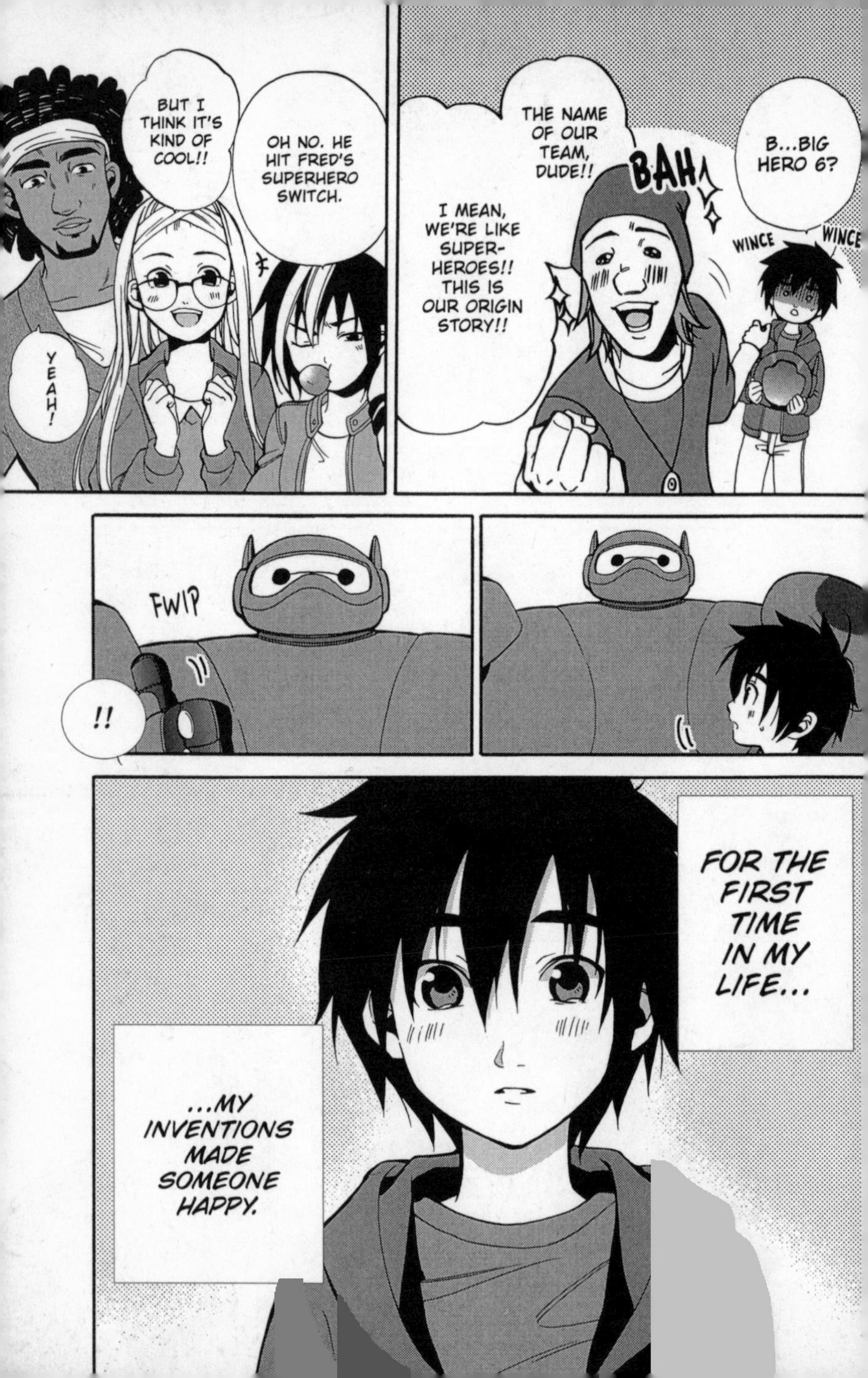
B...BIG HERO 6?
WINCE
WINCE
BAH
THE NAME OF OUR TEAM, DUDE!!
I MEAN, WE'RE LIKE SUPER-HEROES!! THIS IS OUR ORIGIN STORY!!
OH NO. HE HIT FRED'S SUPERHERO SWITCH.
BUT I THINK IT'S KIND OF COOL!!
YEAH!
FWIP
!!
FOR THE FIRST TIME IN MY LIFE...
...MY INVENTIONS MADE SOMEONE HAPPY.

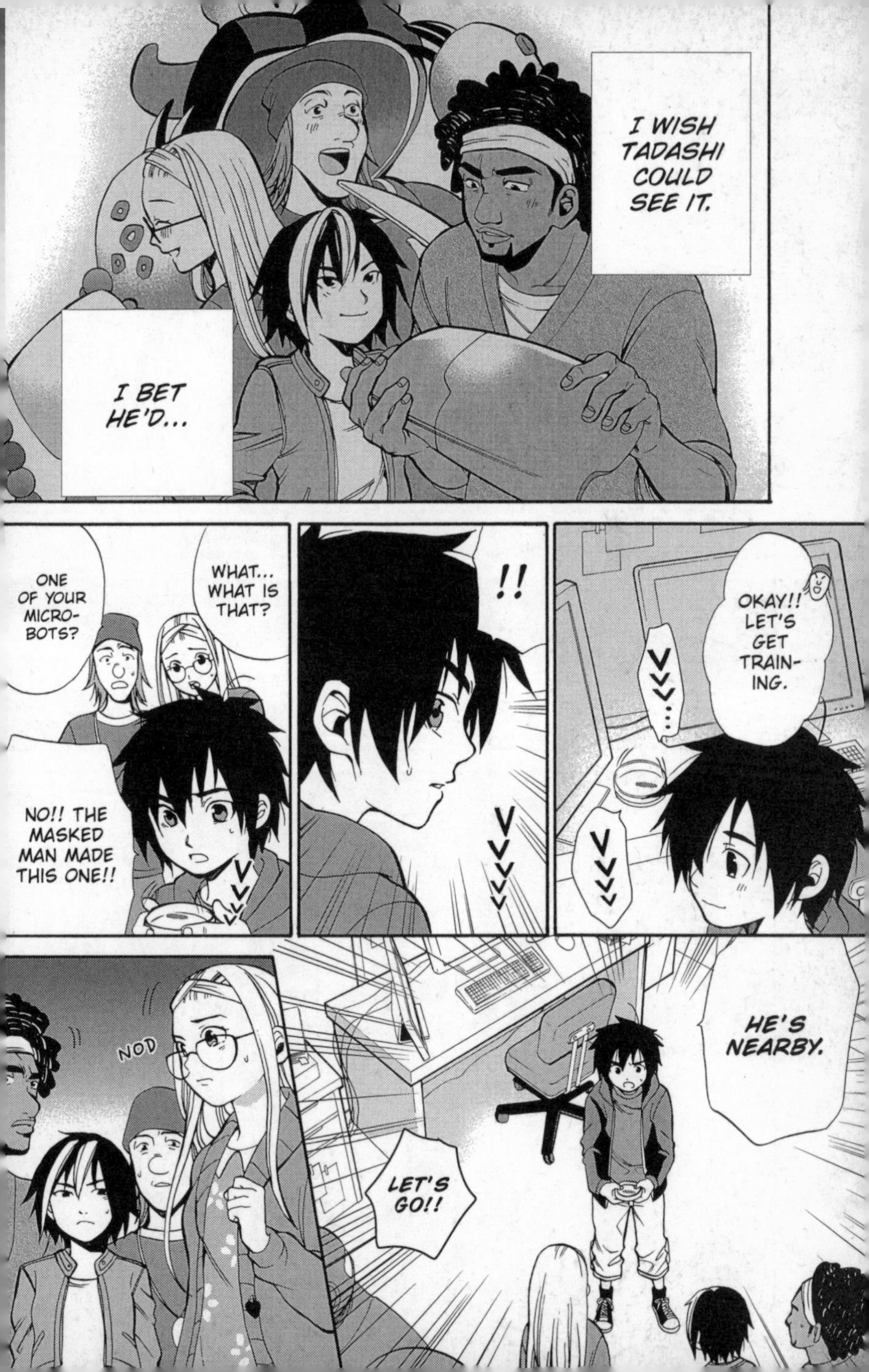
I WISH TADASHI COULD SEE IT.
I BET HE'D...
OKAY!! LET'S GET TRAINING.
!!
WHAT... WHAT IS THAT?
ONE OF YOUR MICRO-BOTS?
NO!! THE MASKED MAN MADE THIS ONE!!
HE'S NEARBY.
LET'S GO!!
NOD

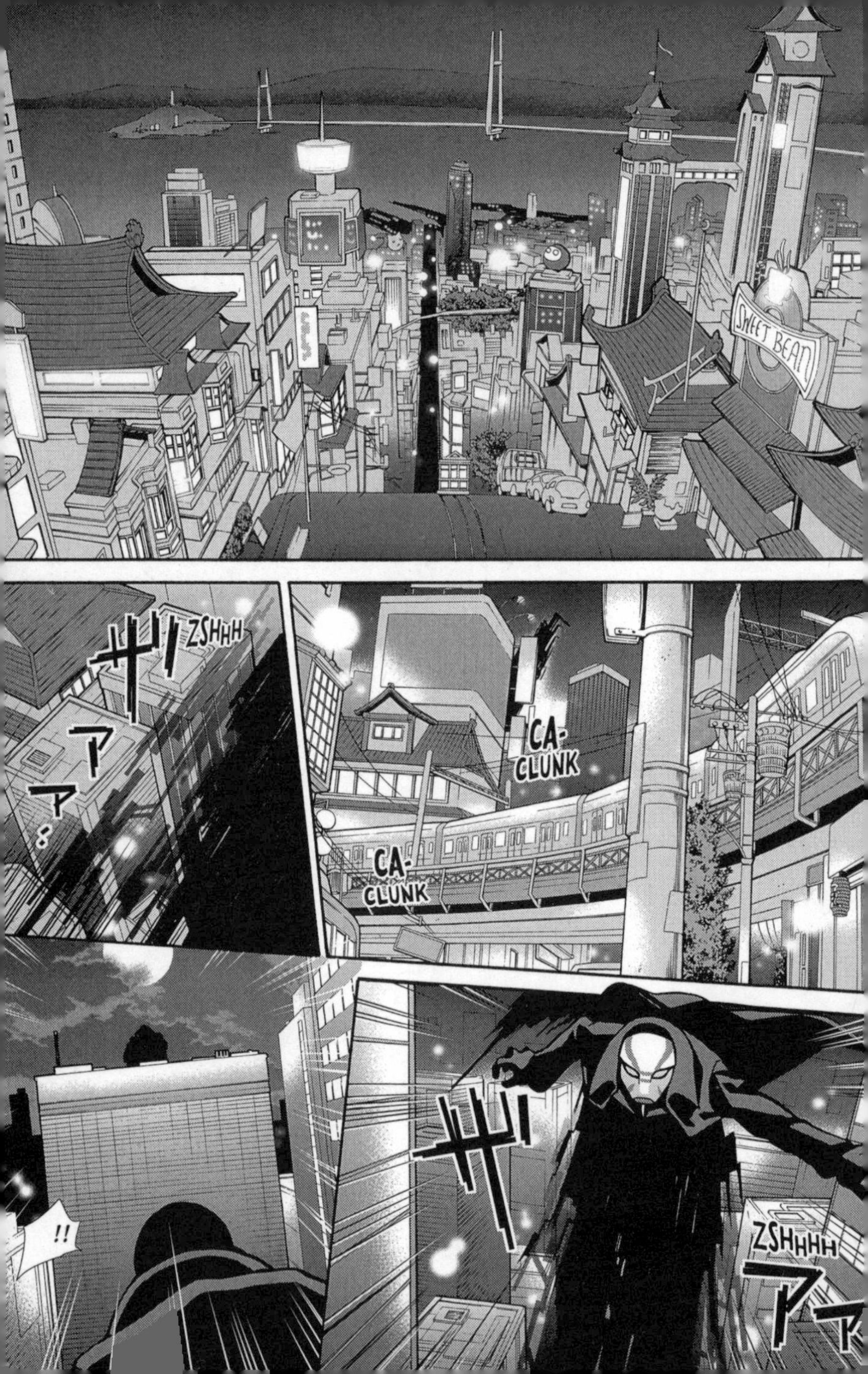
SWEET BEAN
CA-CLUNK
CA-CLUNK
ZSHHH
ZSHHHH
!!

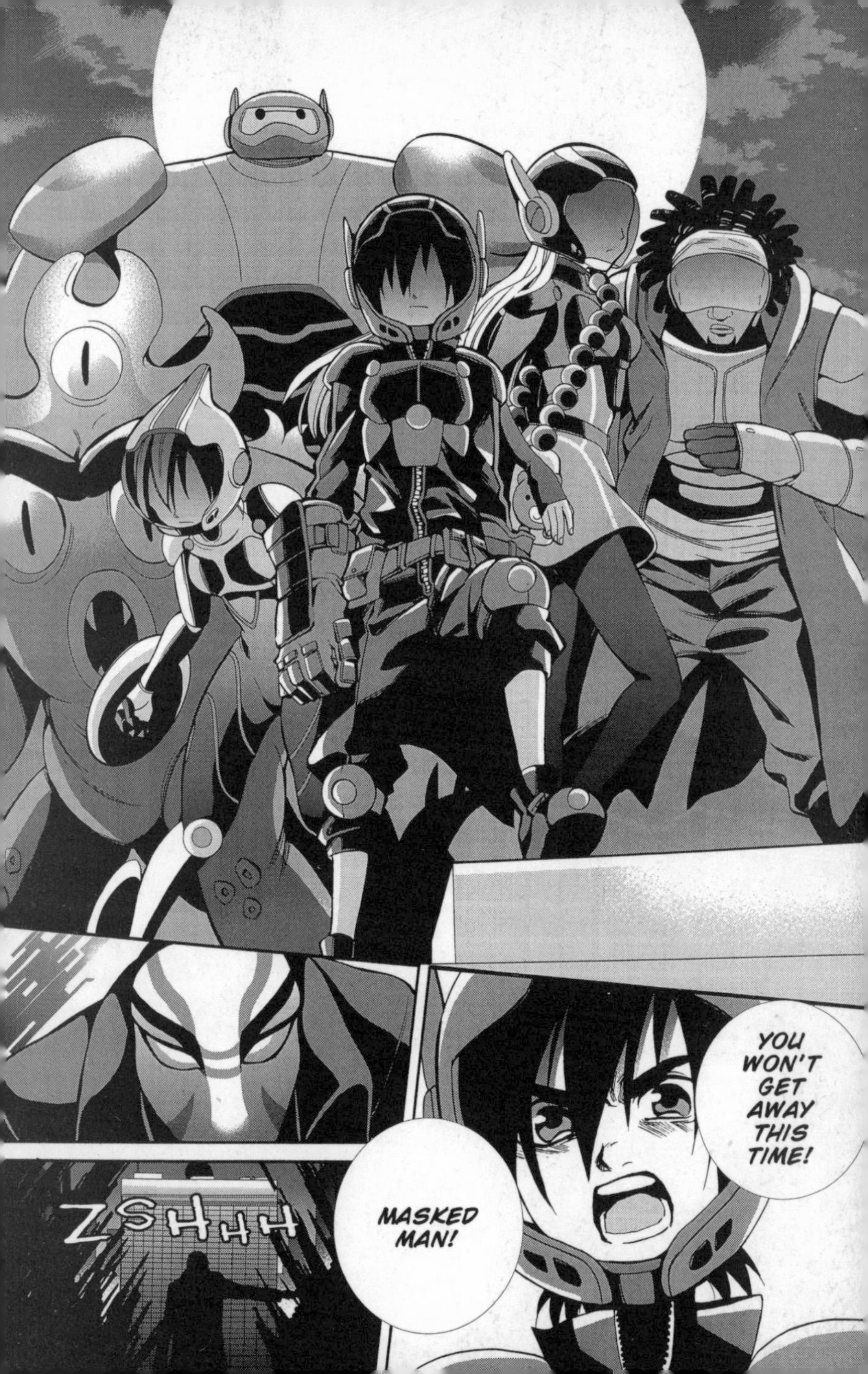
YOU WON'T GET AWAY THIS TIME!
MASKED MAN!
ZSHHH

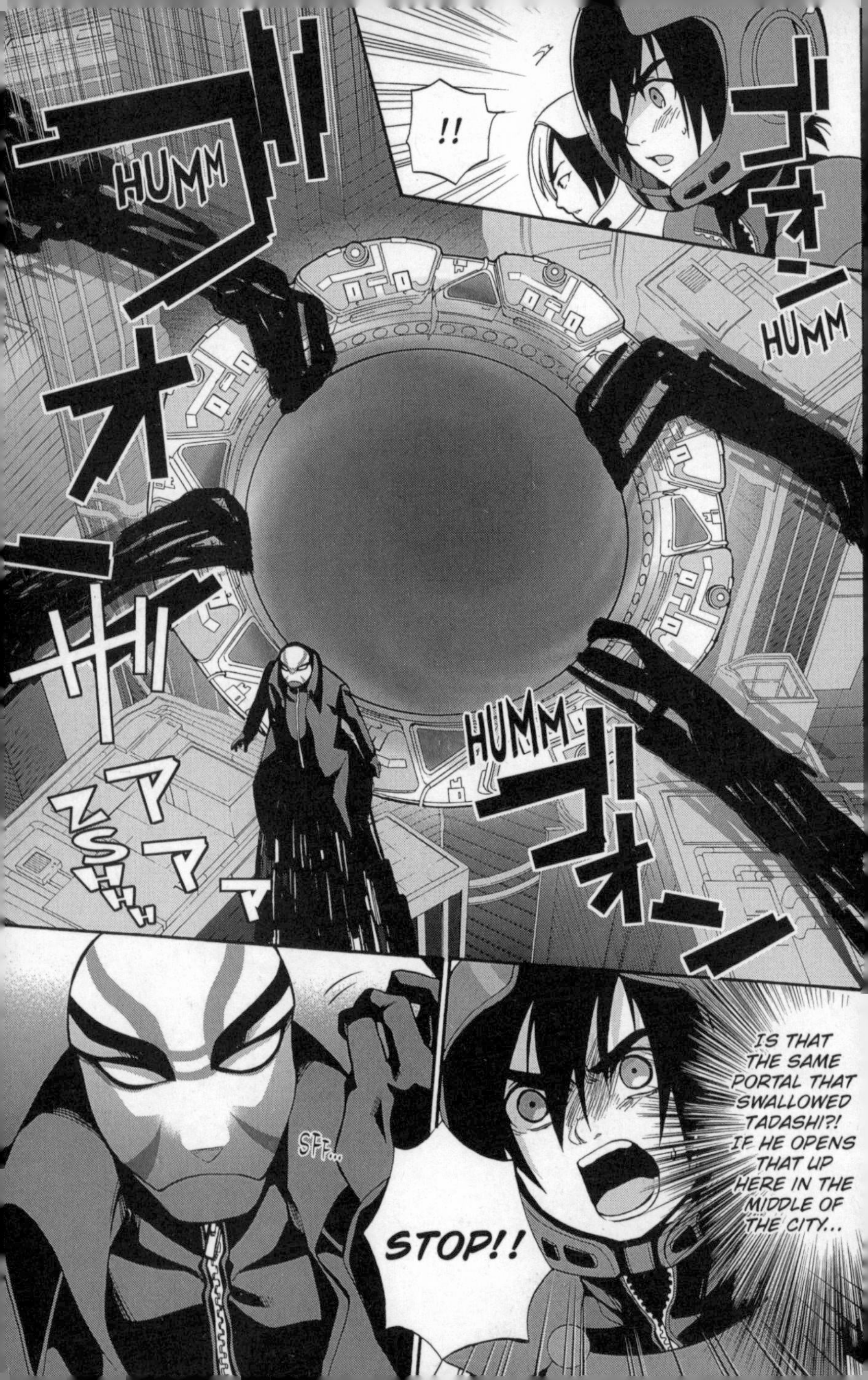
!!
HUMM
HUMM
HUMM
HUMM
ZSHHHH
IS THAT THE SAME PORTAL THAT SWALLOWED TADASHI?! IF HE OPENS THAT UP HERE IN THE MIDDLE OF THE CITY...
STOP!!
SFF...

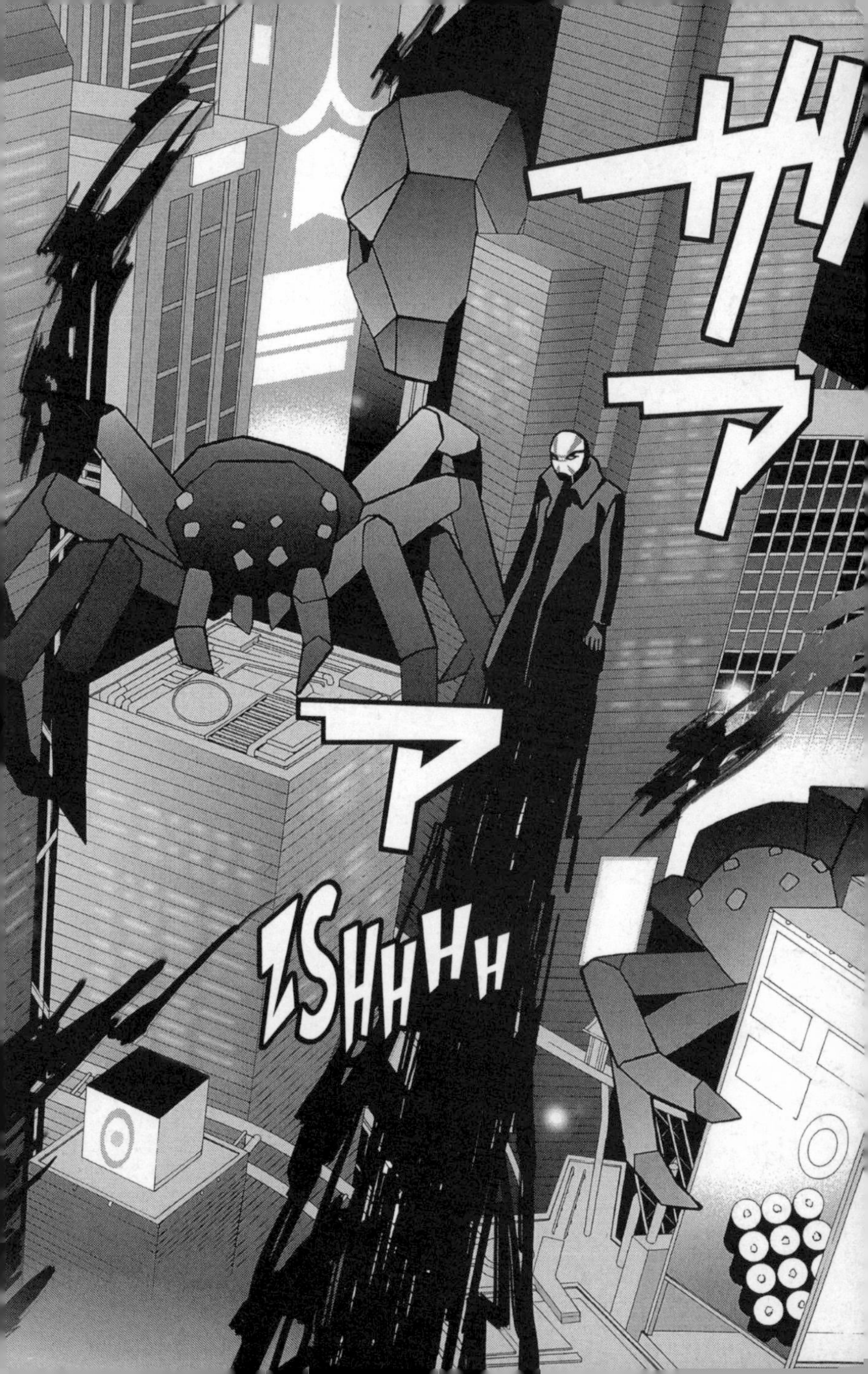
ザアアー
ZSHHHH

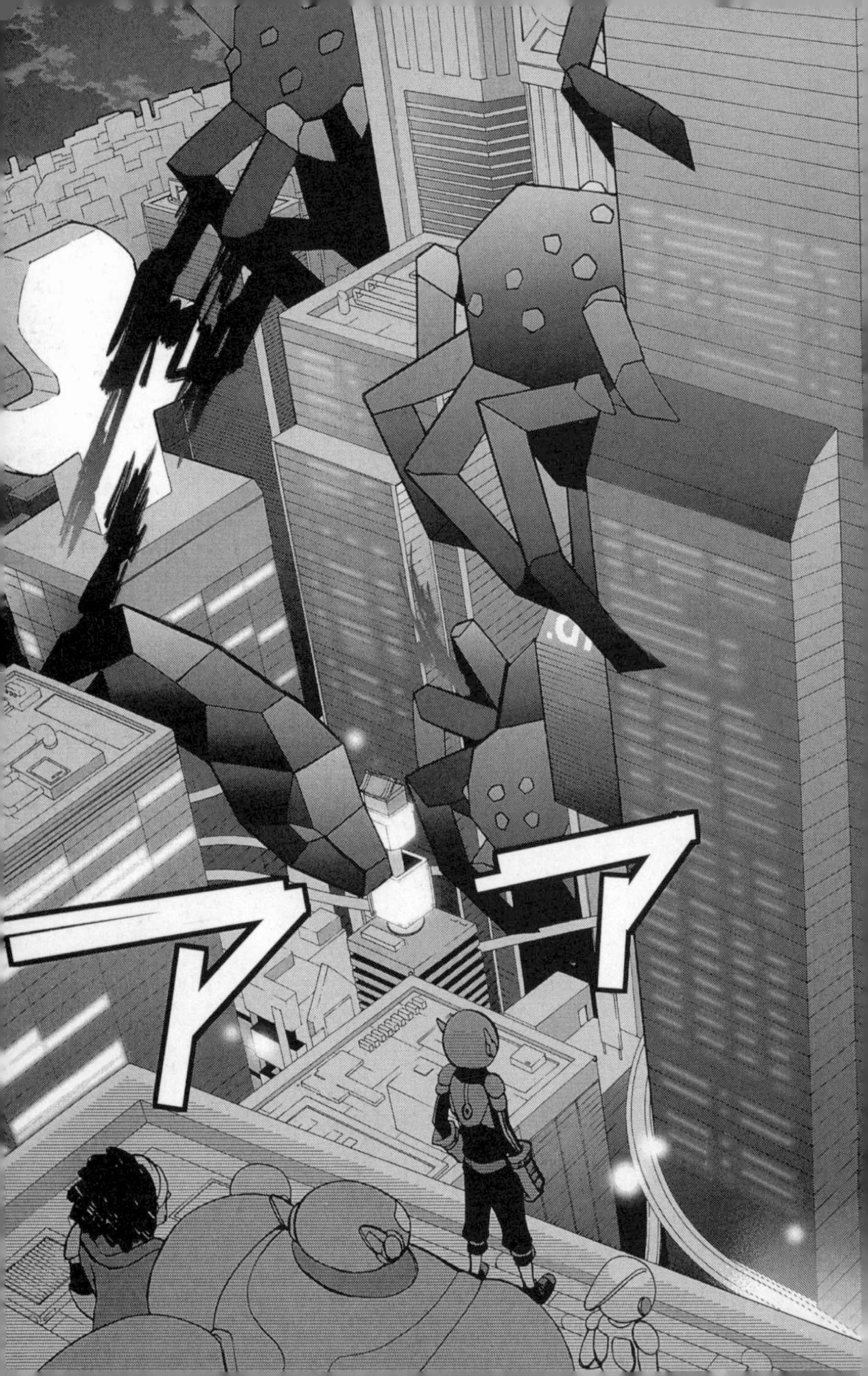

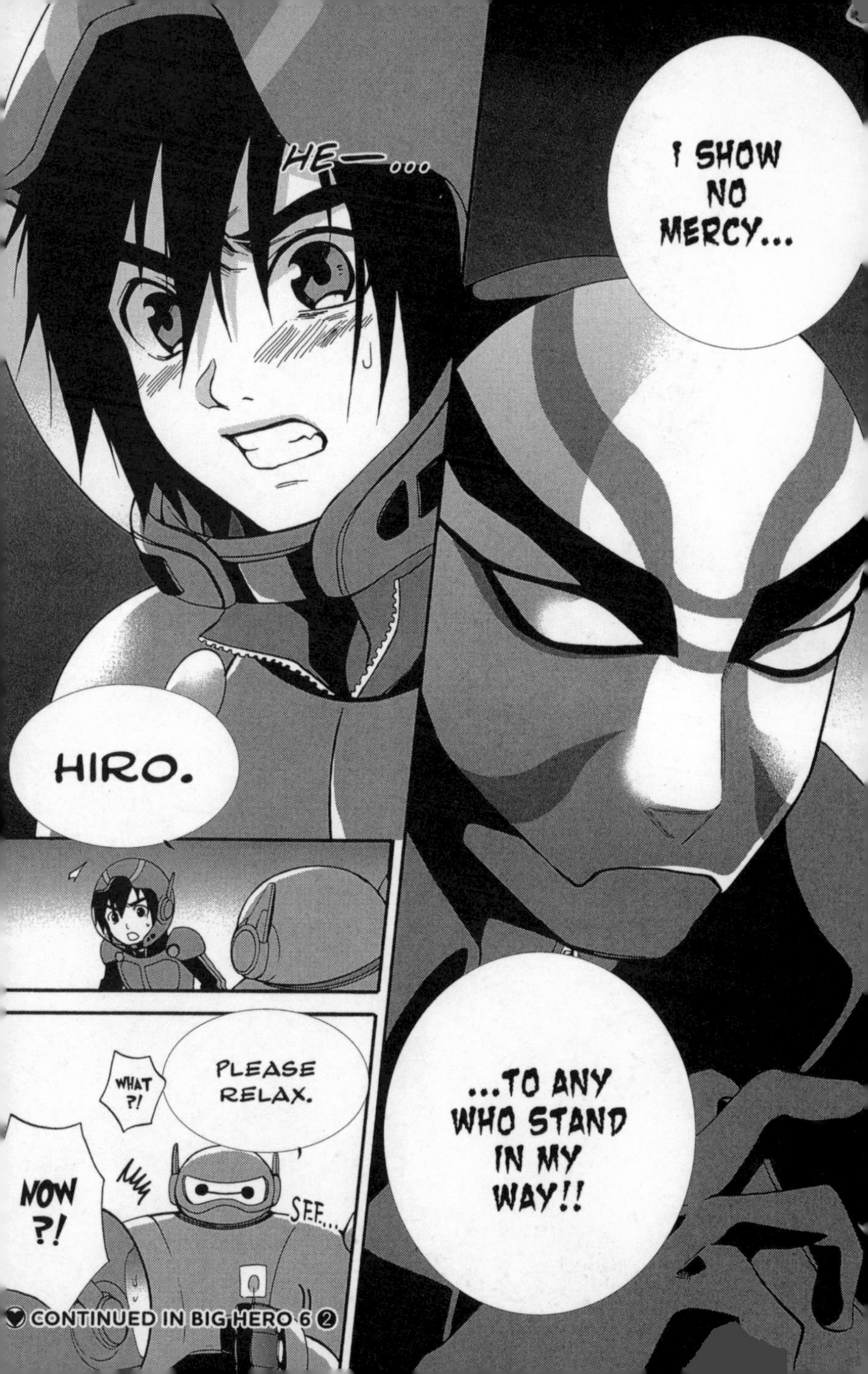
I SHOW NO MERCY...
...TO ANY WHO STAND IN MY WAY!!
HE—...
HIRO.
PLEASE RELAX.
WHAT?!
NOW?!
SFF...

CONTINUED IN BIG HERO 6 ②

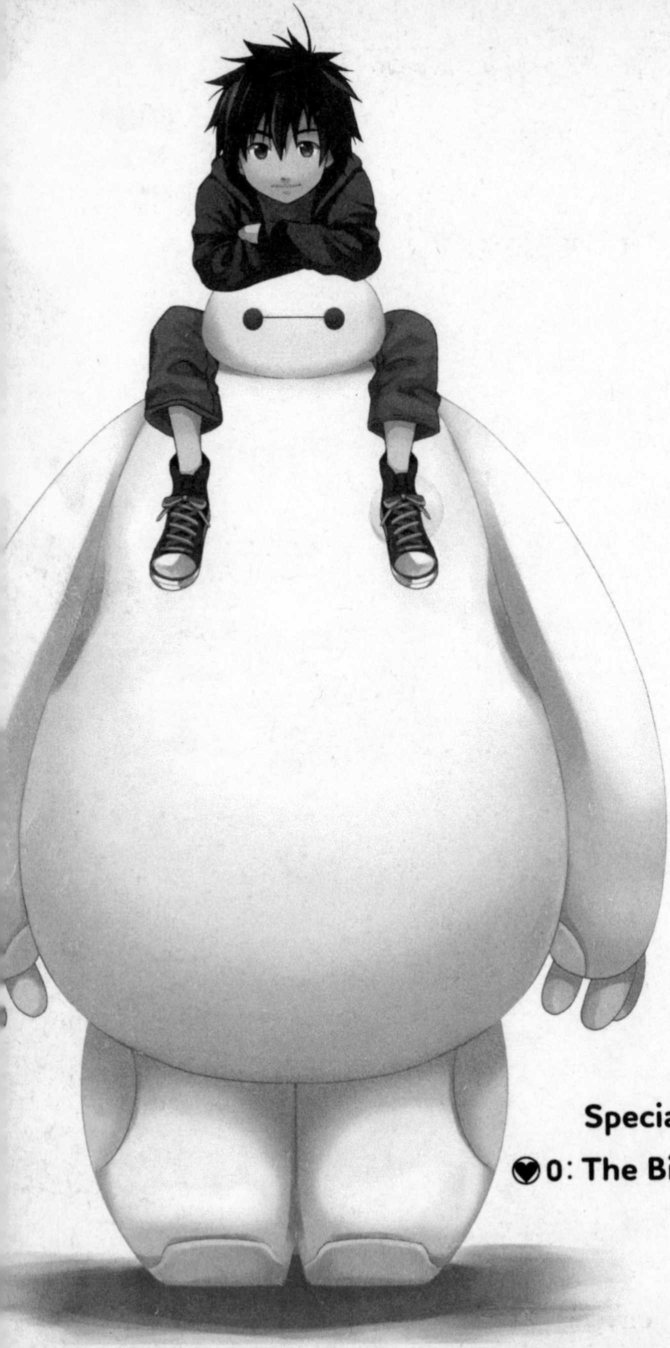

Special Chapter

♥0: The Birth of Baymax

Disney

BIG HERO 6

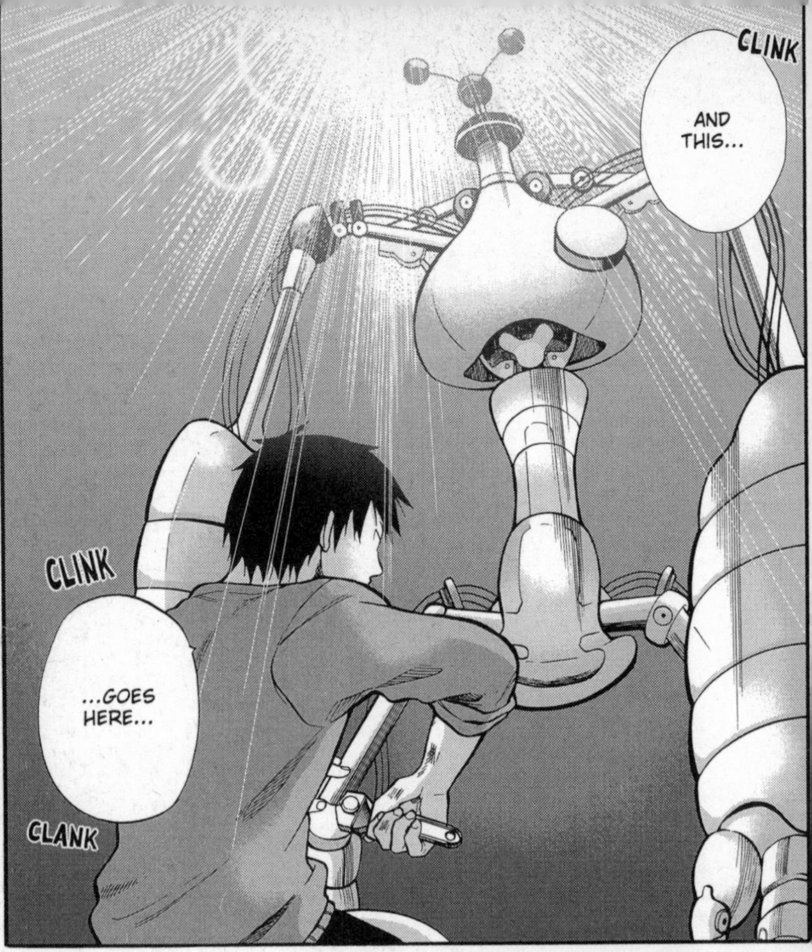
CLINK
AND THIS...
CLINK
...GOES HERE...
CLANK
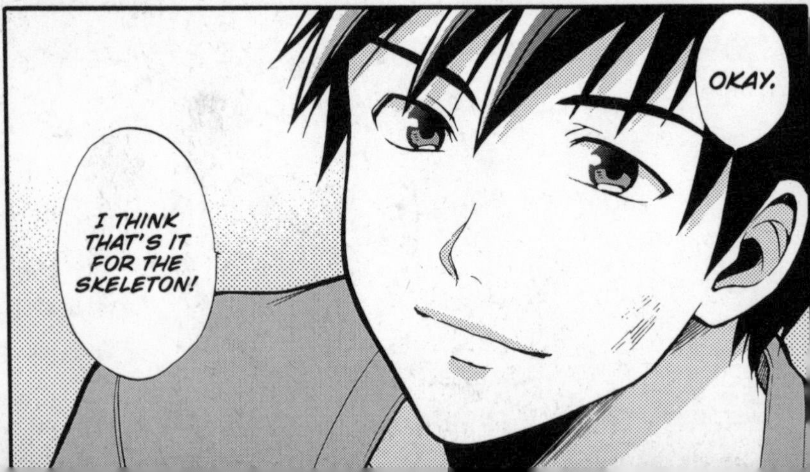
OKAY.
I THINK THAT'S IT FOR THE SKELETON!

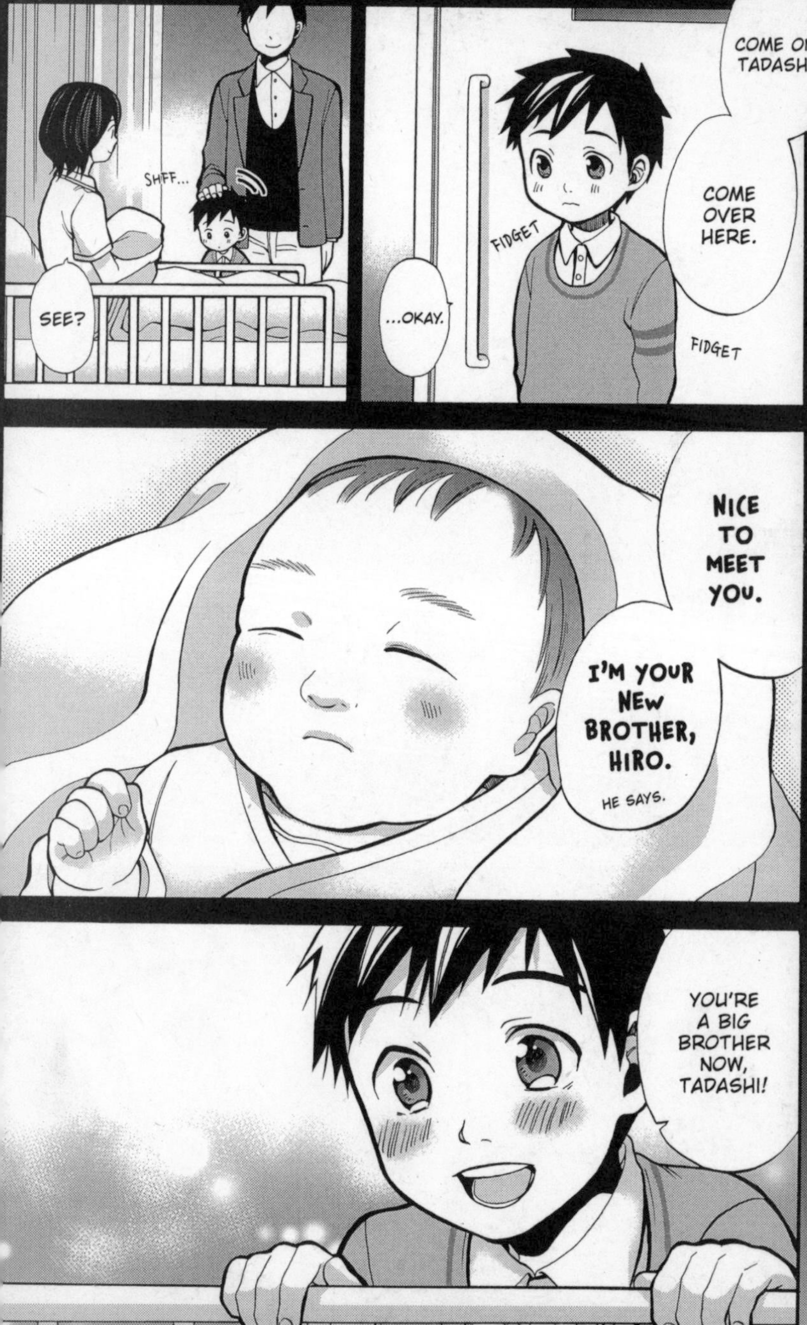
COME ON, TADASHI.
COME OVER HERE.
FIDGET
...OKAY.
FIDGET
SHFF...
SEE?
NICE TO MEET YOU.
I'M YOUR NEW BROTHER, HIRO.
HE SAYS.
YOU'RE A BIG BROTHER NOW, TADASHI!

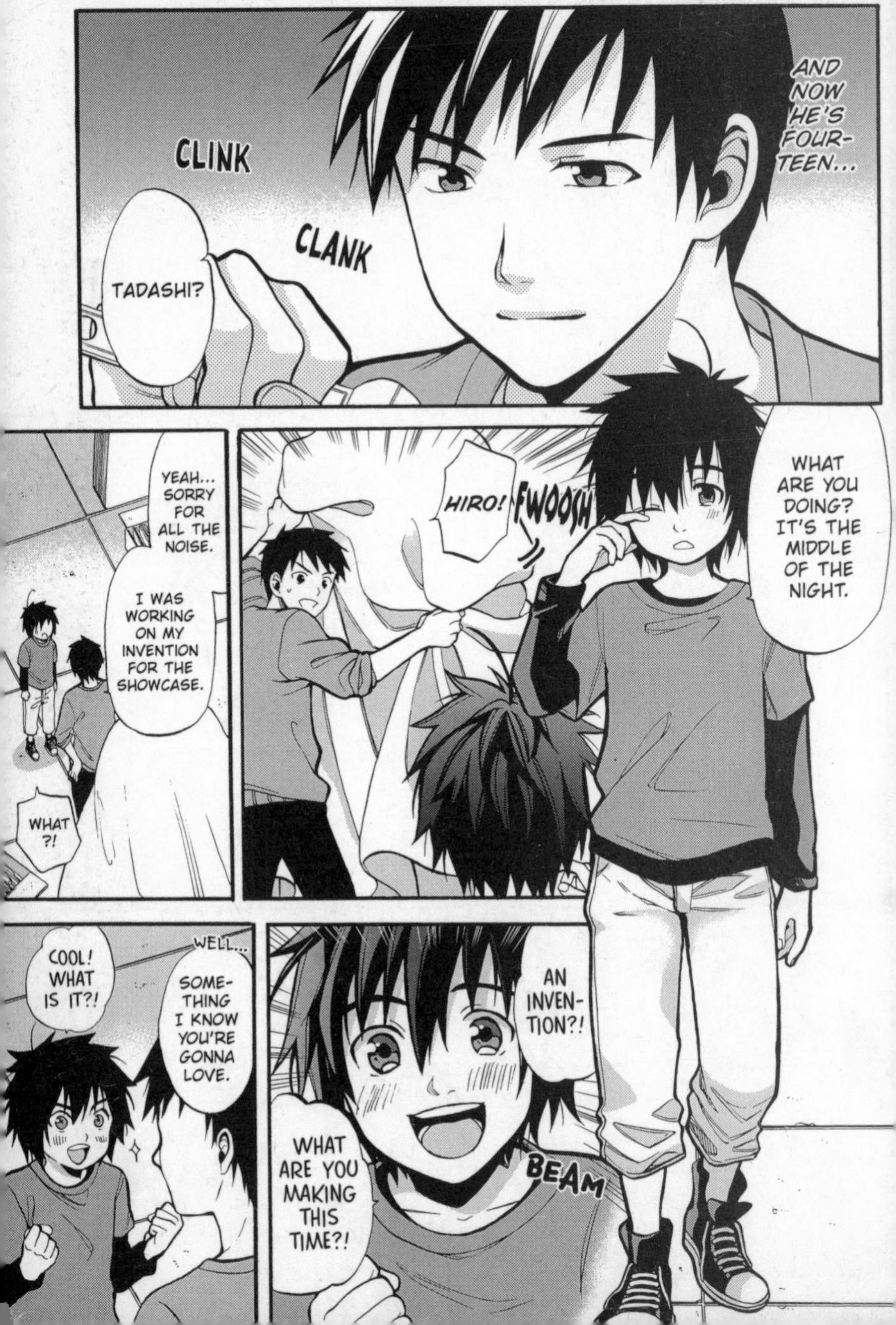
AND NOW HE'S FOURTEEN...
CLINK
CLANK
TADASHI?
WHAT ARE YOU DOING? IT'S THE MIDDLE OF THE NIGHT.
HIRO!
FWOOSH
YEAH... SORRY FOR ALL THE NOISE.
I WAS WORKING ON MY INVENTION FOR THE SHOWCASE.
WHAT?!
AN INVENTION?!
WHAT ARE YOU MAKING THIS TIME?!
BEAM
WELL...
SOMETHING I KNOW YOU'RE GONNA LOVE.
COOL! WHAT IS IT?!

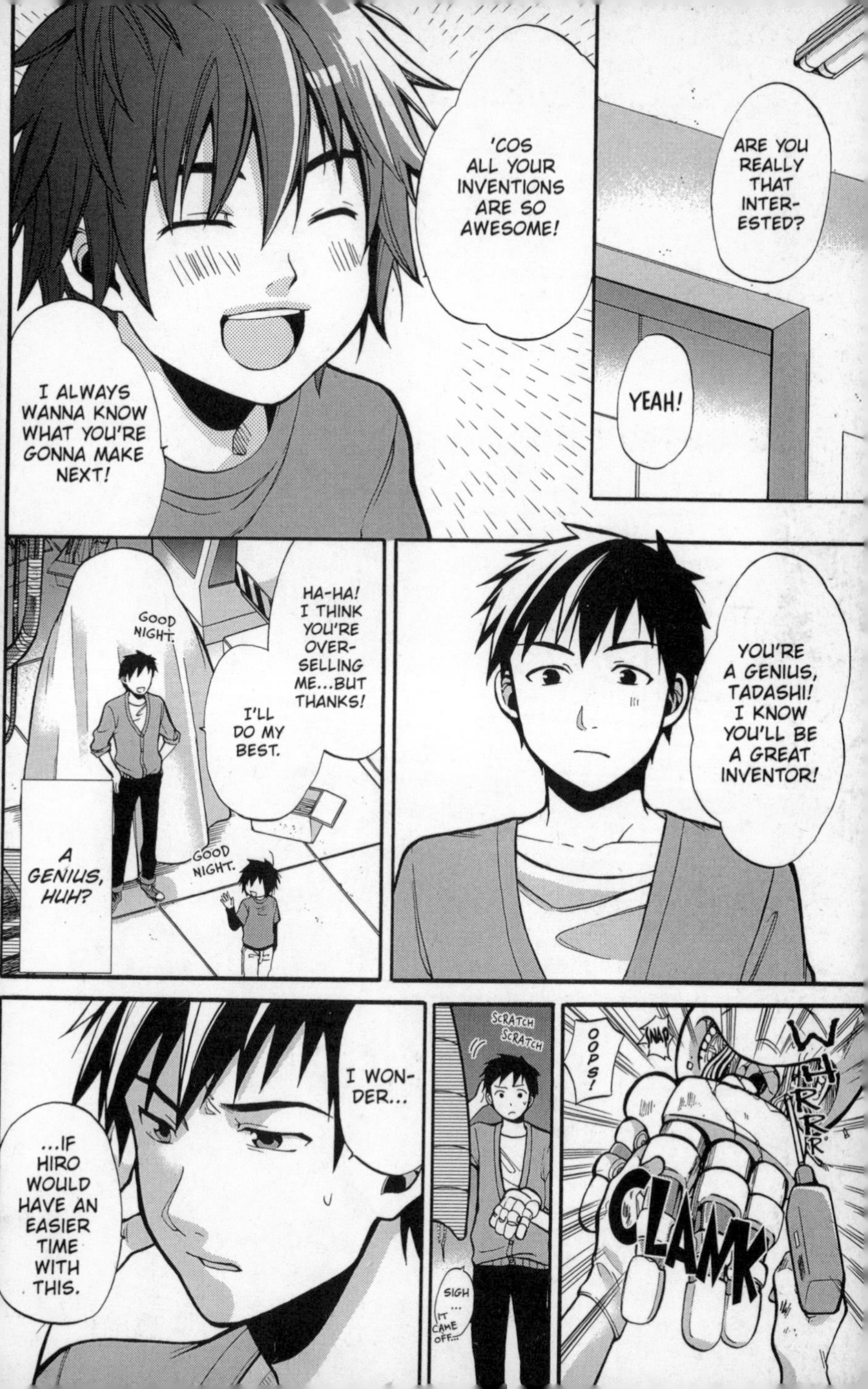
ARE YOU REALLY THAT INTER-ESTED?
YEAH!
'COS ALL YOUR INVENTIONS ARE SO AWESOME!
I ALWAYS WANNA KNOW WHAT YOU'RE GONNA MAKE NEXT!
YOU'RE A GENIUS, TADASHI! I KNOW YOU'LL BE A GREAT INVENTOR!
HA-HA! I THINK YOU'RE OVER-SELLING ME...BUT THANKS!
I'LL DO MY BEST.
GOOD NIGHT.
GOOD NIGHT.
A GENIUS, HUH?
WHRRR
SNAP
OOPS!
CLAMK
SCRATCH SCRATCH
SIGH ...
IT CAME OFF...
I WON-DER...
...IF HIRO WOULD HAVE AN EASIER TIME WITH THIS.

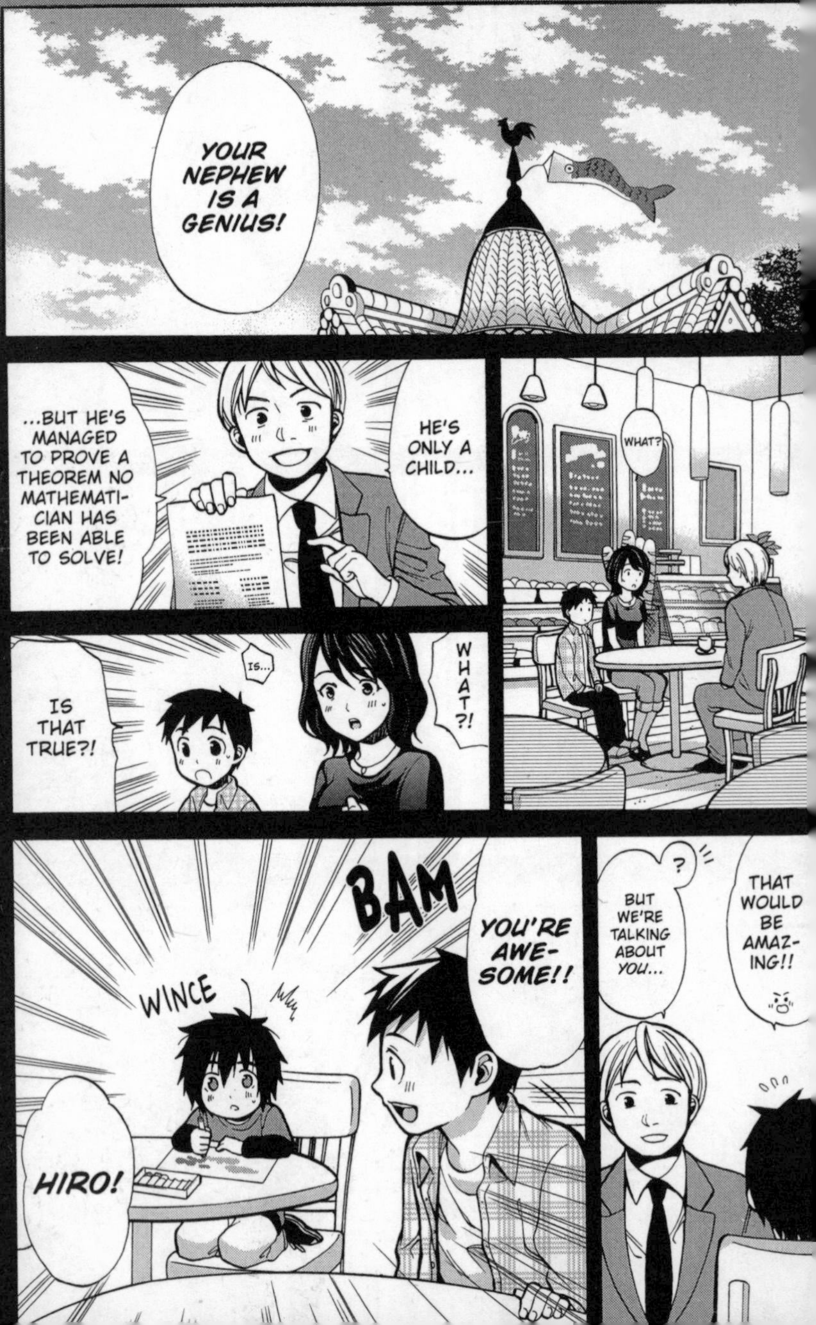
YOUR NEPHEW IS A GENIUS!
WHAT?
HE'S ONLY A CHILD...
...BUT HE'S MANAGED TO PROVE A THEOREM NO MATHEMATI-CIAN HAS BEEN ABLE TO SOLVE!
WHAT?!
IS...
IS THAT TRUE?!
THAT WOULD BE AMAZ-ING!!
?
BUT WE'RE TALKING ABOUT YOU...
BAM
YOU'RE AWE-SOME!!
WINCE
HIRO!

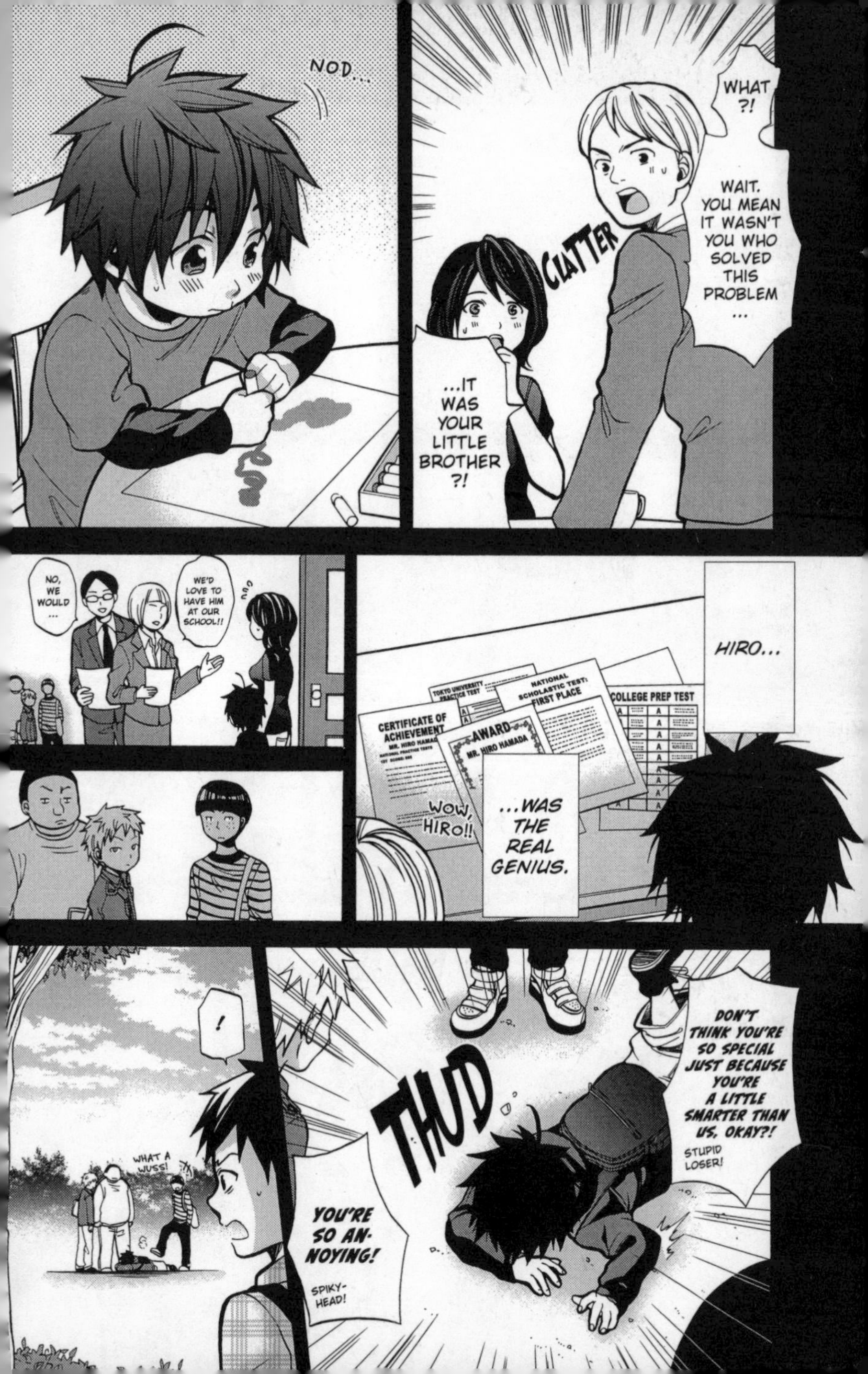
WHAT?!
WAIT. YOU MEAN IT WASN'T YOU WHO SOLVED THIS PROBLEM...
CLATTER
...IT WAS YOUR LITTLE BROTHER?!
NOD...
HIRO...
TOKYO UNIVERSITY PRACTICE TEST
NATIONAL SCHOLASTIC TEST: FIRST PLACE
COLLEGE PREP TEST
CERTIFICATE OF ACHIEVEMENT
MR. HIRO HAMADA
AWARD
MR. HIRO HAMADA
WOW, HIRO!!
...WAS THE REAL GENIUS.
WE'D LOVE TO HAVE HIM AT OUR SCHOOL!!
NO, WE WOULD...
THUD
DON'T THINK YOU'RE SO SPECIAL JUST BECAUSE YOU'RE A LITTLE SMARTER THAN US, OKAY?!
STUPID LOSER!
YOU'RE SO AN-NOYING!
SPIKY-HEAD!
!
WHAT A WUSS!

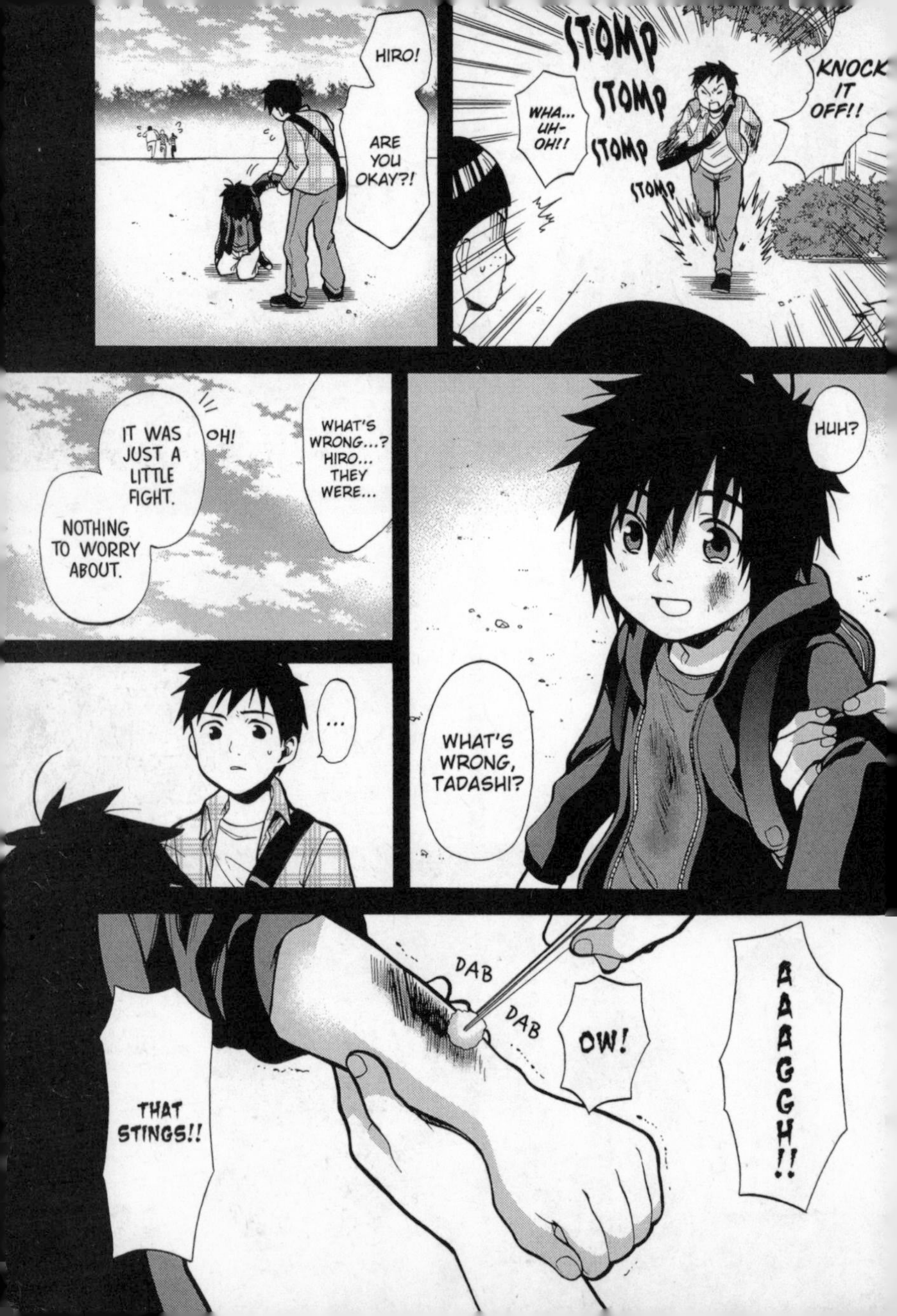
KNOCK IT OFF!!
STOMP
STOMP
STOMP
STOMP
WHA... UH-OH!!
HIRO!
ARE YOU OKAY?!
HUH?
WHAT'S WRONG, TADASHI?
WHAT'S WRONG...? HIRO... THEY WERE...
OH!
IT WAS JUST A LITTLE FIGHT.
NOTHING TO WORRY ABOUT.
...
AAAGGH!!
OW!
DAB
DAB
THAT STINGS!!

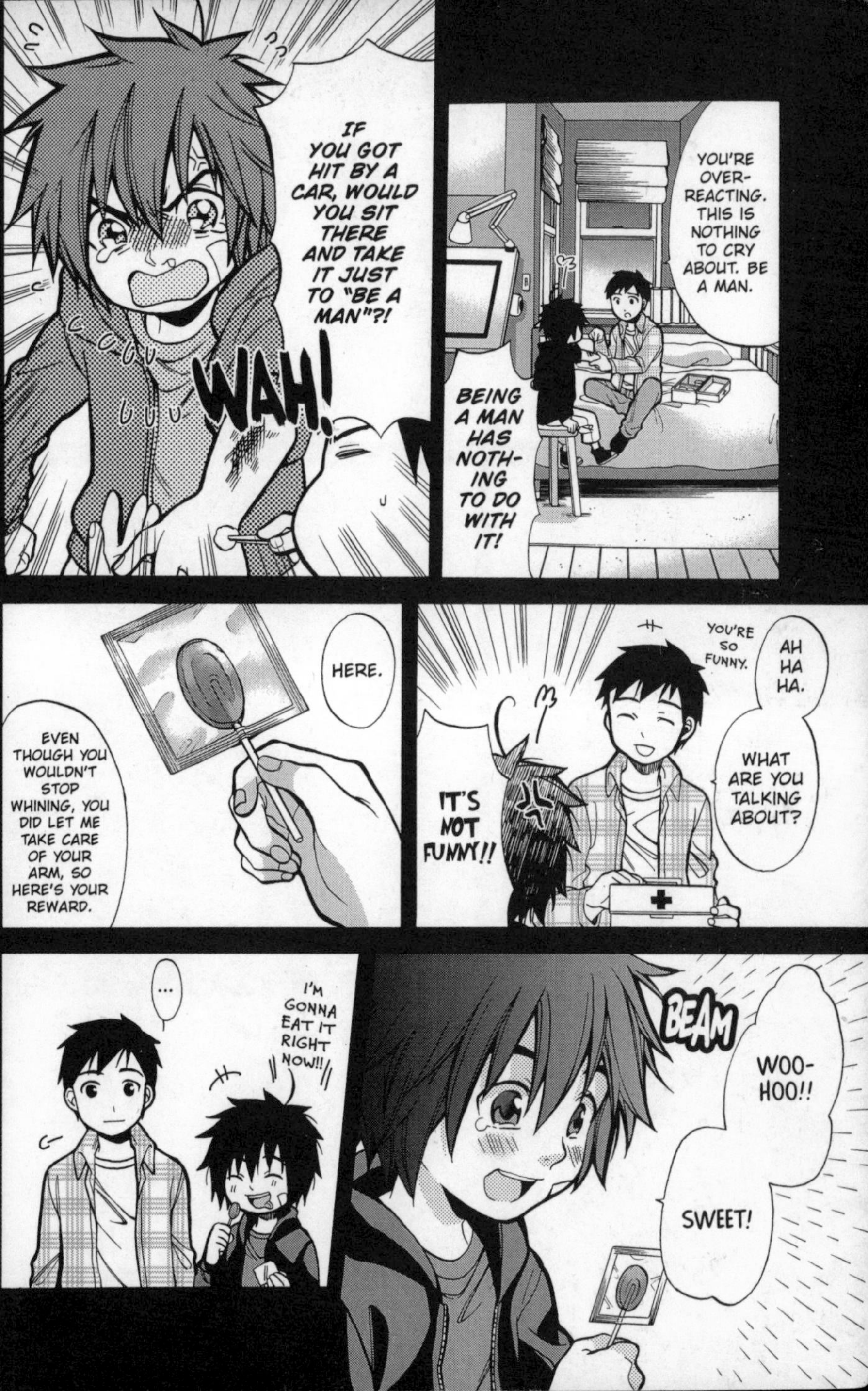
YOU'RE OVER-REACTING. THIS IS NOTHING TO CRY ABOUT. BE A MAN.
BEING A MAN HAS NOTHING TO DO WITH IT!
IF YOU GOT HIT BY A CAR, WOULD YOU SIT THERE AND TAKE IT JUST TO "BE A MAN"?!
WAH!
AH HA HA.
YOU'RE SO FUNNY.
WHAT ARE YOU TALKING ABOUT?
IT'S NOT FUNNY!!
HERE.
EVEN THOUGH YOU WOULDN'T STOP WHINING, YOU DID LET ME TAKE CARE OF YOUR ARM, SO HERE'S YOUR REWARD.
BEAM
WOO-HOO!!
SWEET!
I'M GONNA EAT IT RIGHT NOW!!
...

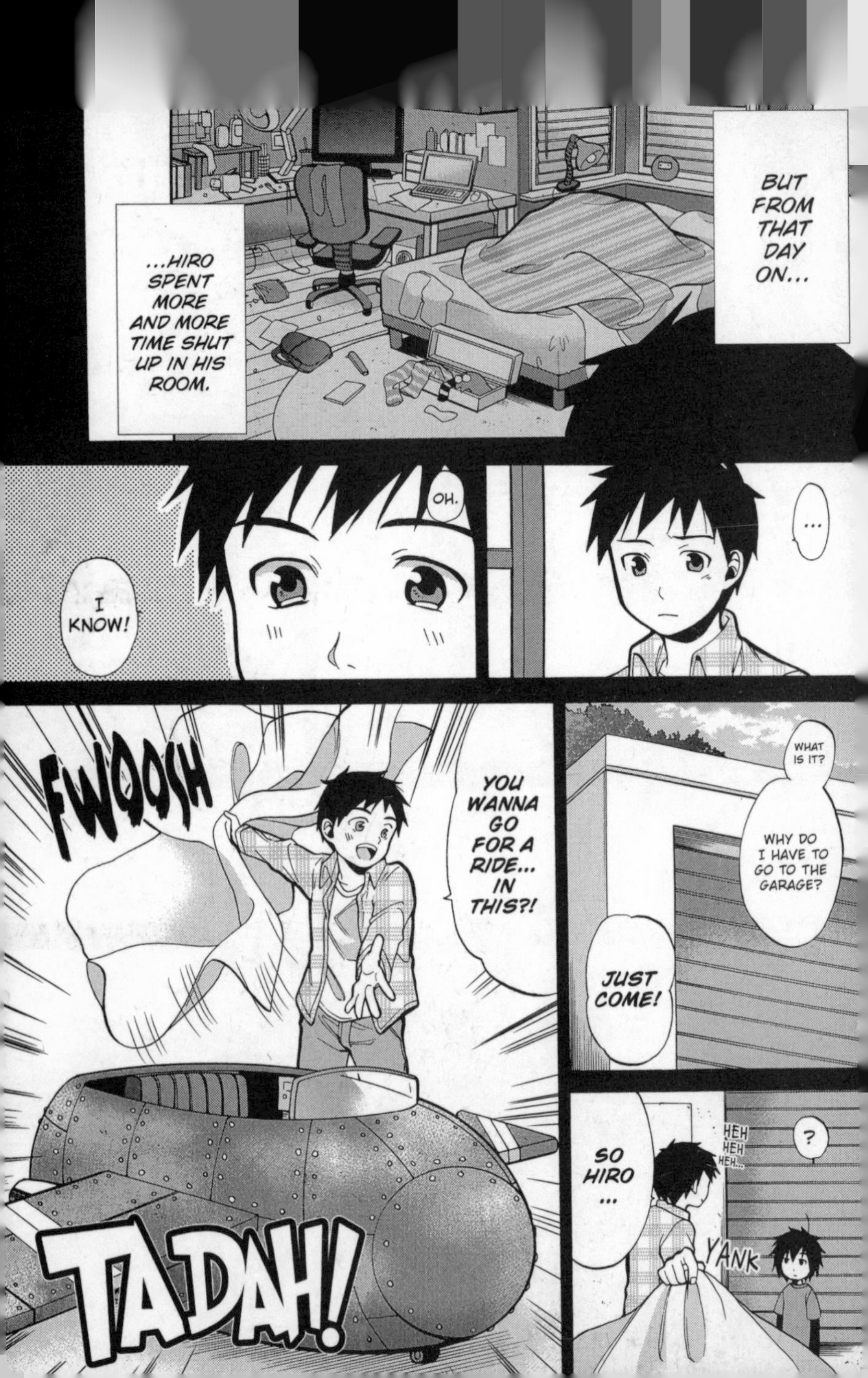
BUT FROM THAT DAY ON...
...HIRO SPENT MORE AND MORE TIME SHUT UP IN HIS ROOM.
...
OH.
I KNOW!
WHAT IS IT?
WHY DO I HAVE TO GO TO THE GARAGE?
JUST COME!
?
HEH HEH HEH...
SO HIRO ...
YANK
YOU WANNA GO FOR A RIDE... IN THIS?!
FWOOSH
TADAH!

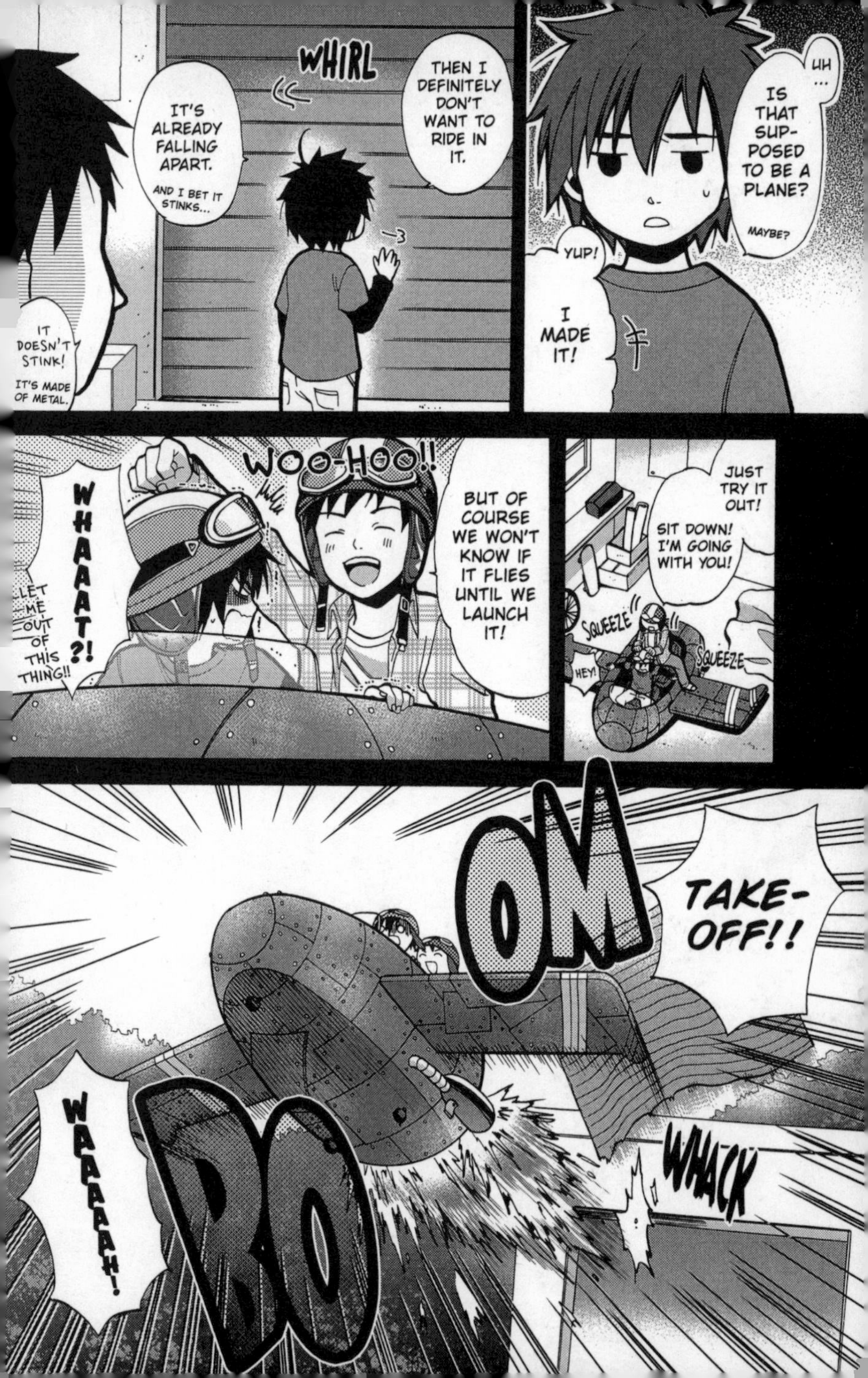
UH...
IS THAT SUP-POSED TO BE A PLANE?
MAYBE?
YUP!
I MADE IT!
THEN I DEFINITELY DON'T WANT TO RIDE IN IT.
WHIRL
IT'S ALREADY FALLING APART.
AND I BET IT STINKS...
IT DOESN'T STINK!
IT'S MADE OF METAL.
JUST TRY IT OUT!
SIT DOWN! I'M GOING WITH YOU!
SQUEEZE
SQUEEZE
HEY!
WOO-HOO!!
BUT OF COURSE WE WON'T KNOW IF IT FLIES UNTIL WE LAUNCH IT!
WHAAAAT?!
LET ME OUT OF THIS THING!!
TAKE-OFF!!
BOOM
WHACK
WAAAAAH!

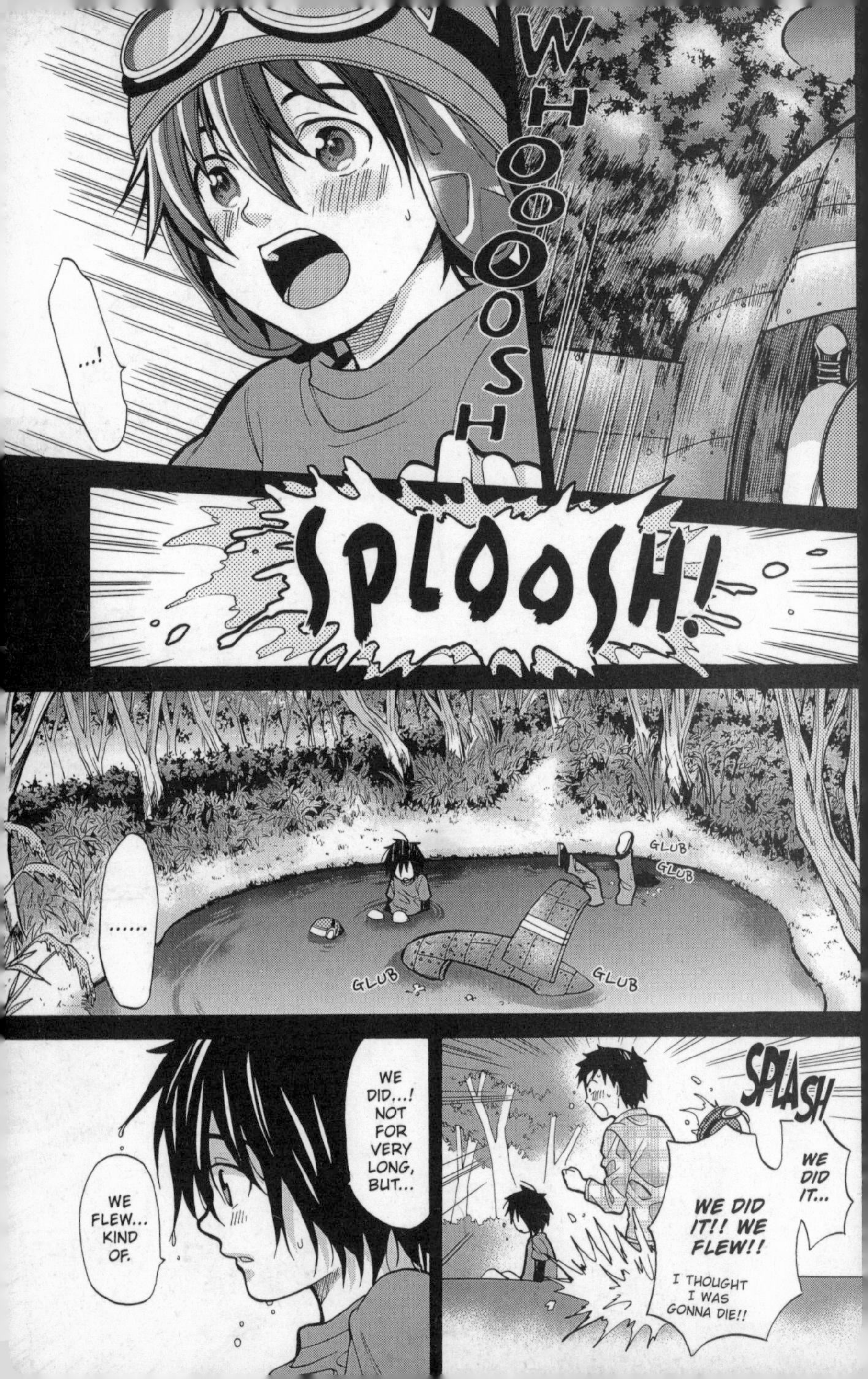
WHOOOOSH
...!
SPLOOSH!
GLUB
GLUB
GLUB
GLUB
......
SPLASH
WE DID IT...
WE DID IT!! WE FLEW!!
I THOUGHT I WAS GONNA DIE!!
WE DID...! NOT FOR VERY LONG, BUT...
WE FLEW... KIND OF.

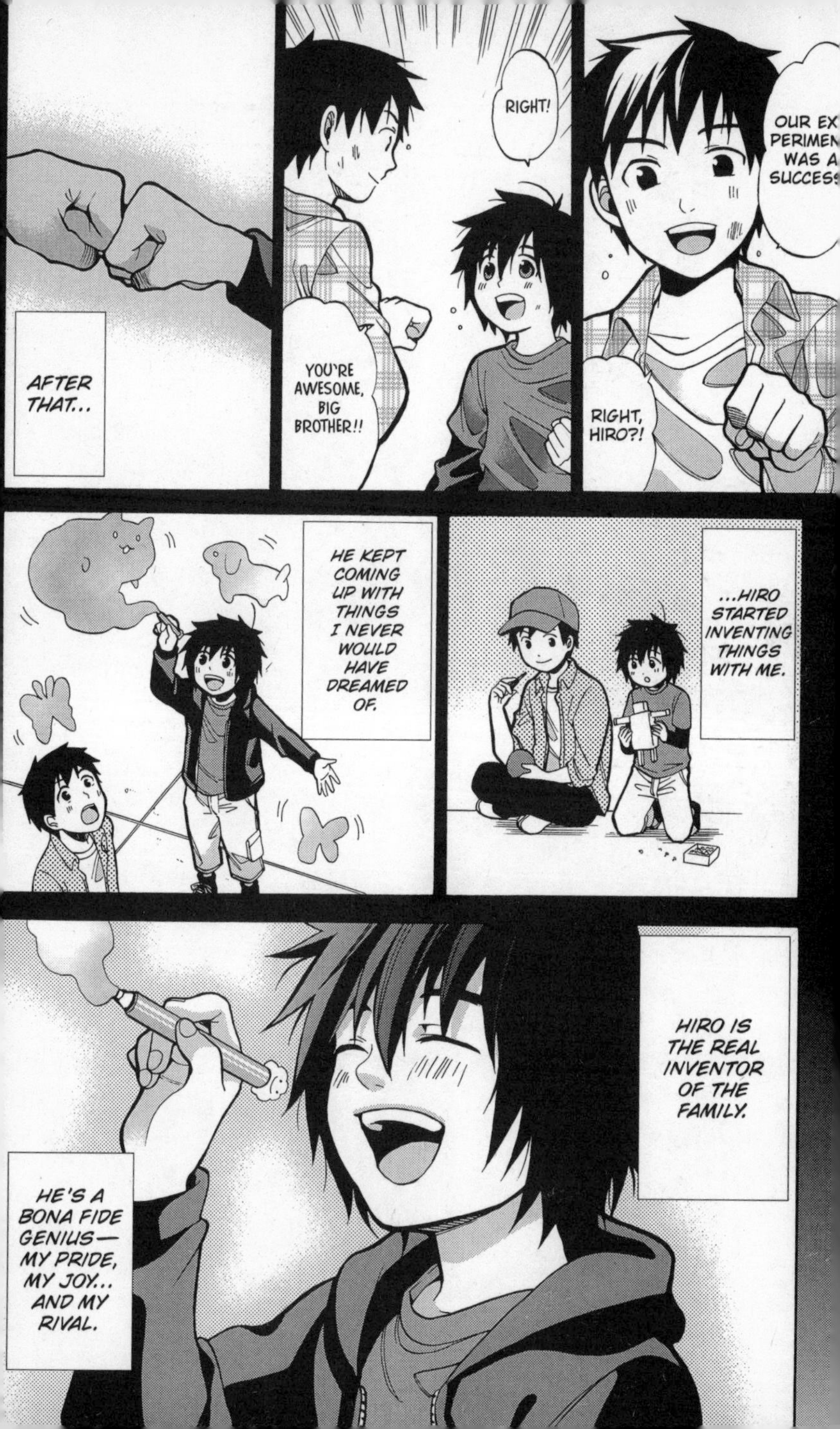
OUR EX PERIMEN WAS A SUCCESS
RIGHT, HIRO?!
RIGHT!
YOU'RE AWESOME, BIG BROTHER!!
AFTER THAT...
...HIRO STARTED INVENTING THINGS WITH ME.
HE KEPT COMING UP WITH THINGS I NEVER WOULD HAVE DREAMED OF.
HIRO IS THE REAL INVENTOR OF THE FAMILY.
HE'S A BONA FIDE GENIUS— MY PRIDE, MY JOY... AND MY RIVAL.

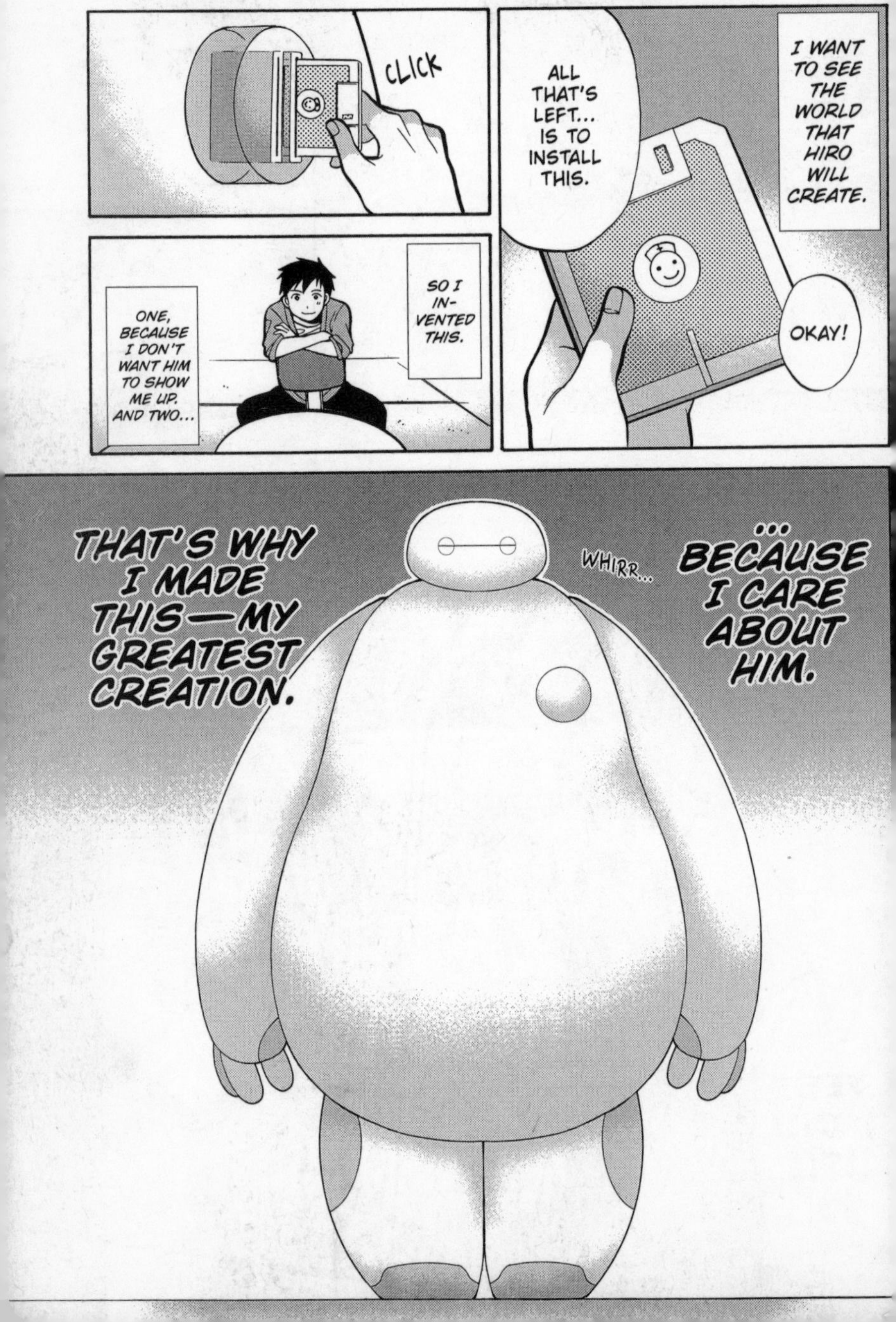
I WANT TO SEE THE WORLD THAT HIRO WILL CREATE.
ALL THAT'S LEFT... IS TO INSTALL THIS.
OKAY!
CLICK
SO I IN-VENTED THIS.
ONE, BECAUSE I DON'T WANT HIM TO SHOW ME UP. AND TWO...
...BECAUSE I CARE ABOUT HIM.
WHIRR...
THAT'S WHY I MADE THIS—MY GREATEST CREATION.

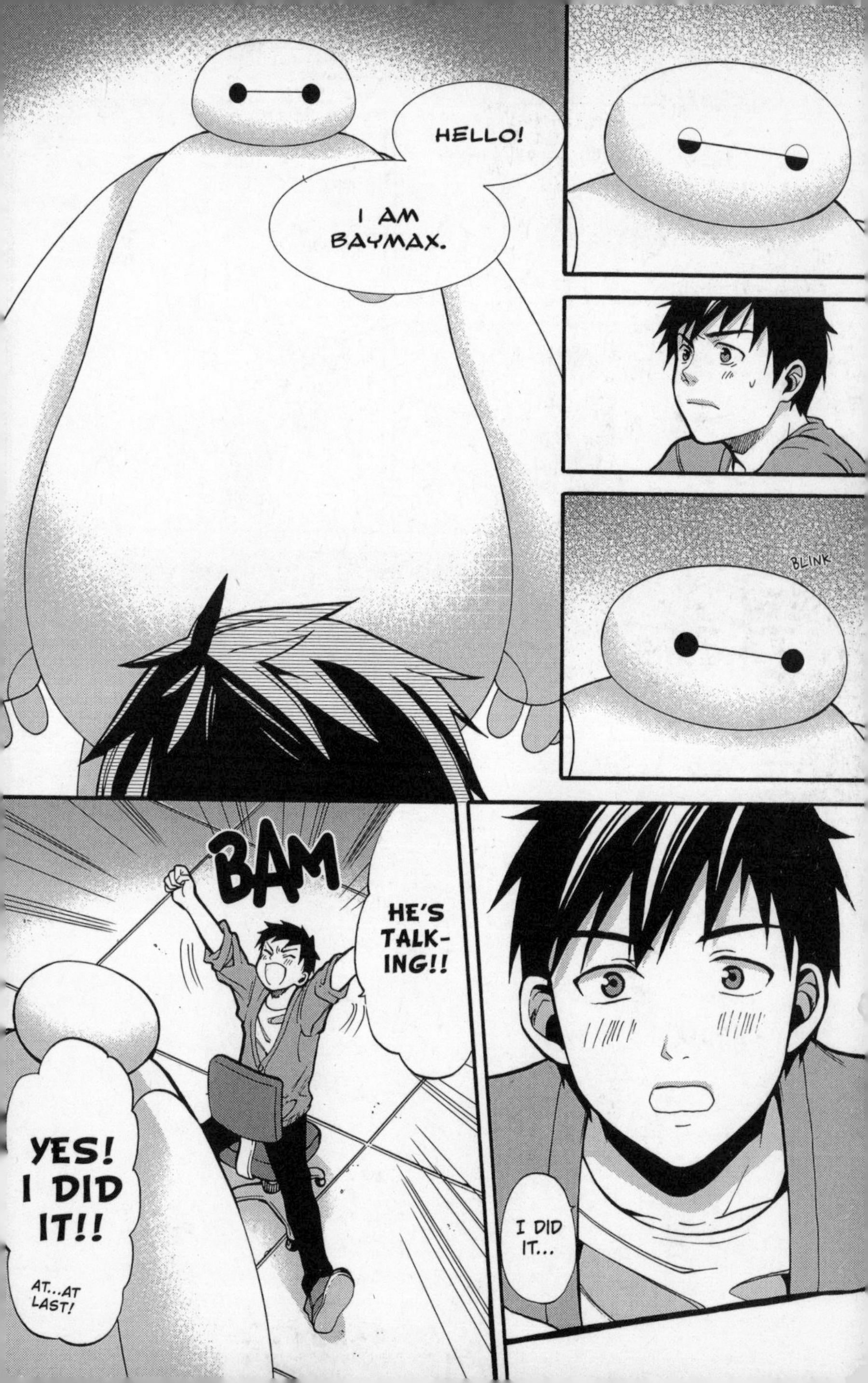
BLINK
HELLO!
I AM BAYMAX.
I DID IT...
HE'S TALKING!!
BAM
YES! I DID IT!!
AT...AT LAST!

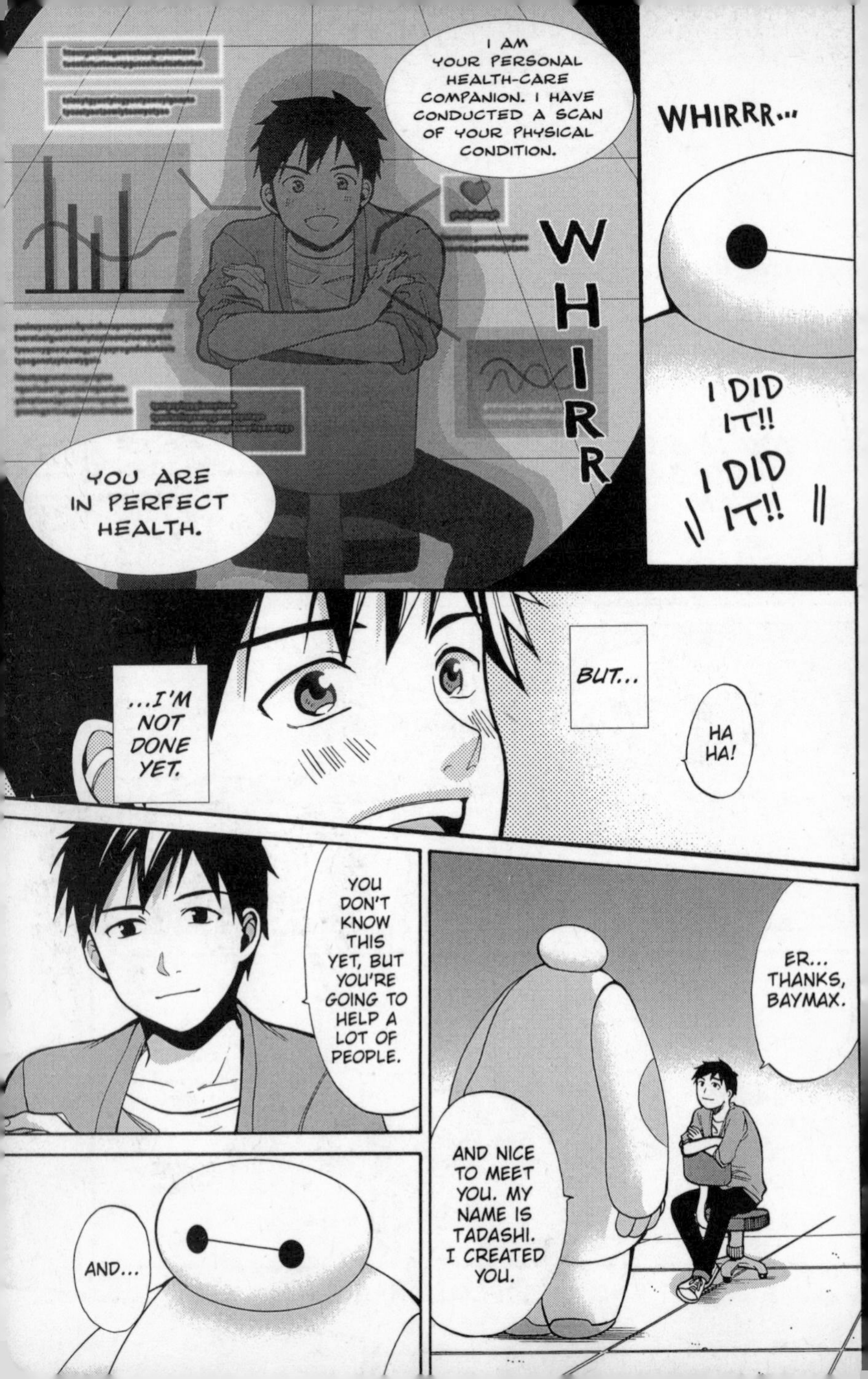
WHIRRR...
I DID IT!! I DID IT!!
I AM YOUR PERSONAL HEALTH-CARE COMPANION. I HAVE CONDUCTED A SCAN OF YOUR PHYSICAL CONDITION.
WHIRRR
YOU ARE IN PERFECT HEALTH.
HA HA!
BUT...
...I'M NOT DONE YET.
ER... THANKS, BAYMAX.
AND NICE TO MEET YOU. MY NAME IS TADASHI. I CREATED YOU.
YOU DON'T KNOW THIS YET, BUT YOU'RE GOING TO HELP A LOT OF PEOPLE.
AND...

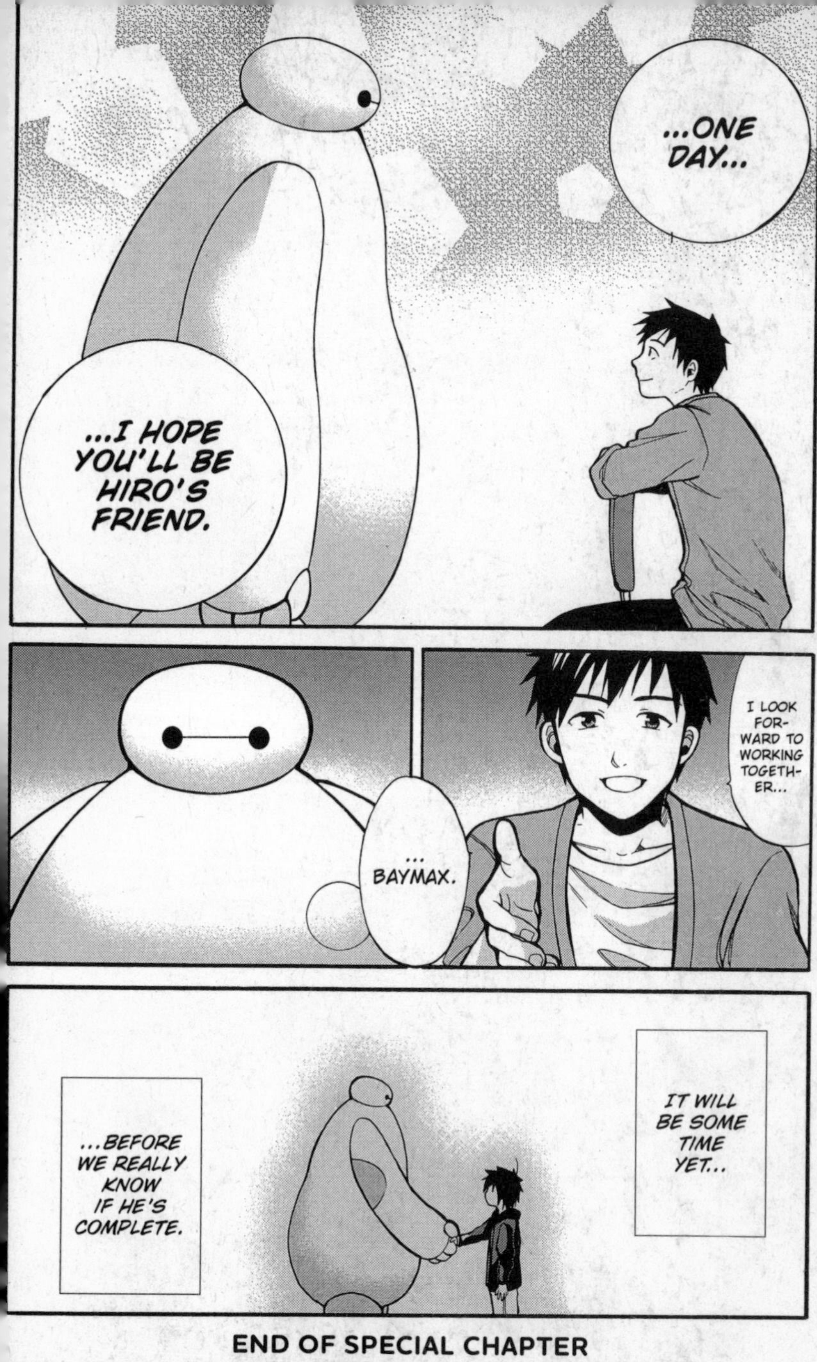
...ONE DAY...
...I HOPE YOU'LL BE HIRO'S FRIEND.
I LOOK FOR- WARD TO WORKING TOGETH- ER...
... BAYMAX.
IT WILL BE SOME TIME YET...
...BEFORE WE REALLY KNOW IF HE'S COMPLETE.

END OF SPECIAL CHAPTER

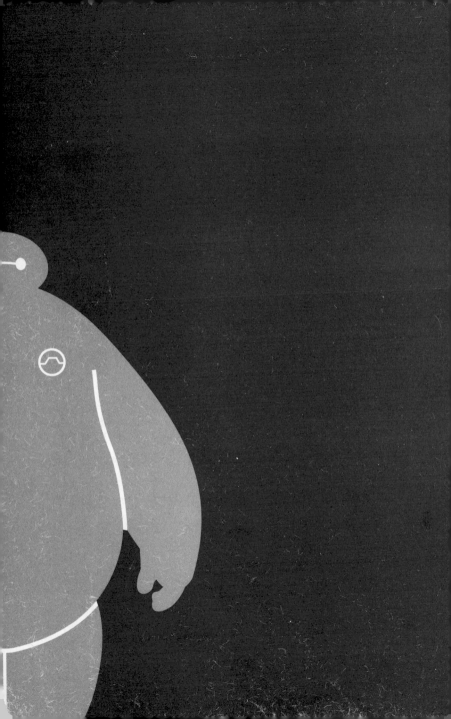

BIG HERO 6 ❶

HARUKI UENO

ORIGINAL CONCEPT:
MARVEL WORLDWIDE, INC.

Translation: Alethea and Athena Nibley • Lettering: Lys Blakeslee

Yen Press
1290 Avenue of the Americas
New York, NY 10104

www.YenPress.com

Yen Press is an imprint of Yen Press, LLC. The Yen Press name and logo are
trademarks of Yen Press, LLC.

The publisher is not responsible for websites (or their content) that are not
owned by the publisher.

First Yen Press Edition: March 2015

ISBN: 978-0-316-26389-4

10 9

BVG

Printed in the United States of America